The Truly Disadvantaged

William Julius Wilson
The Truly Disadvantaged

The Inner City, the Underclass, and Public Policy

SECOND EDITION

The University of Chicago Press
Chicago and London

The University of Chicago Press, Chicago 60637
The University of Chicago Press, Ltd., London
© 1987, 2012 by The University of Chicago
All rights reserved. Published 1987.
Second edition 2012
Printed in the United States of America

21 20 19 18 17 16 15 14 13 12   1 2 3 4 5

ISBN-13: 978-0-226-90126-8 (paper)
ISBN-10: 0-226-90126-2 (paper)

Library of Congress Cataloging-in-Publication Data

Wilson, William J., 1935–
    The truly disadvantaged : the inner city, the underclass, and public
policy / William Julius Wilson. — Second edition.
        p. cm.
    Includes bibliographical references and index.
    ISBN-13: 978-0-226-90126-8 (paperback : alkaline paper)
    ISBN-10: 0-226-90126-2 (paperback : alkaline paper) 1. Urban
poor—United States. 2. Inner cities—United States. 3. Urban
policy—United States. 4. African Americans—Economic conditions.
5. African Americans—Social conditions. 6. United States—Race
relations. I. Title.

    HV4045.W55 2012

    362.50973—dc23

                                        2011043241

Portions of this book previously appeared in somewhat different
form in *Minority Report*, edited by Leslie W. Dunbar, published by
Pantheon Books in 1984; *The New Urban Reality*, edited by Paul
Peterson, published by The Brookings Institution in 1985; *Society*,
vol. 21 (November/December 1983); *Yale Law and Policy Review*, vol.
2 (Spring 1984); and the *Social Service Review*, vol. 57 (December
1985). Chapter 3 is a slightly revised version of an article from *Fighting
Poverty*, edited by S. Danziger and D. Weinberger, published in 1986
and used with permission by Harvard University Press, copyright ©
by the Board of Regents of the University of Wisconsin System. The
Appendix is reproduced, with permission, from the *Annual Review of
Sociology*, vol. 11. © 1985 by Annual Reviews, Inc.

♾This paper meets the requirements of ANSI/NISO Z39.48-1992
(Permanence of Paper).

Contents

Preface

In 1978 the University of Chicago Press published my controversial book, *The Declining Significance of Race*. I had hoped that the major academic contribution of that book would be to explain racial change in America within a macrohistorical-theoretical framework. But there was another contribution I had hoped to make—I wanted to call attention to the worsening condition of the black underclass, in both absolute and relative terms, by relating it to the improving position of the black middle class.

The Declining Significance of Race generated controversy not only within academic quarters but in the popular media as well. At the time of publication, heightened awareness of racial issues had been created because changing social structures altered many traditional patterns of race relations and because the state was inextricably involved in the emerging controversy over affirmative action.

In the initial months following publication of the book, it seemed that critics were so preoccupied with what I had to say about the improving conditions of the black middle class that they virtually ignored my more important arguments about the deteriorating conditions of the black underclass. The view was often expressed that since all blacks are suffering there is no need to single out the black poor.

During the controversy over *The Declining Significance of Race* I committed myself to doing two things: (1) I would address the problems of the ghetto underclass in a comprehensive analysis; and (2) I would spell out, in considerable detail, the policy implications of my work. These two commitments provided direction for the writing of *The Truly Disadvantaged*. The first commitment grew out of my personal and academic reaction to the early critics' almost total preoccupation with my arguments concerning the black middle class. Indeed, it was only after I began writing *The Truly Disadvantaged* that serious scholars (particularly those working in fields such as urban poverty, social welfare, and public policy) were beginning to focus on my analysis of the underclass in *The Declining Significance of Race*.

The second commitment was a reaction to those critics who either labeled me a neoconservative or directly or indirectly tried to associate *The Declining Significance of Race* with the neoconservative movement. Although I am a social democrat, and probably to the left politically of an overwhelming majority of these critics, and although some of the most positive reviews and discussions of *The Declining Significance of Race* have come from those of the democratic Left, the title of my book readily lends itself to the assumption that I am a black conservative. Nonetheless, because I did not spell out the policy implications of *The Declining Significance of Race* in the first edition, it was possible for people to read selectively my arguments and draw policy implications significantly different from those that I would personally draw. Herbert Gans's discussion of the failure of the controversial Moynihan report to offer policy recommendations is relevant here. Gans states that "the vacuum that is created when no recommendations are attached to a policy proposal can easily be filled by undesirable solutions and the report's conclusions can be conveniently misinterpreted."[1] In the second edition of *The Declining Significance of Race*, published in 1980, I wrote an epilogue in which the policy implications of my work were underlined in sharp relief, but by then the views of many readers of the first edition had already solidified.

If the idea for the *The Truly Disadvantaged* grew out of controversy over *The Declining Significance of Race*, does it mean that the former will also generate controversy? It will be controversial. *The Truly Disadvantaged* challenges liberal orthodoxy in analyzing inner-city problems; discusses in candid terms the social pathologies of the inner city; establishes a case for moving beyond race-specific policies to ameliorate inner-city social conditions to policies that address the broader problems of societal organization, including economic organization; and advances a social democratic public-policy agenda designed to improve the life chances of truly disadvantaged groups such as the ghetto underclass by emphasizing programs to which the more advantaged groups of all races can positively relate.

It should be emphasized, however, that many of the central theoretical arguments of *The Truly Disadvantaged* were inspired not by the debate over *The Declining Significance of Race* but by my travels to inner-city neighborhoods in the city of Chicago in the past several years and by my perception of social changes, including changes in the class structure, in inner-city neighborhoods. The essays in part 1 of *The Truly Disadvantaged* describe these changes in some detail and address the question of why the social conditions of the ghetto underclass have deteriorated so rapidly in recent years.

The first chapter in part 1 briefly discusses these social changes, considers the current controversy over the use of the term *underclass*, and attempts to explain why the liberal perspective on the ghetto underclass has declined in influence in recent years. The chapter concludes with a discussion of how liberals can recapture a position of leadership in the public policy forum now dominated by conservative spokespersons. Chapter 2 describes in considerable detail the problems of violent crime, out-of-wedlock births, female-headed families, and welfare dependency in the inner city and argues that recent increases in these rates of social dislocation cannot be accounted for by the easy explanation of racism. Instead these problems have to be related to a complex web of other factors, such as the changes in the urban economy, which have produced extraordinary rates of black joblessness that exacerbate other social problems in the ghetto, and the class transformation of the inner city. Chapters 3 and 4 critically examine the popular welfare state explanations of the rise of social dislocations among the ghetto underclass and, in the process, focus more specifically on the association between joblessness and rates of female-headed families. Chapter 3 introduces and provides national data on the "male marriageable pool index"; chapter 4 presents regional data on this index and relates these data to regional figures on female headship. This chapter also considers the relationship between structural changes in the regional economy and both the "male marriageable pool index" and female headship.

The essays in part 2 of *The Truly Disadvantaged* critically examine public policy approaches to the problems of the ghetto underclass. Chapter 5 reveals the shortcomings of race-specific policies, including affirmative action, in addressing the problems of the ghetto underclass by arguing that minority members from the more advantaged families profit disproportionately from such policies because they are disproportionately represented among those of their racial group most qualified for preferred positions. This chapter argues, therefore, that the amelioration of the conditions of the truly disadvantaged minority members such as the ghetto underclass requires policies that are not race-specific. Chapter 6 extends the analysis presented in chapter 5 by examining the limitations of both the race relations vision and the War on Poverty vision in explaining the problems of the ghetto underclass and in proposing public policy solutions. This chapter argues that because these visions do not relate the problems of minority poverty directly to the broader problems of economic organization, they provide few satisfactory explanations for the sharp rise in inner-city social dislocations since 1970. The lack of adequate liberal explanations cleared the path for the emergence of conservative public policy arguments on the need to change the values and behavior of the minority poor. Finally, chapter 7 integrates and summarizes the basic arguments in the preceding chapters and then recommends a comprehensive public policy agenda to improve the life chances of truly disadvantaged groups such as the ghetto underclass. An important feature of this agenda is that it includes programs to attract and sustain the support of the more advantaged groups of all races and class backgrounds.

In preparing this book I benefited greatly from an award from the Ford Foundation to support the writing of humanistic nonfiction books on major social issues in contemporary society and a grant from the Spencer Foundation. Both of these awards allowed me to reduce my teaching load during the 1982–83 academic year to devote more time to writing, and to hire two marvelous research assistants, Robert Aponte and Kathryn Neckerman, who helped to collect and analyze data for this study. Also, Neckerman coauthored chapter 3, "Poverty and Family Structure: The Widening Gap between Evidence and Public Policy Issues"; both Aponte and Neckerman helped write chapter 4, "Joblessness versus Welfare Effects: A Further Reexamination." The appendix, "Urban Poverty: A State-of-the-Art Review of the Literature," was coauthored by Aponte. I would also like to acknowledge the work of two other research assistants, Loic Wacquant, who developed the maps on the spread of poverty and unemployment in community areas in Chicago, and Patricia Potter, who (along with Wacquant) collected the data for the concentration of inner-city poverty (see Chapter 2).

I also benefited from a year in residence as a fellow at the Center for the Study of Behavioral Sciences at Stanford University during the 1981–82 academic year. There I did a good deal of the initial reading for this study and, partly through participation in a series of stimulating seminars at the center with some of the leading social policy experts in the country, developed ideas about economic and social welfare policy.

Finally, I benefited from the helpful comments of Bernard Gifford (dean of the School of Education, University of California, Berkeley) and Ira Katznelson (dean of the Graduate Faculties, New School for Social Research). Gifford and Katznelson read the first draft of this manuscript and provided detailed written criticisms and suggestions that were very helpful in the revisions of the final draft.

I have dedicated this book to my wife, Beverly, who I am sure does not realize how important she has been in my intellectual development. Just as with my previous books, she edited the entire manuscript and was an insightful critic. But she does something that is even more important—her enthusiasm for my work has had a rejuvenating effect that allowed me to overcome periods of fatigue during the latter stages of writing and helped me to complete this book despite extreme local and national demands on my time.

1

The Ghetto Underclass, Poverty, and Social Dislocations

1   Cycles of Deprivation and the Ghetto Underclass Debate

In the mid-1960s, urban analysts began to speak of a new dimension to the urban crisis in the form of a large subpopulation of low-income families and individuals whose behavior contrasted sharply with the behavior of the general population.[1] Despite a high rate of poverty in ghetto neighborhoods throughout the first half of the twentieth century, rates of inner-city joblessness, teenage pregnancies, out-of-wedlock births, female-headed families, welfare dependency, and serious crime were significantly lower than in later years and did not reach catastrophic proportions until the mid-1970s.

These increasing rates of social dislocation signified changes in the social organization of inner-city areas. Blacks in Harlem and in other ghetto neighborhoods did not hesitate to sleep in parks, on fire escapes, and on rooftops during hot summer nights in the 1940s and 1950s, and whites frequently visited inner-city taverns and nightclubs.[2] There was crime, to be sure, but it had not reached the point where people were fearful of walking the streets at night, despite the overwhelming poverty in the area. There was joblessness, but it was nowhere near the proportions of unemployment and labor-force nonparticipation that have gripped ghetto communities since 1970. There were single-parent families, but they were a small minority of all black families and tended to be incorporated within extended family networks and to be headed not by unwed teenagers and young adult women but by middle-aged women who usually were widowed, separated, or divorced. There were welfare recipients, but only a very small percentage of the families could be said to be welfare-dependent. In short, unlike the present period. inner-city communities prior to 1960 exhibited the features of social organization—including a sense of community, positive neighborhood identification, and explicit norms and sanctions against aberrant behavior.[3]

Although liberal urban analysts in the mid-1960s hardly provided a definitive explanation of changes in the social organization of inner-city neighborhoods, they forcefully and candidly discussed the rise of social

3

dislocations among the ghetto underclass. "The symptoms of lower-class society affect the dark ghettos of America—low aspirations, poor education, family instability, illegitimacy, unemployment, crime, drug addiction, and alcoholism, frequent illness and early death," stated Kenneth B. Clark, liberal author of a 1965 study of the black ghetto. "But because Negroes begin with the primary affliction of inferior racial status, the burdens of despair and hatred are more pervasive."[4] In raising important issues about the experiences of inequality, liberal scholars in the 1960s sensitively examined the cumulative effects of racial isolation and chronic subordination on life and behavior in the inner city. Whether the focus was on the social or the psychological dimensions of the ghetto, facts of inner-city life "that are usually forgotten or ignored in polite discussions" were vividly described and systematically analyzed.[5]

Indeed, what was both unique and important about these earlier studies was that discussions of the experiences of inequality were closely tied to discussions of the structure of inequality in an attempt to explain how the economic and social situations into which so many disadvantaged blacks are born produce modes of adaptation and create norms and patterns of behavior that take the form of a "self-perpetuating pathology."[6] Nonetheless, much of the evidence from which their conclusions were drawn was impressionistic—based mainly on data collected in ethnographic or urban field research that did not capture long-term trends.[7] Indeed, the only study that provided at least an abstract sense of how the problem had changed down through the years was the Moynihan report on the Negro family, which presented decennial census statistics on changing family structure by race.[8]

However, the controversy surrounding the Moynihan report had the effect of curtailing serious research on minority problems in the inner city for over a decade, as liberal scholars shied away from researching behavior construed as unflattering or stigmatizing to particular racial minorities. Thus, when liberal scholars returned to study these problems in the early 1980s, they were dumbfounded by the magnitude of the changes that had taken place and expressed little optimism about finding an adequate explanation. Indeed, it had become quite clear that there was little consensus on the description of the problem, the explanations advanced, or the policy recommendations proposed. There was even little agreement on a definition of the term *underclass*. From the perspective of liberal social scientists, policymakers, and others, the picture seemed more confused than ever.

However, if liberals lack a clear view of the recent social changes in the inner city, the perspective among informed conservatives has crystallized around a set of arguments that have received increasing public attention. Indeed, the debate over the problems of the ghetto underclass has been dominated in recent years by conservative spokespersons as the views of liberals have gradually become more diffused and ambiguous. Liberals have traditionally emphasized how the plight of disadvantaged groups can be related to the problems of the broader society, including problems of discrimination and social-class subordination. They have also emphasized the need for progressive social change, particularly through governmental programs, to open the opportunity structure. Conservatives, in contrast, have traditionally stressed the importance of different group values and competitive resources in accounting for the experiences of the disadvantaged; if reference is made to the larger society, it is in terms of the assumed adverse effects of various government programs on individual or group behavior and initiative.

In emphasizing this distinction, I do not want to convey the idea that serious research or discussion of the ghetto underclass is subordinated to ideological concerns. However, despite pious claims about objectivity in social research, it is true that values influence not only our selection of problems for investigation but also our interpretation of empirical data. And although there are no logical rules of discovery that would invalidate an explanation simply because it was influenced by a particular value premise or ideology, it is true that attempts to arrive at a satisfactory explanation may be impeded by ideological blinders or views restricted by value premises. The solution to this problem is not to try to divest social investigators of their values but to encourage a free and open discussion of the issues among people with different value premises in order that new questions can be raised, existing interpretations challenged, and new research stimulated.

I believe that the demise of the liberal perspective on the ghetto underclass has made the intellectual discourse on this topic too one-sided. It has made it more difficult to achieve the above objective and has ultimately made it less likely that our understanding of inner-city social dislocations will be enhanced. With this in mind I should like to explain, in the ensuing discussion in this chapter, why the liberal perspective on the ghetto underclass has receded into the background and why the conservative perspective enjoys wide and increasing currency. I should then like to suggest how the liberal perspective might be refocused to challenge the now-dominant conservative views on the ghetto underclass and, more important, to provide a more balanced intellectual discussion of why the problems in the inner city sharply increased when they did and in the way that they did.

The Declining Influence of the Liberal Perspective on the Ghetto Underclass

The liberal perspective on the ghetto underclass has become less persuasive and convincing in public discourse principally because many of
those who represent traditional liberal views on social issues have been
reluctant to discuss openly or, in some instances, even to acknowledge
the sharp increase in social pathologies in ghetto communities. This is
seen in the four principal ways in which liberals have recently addressed the subject. In describing these four approaches I want it to be
clear that some liberals may not be associated with any one of them,
some with only one, and others with more than one. But I believe that
these approaches represent the typical, recent liberal reactions to the
ghetto underclass phenomenon and that they collectively provide a
striking contrast to the crystallized, candid, and forceful liberal perspective of the mid-1960s. Let me elaborate.

One approach is to avoid describing any behavior that might be construed as unflattering or stigmatizing to ghetto residents, either because of a fear of providing fuel for racist arguments or because of a
concern of being charged with "racism" or with "blaming the victim."
Indeed, one of the consequences of the heated controversy over the
Moynihan report on the Negro family is that liberal social scientists,
social workers, journalists, policymakers, and civil rights leaders have
been, until very recently, reluctant to make any reference to race at all
when discussing issues such as the increase of violent crime, teenage
pregnancy, and out-of-wedlock births. The more liberals have avoided
writing about or researching these problems, the more conservatives
have rushed headlong to fill the void with popular explanations of
inner-city social dislocations that much of the public finds exceedingly
compelling.

A second liberal approach to the subject of underclass and urban
social problems is to refuse even to use terms such as *underclass*. As
one spokesman put it: "'Underclass' is a destructive and misleading
label that lumps together different people who have different problems. And that it is the latest of a series of popular labels (such as the
'lumpen proletariat,' 'undeserving poor,' and the 'culture of poverty')
that focuses on individual characteristics and thereby stigmatizes the
poor for their poverty."[9] However, the real problem is not the term
underclass or some similar designation but the fact that the term has
received more systematic treatment from conservatives, who tend to
focus almost exclusively on individual characteristics, than from liberals, who would more likely relate these characteristics to the broader
problems of society. While some liberals debate whether terms such as

underclass should even be used, conservatives have made great use of them in developing popular arguments about life and behavior in the inner city.[10]

Regardless of which term is used, one cannot deny that there is a heterogeneous grouping of inner-city families and individuals whose behavior contrasts sharply with that of mainstream America. The real challenge is not only to explain why this is so, but also to explain why the behavior patterns in the inner city today differ so markedly from those of only three or four decades ago. To obscure these differences by eschewing the term *underclass*, or some other term that could be helpful in describing changes in ghetto behavior, norms, and aspirations, in favor of more neutral designations such as *lower class* or *working class* is to fail to address one of the most important social transformations in recent United States history.

Indeed, the liberal argument to reject the term *underclass* reflects the lack of historical perspective on urban social problems. We often are not aware of or lose sight of the fact that the sharp increase in inner-city dislocations has occurred in only the last several years. Although a term such as *lumpen proletariat* or *underclass* might have been quite appropriate in Karl Marx's description of life and behavior in the slums of nineteenth-century England, it is not very appropriate in descriptions of life and behavior in America's large urban ghettos prior to the mid-twentieth century. Indeed, in the 1940s, 1950s, and as late as the 1960s such communities featured a vertical integration of different segments of the urban black population. Lower-class, working-class, and middle-class black families all lived more or less in the same communities (albeit in different neighborhoods), sent their children to the same schools, availed themselves of the same recreational facilities, and shopped at the same stores. Whereas today's black middle-class professionals no longer tend to live in ghetto neighborhoods and have moved increasingly into mainstream occupations outside the black community, the black middle-class professionals of the 1940s and 1950s (doctors, teachers, lawyers, social workers, ministers) lived in higher-income neighborhoods of the ghetto and serviced the black community. Accompanying the black middle-class exodus has been a growing movement of stable working-class blacks from ghetto neighborhoods to higher-income neighborhoods in other parts of the city and to the suburbs. In the earlier years, the black middle and working classes were confined by restrictive covenants to communities also inhabited by the lower class; their very presence provided stability to inner-city neighborhoods and reinforced and perpetuated mainstream patterns of norms and behavior.[11]

This is not the situation in the 1980s. Today's ghetto neighborhoods are populated almost exclusively by the most disadvantaged segments of the black urban community, that heterogeneous grouping of families and individuals who are outside the mainstream of the American occupational system. Included in this group are individuals who lack training and skills and either experience long-term unemployment or are not members of the labor force, individuals who are engaged in street crime and other forms of aberrant behavior, and families that experience long-term spells of poverty and/or welfare dependency. These are the populations to which I refer when I speak of the *underclass*. I use this term to depict a reality not captured in the more standard designation *lower class*.

In my conception, the term *underclass* suggests that changes have taken place in ghetto neighborhoods, and the groups that have been left behind are collectively different from those that lived in these neighborhoods in earlier years. It is true that long-term welfare families and street criminals are distinct groups, but they live and interact in the same depressed community and they are part of the population that has, with the exodus of the more stable working- and middle-class segments, become increasingly isolated socially from mainstream patterns and norms of behavior. It is also true that certain groups are stigmatized by the label *underclass*, just as some people who live in depressed central-city communities are stigmatized by the term *ghetto* or *inner city*, but it would be far worse to obscure the profound changes in the class structure and social behavior of ghetto neighborhoods by avoiding the use of the term *underclass*. Indeed, the real challenge is to describe and explain these developments accurately so that liberal policymakers can appropriately address them. And it is difficult for me to see how this can be accomplished by rejecting a term that aids in the description of ghetto social transformations.

A third liberal approach to the subject of problems in the inner city and the ghetto underclass is to emphasize or embrace selective evidence that denies the very existence of an urban underclass. We have seen this approach in two principal ways. First, in the aftermath of the controversy over Daniel Patrick Moynihan's unflattering depiction of the black family, a number of liberals, particularly black liberals, began in the late 1960s and early 1970s to emphasize the positive aspects of the black experience.[12] Thus earlier arguments, which asserted that some aspects of ghetto life were pathological,[13] were rejected and replaced with those that accented the strengths of the black community. Arguments extolling the strengths and virtues of black families replaced those that described the breakup of black families. In fact, aspects of ghetto behavior described as pathological in the studies of the mid-1960s were reinterpreted or redefined as functional because, it was argued, blacks were demonstrating their ability to survive and even flourish in an economically depressed and racist environment. Ghetto families were portrayed as resilient and capable of adapting creatively to an oppressive society. These revisionist arguments purporting to "liberate" the social sciences from the influence of racism helped shift the focus of social scientists away from discussions of the consequences of racial isolation and economic class subordination to discussions of black achievement. Since the focus was solely on black achievement, little attention was paid to internal differences within the black community. Moreover, since the problems were defined in racial terms, very little discussion was devoted either to problems created by economic shifts and their impact on the poor black community or to the need for economic reform. In short, such arguments effectively diverted attention from the appropriate solutions to the dreadful economic condition of poor blacks and made it difficult for blacks to see, in the words of one perceptive observer, "how their fate is inextricably tied up with the structure of the American economy."[14]

More recently, in response to arguments by conservatives that a growing number of inner-city residents get locked into a culture of poverty and a culture of welfare, some liberals have been quick to cite research indicating that only a small proportion of Americans in poverty and on welfare are persistently poor and persistently on welfare. The problem of long-term poverty and welfare dependency began to receive detailed and systematic empirical attention when it became possible to track the actual experiences of the poor and those who receive welfare with adequate longitudinal data provided by the Michigan Panel Study of Income Dynamics (PSID). A series of initial studies based on the PSID revealed that only a very small percentage of those in poverty and on welfare were long-term cases. For example, one study found that only 3 percent of the population was poor throughout a ten-year time span;[15] another study reported that only 2.2 percent of the population was poor eight of the ten years (1968–78) covered in the research.[16] These studies have been widely cited and have been said to provide powerful evidence against the notion of an underclass.[17]

However, more recent studies based on the PSID data seriously challenge interpretations based on these findings.[18] Specifically, these studies revealed that the previous PSID research on spells of poverty and welfare dependency observed over a fixed time frame—say, eight or ten years—underestimated the length of spells because some individuals who appear to have short spells of poverty or welfare receipt are actually beginning or ending long spells. To correct for this prob-

lem, the more recent studies first identified spells of poverty and welfare receipt, then calculated exit probabilities by year to estimate the
duration of spells. With this revised methodology it was found that,
although most people who become poor during some point in their
lives experience poverty for only one or two years, a substantial subpopulation remains in poverty for a very long time. Indeed, these long-
term poor constitute about 60 percent of those in poverty at any given
point in time and are in a poverty spell that will last eight or more
years. Furthermore, families headed by women are likely to have longer spells of poverty—at a given point in time, the average child who
became poor when the family makeup changed from married-couple to
female-headed is in the midst of a poverty spell lasting almost twelve
years. It was reported that "some 20 percent of poverty spells of children begin with birth. When they do, they tend to last ten years. The
average poor black child today appears to be in the midst of a poverty
spell which will last for almost two decades."[19] Similar findings were
reported on spells of welfare receipt. Long-term welfare mothers tend
to belong to racial minorities, were never married, and are high school
dropouts.

Thus, despite the findings and interpretations of earlier PSID reports on long-term poverty and welfare dependency, there is still a
firm basis for accepting the argument that a ghetto underclass has
emerged and exhibits the problems of long-term poverty and welfare
dependency. Accordingly, liberal attempts to deny the existence of an
underclass on the basis of the earlier optimistic Michigan panel studies
now seem especially questionable.

Finally, a fourth liberal approach to the subject of the ghetto underclass and urban social problems is to acknowledge the rise in inner-city
social dislocations while emphasizing racism as the explanation of these
changes. There are two basic themes associated with this thesis. The
more popular theme is that the cycle of pathology characterizing the
ghetto can only be comprehended in terms of racial oppression and
that "the racial dehumanization Americans permit is a symptom of the
deep-seated, systematic and most dangerous social disease of racism."[20] In response to this argument, I should like to emphasize that
no serious student of American race relations can deny the relationship
between the disproportionate concentration of blacks in impoverished
urban ghettos and historic racial subjugation in American society. But
to suggest that the recent rise of social dislocations among the ghetto
underclass is due mainly to contemporary racism, which in this context
refers to the "conscious refusal of whites to accept blacks as equal
human beings and their willful, systematic effort to deny blacks equal

opportunity,"[21] is to ignore a set of complex issues that are difficult to explain with a race-specific thesis. More specifically, it is not readily apparent how the deepening economic class divisions between the haves and have-nots in the black community can be accounted for when this thesis is invoked,[22] especially when it is argued that this same racism is directed with equal force across class boundaries in the black community.[23] Nor is it apparent how racism can result in a more rapid social and economic deterioration in the inner city in the post–civil rights period than in the period that immediately preceded the notable civil rights victories. To put the question more pointedly, even if racism continues to be a factor in the social and economic progress of some blacks, can it be used to explain the sharp increase in inner-city social dislocations since 1970? Unfortunately, no one who supports the contemporary racism thesis has provided adequate or convincing answers to this question.

The problem is that the proponents of the contemporary racism thesis fail to distinguish between the past and the present effects of racism on the lives of different segments of the black population. This is unfortunate because once the effects of historic racism are recognized it becomes easier to assess the importance of current racism in relation to nonracial factors such as economic-class position and modern economic trends. Moreover, once this distinction is made it clears the way for appropriate policy recommendations. Policy programs based on the premise that the recent rise of social dislocations, such as joblessness, in the inner city is due to current racism will be significantly different from policy programs based on the premise that the growth of these problems is due more to nonracial factors.

However, some liberals know that "racism is too easy an explanation" because, in the words of Michael Harrington, it implies "that the social and economic disorganization faced by black Americans was the result of the psychological state of mind of white America, a kind of deliberate—and racist—ill will." Harrington goes on to acknowledge that such racism exists and has to be vigorously fought, but he emphasizes that "it is a relatively simple part of the problem. For there is an economic structure of racism that will persist even if every white who hates blacks goes through a total conversion." In this more complex version, racism is seen not as a state of mind but as "an occupational hierarchy rooted in history and institutionalized in the labor market."[24] Also, it is argued that this economic structure of racism will become even more oppressive in the future because massive economic trends in the economy—the technological revolution, the internation-

alization of capital, and the world division of labor—will have an adverse effect in areas where blacks have made the most significant gains.

The problem with this argument is not the association between economic shifts and the deteriorating economic position of some blacks,
which I believe is true and should be emphasized, but that this whole
question is discussed in terms of an "economic structure of racism." In
other words, complex problems in the American and worldwide economies that ostensibly have little or nothing to do with race, problems
that fall heavily on much of the black population but require solutions
that confront the broader issues of economic organization, are not
made more understandable by associating them directly or indirectly
with racism. Indeed, because this term has been used so indis-
criminately, has so many different definitions, and is often relied on to
cover up lack of information or knowledge of complex issues, it frequently weakens rather than enhances arguments concerning race. In-
discriminate use of this term in any analysis of contemporary racial
problems immediately signals that the arguments typify worn-out
themes and make conservative writers more interesting in comparison
because they seem, on the surface at least, to have some fresh ideas.

Thus, instead of talking vaguely about an economic structure of racism, it would be less ambiguous and more effective to state simply that
a racial division of labor has been created due to decades, even centuries, of discrimination and prejudice; and that because those in the
low-wage sector of the economy are more adversely affected by imper-
sonal economic shifts in advanced industrial society, the racial division
of labor is reinforced. One does not have to "trot out" the concept of
racism to demonstrate, for example, that blacks have been severely
hurt by deindustrialization because of their heavy concentration in the
automobile, rubber, steel, and other smokestack industries.[25]

In sum, the liberal perspective on the ghetto underclass and inner-
city social dislocations is less persuasive and influential in public discourse today because many of those who represent the traditional liberal
views on social issues have failed to address straightforwardly the rise of
social pathologies in the ghetto. As I have attempted to show, some
liberals completely avoid any discussion of these problems, some eschew terms such as *underclass*, and others embrace selective evidence
that denies the very existence of an underclass and behavior associated
with the underclass or rely on the convenient term *racism* to account for
the sharp rise in the rates of social dislocation in the inner city. The
combined effect of these tendencies is to render liberal arguments ineffective and to enhance conservative arguments on the underclass, even
though the conservative thesis is plagued with serious problems of in-

terpretation and analysis. It is to the conservative perspective that I now turn.

The Increasing Influence of the Conservative Perspective on the Underclass

If the most forceful and influential arguments on the ghetto underclass in the 1960s were put forth by liberals, conservative arguments have moved to the forefront in the 1980s, even though they have undergone only slight modification since the 1960s. Indeed, many students of social behavior recognize that the conservative thesis represents little more than the application of the late Oscar Lewis's culture-of-poverty arguments to the ghetto underclass.[26] Relying on participant observation and life-history data to analyze Latin American poverty, Lewis described the culture of poverty as "both an adaptation and a reaction of the poor to their marginal position in a class stratified, highly individuated, capitalistic society."[27] However, he also noted that once the culture of poverty comes into existence, "it tends to perpetuate itself from generation to generation because of its effect on the children. By the time slum children are age six or seven," argued Lewis, "they have usually absorbed the basic values and attitudes of their subculture and are not psychologically geared to take full advantage of changing conditions or increased opportunities which may occur in their life-time."[28]

Although Lewis was careful to point out that basic structural changes in society may alter some of the cultural characteristics of the poor, conservative students of inner-city poverty who have built on his thesis have focused almost exclusively on the interconnection between cultural traditions, family history, and individual character. For example, they have argued that a ghetto family that has had a history of welfare dependency will tend to bear offspring who lack ambition, a work ethic, and a sense of self-reliance.[29] Some even suggest that ghetto underclass individuals have to be rehabilitated culturally before they can advance in society.[30]

In the 1960s, before the civil rights revolution ran its course and before the Great Society programs began to wind down, such arguments were successfully beaten back by forceful liberal critics who blamed society for the plight of the ghetto underclass and who called for progressive social reforms to improve their economic and social chances in life. There was considerable optimism and confidence among liberals in the latter half of the 1960s not only because they felt they understood the problems of the inner city, but also because they believed they had the potential solution in the form of Great Society and civil rights programs. Conservative students of urban poverty worked in an intimidating atmosphere, and those who dared to write or speak out on the subject received the full brunt of the liberal onslaught.[31]

Arguments that associated ghetto-specific behavior (i.e., behavior that departs from mainstream patterns) with ingrained cultural characteristics (that whole array of norms, values, orientations, and aspirations) received the most attention from liberal critics in the 1960s. These critics contended that ghetto-specific behavior is largely due to segregation, limited opportunities, and external obstacles against advancement—which were determined by different historical circumstances. They further argued that even if one were able to demonstrate a direct relationship between ghetto-specific behavior and values or other cultural traits, this would be only the first step in a proper social analysis. Analysis of the historical and social roots of these cultural differences represents the succeeding and, indeed, more fundamental step.[32]

In short, liberal scholars in the 1960s argued that cultural values do not ultimately determine behavior or success. Rather, cultural values emerge from specific social circumstances and life chances and reflect one's class and racial position. Thus, if underclass blacks have limited aspirations or fail to plan for the future, it is not ultimately the product of different cultural norms but the consequence of restricted opportunities, a bleak future, and feelings of resignation resulting from bitter personal experiences. Accordingly, behavior described as socially pathological and associated with the ghetto underclass should be analyzed not as a cultural aberration but as a symptom of class and racial inequality.[33] As economic and social opportunities change, new behavioral solutions originate and develop into patterns, later to be complemented and upheld by norms. If new situations appear, both the patterns of behavior and the norms eventually undergo change. "Some behavioral norms are more persistent than others," wrote Herbert Gans in 1968, "but over the long run, all of the norms and aspirations by which people live are nonpersistent: they rise and fall with changes in situations."[34]

In the 1960s liberals effectively used this thesis not only to challenge the conservative arguments about culture and underclass behavior but also to explain why ghetto communities were so different from mainstream communities. The assertions about the relationship between culture and social structure were rendered plausible by evidence reported and interpreted in a series of urban field studies in the later

1960s.[35] On the other hand, conservative assertions about underclass life and behavior were weakened because of a lack of direct evidence and because they seemed to be circular in the sense that cultural values were inferred from the behavior of the underclass to be explained, and then these values were used as the explanation of the behavior.[36]

Thus, by the end of the 1960s, the most forceful and persuasive arguments on the ghetto underclass had been provided by liberals, not conservatives. A few years later, just the opposite would be true, even though the conservative thesis of the interplay between cultural tradition, family biography, and individual character remains largely unchanged. To understand this development, it is important to note the unsettling effect of the heated controversy over the Moynihan report on those who represent traditional liberal views.

As I mentioned previously, liberals became increasingly reluctant to research, write about, or publicly discuss inner-city social dislocations following the virulent attacks against Moynihan. Indeed, by 1970 it was clear to any sensitive observer that if there was to be research on the ghetto underclass that would not be subjected to ideological criticism, it would be research conducted by minority scholars on the strengths, not the weaknesses, of inner-city families and communities.[37] Studies of ghetto social pathologies, even those organized in terms of traditional liberal theories, were no longer welcomed in some circles. Thus, after 1970, for a period of several years, the deteriorating social and economic conditions of the ghetto underclass were not addressed by the liberal community as scholars backed away from research on the topic, policymakers were silent, and civil rights leaders were preoccupied with the affirmative action agenda of the black middle class.

By 1980, however, the problems of inner-city social dislocations had reached such catastrophic proportions that liberals were forced to readdress the question of the ghetto underclass, but this time their reactions were confused and defensive. The extraordinary rise in inner-city social dislocations following the passage of the most sweeping antidiscrimination and antipoverty legislation in the nation's history could not be explained by the 1960 explanations of ghetto-specific behavior. Moreover, because liberals had ignored these problems throughout most of the 1970s, they had no alternative explanations to advance and were therefore ill prepared to confront a new and forceful challenge from conservative thinkers. The result was a diffused and confused reaction typified by the four responses to the subject that I discussed above.

The new conservative challenge does not represent a change in the basic premise of the interplay among cultural tradition, family biography, and individual character; rather, it builds on this premise with the argument that the growth of liberal social policies has exacerbated, not alleviated, ghetto-specific cultural tendencies and problems of inner-city social dislocations. Widely read neoconservative books such as *Thinking about Crime, Wealth and Poverty, Civil Rights: Rhetoric or Reality,* and *Losing Ground* present a range of arguments on the negative effects of liberal social policy on the behavior and values of the ghetto underclass.[38] Thus liberal changes in the criminal justice system are said to have decreased the sanctions against aberrant behavior and thereby contributed to the rise of serious inner-city crime since 1965; affirmative action pressures are linked with the deteriorating plight of the underclass because, while they increase the demand for highly qualified minority members, they decrease the demand for the less qualified due to the cost, particularly at times of discharge and promotion; and the Great Society and other social welfare programs have been self-defeating because they have made people less self-reliant, promoted joblessness, and contributed to the rise of out-of-wedlock births and female-headed families. Thus, unlike their liberal counterparts, conservatives have attempted to explain the sharp rise in the rates of social dislocation among the ghetto underclass, and their arguments, which strike many as new and refreshing, have dominated public discourse on this subject for the last several years. But there are signs that this is beginning to change. There are signs of a liberal revival. And the spark for this revival, I believe, is Charles Murray's provocative book, *Losing Ground.*

Probably no work has done more to promote the view that federal programs are harmful to the poor. As reported in a recent *New York Times* editorial, "This year's budget-cutter bible seems to be 'Losing Ground,' Charles Murray's book appraising social policy in the last 30 years. The Reagan budget . . . is likely to propose deep reductions in education, child nutrition and housing assistance, and elimination of programs like the Job Corps, revenue sharing and urban development grants. In agency after agency, officials cite the Murray book as a philosophical base for these proposals, for it concludes that social-welfare programs, far from relieving poverty, increase it and should be stopped."[39] Indeed, *Losing Ground* not only attributes increasing poverty to programs such as those of the Great Society, it also explains increasing rates of joblessness, crime, out-of-wedlock births, female-headed families, and welfare dependency, especially among the ghetto underclass, in terms of such programs as well. Murray argues that recent changes in social policy have effectively changed the rewards and penalties that govern human behavior.

Losing Ground initially drew rave reviews in a variety of newspapers and periodicals, partly because Murray seemed to have marshaled an impressive array of statistics to support his arguments. But following that, critics from liberal quarters awakened and responded with powerful criticisms that have devastated the central core of Murray's thesis.[40] For example, whereas Murray maintains that the availability of food stamps and increases in Aid for Families with Dependent Children (AFDC) payments have had a negative effect on poor black family formation and work incentives, liberal critics have appropriately pointed out that the real value of these two combined programs increased only from 1960 to 1972; after that time, their real value declined sharply because states neglected to adjust AFDC benefit levels to inflation, yet "there were no reversals in the trends of either family composition or work effort."[41] Moreover, in 1975, Congress enacted the Earned Income Tax Credit, which further expanded the advantages of working, for the poor. Thus, if welfare incentives lead to black joblessness and family dissolution as Murray argues, "these trends should have reversed themselves in the 1970s, when the relative advantage of work over welfare increased sharply."[42] They did not, of course; black joblessness, female-headed families, and illegitimacy soared during the 1970s.

Whereas Murray contends that despite substantial increases in spending on social programs, from 1968 to 1980 the poverty rate failed to drop—thus indicating that these programs were not successful— liberal critics argue that Murray "neglects the key facts that contradict his message," namely, that the unemployment rate in 1980 was twice that of 1968.[43] When unemployment increases, poverty also rises. What Murray fails to consider, they argue, is that many people slipped into poverty because of the economic downturn and were lifted out by the broadening of benefits. According to Robert Greenstein, director of the Center on Budget and Policy Priorities in Washington, D.C., "The two trends roughly balanced each other and the poverty rate remained about the same" from 1968 to 1980.[44]

Murray, on the other hand, maintains that the slowing of the economy had nothing at all to do with the failure of the poverty rate to decline in the 1970s. He argues that the economy, according to the Gross National Product (GNP), grew more in the 1970s than in the 1950s, when the poverty rate dropped. Liberal critics have responded with the argument that, although growth in the GNP does create jobs, in the 1970s the growth was insufficient to handle the "unusually large numbers of women and young people (from the baby boom generation) who were entering the job market," resulting in an increase in unemployment. Moreover, real wages, which had risen steadily in the 1950s and 1960s, stopped growing in the 1970s. Greenstein states that "when unemployment rises and real wages fall, poverty increases—and low income groups (especially black males) are affected the most." Thus, liberal critics maintain that far from being unimportant, the economy was the major cause of the failure of poverty to decline in the 1970s. If it had not been for the benefit programs that Murray attacks, the poverty rate would have risen further still.[45]

Murray's book has indeed "lit a fire" under liberals; if these and other responses are any indication, we could be seeing the beginnings of a major revival in the liberal approach to the ghetto underclass phenomenon. But the responses are still largely in reaction to what conservative thinkers are saying. In conclusion I should like to suggest how the liberal perspective might be refocused to provide the kind of intellectual and social policy leadership needed to balance the public discourse on the ghetto underclass.

Conclusion: Toward a Refocused Liberal Perspective

If the liberal perspective on the ghetto underclass is to regain the influence it has lost since the 1960s, it will be necessary to do more than simply react to what conservative scholars and policymakers are saying. Liberals will also have to propose thoughtful explanations of the rise in inner-city social dislocations. Such explanations should emphasize the dynamic interplay between ghetto-specific cultural characteristics and social and economic opportunities. This would necessitate taking into account the effects not only of changes in American economic organization but also of demographic changes and changes in the laws and policies of the government as well. In this connection, the relationships between joblessness and family structure, joblessness and other social dislocations (crime, teenage pregnancy, welfare dependency, etc.), and joblessness and social orientation among different age-groups would receive special attention.

However, thoughtful explanations of the recent rise in the problems of the underclass depend on careful empirical research. It is not sufficient to rely solely on census data and other secondary sources. Liberals will have to augment such information with empirical data on the ghetto underclass experience and on conditions in the broader society that have shaped and continue to shape that experience. This calls for a number of different research strategies ranging from survey to ethnographic to historical.

But first, liberals will have to change the way they have tended to approach this subject in recent years. They can no longer afford to be timid in addressing these problems, to debate whether or not concepts such as the *underclass* should even be used, to look for data to deny the very existence of an underclass, or, finally, to rely heavily on the easy explanation of racism.

These are my suggestions for refocusing the liberal perspective. It will not be easy and there is a lot of work to be done. But such an effort is needed if we are to provide a more balanced public discourse on the problems of the ghetto underclass. In the ensuing chapters, I follow these suggestions in an attempt to describe the growing problems of urban social dislocations in the inner city, explain why these problems sharply increased when they did and in the way that they did, and then use this analysis to suggest a comprehensive policy agenda that moves beyond race-specific issues to confront more fundamental problems associated with changes in advanced industrial society, changes that have had a significant impact on life and experience in the inner city.

2 Social Change and Social Dislocations in the Inner City

The social problems of urban life in the United States are, in large measure, the problems of racial inequality. The rates of crime, drug addiction, out-of-wedlock births, female-headed families, and welfare dependency have risen dramatically in the last several years, and they reflect a noticeably uneven distribution by race. As emphasized in the previous chapter, liberal social scientists, journalists, policymakers, and civil rights leaders have nonetheless been reluctant to face this fact. Often analysts make no reference to race at all when discussing issues such as crime and teenage pregnancy, except to emphasize the deleterious effects of racial discrimination or of the institutionalized inequality of American society.

As I argued in the previous chapter, one of the reasons social scientists have been reluctant to research these problems until very recently may have been the virulent attacks on the Moynihan report in the latter half of the 1960s.[1] There is no need here for detailed discussion of the controversy surrounding the report, which like so many controversies over social issues raged in great measure because of distortions and misinterpretations. However, it should be pointed out that various parts of Moynihan's arguments had been raised previously by such persons as Kenneth B. Clark, E. Franklin Frazier, and Bayard Rustin.[2] Like Rustin, Moynihan argued that as antidiscrimination legislation breaks down barriers to black liberty, issues of equality will draw attention away from issues of liberty; in other words, concerns for equal resources enabling blacks to live comparable to whites in material ways will exceed concerns of freedom. The simple removal of legal barriers will not achieve the goal of equality, he maintained, because the cumulative effects of discrimination make it very nearly impossible for a majority of black Americans to take advantage of opportunities provided by civil rights laws. He observed, in this connection, that "the Negro community is dividing between a stable middle-class group that is steadily growing stronger and more successful, and an increasingly disorganized and disadvantaged lower-class group."[3]

Like Clark, Moynihan emphasized that family deterioration—as revealed in urban blacks' rising rates of broken marriages, female-headed homes, out-of-wedlock births, and welfare dependency—was one of the central problems of the black lower class. And as had Frazier, Moynihan argued that the problems of the black family, which present major obstacles to black equality, derive from previous patterns of inequality that originated in the slavery experience and have been maintained and reinforced by years of racial discrimination. He concluded his report by recommending a shift in the direction of federal civil rights activities to "bring the Negro American to full and equal sharing in the responsibilities and rewards of citizenship" and thereby to increase "the stability and resources of the Negro American family."[4]

The vitriolic criticism of the Moynihan report, which paid far more attention to Moynihan's unflattering depiction of the black family in the urban ghetto than to his historical analysis of the black family's special plight or to his proposed remedies, helped create an atmosphere that discouraged many social scientists from researching certain aspects of lower-class black life.[5] Meanwhile, significant developments were unfolding in ghetto communities across the United States that profoundly affected the lives of millions of blacks and dramatically revealed that the problems earlier described by Clark, Moynihan, and others had reached catastrophic proportions. To be more specific, one-quarter of all black births occurred outside of marriage in 1965, the year Moynihan wrote his report on the Negro family, and by 1980 57 percent were; in 1965 nearly 25 percent of all black families were headed by women, and by 1980 43 percent were;[6] partly as a result, welfare dependency among poor blacks has mushroomed. And perhaps the most dramatic indicator of the extent to which social dislocations have afflicted urban blacks is crime, especially violent crime, which has increased sharply in recent years. Finally, these growing social problems have accompanied increasing black rates of joblessness.

Although these problems are heavily concentrated in urban areas, it would be a serious mistake to assume that they afflict all segments of the urban minority community. Rather, these problems disproportionately plague the ghetto underclass.

The Tangle of Pathology in the Inner City

When figures on black crime, teenage pregnancy, female-headed families, and welfare dependency are released to the public without sufficient explanation, racial stereotypes are reinforced. And the tendency of liberal social scientists either to ignore these issues or to address them in circumspect ways does more to reinforce than to undermine racist perceptions.

These problems cannot be accounted for simply in terms of racial discrimination or in terms of a culture of poverty. Rather, they must be seen as having complex sociological antecedents that range from demographic changes to problems of economic organization. But before turning to these explanatory factors, I should like to outline the growing problems of social dislocation in the inner city, beginning first with violent crime.

Race and Violent Crime

Only one of nine persons in the United States is black; yet in 1984 nearly one of every two persons arrested for murder and nonnegligent manslaughter was black, and 41 percent of all murder victims were black. As Norval Morris and Michael Tonry indicate, "Homicide is the leading cause of death of black men and women aged 25 to 34." Furthermore, 61 percent of all persons arrested for robbery and 38 percent of those arrested for aggravated assault in 1984 were black. Moreover, the rate of black imprisonment in 1984 was 6.25 times greater than the rate of white imprisonment.[7]

The disproportionate involvement of blacks in violent crime is clearly revealed in the data on city arrests collected by the Federal Bureau of Investigation (FBI). Blacks constitute 13 percent of the population in cities, but, as reported in table 2.1, they account for over half of all city arrests for violent crimes. More than half of those arrested in cities for murders and nonnegligent manslaughter, more than half of those arrested for forcible rape, and 64 percent of those arrested for robbery are black. The rate of black crime is even greater in large urban areas where blacks constitute a larger percentage of the population. Although the FBI does not provide data on arrest by size of city and race, the magnitude and social significance of the problems of violent black crimes in large metropolises can perhaps be revealed by examining data on murder rates provided by the Chicago Police Department.[8]

The 1970s was a violent decade in the history of Chicago. The number of violent crimes in the city began to rise in the mid-1960s and reached record levels in the 1970s. The number of homicides jumped from 195 in 1965 to 810 in 1970. During the severe recession year of 1974, the city experienced a record 970 murders (30.8 per 100,000 population) and 4,071 shooting assaults. Despite the record number of homicides in Chicago in 1974, Chicago's murder rate was actually lower than those in Detroit, Cleveland, Washington, D.C., and Bal-

TABLE 2.1
Arrests in Cities, by Type of Offense and Race, 1984

Offence	Racial Distribution			
	White (%)	Black (%)	American Indian or Alaskan Native (%)	Asian or Pacific Islander (%)
Violent crime	48.6	50.2	0.7	0.6
Murder and nonnegligent manslaughter	46.7	52.0	0.6	0.8
Forcible rape	46.4	52.3	0.7	0.6
Robbery	35.2	63.7	0.4	0.7
Aggravated assault	56.1	42.5	0.8	0.6
Property crime	66.1	32.0	1.1	0.9
Burglary	66.2	32.4	0.8	0.6
Larceny-theft	66.1	31.7	1.2	1.0
Motor vehicle theft	63.6	34.6	0.9	0.9
Arson	74.2	24.3	0.8	0.7
Crime total index[a]	62.5	35.6	1.0	0.8

Source: U.S. Department of Justice, Uniform Crime Reports for the United States, 1984 (Washington, D.C.: Government Printing Office, 1985).

[a] Percentage of all crimes by each ethnic group.

timore.[9] In 1981, another recession year, 877 murders were committed in Chicago, the second highest number ever; yet its rate placed Chicago only fifth among the ten largest urban areas in the country (see table 2.2).

In Chicago, like other major urban centers, blacks are not only more likely to commit murder, they are also more likely to be victims of murder. During the 1970s, 8 of every 10 murderers in Chicago were black, as were 7 of every 10 murder victims. In 1983, 513 blacks (other than Hispanic), 108 Hispanics, and 95 whites (other than Hispanic) were victims of murder; of known perpetrators that year, 515 were black, 102 were Hispanic, and 58 were white. In 1970 only 56 of the murder victims were Hispanic, compared with 135 white and 607 black victims. Age changes in the Hispanic population accounted in large measure for their increased involvement in violent crimes—a matter that will be discussed later in greater detail.

Homicides in Chicago were overwhelmingly intraracial or intra-ethnic. During the 1970s, of those murders where the ethnicity of the offender was known, 98 percent of black homicides were committed by

TABLE 2.2
Murder Rates per 100,000 Population of Ten Largest U.S. Cities, 1979–1984

City	1979		1980		1981		1982		1983		1984		Six-Year Average	
	Rate	Rank	Rate	Rank	Rate	Rank	Rate	Rank	Rate	Rank	Rate	Rank	Rate	Rank
Detroit	35.9	3	45.7	2	42.1	1	43.4	1	49.3	1	45.3	1	43.6	1
Cleveland	45.6	1	46.3	1	40.7	2	34.0	3	25.9	6	28.0	4	36.8	2
Houston	40.3	2	39.1	3	NA	NA	40.4	2	32.5	2	26.2	6	35.7	3
Dallas	34.8	4	35.4	4	31.8	4	31.5	4	26.8	4	29.8	2	31.7	4
Washington	27.4	8	31.5	6	35.1	3	30.7	5	29.4	3	28.1	3	30.4	5
Los Angeles	27.4	7	34.2	5	29.0	6	27.4	7	26.0	5	24.1	8	28.0	6
Baltimore	31.0	5	27.5	8	28.6	7	28.4	6	25.0	7	27.3	5	28.0	7
Chicago	28.0	6	28.9	7	29.1	5	22.2	9	24.1	8	24.6	7	26.2	8
New York	24.4	9	25.8	10	25.8	8	23.5	8	22.8	9	20.2	9	23.8	9
Philadelphia	21.9	10	25.9	9	21.5	9	19.7	10	18.4	10	15.8	10	20.5	10

Sources: U.S. Department of Justice, *Uniform Crime Reports for the United States, 1980, 1981, 1982, 1983, 1984, 1985* (Washington, D.C.: Government Printing Office, 1981, 1982, 1983, 1984, 1985, 1986).

Notes: The 1979 rate for Los Angeles is slightly higher than that for Washington, D.C., before rounding. The six-year average is slightly higher for Los Angeles than for Baltimore before rounding. The top ten cities in population in the 1970 census (above) are not the same as those of the 1980 census.

other blacks, 75 percent of Hispanic homicides were committed by other Hispanics, and 51.5 percent of white homicides were committed by other whites. This pattern held for the most recent year for which homicide data are available. In 1983, 98 percent of the known perpetrators of black homicide were black, 81 percent of perpetrators of Hispanic homicide were Hispanic, and 52 percent of perpetrators of white homicide were white.[10]

In examining the figures on homicide in Chicago it is important to recognize that the rates vary significantly according to the economic status of the community, with the highest rates of violent crime associated with the communities of the underclass. More than half of the 1983 murders and aggravated assaults in Chicago occurred in seven of the city's twenty-four police districts, the areas with a heavy concentration of low-income black and Latino residents.[11]

The most violent area is the overwhelmingly black Wentworth Avenue police district on the South Side of Chicago. Indeed, in 1983, 81 murders (11 percent of city total) and 1,691 aggravated assaults (13 percent of city total) occurred in this four-square-mile district which contains only 3.4 percent of the city's total population.[12]

The Wentworth figures on violent crime are high partly because the Robert Taylor Homes, the largest public-housing project in the city of Chicago, is located there. Robert Taylor Homes is a complex of twenty-eight sixteen-story buildings covering ninety-two acres. The official population in 1980 was almost 20,000, but, according to a recent report, "there are an additional 5,000 to 7,000 adult residents who are not registered with the housing authority."[13] In 1983 all of the registered households were black and 69 percent of the official population were minors. The median family income was $5,470. Ninety-three percent of the families with children were headed by a single parent. Eight-three percent of the (nonelderly headed) families with children received Aid to Families with Dependent Children (AFDC).[14] Unemployment was estimated to be 47 percent in 1980. Although in 1980 only a little more than 0.5 percent of Chicago's more than 3 million people lived in the Robert Taylor Homes, "11 percent of the city's murders, 9 percent of its rapes, and 10 percent of its aggravated assaults were committed in the project."[15]

Robert Taylor Homes is by no means the only violent large housing project in Chicago. For example, Cabrini-Green, the second largest, experienced a rash of violent crimes in early 1981 that prompted Chicago's then mayor Jane Byrne to take up residence there for several weeks to help stem the tide. Cabrini-Green includes eighty-one high- and low-rise buildings covering seventy acres on Chicago's Near North

Side. In 1983 nearly 13,000 people, almost all black, were officially registered there; but like the Robert Taylor Homes, many more reside there than appear in the records of the Chicago Housing Authority (CHA). Minors were 66 percent of the registered population; 90 percent of the families with children were headed by women; 83 percent of the households were on welfare (AFDC or General Assistance), and 81 percent of the families with children received AFDC in 1983.[16] In a nine-week period beginning in early January 1981, ten Cabrini-Green residents were murdered; thirty-five were wounded by gunshots, including random sniping; and more than fifty firearms were confiscated, "the tip of an immense illegal arsenal," according to the Chicago police.[17]

Family Dissolution and Welfare Dependency

What is true of the structure of families and welfare dependency in the Robert Taylor Homes and Cabrini-Green is typical of all the CHA housing projects. In 1983, of the 25,000 families with children living in CHA projects, only 8 percent were married-couple families, and 80 percent of the family households received AFDC.[18] But female-headed families and welfare dependency are not confined to public-housing projects. The projects simply magnify these problems, which permeate ghetto neighborhoods and to a lesser extent metropolitan areas generally.

The increase in the number of female-headed families in the United States was dramatic during the 1970s. Whereas the total number of families grew by 20 percent from 1970 to 1984, the number of female-headed families increased by 51 percent. Moreover, the number of families headed by women with one or more of their children present in the home increased by 77 percent. If the change in family structure was notable for all families in the 1970s, it was close to phenomenal for blacks and Hispanics. Whereas families headed by white women increased by 63 percent, the number of families headed by black and Hispanic women grew by 108 and 164 percent, respectively.[19]

In 1965 Moynihan expressed great concern that 25 percent of all black families were headed by women. The proportion surpassed 28 percent in 1970, reached 40 percent by 1979, and registered an alarming 43 percent in 1984. By contrast, only 13 percent of white families and 23 percent of Hispanic families were headed by women in 1984, even though each group recorded a significant increase in female-headed families during the 1970s.[20]

In 1984, 73 percent of all female householders resided in metropolitan areas (39 percent in central cities and 34 percent in the adjacent suburbs); of those who were black and Hispanic, 79 and 91 percent respectively lived in metropolitan areas, with 60 percent of the metropolitan blacks and 64 percent of the Hispanics in the central city. The women householders were younger than in previous years. For example, from 1970 to 1984 the number of female heads of families forty-five years or older increased by nearly 1 million (31 percent), while those under forty-five years of age increased by almost 3.3 million (135 percent), resulting in a decline in the median age from 48.2 years in 1979 to 41.4 years in 1984.[21]

Even if a female householder is employed full time, her earnings are usually substantially less than that of a male worker and are not likely to be supplemented with income from a second full-time employed member of the household. For women who head families and are not employed (including those who have never been employed, have dropped out of the labor force to become full-time mothers, or are employed only part time), the economic situation is often desperate. In 1983 the median income of female-headed families ($11,789) was only 43 percent of the median income of husband-wife families ($27,286); the median income of families headed by black women ($7,999) was only 37 percent of the median income of husband-wife black families ($21,840). In 1983, of the roughly 3.6 million families that reported incomes of less than $5,000, 57 percent were headed by women.[22]

The relationship between level of family income and family structure is even more pronounced among black families. As shown in table 2.3, whereas 80 percent of all black families with incomes under $4,000 were headed by women in 1978, only 8 percent with incomes of $25,000 or more were headed by women; in metropolitan areas, the difference was even greater.

Economic hardship has become almost synonymous with black female-headed families: only 30 percent of all poor black families were headed by women in 1959, but by 1978 the proportion reached 74 percent (though it has remained slightly below that level since then), due, as discussed in the next chapter, to the increase in the number of married-couple parents in poverty in recent years. By contrast, 39 percent of all poor white families were headed by women in 1978, after which the white proportion also decreased slightly.[23] Reflecting the growth of black female-headed families, the proportion of black children in married-couple families dropped significantly, from 63 percent in 1970 to 50 percent in 1978 and 46 percent in 1984. Moreover, 46 percent of black children under eighteen years of age resided in families whose incomes were below the poverty level in 1983, and three-fourths of those were in families headed by females.[24]

TABLE 2.3
Proportion of Families at Selected Income Levels, by Race, Head of Household, and Metropolitan Residence, 1978

Race and Income Level ($)	All Families (%)	Families with Female Heads (%)	All Families in Metropolitan Areas (%)	Metropolitan Families with Female Heads (%)
Black				
Under 4,000	15.9	80.3	70.7	85.1
4,000–6,999	16.2	63.8	70.1	71.2
7,000–10,999	18.3	46.2	74.8	50.7
11,000–15,999	16.7	28.9	76.3	31.8
16,000–24,999	19.2	15.3	82.7	15.4
25,000 and over	13.4	7.7	88.5	7.6
White				
Under 4,000	4.3	42.2	52.4	51.0
4,000–6,999	4.7	27.6	56.2	33.7
7,000–10,999	12.7	19.5	57.7	21.8
11,000–15,999	16.9	13.4	59.9	16.7
16,000–24,999	28.8	7.2	66.0	8.5
25,000 and over	29.5	2.9	75.4	3.1

Source: U.S. Bureau of the Census, Current Population Reports, series P-60, no. 123, "Money Income of Families and Persons in the United States, 1978" (Washington, D.C.: Government Printing Office), p. 70.

The rise of female-headed families among blacks corresponds closely with the increase in the ratio of out-of-wedlock births. Only 15 percent of all black births in 1959 were out of wedlock. This figure jumped to roughly 24 percent in 1965 and 57 percent in 1982, almost five times greater than the white ratio. Indeed, despite the far greater white population, in 1982 the number of black babies born out of wedlock (328,879) nearly matched the number of illegitimate white babies.[25] Although the proportion of black births that are outside of marriage is, in part, a function of the general decline in fertility among married blacks (a point discussed below), it is also a reflection of the growing prevalence of out-of-wedlock births among teenagers. For example, despite a sharp drop in the rate of teenage childbearing among both blacks and whites since 1960, the proportion of black teenage births that were out of wedlock increased from only 42 percent in 1960, to 63 percent in 1970, and then to a staggering 89 percent in 1983. A similar pattern occurred among whites—7 percent of the white teenage births were out of wedlock in 1960, 17 percent in 1970, and 39 percent in 1983.[26]

These problems are, to repeat, most acute in ghetto neighborhoods. For example, in the overwhelmingly black and impoverished communities of Chicago (communities with rates of household poverty that exceeded 40 percent in 1980) the proportion of female households increased from 34 to 61 percent in Garfield Park between 1970 and 1980, from 37 to 66 percent in the Near West Side, from 33 to 61 percent in North Lawndale, from 41 to 75 percent in the Near South Side, from 43 to 70 percent in Douglas, from 48 to 78 percent in Oakland, from 40 to 71 percent in Grand Boulevard, from 35 to 70 percent in Washington Park, and from 44 to 65 percent in Riverdale. These alarming trends, in turn, are related to extramarital childbearing. In 1983 nearly three-quarter of all black births in Chicago were out of wedlock, compared to only about half in 1970. Ninety-five percent of all black teenage births in Chicago were out of wedlock in 1983, compared to 75 percent in 1970.[27]

These developments have significant implications for the problems of welfare dependency. In 1977 the proportion of families receiving AFDC that were black (43 percent) slightly exceeded the proportion that were white other than Spanish (42.5 percent), despite the great difference in total population.[28] It is estimated that about 60 percent of the children who are born out of wedlock and are alive and not adopted receive welfare. A study by the Urban Institute pointed out that "more than half of all AFDC assistance in 1975 was paid to women who were or had been teenage mothers."[29]

In this section, I have focused on female-headed families, out-of-wedlock births, and teenage pregnancy because they have become inextricably connected with poverty and dependency. The sharp increase in these and other forms of social dislocations in the inner city (including joblessness and violent crime) offers a difficult challenge to policymakers. Because there has been so little recent systematic research on these problems and a paucity of thoughtful explanations for them, racial stereotypes of life and behavior in the urban ghetto have not been adequately challenged. The physical and social isolation of residents in the urban ghetto is thereby reinforced. The fundamental question is: Why have the social conditions of the urban underclass deteriorated so rapidly since the mid-1960s and especially since 1970?

Toward a Comprehensive Explanation

There is no single explanation for the racial or ethnic variations in the rates of social dislocations I have described. But I should like to suggest several interrelated explanations that represent a comprehensive set of variables—including societal, demographic, and neighborhood variables. In the process, I hope to show that the sources of current problems in the inner city are exceedingly complex and that their amelioration calls for imaginative and comprehensive programs of economic and social reform that are in sharp contrast to the current approaches to social policy in America, which are based on short-term political considerations.

The Effects of Historic and Contemporary Discrimination

Discrimination is the most frequently invoked explanation of social dislocations in the urban ghetto. However, proponents of the discrimination thesis often fail to make a distinction between the effects of historic discrimination, that is, discrimination before the middle of the twentieth century, and the effects of discrimination following that time. They therefore find it difficult to explain why the economic position of poor urban blacks actually deteriorated during the very period in which the most sweeping antidiscrimination legislation and programs were enacted and implemented.[30] Their emphasis on discrimination becomes even more problematic in view of the economic progress of the black middle class during the same period.

There is no doubt that contemporary discrimination has contributed to or aggravated the social and economic problems of the ghetto underclass. But is discrimination greater today than in 1948, when, as shown in table 2.4, black unemployment was less than half the 1980 rate, and the black-white unemployment ratio was almost one-fourth less than the 1980 ratio? Although labor economists have noted the shortcomings of the official unemployment rates as an indicator of the economic conditions of groups, these rates have generally been accepted as one significant measure of relative disadvantage.[31] It is therefore important to point out that it was not until 1954 that the 2:1 unemployment ratio between blacks and whites was reached, and that since 1954, despite shifts from good to bad economic years, the black-white unemployment ratio has shown very little change. There are obviously many reasons for the higher levels of black unemployment since the mid-1950s (including the migration of blacks from a rural subsistence economy to an urban economy with protected labor markets), but to suggest contemporary discrimination as the main factor is to obscure the impact of economic and demographic changes and to leave unexplained the question of why black unemployment was lower not after but before 1950.

The question has also been raised about the association between

TABLE 2.4
Unemployment Rates, by Race, Selected Years, 1948–1984

| Year | Unemployment Rate | | Black-White Unemployment Ratio |
	Black and Other Races	White	
1948	5.9	3.5	1.7
1951	5.3	3.1	1.7
1954	9.0	5.0	2.0
1957	7.9	3.8	2.1
1960	10.2	4.9	2.1
1963	10.8	5.0	2.2
1966	7.3	3.3	2.2
1969	6.4	3.2	2.1
1972	10.0	5.1	2.0
1975	13.8	7.8	1.8
1978	11.9	5.2	2.3
1981	14.2	6.7	2.1
1984	14.4	6.5	2.2

Sources: U.S. Department of Labor, Employment and Training Report of the President (Washington, D.C.: Government Printing Office, 1982); and idem, Employment and
Earnings 32 (Washington, D.C.: Government Printing Office, January 1985).

Notes: The unemployment rate is the percentage of the
civilian labor force aged sixteen and over that is unemployed. "Black and other races" is a U.S. Census Bureau
designation and is used in those cases where data are not
available solely for blacks. However, because about 90
percent of the population so designated is black, statistics
reported for this category generally reflect the condition of
the black population. The black-white unemployment ratio
is the percentage of blacks who are unemployed divided by
the percentage of whites who are unemployed.

contemporary discrimination within the criminal justice systems and
the disproportionate rates of black crime. An answer was provided by
Alfred Blumstein in an important study of the racial disproportionality
in America's state prison populations. Blumstein found that 80 percent
of the disproportionate black incarceration rates during the 1970s could
be attributed to the disproportionate number of blacks arrested and
that the more serious the offense, the stronger the association between
arrest rates and incarceration rates. For example, all but a small fraction of the disproportionate black incarceration rates for homicide, ag-

gravated assault, and robbery could be accounted for by the differential black arrest rates. He points out, therefore, that discrimination probably plays a more important role in the black incarceration rates for less serious crimes. He also states that "even if the relatively large racial differences in handling these offenses were totally eliminated, however, that would not result in a major shift in the racial mix of prison populations."[32]

Thus, if a higher rate of black incarceration is accounted for by a higher rate of arrests, the question moves back a step: is the racial disproportionality in United States prisons largely the result of black bias in arrest? Recent research in criminology demonstrates consistent relationships between the distribution of crimes by race as reported in the arrest statistics of the *Uniform Crime Reports* and the distribution based on reports by victims of assault, robbery, and rape (where contact with the offender was direct).[33] "While these results are certainly short of definitive evidence that there is not bias in arrests," observes Blumstein, "they do strongly suggest that the arrest process, whose demographics we can observe, is reasonably representative of the crime process for at least these serious crime types."[34]

It should also be emphasized that, contrary to prevailing opinion, the black family showed signs of significant deterioration not before, but after, the middle of the twentieth century. Until the publication of Herbert Gutman's impressive historical study on the black family, scholars had assumed that the current problems of the black family could be traced back to slavery. "Stimulated by the bitter public and academic controversy" surrounding the Moynihan report, Gutman presented data that convincingly demonstrated that the black family was not particularly disorganized during slavery or during the early years of blacks' first migration to the urban North beginning after the turn of the century. The problems of the modern black family, he suggests, are a product of more recent social forces.[35]

But are these problems mainly a consequence of present-day discrimination, or are they related to other factors that may have little or nothing to do with race? If contemporary discrimination is the main culprit, why did it produce the most severe problems of urban social dislocation during the 1970s, a decade that followed an unprecedented period of civil rights legislation and ushered in the affirmative action programs? The problem, as I see it, is unraveling the effects of present-day discrimination, on the one hand, and of historic discrimination, on the other.

My own view is that historic discrimination is far more important than contemporary discrimination in explaining the plight of the ghetto underclass, but that a full appreciation of the effects of historic discrimination is impossible without taking into account other historical and contemporary forces that have also shaped the experiences and behavior of impoverished urban minorities.

The Importance of the Flow of Migrants

One of the legacies of historic discrimination is the presence of a large black underclass in central cities. Blacks constituted approximately 23 percent of the population of central cities in 1983, but they were 43 percent of the poor in these cities.[36] In accounting for the historical developments that contributed to this concentration of urban black poverty, I should like to draw briefly upon Stanley Lieberson's work.[37] On the basis of a systematic analysis of early United States censuses and other sources of data, Lieberson concluded that in many spheres of life, including the labor market, blacks were discriminated against far more severely in the early twentieth century than were the new white immigrants from southern, central, and eastern Europe. The disadvantage of skin color, in the sense that the dominant white population preferred whites over nonwhites, is one that blacks shared with the Japanese, Chinese, and other nonwhite groups. However, skin color per se "was not an insurmountable obstacle." Because changes in immigration policy cut off Asian migration to America in the late nineteenth century, the Chinese and Japanese populations did not reach large numbers and, therefore, did not pose as great a threat as did blacks. Lieberson was aware that the "response of whites to Chinese and Japanese was of the same violent and savage character in areas where they were concentrated," but he emphasized that "the threat was quickly stopped through changes in immigration policy." Furthermore, the discontinuation of large-scale immigration from China and Japan enabled those already here to solidify networks of ethnic contacts and to occupy particular occupational niches in small, relatively stable communities.

If different population sizes accounted for much of the difference in the economic success of blacks and Asians, they also helped to determine the dissimilar rates of progress of urban blacks and the new European arrivals. The dynamic factor behind these differences, and perhaps the most important single contributor to the varying rates of urban racial and ethnic progress in the twentieth-century United States, is the flow of migrants. After the changes in immigration policy that halted Asian immigration to America came drastic restrictions on new European immigration. However, black migration to the urban North continued in substantial numbers for several decades. The sizable and continuous migration of blacks from the South to the North, coupled with the curtailment of immigration from eastern, central, and southern Europe, created a situation in which other whites muffled their negative disposition toward the new Europeans and directed their antagonisms against blacks. According to Lieberson, "the presence of blacks made it harder to discriminate against the new Europeans because the alternative was viewed less favorably."[38]

The flow of migrants also made it much more difficult for blacks to follow the path of both the new Europeans and the Asian-Americans in overcoming the negative effects of discrimination by finding special occupational niches. Only a small part of a group's total work force can be absorbed in such specialities when the group's population increases rapidly or is a sizable proportion of the total population. Furthermore, the continuing flow of migrants had a harmful effect on the urban blacks who had arrived earlier. Lieberson points out:

> Sizable numbers of newcomers raise the level of ethnic and/or racial consciousness on the part of others in the city; moreover, if these newcomers are less able to compete for more desirable positions than are the longer-standing residents, they will tend to undercut the position of other members of the group. This is because the older residents and those of higher socioeconomic status cannot totally avoid the newcomers, although they work at it through subgroup residential isolation. Hence, there is some deterioration in the quality of residential areas, schools, and the like for those earlier residents who might otherwise enjoy more fully the rewards of their mobility. Beyond this, from the point of view of the dominant outsiders, the newcomers may reinforce stereotypes and negative dispositions that affect all members of the group.[39]

The pattern of rural black migration that began with the rise of urban industrial centers in the North has been strong in recent years in the South. In Atlanta and Houston, to illustrate, the continuous influx of rural southern blacks, due in large measure to the increasing mechanization of agriculture, has resulted in the creation of large urban ghettos that closely resemble those in the North.[40] The net result in both the North and the South is that as the nation entered the last quarter of this century, its large cities continued to have a disproportionate concentration of low-income blacks who were especially vulnerable to recent structural changes in the economy.

It should be noted, however, that black migration to urban areas has been minimal in recent years. Indeed, between 1970 and 1977 there was actually a net outmigration of 653,000 blacks from the central cities.[41] In most large cities the number of blacks increased only moderately or declined. Increases in the urban black population during the 1970s were mainly due to births,[42] which indicates that for the first time in the twentieth century the ranks of central-city blacks are no longer being replenished by poor migrants. This could result in an improvement in the average socioeconomic status of urban blacks, including a decrease in joblessness, crime, out-of-wedlock births, teenage pregnancy, female-headed families, and welfare dependency. However, although the Asian and newer European immigrants have benefited from a cessation of migration, it is difficult to determine whether the cessation of black migration to the central city will result in noticeable improvement in the status of urban blacks. There are other factors—such as discrimination, structural changes in the economy, and the size of the population—that affect the differential rate of ethnic-group progress at different periods. Moreover, the growing concentration of poverty in inner-city neighborhoods, to be discussed later, could offset any real gains associated with a decrease in urban migration. Nonetheless, one of the major obstacles to urban black advancement—the constant flow of migrants—has been removed.

Hispanics, on the other hand, appear to be migrating to urban areas in increasing numbers. The comparative status of Hispanics as an ethnic group is not entirely clear because comparable data on their types of residence in 1970 are not available. But data collected since 1974 indicate that their numbers in central cities are increasing rapidly because of both immigration and births. Indeed, in several large cities, including Los Angeles, Miami, San Diego, Denver, and Phoenix, they outnumber American blacks.[43] Although the Hispanic population is diverse in nationalities and socioeconomic status—for example, the median income of Mexicans and Cubans is significantly greater than that of Puerto Ricans—they are often identified collectively as a distinct ethnic group because of their common Spanish-speaking origins.[44] Accordingly, the rapid growth of the urban Hispanic population, accompanied by the opposite trend for the urban black population, could contribute significantly to different outcomes for these two groups in the next several decades. More specifically, whereas urban blacks could record a decrease in their rates of joblessness, crime, teenage pregnancy, female-headed homes, and welfare dependency, Hispanics could show a steady increase in each. Moreover, blacks could experience a decrease in the ethnic hostility directed toward them, but Hispanics, with their growing visibility, could be victims of increasing ethnic antagonisms.

However, Hispanics are not the only ethnic group in urban America experiencing a rapid growth in numbers. According to the United States Census Bureau, Asians, who constitute less than 2 percent of the nation's population, were the fastest-growing American ethnic group in the 1970s. Following the liberalization of United States immigration policies, the large influx of immigrants from Southeast Asia and, to a lesser degree, from South Korea and China has been associated with reports of increasing problems, including anti-Asian sentiments, joblessness, and violent crime. According to one report, the nation's economic woes have exacerbated the situation as the newcomers have competed with black, Hispanic, and white urban workers for jobs. Moreover, the steady inpouring of immigrants from Taiwan, Hong Kong, and China has upset the social organization of Chinatowns. Once stable and homogeneous, Chinatowns are now suffering from problems that have traditionally plagued inner-city black neighborhoods, such as joblessness, school dropouts, overcrowding, violent street crime, and gang warfare.[45]

The Relevance of Changes in the Age Structure

The flow of migrants also affects the average age of an ethnic group. For example, the black migration to urban centers—the continual replenishment of urban black populations by poor newcomers—predictably skewed the age profile of the urban black community and kept it relatively young. The higher the median age of a group, the greater its representation in higher income categories and professional positions. It is therefore not surprising that ethnic groups such as blacks and Hispanics, who on average are younger than whites, also tend to have high unemployment and crime rates.[46] As revealed in table 2.5, ethnic groups differ markedly in their median age and in the proportion under age fifteen.

In the nation's central cities in 1977, the median age for whites was 30.3, for blacks 23.9, and for Hispanics 21.8. One cannot overemphasize the importance of the sudden growth of young minorities in the central cities. The number of central-city blacks aged fourteen to twenty-four rose by 78 percent from 1960 to 1970, compared with an increase of only 23 percent for whites of the same age.[47] From 1970 to 1977 the increase in the number of young blacks slackened off somewhat, but it was still substantial. For example, in the central cities the number of blacks aged fourteen to twenty-four increased by 21 percent from 1970 to 1977 and the number of Hispanics by 26 percent, while whites of this age-group decreased by 4 percent.[48]

On the basis of these demographic changes alone one would expect blacks and Hispanics to contribute disproportionately to the increasing

TABLE 2.5
Age Structure of Racial and Ethnic Groups, 1984

Group	Under 15 Years (%)	65 Years and Over (%)	Median Age (years)
White	20.9	12.6	32.2
Black	27.7	8.1	26.3
Hispanic	32.3	4.0	23.7
U.S. Total	21.9	11.9	31.2

Sources: U.S. Bureau of the Census, Current Population Reports, series P-25, no. 965, "Estimates of the Population of the United States, by Age, Sex, and Race, 1980 to 1984" (Washington, D.C.: Government Printing Office, 1985); and idem, Current Population Reports, Series P-20, no. 396, "Persons of Spanish Origin in the United States, March 1982" (Washington, D.C.: Government Printing Office, 1985).

Note: The Hispanic data are for 1982, the last year for which estimates are available.

rates of social dislocation in the central city, such as crime. Indeed, 66 percent of all those arrested for violent and property crimes in American cities in 1980 were under twenty-five years of age.[49]

Youth is not only a factor in crime; it is also associated with out-of-wedlock births, female-headed homes, and welfare dependency. Teenagers accounted for 38 percent of all out-of-wedlock births in 1982, and 78 percent of all illegitimate black births in that year were to teenage and young adult women. The median age of female householders has decreased substantially in recent years, and the explosion of teenage births has contributed significantly to the rise in the number of children on AFDC, from roughly 35 per 1,000 children under eighteen in 1960 to around 114 per 1,000 in 1982.[50]

In short, much of what has gone awry in the inner city is due in part to the sheer increase in the number of young people, especially young minorities. However, as James Q. Wilson has pointed out in his analysis of the proliferation of social problems in the 1960s (a period of general economic prosperity), "changes in the age structure of the population cannot alone account for the social dislocations" of that decade. He argues, for example, that from 1960 to 1970 the rate of unemployment in the District of Columbia increased by 100 percent and the rate of serious crime by over 400 percent, yet the number of young persons between sixteen and twenty-one years of age rose by only 32 percent.

Also, the number of murders in Detroit increased from 100 in 1960 to 500 in 1971, "yet the number of young persons did not quintuple."[51]

Wilson states that the "increase in the murder rate during the 1960s was more than ten times greater than what one would have expected from the changing age structure of the population alone" and "only 13.4 percent of the increase in arrests for robbery between 1950 and 1965 could be accounted for by the increase in the numbers of persons between the ages of ten and twenty-four."[52] Speculating on this problem, Wilson advances the hypothesis that an abrupt rise in the number of young persons has an "exponential effect on the rate of certain social problems." In other words, there may be a "critical mass" of young persons in a given community such that when that mass is reached or is increased suddenly and substantially, "a self-sustaining chain reaction is set off that creates an explosive increase in the amount of crime, addiction, and welfare dependency."[53]

This hypothesis seems to be especially relevant to inner-city neighborhoods and even more so to those with large public-housing projects. Opposition from organized community groups to the construction of public housing in their neighborhoods has "led to massive, segregated housing projects, which become ghettos for minorities and the economically disadvantaged."[54] As the earlier description of the Robert Taylor Homes and Cabrini-Green in Chicago suggests, when large poor families were placed in high-density housing projects in the ghetto, both family and neighborhood life suffered. High crime rates, family dissolution, and vandalism flourished in these projects. In St. Louis, the Pruit-Igoe project, which included about ten thousand adults and children, developed serious problems five years after it opened and "it became so unlivable that it was destroyed in 1976, 22 years after it was built."[55]

In both the housing projects and other inner-city neighborhoods, residents have difficulty identifying their neighbors. They are, therefore, less likely to engage in reciprocal guardian behavior. Events in one part of the block or neighborhood tend to be of little concern to those residing in other parts.[56] These conditions of social disorganization are as acute as they are because of the unprecedented increase in the number of teenage and young adult minorities in these neighborhoods, many of whom are jobless, not enrolled in school, and a source of delinquency, crime, and unrest.

Nonetheless, despite the increase of minority teenagers and young adults, there were 6 percent fewer blacks aged thirteen and under in metropolitan areas in 1977 than in 1970, and 13 percent fewer in the central cities. White children in this age category also decreased during this period by even greater percentages: 17 percent in metropolitan areas and 24 percent in the central cities. By contrast, Hispanic children in this age category increased from 1970 to 1977 by 16 percent in metropolitan areas and 12 percent in the central cities. Thus, just as the change in migration flow could affect the rates of ethnic-group involvement in certain types of social problems, so too could changes in the age structure. Whereas whites and blacks—all other things being equal—could in the near future show a decrease in problems such as joblessness, crime, out-of-wedlock births, teenage pregnancy, family dissolution, and welfare dependency, the growing Hispanic population, owing to rapid increases in births and migration, could very likely experience increasing rates of social dislocation.

The Impact of Basic Economic Changes

The population explosion among minority youths occurred at a time when changes in the economy posed serious problems for unskilled individuals, both in and out of the labor force. Urban minorities have been particularly vulnerable to structural economic changes, such as the shift from goods-producing to service-producing industries, the increasing polarization of the labor market into low-wage and high-wage sectors, technological innovations, and the relocation of manufacturing industries out of the central cities. These economic shifts point out the fact that nearly all of the large and densely populated metropolises experienced their most rapid development during an earlier industrial and transportation era. Today these urban centers are undergoing an irreversible structural transformation from "centers of production and distribution of material goods to centers of administration, information exchange, and higher-order service provision."[57] The central-city labor market, particularly in northern areas, has been profoundly altered in the process.

In a paper on the regional and urban redistribution of people and jobs in the United States, John Kasarda points out that the transformation of major northern metropolises from centers of goods processing to centers of information processing has been accompanied by a major shift in the educational requirements for employment.[58] Whereas job losses in these cities have been greatest in industries with lower educational requirements, job growth has been concentrated in industries that require higher levels of education.

These points are illustrated in table 2.6, which presents employment changes from 1970 to 1984 in industries classified by the average level of education completed by their workers. Industries are divided into those whose workers averaged less than twelve years of schooling (less than high school) in 1982 and those whose workers averaged more than

TABLE 2.6
Central-City Jobs in Industries, by Mean Education of Employees,
1970, 1984 (figures in thousands)

City and Educational Mean of Industry	Number of Jobs 1970	1984	Change 1970–84
New York			
Less than high school	1,445	953	−492
Some higher education	1,002	1,241	239
Philadelphia			
Less than high school	396	224	−172
Some higher education	205	224	39
Boston			
Less than high school	168	124	−44
Some higher education	185	252	67
Baltimore			
Less than high school	187	114	−73
Some higher education	90	105	15
St. Louis			
Less than high school	197	108	−89
Some higher education	98	96	−2
Atlanta			
Less than high school	157	148	−9
Some higher education	92	129	37
Houston			
Less than high school	280	468	188
Some higher education	144	361	217
Denver			
Less than high school	106	111	5
Some higher education	72	131	59
San Francisco			
Less than high school	132	135	3
Some higher education	135	206	71

Source: John D. Kasarda, "The Regional and Urban Redistribution of People and Jobs in the U.S.," paper prepared for the National Research Council Committee on National Urban Policy, National Academy of Sciences, 1986.

thirteen years of education (some higher education). The figures show that all the major northern cities had consistent job losses in industries where employer education averaged less than a high school degree and consistent employment growth in industries where workers on the average acquired some higher education. For example, in New York City the number of jobs in industries with the lower education requisites decreased by 492,000 from 1970 to 1984, whereas those with higher education requisites increased by 239,000. Similar losses and gains occurred in other northern cities. The city of Boston, however, actually added more jobs (67,000) in the higher-education-requisite industries than it lost (44,000) in the lower-education-requisite industries, resulting in an overall growth of 23,000 jobs between 1970 and 1984. Whereas substantial job losses continue in manufacturing and other blue-collar industries in cities in the northeastern region of the country, "their vibrant information-processing sectors are more than compensating for blue-collar job losses, reversing decades of net employment decline."[59]

What are the implications of this transformation of the urban economy for poor minorities? First of all, cities in the North that have experienced the greatest decline of jobs in the lower-education-requisite industries since 1970 have had, at the same time, significant increases in minority residents who are seldom employed in the high-growth industries. Indeed, despite increases in educational attainment since 1970, "black males (over age sixteen) in northern cities are still most concentrated in the education completed category where employment opportunities declined the fastest and are least represented in that category where northern central city employment has most expanded since 1970." This has created "a serious mismatch between the current education distribution of minority residents in large northern cities and the changing education requirements of their rapidly transforming industries bases. This mismatch is one major reason why both unemployment rates and labor-force dropout rates among central-city blacks are much higher than those of central-city residents, and why black unemployment rates have not responded well to economic recovery in many northern cities."[60]

Furthermore, the jobless rate (unemployment and labor-force nonparticipation) among young black males (aged sixteen to twenty-four) has increased sharply since 1969 in the large central cities of the Northeast and Midwest. In the South and West jobless rates among young central-city black males are lower. Kasarda points out that cities in these regions of the United States have either had fewer job losses or have added jobs in industries with lower education requirements. Furthermore, black males in the West not only have lower combined unemployment and labor-force nonparticipation rates than their counterparts in the rest of the nation, they also have higher levels of education. "It is not fortuitous, then, that black males residing in central cities of the West also showed the smallest rises in rates of unemployment and rates of labor-force nonparticipation between 1969 and 1985."[61]

Finally, Kasarda points out that despite the substantial loss of lower-skill jobs in many northern urban centers in recent years, substantial increases in these jobs have occurred nationwide. In the food and drink industry, for example, over 2.1 million nonadministrative jobs were added between 1975 and 1985, which exceeds the total number of production jobs currently available in the combined automobile, steel, and textile industries in this country. "Unfortunately," states Kasarda, "essentially all of the national growth in entry-level and other low education requisite jobs have accrued in the suburbs, exurbs, and non-metropolitan areas far removed from growing concentrations of poorly educated urban minorities."62

Heavily concentrated in central cities, blacks have experienced a deterioration of their economic position on nearly all the major labor-market indicators. Two of these indicators are presented in tables 2.7 and 2.8, which show respectively the proportion who are in the labor force and the fraction who are employed, including those not in the labor force.

Blacks, especially young males, are dropping out of the labor force in significant numbers. The severe problems of joblessness for black teen-

TABLE 2.7

Civilian Labor-Force Participation Rates for Males Aged Sixteen to Thirty-Four, by Race and Age, Selected Years, 1960–1984

Race and Age	1960	1965	1969	1973	1977	1981	1984
Black and Other Races							
16–17	45.6	39.3	37.7	33.6	31.0	30.0	27.0
18–19	71.2	66.7	63.2	61.3	57.5	54.1	55.4
20–24	90.4	89.8	84.4	81.4	77.7	76.6	77.2
25–34	96.2	95.7	94.4	91.4	90.2	88.3	88.2
White							
16–17	46.0	44.6	48.8	52.7	53.8	51.5	47.0
18–19	69.0	65.8	66.3	72.3	74.9	73.5	70.8
20–24	87.8	85.3	82.6	85.8	86.8	87.0	86.5
25–34	97.7	97.4	97.0	96.2	96.0	95.8	95.4

Sources: U.S. Department of Labor, Employment and Training Report of the President (Washington, D.C.: Government Printing Office, 1982); and idem, Employment and Earnings, 32 (January 1985).

Note: "Black and other races" is a U.S. Census Bureau designation and is used in those cases where data are not available solely for blacks. However, because about 90 percent of the population so designated is black, statistics reported for this category generally reflect the condition of the black population.

TABLE 2.8
Employment-Population Ratios for Civilian Males Aged Sixteen to Thirty-Four, by
Race and Age, Selected Years, 1955–1984

Race and Age	1955	1965	1975	1984
Black and Other Races				
16–17	41.1	28.8	18.4	16.2
18–19	66.0	53.4	38.5	34.0
20–24	78.6	81.6	60.3	58.3
25–34	87.6	90.0	80.4	76.3
White				
16–17	42.2	38.0	41.6	37.8
18–19	64.2	58.3	60.3	60.1
20–24	80.4	80.2	74.3	78.0
25–34	95.2	94.9	89.7	89.5

Sources: U.S. Department of Labor, Employment and Training Report of the
President (Washington, D.C.: Government Printing Office, 1982); and idem,
Employment and Earnings, 32 (January 1985).

Notes: The employment-population ratio is the ratio of the employed civilian
population to the total civilian population. This excludes those who are either
institutionalized or in the armed forces. "Black and other races" is a U.S. Census
Bureau designation and is used in those cases where data are not available solely
for blacks. However, because about 90 percent of the population so designated is
black, statistics reported for this category generally reflect the condition of the
black population.

agers and young adults are seen in the figures on changes in the male
civilian labor-force participation rates (table 2.7). The percentage of
black males in the labor force fell sharply between 1960 and 1984 for
those aged sixteen to twenty-four, and somewhat less for those aged
twenty-five to thirty-four. Black males began dropping out of the labor
force in increasing numbers as early as 1965, while white males either
maintained or increased their rate of participation until 1981.

But even these figures do not reveal the severity of joblessness
among younger blacks. Only a minority of noninstitutionalized black
youth are employed. As shown in table 2.8, the percentage of black
male youth who are employed has sharply and steadily declined since
1955, whereas among white males it has increased only slightly for all
categories. The fact that only 58 percent of all black young adult males,
34 percent of all black males aged eighteen to nineteen, and 16 percent
of those aged sixteen to seventeen were employed in 1984 reveals a
problem of joblessness for young black men that has reached catastrophic proportions.

The combined indicators of labor-force participation and employment-population ratios reveal a disturbing picture of black
joblessness, especially among younger blacks. If the evidence presented in recent longitudinal research is correct, joblessness during youth
may have a long-term harmful effect on later success in the labor market.[63] Increasing joblessness during youth is a problem primarily
experienced by lower-income blacks—those already in or near the underclass. To illustrate this fact, table 2.9 provides data on unemployed
teenagers living at home. Of the unemployed teenagers living at home
in 1977, 67 percent were from families with incomes below $10,000.
And among those unemployed teenagers living at home and not enrolled in school, 75 percent were from families with less than $10,000
in income and 41 percent from families with less than $5,000.

   If the increasing black joblessness is due to structural changes in the
economy, it is also a function of the general weakness of the national
economy in recent years. As Frank Levy has clearly shown, the 1973
OPEC oil price increase resulted in both a recession and a rise in inflation which, in turn, decreased real wages by 5 percent in two years.
Levy points out that the OPEC oil increase marked the beginning of a
period of slow growth in labor productivity ("the measured value of
output per hour of labor") which had been the basis of a growth in real
wages of 2.5 to 3.5 percent a year from the end of World War II to
1973. However, from 1973 to 1982 labor productivity grew by less
than .8 percent each year. Although real wages had regained their
1973 levels by 1979, the fall of the Shah of Iran and the subsequent
second OPEC oil price increase effectively renewed the cycle, result-

TABLE 2.9
Unemployed Blacks Aged Sixteen to Nineteen Living at Home, by
School Enrollment Status and Family Income, 1977

Family Income ($)	Total (%)	Enrolled in School (%)	Not in School (%)
Under 5,000	32.1	23.6	41.0
5,000–9,999	34.7	35.7	33.6
10,000–14,999	16.8	20.0	13.4
15,000–24,999	12.0	15.0	9.0
25,000 or more	4.4	5.7	3.0
TOTAL	100.0	100.0	100.0

Source: Anne McDougall Young, "The Difference a Year Makes in
   the Nation's Youth Work Force," Monthly Labor Review 102
   (October 1979):38.

ing in a decade of wage stagnation. Levy carefully notes that it was only because the proportion of the entire population in the labor force increased from 41 to 50 percent between 1970 and today (due in large measure to the increased labor-force participation of women, the coming of age of the large baby boom cohorts and lower birth rates), "GNP per capita (i.e., per man, woman and child) could continue to rise even though GNP per worker (wages) was not doing well." In a period of slow growth in labor productivity, efforts to increase money wages only resulted in more inflation. Policymakers responded by running a slack economy; in other words, by allowing unemployment to rise in order to fight inflation.

As Levy notes, manufacturing industries, a major source of black employment in the twentieth century, are particularly sensitive to a slack economy and therefore have suffered many job losses in recent years, particularly in the older, central city plants. Moreover, low-wage workers and newly hired workers (disproportionately represented by blacks) are most adversely affected by a slack economy. One of the consequences of increasing unemployment, states Levy, is "a growing polarization in the income distribution of black men. . . . Compared to 1969, the proportions of black men with income below $5,000 and above $25,000 have both grown. Thus black men at the top of the distribution were doing progressively better while blacks at the bottom—between a fifth and a quarter of all black men ages 25–55—were doing progressively worse."

Finally, the economic problems of low income blacks have been reinforced by recent demographic factors resulting in a "labor surplus environment." On this point Levy states: "During the decade, women of all ages sharply increased their labor-force participation and the large baby boom cohorts of the 1950's came of age. Between 1960 and 1970, the labor force (nationwide) had grown by 13 million persons. But between 1970 and 1980, the labor force grew by 24 million persons. Because of this growth, we can assume that employers could be particularly choosy about whom they hired. In 1983, the more than half of all black household heads in central city poverty areas had not finished high school, a particular disadvantage in this kind of job market."[64]

The changes associated with the cessation of black migration to the central city and the sharp drop in the number of black children under age thirteen may increase the likelihood that the economic situation of urban blacks will improve in the near future. However, the current problems of black joblessness are so overwhelming that it is just as likely that only a major program of economic reform will be sufficient to prevent a significant proportion of the urban underclass from being permanently locked out of the mainstream of the American occupational system. And the strongest case for this argument is found in those inner-city neighborhoods that have recently undergone a social transformation.

Concentration Effects: The Significance of the Social
Transformation of the Inner City

In the nation's fifty largest cities the poverty population rose by 12 percent and the number of persons living in poverty areas (i.e., census tracts with a poverty rate of at least 20 percent) increased by more than 20 percent from 1970 to 1980, despite a 5 percent reduction in the total population in these cities during this period.[65]

However, if we closely examine population and social changes in the five largest cities in the United States, as determined on the basis of the 1970 census population figures (i.e., New York, Chicago, Los Angeles, Philadelphia, and Detroit), where nearly half of the total poor population of the fifty largest cities in the United States lived in 1980, we get a clearer picture of the magnitude of the changes that have taken place in both the population and the neighborhoods of large metropolises.

Although the total population in these five largest cities decreased by 9 percent between 1970 and 1980, the poverty population increased by 22 percent (see figure 2.1). Furthermore, the population living in poverty areas grew by 40 percent overall, by 69 percent in high-poverty areas (i.e., areas with a poverty rate of at least 30 percent), and by a staggering 161 percent in extreme-poverty areas (i.e., areas with a poverty rate of at least 40 percent).[66] It should be emphasized that these incredible changes took place within just a 10-year period.

Poverty areas, of course, include both poor and nonpoor individuals. It is therefore worth noting that the increase in the poor population in these areas was even more severe than that in the total population. More specifically, the number of poor living in poverty areas in these five largest cities increased by 58 percent overall, by 70 percent in high-poverty areas, and by a whopping 182 percent in the extreme-poverty areas.[67] The extraordinary increase in both the poor and nonpoor populations in the extreme-poverty areas between 1970 and 1980 was due mainly to changes in the demographic characteristics of the black population.

Whereas the total white population in the extreme-poverty areas in the five largest cities increased by 45 percent and the white poor population by only 24 percent, the total black population in these areas increased by 148 percent and the poor black population by 164 percent

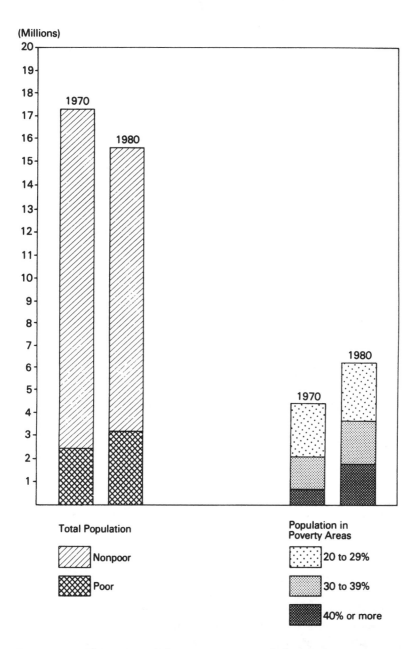

(Millions)

Total Population

    ⬚ Nonpoor

    ⬚ Poor

Population in
Poverty Areas

    ⬚ 20 to 29%

    ⬚ 30 to 39%

    ⬚ 40% or more

**Figure 2.1. Change in population, poverty population, and population in
poverty areas in five largest cities (based on 1970 census), 1970–80.** *Sources:*
U.S. Bureau of the Census. *1970 Census of the Population: Low Income Areas
in Large Cities.* PC-(2)-9B. Washington, D.C.: Government Printing Office,
1973; and *1980 Census of the Population: Low Income Areas in Large Cities.*
PC-2-8D. Washington, D.C.: Government Printing Office, 1985.

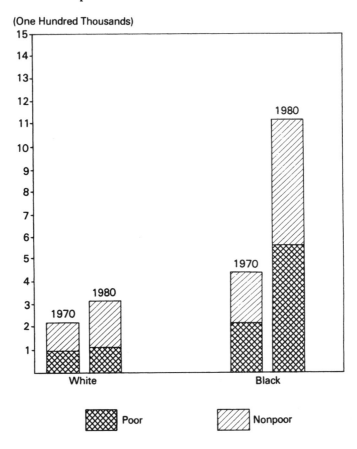

Figure 2.2. Change in population in extreme poverty areas (at least 40% poor) in five largest cities (based on 1970 census) by race, 1970–80. *Sources:* see fig. 2.1.

(see figure 2.2). However, these racial differences become even greater when blacks are compared with non-Hispanic whites. In the 1970 Census the question of "Spanish/Hispanic origin" was asked of only a 5-percent sample of the population; in the 1980 Census this question was asked of everyone. Thus, the data from the 1980 Census make it possible to separate non-Hispanic whites from those whites of Spanish/Hispanic origin who either self-classified themselves as white or marked the category "other" and wrote in entries such as "Mexican," "Puerto Rican," or "Cuban." When these differences are calculated from 1980 Census data, only 47 percent of the more than 306,000 whites living in extreme-poverty areas in these five cities were non-Hispanic, and only 43 percent of the more than 123,000 poor whites in these areas were non-Hispanic. This means that less than 2 percent of the nearly 8 million non-Hispanic whites and only 7 percent of the more than 750,000 poor non-Hispanic whites in these five large central cities lived in extreme-poverty areas in 1980. I will return to the important question of the differences in the ethnic and racial concentration in poverty areas, but first let me examine the factors involved in the growing concentration of urban poverty.

In chapter 1, I emphasized that inner-city neighborhoods have undergone a profound social transformation in the last several years as reflected not only in their increasing rates of social dislocation (including crime, joblessness, out-of-wedlock births, female-headed families, and welfare dependency) but also in the changing economic class structure of ghetto neighborhoods. I pointed out that in the 1940s, and 1950s, and even into the 1960s, these neighborhoods featured a vertical integration of different income groups as lower-, working-, and middle-class professional black families all resided more or less in the same ghetto neighborhoods. I also stated that the very presence of working- and middle-class families enhanced the social organization of inner-city neighborhoods. Finally, I noted that the movement of middle-class black professionals from the inner city, followed in increasing numbers by working-class blacks, has left behind a much higher concentration of the most disadvantaged segments of the black urban population, the population to which I refer when I speak of the ghetto underclass. Sheldon Danziger and Peter Gottschalk have reacted to this thesis and have pointed out that some census tracts could have become more impoverished because "more poor people moved into them or because a greater percentage of existing tract residents became poor." Furthermore, tracts that were not in poverty previously could have become designated poverty areas "either because nonpoor residents moved away or because the number of poor within them increased."[68]

However, if we examine data collected on Chicago community areas from 1970 to 1980, it is clear that several processes are at work resulting in an increase in the number of individuals, particularly minority individuals, living in poverty areas. As shown in figure 2.3, based on the percentage of families with incomes below the poverty line, of the seventy-seven Chicago community areas in 1970 only eight had rates of poverty of at least 30 percent and only one had a rate of poverty that exceeded 40 percent.[69] Over 90 percent of the average population in these eight communities were black in 1970; yet, it is significant to

note that from 1970 to 1980 these communities had a net black migration ("that is, the difference between population at the beginning and
at the end of the time interval 'minus' natural increase")[70] of minus 42
percent. This means that nearly 151,000 blacks departed these communities during this ten-year period, leaving behind a much more
highly concentrated poverty population. Six of these communities
moved from the high- to the extreme-poverty range from 1970 to 1980,
and one had climbed from a 44-percent rate in 1970 to a 61-percent
poverty rate in 1980. Despite the exodus of 151,000 blacks, the *absolute* number of poor families in these eight communities remained
virtually the same (from 26,940 in 1970 to 26,259 in 1980). These data
support the hypothesis that the significant increase in the poverty concentration in these overwhelmingly black communities is related to the
large out-migration of nonpoor blacks.

The increase in the concentration of poverty in Chicago was not confined to these eight neighborhoods, however. Indeed, whereas only
sixteen of Chicago's seventy-seven neighborhoods were designated
community poverty areas in 1970, and whereas only one could be classified as an extreme-poverty area by 1980, as shown in figure 2.4, the
number of community poverty areas had increased to twenty-six, and
nine of these were extreme-poverty areas. In addition to the out-
migration of nonpoor blacks from many of these neighborhoods, some
have become more poor because of the net minus migration of whites
and other nonblacks. This is particularly the case in those twelve community areas with poverty rates in the 20-percent range in 1980. Seven
of these neighborhoods were nonpoverty areas in 1970. Between 1970
and 1980, almost 185,000 whites and other nonblacks departed these
areas, creating a minus net migration of 29 percent.

Thus, despite the fact that each of the community poverty areas in
1970 had lost population by 1980, the remarkable spread of poverty to
other areas by 1980 resulted in a significant increase in the total
number of people living in poor Chicago neighborhoods. It is also the
case that the number of poor people in Chicago who lived both inside
and outside community poverty areas increased by 24 percent from
1970 to 1980 despite an 11-percent decrease in the population. Obviously, part of that increase is due to the rise in the number of people
in these poverty areas who became poor during this period. And perhaps one of the major contributing factors is the increase in
joblessness.

As revealed in figures 2.5 and 2.6, whereas only five community
areas in Chicago had an unemployment rate of at least 15 percent in
1970, by 1980 twenty-five community areas did, and of these, ten (all

Figure 2.3 Chicago Community Poverty Areas, 1970. *Source: Local Community Fact Book: Chicago Metropolitan Area, 1970 and 1980* (Chicago: Chicago Review Press, 1984).

Figure 2.4. Chicago Community Poverty Areas, 1980. *Source:* see fig. 2.3.

Figure 2.5. Unemployment rates in Chicago Community Areas, 1970.
Source: see fig. 2.3.

Figure 2.6. Unemployment rates in Chicago Community Areas, 1980. *Source:* see fig. 2.3.

predominately black and all high-to-extreme community poverty areas) had rates of at least 20-percent unemployment. As I shall argue, increasing joblessness has its most devastating effect in the most highly concentrated poverty areas.

It is the growth of the high- and extreme-poverty areas that epitomizes the social transformation of the inner city, a transformation that represents a change in the class structure in many inner-city neighborhoods as the nonpoor black middle and working classes tend no longer to reside in these neighborhoods, thereby increasing the proportion of truly disadvantaged individuals and families. What are the effects of this growing concentration of poverty on individual and families in the inner city?

I initially raised this question in systematic form in 1985,[71] and my arguments on the changing class structure in the inner city were later picked up in the popular media.[72] However, instead of focusing on the changing situational and structural factors that accompanied the black middle- and working-class exodus from the inner city, arguments in the popular media tended to emphasize a crystallization of a ghetto culture of poverty once black middle-class self-consciously imposed cultural constraints on lower-class culture were removed. Indeed, Nicholas Lemann, in one of two articles titled the "Origins of the Underclass" in the *Atlantic Monthly* goes so far as to suggest that "every aspect of the underclass culture in the ghettos is directly traceable to roots in the South—and not the South of slavery but the South of a generation ago. In fact, there seems to be a strong correlation between underclass status in the North and a family background in the nascent underclass of the sharecropper."[73] However, as discussed in the appendix, the systematic research on urban poverty and recent migration (that is, migration in the second half of the twentieth century) consistently shows that southern-born blacks who have migrated to the urban North experience greater economic success in terms of employment rates, earnings, and welfare dependency than do those urban blacks who were born in the North (see "Urban Poverty and Migration" in the appendix). For example, one study of southern migrants in six large urban areas (New York, Philadelphia, Washington, D.C., Chicago, Detroit, and Los Angeles) points out that "the rapid rise that occurred during the 1960s in the number of persons on welfare resulted mainly from an increase in the number of urban nonmigrants applying for welfare." Northern-born blacks were more likely to receive welfare than southern-born blacks, despite the fact that the level of education of blacks born in the North was higher than that of blacks born in the South. In addition, "the migrants (both men and women) have tended to have higher labor-force participation rates and lower unemployment rates than black natives in the cities in question."[74]

However, the argument that associates the increase of social problems in the inner city with the crystallization of underclass culture obscures some very important structural and institutional changes in the inner city that have accompanied the black middle- and working-class exodus, and leaves the erroneous impression that the sharp increase in social dislocations in the inner city can simply be explained by the ascendancy of a ghetto culture of poverty. The problem is much more complex.

More specifically, I believe that the exodus of middle- and working-class families from many ghetto neighborhoods removes an important "social buffer" that could deflect the full impact of the kind of prolonged and increasing joblessness that plagued inner-city neighborhoods in the 1970s and early 1980s, joblessness created by uneven economic growth and periodic recessions. This argument is based on the assumption that even if the truly disadvantaged segments of an inner-city area experience a significant increase in long-term spells of joblessness, the basic institutions in that area (churches, schools, stores, recreational facilities, etc.) would remain viable if much of the base of their support comes from the more economically stable and secure families. Moreover, the very presence of these families during such periods provides mainstream role models that help keep alive the perception that education is meaningful, that steady employment is a viable alternative to welfare, and that family stability is the norm, not the exception.

Thus, a perceptive ghetto youngster in a neighborhood that includes a good number of working and professional families may observe increasing joblessness and idleness but he will also witness many individuals regularly going to and from work; he may sense an increase in school dropouts but he can also see a connection between education and meaningful employment; he may detect a growth in single-parent families, but he will also be aware of the presence of many married-couple families; he may notice an increase in welfare dependency, but he can also see a significant number of families that are not on welfare; and he may be cognizant of an increase in crime, but he can recognize that many residents in his neighborhood are not involved in criminal activity.

However, in ghetto neighborhoods that have experienced a steady out-migration of middle- and working-class families—communities, in other words, that lack a social buffer—a sudden and/or prolonged increase in joblessness, as existed in the 1970s and first half of the 1980s, creates a ripple effect resulting in an exponential increase in related forms of social dislocation. The ways in which people adapt to the growing problem of long-term joblessness in such neighborhoods are influenced not only by the constraints they face and the opportunities they have, but also by the repeated ways they have responded to such problems in the past.

Thus, in a neighborhood with a paucity of regularly employed families and with the overwhelming majority of families having spells of long-term joblessness, people experience a social isolation that excludes them from the job network system that permeates other neighborhoods and that is so important in learning about or being recommended for jobs that become available in various parts of the city. And as the prospects for employment diminish, other alternatives such as welfare and the underground economy are not only increasingly relied on, they come to be seen as a way of life. Moreover, unlike the situation in earlier years, girls who become pregnant out of wedlock invariably give birth out of wedlock because of a shrinking pool of marriageable, that is, employed, black males (see chap. 3).

Thus, in such neighborhoods the chances are overwhelming that children will seldom interact on a sustained basis with people who are employed or with families that have a steady breadwinner. The net effect is that joblessness, as a way of life, takes on a different social meaning; the relationship between schooling and postschool employment takes on a different meaning. The development of cognitive, linguistic, and other educational and job-related skills necessary for the world of work in the mainstream economy is thereby adversely affected. In such neighborhoods, therefore, teachers become frustrated and do not teach and children do not learn. A vicious cycle is perpetuated through the family, through the community, and through the schools. The consequences are dramatically revealed when figures on educational attainment in the inner-city schools are released. For example, of the 39,500 students who enrolled in the ninth grade of Chicago's public schools in 1980, and who would have normally graduated from high school four years later in the spring of 1984, only 18,500 (or 47 percent) graduated; of these only 6,000 were capable of reading at or above the national twelfth-grade level. However, the situation is even more bleak for those black and Hispanic students who attended segregated inner-city high schools and who represented two-thirds of the original class of 1984. Of the 25,500 ninth-grade black and Hispanic students who were originally enrolled in these segregated, nonselective high schools in Chicago, 16,000 did not graduate. "Of the 9,500 students who did graduate, 4,000 read at or below the junior level and only 2,000 read at or above the national average. In these non-selective segregated high schools, then, only 2,000 of the original class of 25,000 students both completed high school and could read at or above the level considered average in the rest of the country."[75] Although these figures do not indicate the proportion of students who left inner-city schools because they moved out of the neighborhoods in which these schools are located, they, nonetheless, suggest a shockingly high degree of educational retardation in the inner city.

In short, the communities of the underclass are plagued by massive joblessness, flagrant and open lawlessness, and low-achieving schools, and therefore tend to be avoided by outsiders. Consequently, the residents of these areas, whether women and children of welfare families or aggressive street criminals, have become increasingly socially isolated from mainstream patterns of behavior.

If I had to use one term to capture the differences in the experiences of low-income families who live in inner-city areas from the experiences of those who live in other areas in the central city today, that term would be *concentration effects*. The social transformation of the inner city has resulted in a disproportionate concentration of the most disadvantaged segments of the urban black population, creating a social milieu significantly different from the environment that existed in these communities several decades ago.

I have already contrasted the situation of a poor black child living in a stable, vertically class-integrated inner-city community with one who lives in a depressed, unstable, and socially isolated inner-city community. I should also point out that whereas poor blacks are frequently found in isolated poor urban neighborhoods, poor whites rarely live in such neighborhoods. Indeed, as shown in figure 2.7, whereas 68 percent of all poor whites lived in nonpoverty areas in the five large central cities in 1980, only 15 percent of poor blacks and 20 percent of poor Hispanics lived in such areas. And whereas only 7 percent of all poor whites live in the extreme poverty areas, 32 percent of all poor Hispanics and 39 percent of all poor blacks lived in such areas. Accordingly, if one were to conduct a study that simply compared the responses of poor urban whites with those of poor urban blacks independent of concentration effects, that is, without taking into account the different neighborhoods in which poor whites and poor blacks tend to live, one would reach conclusions about attitudes, norms, behavior, and human-capital traits that would be favorable to poor whites and unfavorable to poor blacks. In other words, "simple comparisons between poor whites and poor blacks would be confounded with the fact that poor whites reside in areas which are ecologically and economically very different

(One Hundred Thousands)

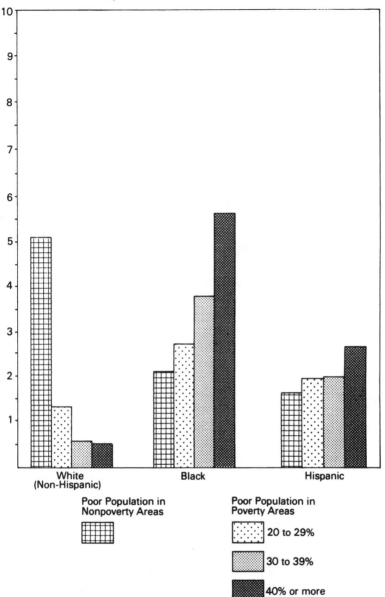

Figure 2.7. Concentration of poor population in nonpoverty and poverty areas in five largest cities (based on 1970 census), 1980. *Source: 1980 Census of the Population: Low Income Areas in Large Cities.* PC-2-8D. Washington, D.C.: Government Printing Office, 1985.

from poor blacks. Any observed relationships involving race would reflect, to some unknown degree, the relatively superior ecological niche
many poor whites occupy with respect to jobs, marriage opportunities,
and exposure to conventional role models."[76]

What is significant to emphasize, however, is that inner-city communities are not only "ecologically and economically very different" from
areas in which poor urban whites tend to reside, they are also very
different from their own ecological and economic makeup of several
decades ago. Take the problem of social networks. Unlike poor urban
whites or even the inner-city blacks of earlier years, the residents of
highly concentrated poverty neighborhoods in the inner city today not
only infrequently interact with those individuals or families who have
had a stable work history and have had little involvement with welfare
or public assistance, they also seldom have sustained contact with
friends or relatives in the more stable areas of the city or in the
suburbs.

The net result is that the degree of social isolation—defined in this
context as the lack of contact or of sustained interaction with individuals and institutions that represent mainstream society—in these
highly concentrated poverty areas has become far greater than we had
previously assumed. What are the affects of this kind of social isolation?

Inner-city social isolation makes it much more difficult for those who
are looking for jobs to be tied into the job network. Even in those
situations where job vacancies become available in an industry near or
within an inner-city neighborhood, workers who live outside the inner
city may find out about these vacancies sooner than those who live near
the industry because the latter are not tied into the job network. This
point is overlooked in the recent widely cited study by David Ellwood.[77] This study questioned the validity of the spatial-mismatch hypothesis because the reported data show that black youth on the west
side of Chicago had as high a jobless rate as black youth on the south
side despite the much higher concentration of employers on the west
side. However, what needs to be considered is youth's lack of access to
the job network in both the west-side and south-side neighborhoods.

Inner-city social isolation also generates behavior not conducive to
good work histories. The patterns of behavior that are associated with a
life of casual work (tardiness and absenteeism) are quite different from
those that accompany a life of regular or steady work (e.g., the habit of
waking up early in the morning to a ringing alarm clock). In neighborhoods in which nearly every family has at least one person who is
steadily employed, the norms and behavior patterns that emanate from
a life of regularized employment become part of the community ge-

stalt. On the other hand, in neighborhoods in which most families do not have a steadily employed breadwinner, the norms and behavior patterns associated with steady work compete with those associated with casual or infrequent work. Accordingly, the less frequent the regular contact with those who have steady and full-time employment (that is, the greater the degree of social isolation), the more likely that initial job performance will be characterized by tardiness, absenteeism, and, thereby, low retention. In other words, a person's patterns and norms of behavior tend to be shaped by those with which he or she has had the most frequent or sustained contact and interaction. Moreover, since the jobs that are available to the inner-city poor are the very ones that alienate even persons with long and stable work histories, the combination of unattractive jobs and lack of community norms to reinforce work increases the likelihood that individuals will turn to either underground illegal activity or idleness or both.

The key theoretical concept, therefore, is not *culture of poverty* but *social isolation*. Culture of poverty implies that basic values and attitudes of the ghetto subculture have been internalized and thereby influence behavior. Accordingly, efforts to enhance the life chances of groups such as the ghetto underclass require, from this perspective, social policies (e.g., programs of training and education as embodied in mandatory workfare) aimed at directly changing these subcultural traits. Social isolation, on the other hand, not only implies that contact between groups of different class and/or racial backgrounds is either lacking or has become increasingly intermittent but that the nature of this contact enhances the effects of living in a highly concentrated poverty area. These concentration effects include the constraints and opportunities in neighborhoods in which the population is overwhelmingly socially disadvantaged—constraints and opportunities that include the kinds of ecological niches that the residents of these neighborhoods occupy in terms of access to jobs and job networks, availability of marriageable partners, involvement in quality schools, and exposure to conventional role models.

The distinction between *social isolation* and *culture of poverty* will be discussed in greater detail in chapter 6. For now let me say that to emphasize the concept *social isolation* does not mean that cultural traits are irrelevant in understanding behavior in highly concentrated poverty areas; rather, it highlights the fact that culture is a response to social structural constraints and opportunities. From a public-policy perspective, this would mean shifting the focus from changing subcultural traits (as suggested by the "culture of poverty" thesis) to changing the structure of constraints and opportunities. The increasing social isolation of the inner city is a product of the class transformation of the inner city, including the growing concentration of poverty in inner-city neighborhoods. And the class transformation of the inner city cannot be understood without considering the effects of fundamental changes in the urban economy on the lower-income minorities, effects that include joblessness and that thereby increase the chances of long-term residence in highly concentrated poverty areas.

Conclusion

In this chapter, I have tried to show that the factors associated with the recent increases in social dislocation among the ghetto underclass are complex and cannot be reduced to the easy explanation of racism or racial discrimination. Although present-day discrimination undoubtedly has contributed to the increasing social and economic woes of the ghetto underclass, I have argued that these problems have been due far more to a complex web of other factors that include shifts in the American economy—which have produced extraordinary rates of black joblessness that have exacerbated other social problems in the inner city—the historic flow of migrants, changes in the urban minority age structure, population changes in the central city, and the class transformation of the inner city.

However, as discussed in the previous chapter, conservative scholars have placed far more emphasis on ghetto culture and the liberal welfare state as factors related to the increase in inner-city social dislocations. I have already argued against elevating the culture-of-poverty thesis to central explanatory importance and, to repeat, I will elaborate on this position in chapter 6. However, in the next two chapters the welfare-state explanation of the rise of inner-city social dislocations will be critically assessed. In the process, the relationship of basic economic changes and joblessness to the rise of black female-headed families, out-of-wedlock births, and welfare dependency will be more firmly established.

3   Poverty and Family Structure
The Widening Gap Between Evidence
and Public Policy Issues
with Kathryn Neckerman

In the early and mid-1960s social scientists such as Kenneth B. Clark, Lee Rainwater, and Daniel Patrick Moynihan discussed in clear and forceful terms the relationship between black poverty and family structure and sounded the alarm even then that the problems of family dissolution among poor blacks were approaching catastrophic proportions.[1] These writers emphasized that the rising rates of broken marriages, out-of-wedlock births, female-headed families, and welfare dependency among poor urban blacks were the products not only of race-specific experiences, but also of structural conditions in the larger society, including economic relations. And they underlined the need to address these problems with programs that would attack structural inequality in American society and thereby, in the words of Moynihan, "bring the Negro American to full and equal sharing in the responsibilities and rewards of citizenship."[2]

There is a distinct difference in the way the problems of poverty and family structure were viewed in the major studies of the 1960s and the way they are viewed today, however. Unlike the earlier studies, discussions in the current research of the relationship between black family instability and male joblessness have been overshadowed by discussions that link family instability with the growth of income transfers and in-kind benefits. Because, as we demonstrate in this chapter, the factors associated with the rise of single-parent families—not only among blacks, but among whites as well—are sufficiently complex to preclude overemphasis on any single variable, the recent trend among scholars and policymakers to neglect the role of male joblessness while emphasizing the role of welfare is especially questionable. But first let us examine the problem of poverty and family structure in its historical context.

Poverty and Family Structure in Historical Perspective

In the early twentieth century the vast majority of both black and white low-income families were intact. Although national information on fami-

63

ly structure was not available before the publication of the 1940 census, studies of early manuscript census forms of individual cities and counties make it clear that even among the very poor, a substantial majority of both black and white families were two-parent families. Moreover, most of the women heading families in the late nineteenth and early twentieth centuries were widows. Evidence from the 1940 census indicates that divorce and separation were relatively uncommon.[3]

It is particularly useful to consider black families in historical perspective because social scientists have commonly assumed that the recent trends in black family structure that are of concern in this chapter could be traced to the lingering effects of slavery. E. Franklin Frazier's classic statement of this view in *The Negro Family in the United States* informed all subsequent studies of the black family, including the Moynihan report.[4] But recent research has challenged assumptions about the influence of slavery on the character of the black family. Reconstruction of black family patterns from manuscript census forms has shown that the two-parent, nuclear family was the predominant family form in the late nineteenth and early twentieth centuries. Historian Herbert Gutman examined data on black family structure in the northern urban areas of Buffalo and Brooklyn, New York; in the southern cities of Mobile, Alabama, of Richmond, Virginia, and of Charleston, South Carolina; and in several counties and small towns during this period. He found that between 70 percent and 90 percent of black households were "male-present" and that a majority were nuclear families.[5] Similar findings have been reported for Philadelphia, for rural Virginia, for Boston, and for cities of the Ohio Valley.[6] This research demonstrates that neither slavery, nor economic deprivation, nor the migration to urban areas affected black family structure by the first quarter of the twentieth century.

However, the poverty and degraded conditions in which most blacks lived were not without their consequences for the family. For the most part, the positive association between intact family structure and measures of class, such as property ownership, occupation, or literacy, generally reflected the higher rate of mortality among poor men.[7] Widowhood accounted for about three-quarters of female-headed families among blacks, Germans, Irish, and native white Americans in Philadelphia in 1880.[8] In addition, men sometimes had to live apart from their families as they moved from one place to another in search of work.[9] Given their disproportionate concentration among the poor in America, black families were more strongly affected by these conditions and therefore were more likely than white families to be female headed. For example, in Philadelphia in 1880, 25.3 percent of all black families were female headed, compared to only 13.6 percent of all native white families.

The earliest detailed national census information on family structure is available from the 1940 census. In 1940 female-headed families were more prevalent among blacks than among whites, and among urbanites than among rural residents for both groups. Yet, even in urban areas, 72 percent of black families with children under eighteen were male headed. Moreover, irrespective of race and residence, most women heading families were widows.

The two-parent nuclear family remained the predominant type for both blacks and whites up to World War II. As shown in table 3.1, 10 percent of white families and 18 percent of black families were female

TABLE 3.1
Percentage of Female-Headed Families, No Husband Present, by
Race and Spanish Origin, 1940–1983

Year	White	Black	Spanish Origin	Total Families
1940	10.1	17.9	—	—
1950	8.5	17.6[a]	—	9.4
1960	8.1	21.7	—	10.0
1965	9.0	24.9	—	10.5
1970	9.1	28.3	—	10.8
1971	9.4	30.6	—	11.5
1972	9.4	31.8	—	11.6
1973	9.6	34.6	16.7	12.2
1974	9.9	34.0	17.4	12.4
1975	10.5	35.3	18.8	13.0
1976	10.8	35.9	20.9	13.3
1977	10.9	37.1	20.0	13.6
1978	11.5	39.2	20.3	14.4
1979	11.6	40.5	19.8	14.6
1980	11.6	40.2	19.2	14.6
1981	11.9	41.7	21.8	15.1
1982	12.4	40.6	22.7	15.4
1983	12.2	41.9	22.8	15.4

Sources: U.S. Bureau of the Census, Current Population Reports, series P-20, nos. 153, 218, 233, 246, 258, 276, 291, 311, 326, 340, 352, 366, 371, 381, and 388, "Household and Family Characteristics" (Washington, D.C.: Government Printing Office, 1965, 1970–1984); and idem, Current Population Reports, series P-20, nos. 267 and 290, "Persons of Spanish Origins in the United States" (Washington, D.C.: Government Printing Office, 1974 and 1975).

[a] Black and other.

headed in 1940. The relative stability in gross census figures on female-headed families between 1940 and 1960 obscures the beginnings of current trends in family breakup. More specifically, while widowhood fell significantly during those two decades, marital dissolution was rising.[10] Furthermore, the proportion of out-of-wedlock births was growing. By the 1960s, the proportion of female-headed families had begun to increase significantly among blacks, rising from 22 percent in 1960 to 28 percent in 1970, and then to 42 percent by 1983. This proportion also rose among white families, from 8 percent in 1960 to 12 percent in 1983. The increase in female-headed families with children under eighteen is even more dramatic. By 1983, almost one out of five families with children under eighteen were headed by women, including 14 percent of white families, 24 percent of Spanish-origin families, and 48 percent of black families.[11] To understand the nature of these shifts, it is necessary to disaggregate these statistics and consider factors such as changes in fertility rates, marital status, age structure, and living arrangements.

Changing Family Structure and Demographic Correlates

The unprecedented increases in the proportion of births out of wedlock are a major contributor to the rise of female-headed families in the black community. In 1980, 68 percent of births to black women ages fifteen to twenty-four were outside of marriage, compared to 41 percent in 1955. According to 1981 figures, almost 30 percent of all young single black women have borne a child before the age of twenty.[12] The incidence of out-of-wedlock births has risen to unprecedented levels for young white women as well, although both rates and ratios remain far below those for black women (see table 3.2).

These increases in births outside of marriage reflect trends in fertility and marital status, as well as changes in population composition. Age-specific fertility rates for both white and black women have fallen since the peak of the baby boom in the late 1950s. Even fertility rates for teenagers (ages fifteen to nineteen) have fallen overall. What these figures obscure, however, is that the fertility rates of young unmarried women have risen or declined only moderately, while those of married women of these ages have fallen more substantially (see table 3.2). In addition, growing proportions of young women are single. For instance, the percentage of never-married women increased dramatically between 1960 and 1980, from 29 percent to 47 percent for whites, and from 30 percent to 69 percent for blacks.[13] Recent data show not only

TABLE 3.2
Fertility Rates and Ratios by Race and Age, 1960–1980

Age-group and Year	Fertility Rate Black	Fertility Rate White	Marital Fertility Rate Black	Marital Fertility Rate White	Nonmarital Fertility Rate Black	Nonmarital Fertility Rate White	Illegitimacy Ratio Black	Illegitimacy Ratio White
Ages 15–19								
1960	158.2	79.4	659.3	513.0	76.5	6.6	421.5	71.6
1965	136.1	60.7	602.4	443.2	75.8	7.9	492.0	114.3
1970	133.4	57.4	522.4	431.8	90.8	10.9	613.5	171.0
1975	106.4	46.4	348.0	311.8	86.3	12.0	747.2	229.0
1980	94.6	44.7	344.0	337.6	83.0	16.0	851.5	329.8
Ages 20–24								
1960	294.2	194.9	361.8	352.5	166.5	18.2	199.6	21.9
1965	247.3	138.8	293.3	270.9	152.6	22.1	229.9	38.4
1970	196.8	145.9	267.6	244.0	120.9	22.5	295.0	51.8
1975	141.0	108.1	192.4	179.6	102.1	15.5	399.5	60.9
1980	145.0	112.4	232.8	198.2	108.2	22.6	560.2	114.9
Ages 25–29								
1960	214.6	252.8	225.0	220.5	171.8	18.2	141.3	11.4
1965	188.1	189.8	188.6	177.3	164.7	24.3	162.8	18.8
1970	140.1	163.4	159.3	164.9	93.7	21.1	180.6	20.7
1975	108.7	108.2	130.8	132.4	73.2	14.8	226.8	26.2
1980	115.5	109.5	149.7[a]	148.4[a]	79.1	17.3	361.7	50.2

Sources: National Center for Health Statistics, *Vital Statistics of the United States,* annual volumes 1960–1975 and 1984 (Washington, D.C.: Government Printing Office).

[a] Marital fertility rates for 1980 are unavailable; 1979 figures are substituted.

that the incidence of premarital conception has increased, but also that the proportion of those premarital pregnancies legitimated by marriage has decreased.[14] Thus, out-of-wedlock births now comprise a far greater proportion of total births than they did in the past, particularly for black women (see table 3.2). The black "illegitimacy ratio" has increased so precipitously in recent years not because the rate of extramarital births has substantially increased, but because the percentage of women married and the rate of marital fertility have both declined significantly.

The decline in the proportion of women who are married and living with their husbands is a function of both a sharp rise in separation and divorce rates and the substantial increase in the percentage of never-married women. The combined impact of these trends has been partic-

ularly drastic for black women as the proportion married and living
with their husbands fell from 52 percent in 1947 to 34 percent in
1980.[15] As set out in table 3.3, black women have much higher separation and divorce rates than white women, although the differences are
exaggerated because of a higher rate of remarriage among white wom-
en.[16] Whereas white women are far more likely to be divorced than
separated, black women are more likely to be separated than divorced.
Indeed, a startling 22 percent of all married black women are separated
from their husbands.[17]

Just as important a factor in the declining proportion of black women
who are married and living with their husbands is the increase in the
percentage of never-married women. Indeed, as shown in table 3.3,
the proportion of never-married black women increased from 65 percent in 1960 to 82 percent in 1980 for those ages fourteen to twenty-
four and from 8 percent to 21 percent for those ages twenty-five to
forty-four. On the other hand, while the proportion of black women
who are separated or divorced increased from 22 percent in 1960 to 31
percent in 1980 for those ages twenty-five to forty-four, and from 17
percent to 25 percent for those ages forty-five to sixty-four, the fraction
divorced or separated actually fell for younger women.

For young women, both black and white, the increase in the percentage of never-married women largely accounts for the decline in the
proportion married with husband present (see table 3.3). For black
women ages twenty-five to forty-four, increases in both the percentage
of never-married women and in martial dissolution were important; for
white women of the same age-group, marital dissolution is the more
important factor. Marriage has not declined among white women ages
forty-five to sixty-four; however, among black women in the same age-
group, the proportion married with husband present has fallen, due
mainly to increases in marital dissolution.

Although trends in fertility and marital status are the most important
contributors to the rise of female-headed families, the situation has
been exacerbated by recent changes in the age structure, which have
temporarily increased the proportion of young women in the population, particularly in the black population. Whereas in 1960, only 36
percent of black women ages fifteen to forty-four were between fifteen
and twenty-four years of age, by 1975 that proportion had increased to
46 percent; the comparable increase for white women was from 34
percent in 1960 to 42 percent in 1975.[18] These changes in the age
structure increase the proportion of births occurring to young women
and, given the higher out-of-wedlock birth ratios among young wom-

TABLE 3.3
Marital Status of Women by Race and Age, 1947–1980

Age-group and Marital Status	1947		1960		1970		1980	
	White	Black	White	Black	White	Black	White	Black
Ages 14–24								
Married[a]	33.5	30.9	33.6	25.7	29.6	21.3	26.8[b]	13.1[b]
Never married	62.9	59.5	63.3	65.0	66.4	72.3	68.6	82.4
Separated/divorced/husband absent	3.3	8.4	3.0	9.0	3.8	6.2	4.5	4.3
Widowed	0.4	1.3	0.1	0.3	0.1	0.1	0.1	0.2
Ages 25–44								
Married	80.3	67.2	85.1	64.9	85.0	62.0	75.5	44.7
Never married	11.5	10.5	6.8	8.2	6.3	12.2	9.8	21.3
Separated/divorced/husband absent	5.8	14.4	6.3	22.4	7.6	22.2	13.6	30.8
Widowed	2.4	8.0	1.8	4.5	1.2	3.6	1.1	3.2
Ages 45–64								
Married	70.2	57.6	74.1	52.8	73.5	54.1	74.0	46.0
Never married	8.0	5.3	6.4	5.3	5.9	4.7	4.4	6.8
Separated/divorced/husband absent	5.0	8.3	5.7	16.6	7.3	20.4	9.8	25.4
Widowed	16.8	28.5	13.7	25.3	13.3	20.4	11.8	21.8

Sources: U.S. Bureau of the Census, *Current Population Reports*, series P-20, no. 10, "Characteristics of Single, Married, Widowed, and Divorced Persons in 1947" (Washington, D.C.: Government Printing Office, 1948); idem, *Current Population Reports*, series P-20, nos. 153 and 218, "Marital Status and Family Status" (Washington, D.C.: Government Printing Office, 1960 and 1970); idem, *Current Population Reports*, series P-20, no. 365, "Marital Status and Living Arrangements, March 1980" (Washington, D.C.: Government Printing Office, 1981).

[a] Married, husband present.
[b] Includes only ages 15–24.

en, inflate the proportion of all births that occur outside of marriage as well.

Finally, the rise in the proportion of female-headed families reflects an increasing tendency for women to form independent households rather than to live in subfamilies. Until recently, Census Bureau coding procedures caused the number of subfamilies to be significantly underestimated;[19] therefore, an accurate time series is impossible. However, other research suggests that women are becoming more likely to form their own households. For example, Cutright's analysis of components of growth in female-headed families between 1940 and 1970 indicates that 36 percent of the increase in numbers of female family heads between the ages of fifteen and forty-four can be attributed to the higher propensity of such women to form their own households.[20] Bane and Ellwood show that these trends continued during the 1970s.[21] In the period 1969 to 1973, 56 percent of white children and 60 percent of black children born into single-parent families lived in households headed by neither mother nor father (most lived with grandparents). During the years 1974 to 1979, those proportions declined to 24 percent for white children and 37 percent for black children.

Thus, young women comprise a greater proportion of single mothers than ever before. For example, while in 1950, only 26 percent of black female family heads and 12 percent of white female family heads were under the age of thirty-five, in 1983 those proportions had risen to 43 percent for blacks and 29 percent for whites. The number of black children growing up in fatherless families increased by 41 percent between 1970 and 1980, and most of this growth has occurred in families in which the *mother has never been married.*[22] This is not surprising, according to Bane and Ellwood's research: whereas the growth of the number of single white mothers over the last decade is mainly due to the increase in separation and divorce, the growth of the number of single black mothers is "driven by a dramatic decrease in marriage and increase in fertility among never-married women."[23] In 1982 the percentage of black children living with both parents had dipped to 43 percent, only roughly half of the proportion of white children in two-parent homes.

As Bane and Ellwood point out, "Never married mothers are more likely than divorced, separated or widowed mothers to be younger and to be living at home when they have their children."[24] Younger mothers tend to have less education, less work experience, and thus fewer financial resources. Therefore they are more likely initially to form subfamilies, drawing support from parents and relatives. However, it appears that most children of single mothers in subfamilies spend only a small part of their lives in such families. On the basis of an analysis of data from the Panel Study of Income Dynamics (PSID) for the period 1968 to 1979, Bane and Ellwood suggest that by the time children born into subfamilies reach age six, two-thirds will have moved into different living arrangements. Among blacks, two-thirds of the moves are into independent female-headed families, whereas among whites two-thirds are into two-parent families. However, whether the focus is on subfamilies or on independent female-headed families, less than 10 percent of white children and almost half of the black children born into non-two-parent families remain in such families "for their entire childhood."[25] And, as discussed in the next section, these families are increasingly plagued by poverty.

The Poverty Status of Female-Headed Families

As emphasized in the previous chapter, the rise of female-headed families has had dire social and economic consequences because these families are far more vulnerable to poverty than are other types of families. Indeed, sex and marital status of the head are the most important determinants of poverty status for families, especially in urban areas. The poverty rate of female-headed families was 36.3 percent in 1982, while the rate for married-couple families was only 7.6 percent. For black and Spanish-origin female-headed families in 1982, poverty rates were 56.2 percent and 55.4 percent respectively.[26]

Female-headed families comprise a growing proportion of the poverty population. Individuals in female-headed families made up fully a third of the poverty population in 1982. Forty-six percent of all poor families and 71 percent of all poor black families were female headed in 1982. These proportions were higher for metropolitan areas, particularly for central cities, where 60 percent of all poor families and 78 percent of all poor black families were headed by women.[27] The proportion of poor black families headed by women increased steadily from 1959 to 1977, from less than 30 percent to 72 percent, and has remained slightly above 70 percent since then. The total number of poor black female-headed families continued to grow between 1977 and 1982, increasing by 373,000; the proportion of the total number of poor black families did not continue to increase only because of the sharp rise in the number of male-headed families in poverty during this period (from 475,000 to 622,000 in 1982). The proportion of poor white families headed by women also increased from less than 20 percent in

1959 to a high of almost 40 percent in 1977, and then dropping to 35 percent in 1983.

Female-headed families are not only more likely to be in poverty, they are also more likely than male-headed families to be persistently poor. For example, Duncan reports, on the basis of data from the Michigan PSID, that 61 percent of those who were persistently poor over a ten-year period were in female-headed families, a proportion far exceeding the prevalence of female-headed families in the general population.[28]

Causes of the Rise in Female-Headed Families

As the foregoing discussion suggests, to speak of female-headed families and out-of-wedlock births is to emphasis that they have become inextricably tied up with poverty and dependency, often long term. The sharp rise in these two forms of social dislocation is related to the demographic changes in the population that we discussed in the previous section. For example, the drop in the median age of women heading families would lead one to predict a higher rate of poverty among these families, all other things being equal. We only need to consider that young women who have a child out of wedlock, the major contributor to the drop in median age of single mothers, are further disadvantaged by the disruption of their schooling and employment.

However, while a consideration of demographic changes may be important to understand the complex nature and basis of changes in family structure, it is hardly sufficient. Indeed, changes in demographic factors are generally a function of broader economic, political, and social trends. For example, the proportion of out-of-wedlock births has risen among young black women, as a result of a decline in both marriage and marital fertility, coupled with relative stability in out-of-wedlock birth rates (i.e., the number of births per 1,000 unmarried women). This increase in the proportion of extramarital births could be mainly a function of the increasing difficulty of finding a marriage partner with stable employment, or of changes in social values regarding out-of-wedlock births, or of increased economic independence afforded women by the availability of income transfer payments. Broader social and economic forces may also be influencing married women to have fewer children. In the previous chapter the factors associated with the rise of social dislocations, including female-headed families, in the inner city were examined. In this section we extend that discussion by delineating the role of broader social and economic forces not only on trends in family formation in the inner city, but on national trends in family formation as well. In the process we hope to establish the argument that despite the complex nature of the problem, the weight of existing evidence suggests that the problems of male joblessness could be the single most important factor underlying the rise in unwed mothers among poor black women. Yet, this factor has received scant attention in recent discussions of the decline of intact families among the poor. Let us first examine the contribution of other factors, including social and cultural trends and the growth of income transfers, which in recent years has become perhaps the single most popular explanation of changes in family formation and family structure.

The Role of Changing Social and Cultural Trends

Extramarital fertility among teenagers if of particular significance to the rise of female-headed families. Out-of-wedlock birth rates for teens are generally not falling as they are for older women. Almost 40 percent of all illegitimate births are to women under age twenty.[29] Moreover, adolescent mothers are the most disadvantaged of all female family heads because they are likely to have their schooling interrupted, experience difficulty finding employment, and very rarely receive child support. They are also the most likely to experience future marital instability and disadvantages in the labor market.

Any attempt to explain the social and cultural factors behind the rise of out-of-wedlock teenage fertility must begin with the fact that most teenage pregnancies are reportedly unwanted. Surveys by Zelnik and Kantner have consistently shown that the majority of premarital pregnancies are neither planned nor wanted. In 1979, for instance, 82 percent of premarital pregnancies in fifteen- to nineteen-year-olds (unmarried at the time the pregnancy was resolved) were unwanted.[30]

However, unpublished tabulations from a recent Chicago study of teenage pregnancy indicate that adolescent black mothers reported far fewer pregnancies to be unwanted than did their white counterparts. Moreover, as Dennis Hogan has stated, the Chicago data suggest that "it is not so much that single motherhood is unwanted as it is that it is not sufficiently 'unwanted.' Women of all ages without a strong desire to prevent a birth tend to have limited contraceptive success."[31] This argument would seem especially appropriate to poor inner-city black neighborhoods. In this connection, Kenneth Clark has argued that

In the ghetto, the meaning of the illegitimate child is not ultimate disgrace. There is not the demand for abortion or for surrender of the child that one finds in more privileged communities. In the middle class, the disgrace of illegitimacy is tied to personal and family aspirations. In lower-class families, on the other hand, the girl loses only some of her already limited options by having an illegitimate child; she is not going to make a "better marriage" or improve her economic and social status either way. On the contrary, a child is a symbol of the fact that she is a woman, and she may gain from having something of her own. Nor is the boy who fathers an illegitimate child going to lose, for where is he going? The path to any higher status seems closed to him in any case.[32]

Systematic evidence of expected parenthood prior to first marriage is provided in two studies by Hogan. Drawing upon data collected in a national longitudinal survey of high school students conducted for a National Center for Educational Statistics study (described from here on as the High School and Beyond data), Hogan found that whereas only 1 percent of the white females and 1.4 percent of the white males who were single and childless in 1980 expected to become parents prior to first marriage, 16.5 percent of black females and 21 percent of black males expected parenthood before first marriage. In a follow-up study that focused exclusively on black female adolescents and excluded respondents "who were pregnant or near marriage at the time of the initial interview [1980]," Hogan found that only 8.7 percent expected to become single mothers in 1980, and of these, 19.5 percent actually became unmarried mothers by 1982.[33] On the other hand, of the 91 percent who reported that they *did not* expect to become unmarried mothers, only 7.4 percent gave birth to a child by 1982. Unpublished data from this same study reveal that 20.1 percent of the black girls becoming single mothers by 1982 *expected* to do so in 1980.[34] Thus, although only a small percentage of these adolescent girls expected to become single mothers, those who expressed that view were almost three times as likely to become single mothers as the overwhelming majority who did not.

A number of social structural factors that may influence the development of certain behavior norms may also be directly related to single parenthood. Hogan's research shows that girls from married-couple families and those from households with both mother and grandparent are much less likely to become unwed mothers than those from independent mother-headed households or nonparental homes. The fact that the rate of premarital parenthood of teens who live with both their single mothers and one (usually the grandmother) or more grandparents is as low as that of teens who live in husband-wife families suggests that "the critical effects of one-parent families are not so much attributable to the mother's example of single parenthood as an acceptable status as to the poverty and greater difficulty of parental supervision in one-adult families."[35] Furthermore, Hogan and Kitagawa's analysis of the influences of family background, personal characteristics, and social milieu on the probability of premarital pregnancy among black teenagers in Chicago indicates that those from nonintact families, lower social class, and poor and highly segregated neighborhoods have significantly higher fertility rates. Hogan and Kitagawa estimated that 57 percent of the teenage girls from high-risk social environments (lower class, poor inner-city neighborhood residence, female-headed family, five or more siblings, a sister who is a teenager mother, and loose parental supervision of dating) will become pregnant by age eighteen compared to only 9 percent of the girls from low-risk social backgrounds.[36]

Social structural factors also appear to affect the timing of marriage. Hogan reports that although black teenagers expect to become parents at roughly the same ages as whites, they expect to become married at later ages. Analysis of the High School and Beyond data reveals that when social class is controlled, black adolescents have expected age-specific rates of parenthood that are only 2 percent lower than those of whites, but expected age-specific rates of marriage that are 36 percent lower.[37] While Hogan notes that many whites are delaying marriage and parenthood because of educational or career aspirations, he attributes blacks' expectations of late marriage to the poor "marriage market" black women face. Indeed, available research has demonstrated a direct connection between the early marriage of young people and an encouraging economic situation, advantageous government transfer programs, and a balanced sex ratio.[38] These conditions are not only more likely to obtain for young whites than for young blacks, but as we try to show, they have become increasingly problematic for blacks.

This evidence suggests therefore that attitudes and expectations concerning marriage and parenthood are inextricably linked with social structural factors. Since we do not have systematic longitudinal data on the extent to which such attitudes and aspirations have changed in recent years, we can only assume that some changes have indeed occurred and that they are likely to be responses to broader changes in the society. This is not to ignore the import of normative or cultural explanations, rather it is to underline the well-founded sociological generalization that group variations in behavior, norms, and values often reflect variations in group access to channels of privilege and influence. When this connection is overlooked, explanations of problems such as premarital parenthood or female-headed families may focus on the norms and aspirations of individuals, and thereby fail to address the ultimate sources of the problem, such as changes in the structure of opportunities for the disadvantaged.

It is also important to remember that there are broader social and cultural trends in society that affect in varying degrees the behavior of all racial and class groups. For instance, sexual activity is increasingly prevalent among all teenagers. Growing proportions of adolescents have had sexual experience: according to one survey, the proportion of metropolitan teenage women who reported having premarital intercourse increased from 30 percent in 1971 to 50 percent in 1979. These proportions have risen particularly for white adolescents, thereby narrowing the differentials in the incidence of sexual activity. And they have more than offset the increase in contraceptive use over the past decade, resulting in a net increase in premarital pregnancy.[39] Rising rates of sexual activity among middle-class teens may be associated with various social and cultural trends such as the "sexual revolution," the increased availability of birth control and abortion, and perhaps the growing sophistication of American adolescents, or their adoption of adult social behavior at an increasingly early age. While these trends may also have influenced the sexual behavior of teens from disadvantaged backgrounds, it is difficult to assess their effects independent of the complex array of other factors. Our meager state of knowledge permits us only to say that they probably have some effect, but we do not have even a rough idea as to the degree.

Although our knowledge of the effect of social and cultural trends on the rise of extramarital fertility is scant, we know a little more about the effect of some of these trends on marital dissolution. Multivariate analyses of marital splits suggest that women's labor-force participation and income significantly increase marital dissolution among white women.[40] Labor-force participation rates of white women have nearly doubled from 1940 to 1980 (from 25.6 percent to 49.4 percent), in part due to a decline in marriage and in part to an increase in labor-force participation among married women, particularly those with children. The labor-force participation of black women has also increased, but not as dramatically (from 39.4 percent in 1940 to 53.3 percent in 1980);[41] black women have always worked in greater proportions than white women, a pattern that still holds today for all age-groups except women ages sixteen to twenty-four, an age category with high fertility rates.

Accompanying the increasing labor-force participation of women has been the rise of the feminist movement, which validates work as a source of both independence from men and personal fulfillment, and which has provided practical support not only through legal and political action but also through its role in promoting organizational resources for women in the labor market. Feminism as a social and cultural movement may have directly influenced the marriage decisions of women; it may also have indirectly affected these decisions through its role in women's more active participation in the labor market. In the absence of systematic empirical data, the effect of the feminist movement on the marital dissolution of women, particularly white women, can only be assumed.

It can be confidently asserted, however, that women's increasing employment makes marital breakup financially more viable than in the past. Although marital dissolution means a substantial loss of income, and sometimes severe economic hardship—median income of white female-headed families in 1979 was $11,452, compared to $21,824 for white married-couple families[42]— most white women can maintain their families above poverty with a combination of earnings and income from other sources such as alimony, child support, public-income transfers, personal wealth, and assistance from families. In 1982, 70 percent of white female-headed families were living above the poverty line.[43] In addition, many white single mothers remarry. For most black women facing marital dissolution, the situation is significantly different, not only because they tend to have fewer resources and are far less likely to remarry, but also because the major reasons for their increasing rates of marital disintegration have little to do with changing social and cultural trends.

The Role of Welfare

A popular explanation for the rise of female-headed families and out-of-wedlock births has been the growth of liberal welfare policies, in particular, broadened eligibility for income transfer programs, increases in benefit levels, and the creation of new programs such as Medicaid and food stamps. Charles Murray, for example, argues that relaxed restrictions and increasing benefits of AFDC enticed lower-class women to forego marriage or prolong childlessness in order to qualify for increasingly lucrative benefits.[44] Likewise, Robert Gordon depicts "welfare provisions as a major influence in the decline in two-adult households in American cities."[45]

The effect of welfare on out-of-wedlock births and marital instability became even more of an issue after the costs and caseloads of public assistance programs dramatically increased during the late 1960s and early 1970s. Since that time, a good deal of research has addressed this issue. Because all states have AFDC and food stamp programs, there can be no true test of the effects of welfare on family structure: there is no "control" population that has not been exposed to these welfare programs. However, substantial interstate variations in levels of AFDC benefits and in eligibility rules have provided opportunities for researchers to test the effects of program characteristics. Most studies have examined the level of welfare benefits as one of the determinants of a woman's choice between marriage and single parenthood. Some use aggregate data; others use individual-level data; still others examine the effect of providing cash transfers to intact families under special conditions, such as the Income Maintenance Experiments. But whether the focus is on the relationship between welfare and out-of-wedlock births or that between welfare and marital dissolution, the results have been inconclusive at best.

Many of the studies concerning welfare and out-of-wedlock births have compared illegitimacy rates or ratios across states with varying AFDC benefit levels. Cutright found no association between out-of-wedlock birth rates and benefit levels in 1960 or 1970. Using aggregate data, Winegarden's state-level analysis showed no association between measures of fertility and benefit levels, although he did report a small positive association with benefit availability. Fechter and Greenfield and Moore and Caldwell both used state-level cross-sectional data in a multivariate analysis and found no effects of welfare benefit levels on out-of-wedlock births. Finally, Vining showed that for blacks, the illegitimacy ratio in the South was only slightly lower than in non-southern states, despite levels of AFDC payments that were less than half those of the rest of the country; for whites, the difference was somewhat larger.[46]

This type of research is vulnerable to the criticism that, in Vining's words, "the overall incidence of illegitimacy could have been rising over time in concert with an overall rise in welfare payments, despite the lack of correlation between cross-state variation in illegitimacy and cross-state variation in welfare levels at any point in time."[47] However, despite frequent references in the literature to rising welfare expenditures, benefit levels have fallen in real terms over the past ten years, while illegitimacy ratios have continued to rise. Both Cutright and Ellwood and Bane examined changes over time in state benefit levels and in illegitimate birth rates and found no association.[48]

Other studies using different approaches and data sets have also yielded inconclusive, largely negative, results. Placek and Hendershot analyzed retrospective interviews of three hundred welfare mothers and found that when the women were on welfare, they were significantly *less* likely to refrain from using contraceptives, *less* likely to desire an additional pregnancy, and *less* likely to become pregnant. Similarly, Presser and Salsberg, using a random sample of New York women who had recently had their first child, reported that women on public assistance desired fewer children than women not on assistance, and were less likely to have planned their first birth. Based on a longitudinal study of low-income New York City women, Polgar and Hiday reported that women having an additional birth over a two-year period were no more likely to be receiving welfare at the start of the period than women who did not get pregnant. Moore and Caldwell reported no relationship between characteristics of AFDC programs and out-of-wedlock pregnancy and childbearing from a microlevel analysis of survey data.[49] Ellwood and Bane examined out-of-wedlock birth rates among women likely and unlikely to qualify for AFDC if they became single mothers, and found no significant effect of welfare benefit levels; a comparison of married and unmarried birth rates in low- and high-benefit states also yielded no effects.[50]

Finally, results from the Income Maintenance Experiments have been inconclusive. Reports from the New Jersey experiments indicate no effect. In the Seattle and Denver experiments, effects of income maintenance payments on fertility varied by race/ethnicity: white recipients had significantly lower fertility, Mexican-Americans had higher fertility, and blacks showed no effect.[51] Because of the relatively short duration of the study, it is not clear if maintenance payments affected completed fertility or simply the timing of births.

The results of studies focusing on the relationship between welfare and family stability have also been inconclusive. Researchers using aggregate data ordinarily look for correlations between rates of female family headship and size of AFDC payments, while controlling for other variables. In some studies, the unit of analysis is the state; in others, most notably Honig and Ross and Sawhill, various metropolitan areas were examined.[52] Analytic models used in most of these studies are similar, but disagreement over specification of the variables and other aspects of the analysis has produced mixed results. Honig found positive effects for AFDC payments on female family headship, although by 1970 the effects had diminished; Minarik and Goldfarb reported insignificant negative effects; Ross and Sawhill found significant positive effects for nonwhites, but not for whites; and Cutright and Madras found that AFDC benefits did not affect marital disruption, but did increase the likelihood that separated or divorced mothers would head their own households.[53]

As Ellwood and Bane observed, despite the sophistication of some of these multivariate analyses of aggregate data, the analyses have "largely ignored the problems introduced by largely unmeasurable differences between states."[54] Introducing a unique and resourceful solution to these problems, they present estimates of welfare effects based on comparisons of marital dissolution and living arrangements among mothers likely and unlikely to be AFDC recipients, and among women who are or are not mothers (and thus eligible for AFDC), in high- and low-benefit states. They also examine changes over time in benefit levels and family structure. The findings based on these three different comparisons are remarkably similar. Ellwood and Bane estimate that in 1975, a $100 increase in AFDC benefits would have resulted in a 10 percent increase in the number of divorced or separated mothers, with a more substantial effect for young women; the same increase in AFDC benefits would have contributed to an estimated 25 percent to 30 percent increase in the formation of independent households, again with much more substantial effects for young mothers.[55]

Studies using individual-level data have yielded mixed results, with some finding modest effects, and some reporting no effect at all of welfare on marital dissolution or family headship. Hoffman and Holmes analyzed Michigan PSID data and reported that low-income families living in states with high AFDC benefits were 6 percent more likely than the average to dissolve their marriages, while similar families in states with low-benefit levels were 6 percent less likely to do so. Ross and Sawhill, in a similar analysis of the same data, found no significant welfare effects, even in a regression performed separately for low-income families. In a recent study, Danziger et al. modeled headship choices using data from 1968 and 1975 *Current Population Surveys* and concluded that a reduction in welfare benefits would result in only a slight decrease in the number of female household heads; the authors also reported that the increase in female-headed families between 1968 and 1975 was greater than the model would have predicted given the changes in the relative economic circumstances of female heads and married women occurring during that period.[56] It seems likely that the decreasing supply of "marriageable men" (examined below) is a constraint on women's marriage decisions that is not accounted for in the model.

Studies of intact families receiving income transfers under the Income Maintenance Experiments show that providing benefits to two-parent families did not tend to reduce marital instability: the split rates for these families were higher, not lower, than those of comparable low-income families, although the results were not consistent across maintenance levels. The Income Maintenance Experiments "increased the proportion of families headed by single females. For blacks and whites, the increase was due to the increase in dissolution; for

Chicanos, the increase was due to the decrease in the marital formation rates." Groeneveld, Tuma, and Hannan speculate that nonpecuniary factors such as the stigma, transaction costs, and lack of information associated with the welfare system caused the income maintenance program to have a greater effect on women's sense of economic independence.[57]

To sum up, this research indicates that welfare receipt or benefit levels have no effect on the incidence of out-of-wedlock births. Aid to Families with Dependent Children payments seem to have a substantial effect on living arrangements of single mothers, but only a modest impact on separation and divorce. The extent to which welfare deters marriage or remarriage among single mothers is addressed only indirectly, in studies of the incidence of female-headed households, and here the evidence is inconclusive.

However, if the major impact of AFDC is on the living arrangements of single mothers, it could ultimately have a greater influence on family structure. As we emphasized in our discussion of Hogan's research on the premarital parenthood of adolescents, young women from independent mother-headed households are more likely to become unwed mothers than those from married-couple families and those from female-headed subfamilies living in the homes of their grandparents.[58]

Nonetheless, the findings from Ellwood and Bane's impressive research, and the inconsistent results of other studies on the relationship between welfare and family structure, and welfare and out-of-wedlock births, raise serious questions about the current tendency to blame changes in welfare policies for the decline in the proportion of intact families and legitimate births among the poor. As Ellwood and Bane emphatically proclaim, "Welfare simply does not appear to be the underlying cause of the dramatic changes in family structure of the past few decades."[59] The factor that we have identified as the underlying cause is discussed in the next section.

The Role of Joblessness

Although the structure of the economy and the composition of the labor force have undergone significant change over the last forty years, the labor-force participation patterns of white men have changed little. The labor-force participation rate of white men declined from 82 percent in 1940 to 76 percent in 1980, in part because of a drop in the labor-force activity of men over the age of fifty-five (from 83.9 percent to 72.2 percent for those ages fifty-five to sixty-four).[60] Labor-force participation of white men ages twenty-four and under actually increased over the past decade.

For blacks, the patterns are different. The labor-force participation of black men declined substantially, from 84 percent in 1940 to 67 percent in 1980.[61] Labor-force trends for older black men parallel those of white men of the same ages. But the decline in labor-force participation of young black men and, to a lesser extent, prime-age black men has occurred, while the participation of comparable white men has either increased or remained stable.

Economic trends for black men, especially young black men, have been unfavorable since the end of World War II. While the status of young blacks who are employed has improved with the percentage of white-collar workers among all black male workers, rising from 5 percent in 1940 to 27 percent in 1983, the proportion of black men who are employed has dropped from 80 percent in 1930 to 56 percent in 1983. Unemployment rose sharply for black male teenagers during the 1950s and remained high during the prosperous 1960s; similarly, unemployment rates for black men twenty to twenty-four years of age rose sharply during the mid-1970s and have remained high. In 1979, when the overall unemployment rate had declined to 5.8 percent, the rate for black male teenagers was 34.1 percent.[62] In addition, while blacks have historically had higher labor-force participation levels, by the 1970s labor-force participation of black men had fallen below that of white men for all age-groups, with particularly steep declines for those ages twenty-four and younger (see chap. 2, table 2.7).

The adverse effects of unemployment and other economic problems of family stability are well established in the literature. Studies of family life during the Great Depression document the deterioration of marriage and family life following unemployment. More recent research, based on longitudinal data sets such as the PSID and the National Longitudinal Study or on aggregate data, shows consistently that unemployment is related to marital instability and the incidence of female-headed families. Indicators of economic status such as wage rates, income, or occupational status may also be related to marital instability or female headedness, although the evidence is not as consistent. For instance, while Cutright's analysis of 1960 census data indicates that divorce and separation rates are higher among lower-income families, Sawhill et al. find that unemployment, fluctuations in income, and lack of assets are associated with higher separation rates, but that the level of the husband's earnings has an effect only among low-income black families. However, Cohen reports that when the husband's age is controlled, the higher the husband's earnings, the less likely both black and white couples are to divorce.[63]

Nonetheless, the weight of the evidence on the relationship between the employment status of men, and family life and married life suggests that the increasing rate of joblessness among black men merits serious consideration as a major underlying factor in the rise of black single mothers and female-headed households. Moreover, when the factor of joblessness is combined with high black-male mortality and incarceration rates,[64] the proportion of black men in stable economic situations is even lower than that conveyed in the current unemployment and labor-force figures.

The full dimensions of this problem are revealed in figures 3.1 through 3.6, which show the effect of male joblessness trends, in combination with the effects of male mortality and incarceration rates, by presenting the rates of employed civilian men to women of the same race and age-group.[65] This ratio may be described as a "male marriageable pool index." The number of women is used as the denominator in order to convey the situation of young women in the "marriage market." Figures 3.1 to 3.3, for men sixteen to twenty-four years of age, show similar patterns: a sharp decline in the nonwhite ratios beginning in the 1960s, which is even more startling when compared with the rising ratios for white men. Figures 3.4 to 3.6, for men twenty-five to fifty-four years of age, show a more gradual decline for black men relative to white men. Clearly, what our "male marriageable pool index" reveals is a long-term decline in the proportion of black men, and particularly young black men, who are in a position to support a family.

As we noted above, the relationship between joblessness and marital instability is well established in the literature. Moreover, available evidence supports the argument that among blacks, increasing male joblessness is related to the rising proportions of families headed by women.[66] By contrast, for whites, trends in male employment and earnings appear to have little to do with the increase in female-headed families. Although lower-income families have higher rates of marital dissolution, trends in the employment status of white men since 1960 cannot explain the overall rise in white separation and divorce rates.

It seems likely that the chief cause of the rise of separation and divorce rates among whites is the increased economic independence of white women as indicated by their increasing employment and improving occupational status. It is not that this growing independence gives white women a financial incentive to separate from or to divorce their husbands; rather, it makes dissolution of a bad marriage a more viable alternative than in the past. That the employment status of white males is not a major factor in white single motherhood or female-headed families can perhaps also be seen in the higher rate of remarriage among white women and the significantly earlier age of first mar-

riage. By contrast, the increasing delay of first marriage and the low
rate of remarriage among black women seem to be directly tied to the
increasing labor-force problems of men.

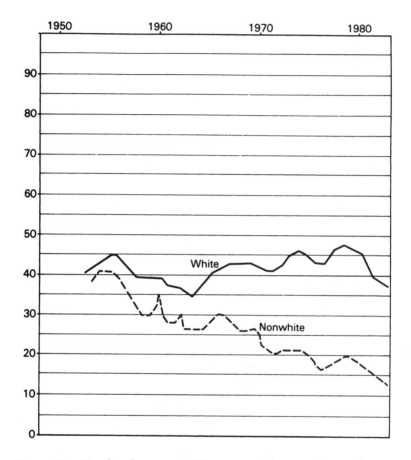

**Figure 3.1.   Employed men per 100 women of the same age and race—
sixteen and seventeen years of age, 1954–82.** *Sources:* U.S. Bureau of Labor
Statistics, *Handbook of Labor Statistics,* Bulletin 2070 (Washington, D.C.:
Government Printing Office, 1980); idem, *Employment and Earnings.* The
denominators, the number of women by age and race, are taken from U.S.
Bureau of the Census, *Current Population Reports,* series P-25, no. 721,
"Estimates of the United States by Age, Sex, and Race, 1970 to 1977" (Wash-
ington, D.C.: Government Printing Office, 1978); and idem, *Current Popula-
tion Reports,* series P-25, "Estimates of the Population of the United States by
Age, Sex, and Race, 1980 to 1982" (Washington, D.C.: Government Printing
Office, 1983).

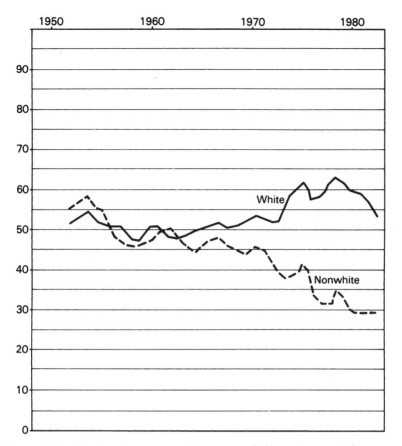

Figure 3.2. Employed men per 100 women of the same age and race—
eighteen and nineteen years of age, 1954–82. *Sources:* see fig. 3.1.

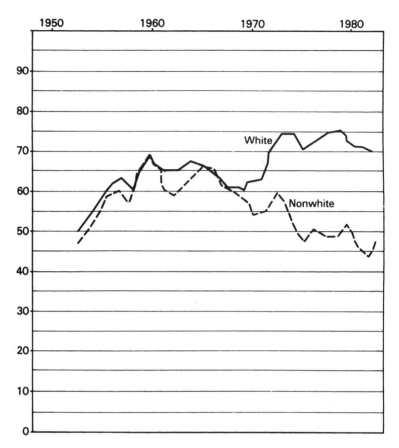

Figure 3.3.   Employed men per 100 women of the same age and race—
twenty and twenty-four years of age, 1954–82. *Sources:* see fig. 3.1.

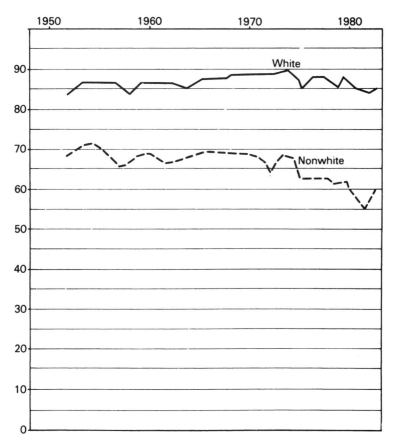

Figure 3.4. Employed men per 100 women of the same age and race—
twenty-five and thirty-four years of age, 1954–82. *Sources:* see fig. 3.1.

Figure 3.5. Employed men per 100 women of the same age and race—thirty-five and forty-four years of age, 1954–82. *Sources:* see fig. 3.1.

Figure 3.6.   Employed men per 100 women of the same age and race—forty-five and fifty-four years of age, 1954–82. *Sources:* see fig. 3.1.

Conclusion

In the 1960s scholars readily attributed black family deterioration to the problems of male joblessness. However, in the last ten to fifteen years, in the face of the overwhelming focus on welfare as the major source of black family breakup, concerns about the importance of male joblessness have receded into the background. We argue in this chapter that the available evidence justifies renewed scholarly and public policy attention to the connection between the disintegration of poor families and black male prospects for stable employment.

We find that when statistics on black family structure are disaggregated to reveal changes in fertility rates, marital status, age structure, and residence patterns, it becomes clear, first of all, that the black "illegitimacy ratio" has increased rapidly not so much because of an increase in the incidence of out-of-wedlock births, but mainly because both the rate of marital fertility and the percentage of women married and living with their husbands has declined significantly. And the sharp reduction of the latter is due both to the rise in black divorce and separation and to the increase in the percentage of never-married women. Inextricably connected with these trends are changes in the age structure, which have increased the fraction of births to young women and thereby inflated the proportion of all births occurring outside of marriage. The net result has been a 41 percent increase in the number of black children growing up in fatherless families during the 1970s, with most of this increase occurring in families in which the mother has never been married. Furthermore, the substantial racial differences in the timing of first marriage and the rate of remarriage underscore the persistence of black female headedness. And what makes all of these trends especially disturbing is that female-headed families are far more likely than married-couple families to be not only poor, but mired in poverty for long periods of time.

Although changing social and cultural trends have often been invoked to explain some of the dynamic changes in the structure of the family, they appear to have more relevance for shifts in family structure among whites. And contrary to popular opinion, there is little evidence to provide a strong case for welfare as the primary cause of family breakups, female-headed households, and out-of-wedlock births. Welfare does seem to have a modest effect on separation and divorce, especially for white women, but recent evidence suggests that its total effect on the size of the population of female householders is small. As shown in Ellwood and Bane's impressive study, if welfare does have a major influence on female-headed families, it is in the living arrangements of single mothers.[67] We explained why this could ultimately and indirectly lead to an increase in female family headship.

By contrast, the evidence for the influence of male joblessness is much more persuasive. Research has demonstrated, for example, a connection between the early marriage of young people and an encouraging economic situation. In this connection, we have tried to show that black women are more likely to delay marriage and less likely to remarry. We further noted that although black teenagers expect to become parents at about the same ages as whites, they expect to marry at later ages. And we argue that both the black delay in marriage and the lower rate of remarriage, each of which is associated with high percentages of out-of-wedlock births and female-headed households, can be directly tied to the labor-market status of black males. As we have documented, black women, especially young black women, are facing a shrinking pool of "marriageable" (i.e., economically stable) men.

White women are not faced with this problem. Indeed, our "male marriageable pool index" indicates that the number of employed white men per one hundred white women in different age categories has either remained roughly the same or has increased since 1954. We found little reason, therefore, to assume a connection between the rise in female-headed white families and changes in white male employment. That the pool of "marriageable" white men has not shrunk over the years is reflected, we believe, in the earlier age of first marriage and higher rate of remarriage among white women. For all these reasons, we hypothesize that increases in separation and divorce among whites are due chiefly to the increased economic independence of white women and related social and cultural factors.

Despite the existence of evidence suggesting that the increasing inability of many black men to support a family is the driving force behind the rise of female-headed families, in the last ten to fifteen years welfare has dominated explanations of the increase in female headship. The commonsense assumption that welfare regulations break up families, affirmed by liberals and conservatives alike, buttressed the welfare explanations of trends in family structure. The Subcommittee on Fiscal Policy of the Joint Economic Committee initiated a program of research on the topic in 1971; according to Cutright and Madras, recognition of the increasing monetary value of noncash benefits, in the context of economic theories of marriage,[68] persuaded the subcommittee that welfare was related to the rise of female-headed families despite inconclusive evidence. And despite frequent references to rising social welfare expenditures, the real value of welfare benefits has declined over the past ten years while the number and proportion of female-headed families continue to climb.

Only recently has it been proposed that the rise in female-headed families among blacks is related to declining employment rates among black men.[69] Evidence such as that displayed in figures 3.1 to 3.6 and in other studies discussed in this chapter makes a compelling case for once again placing the problem of black joblessness as a top-priority item in public policy agendas designed to enhance the status of poor black families.

4   Joblessness versus Welfare Effects
A Further Reexamination
with Robert Aponte and Kathryn Neckerman

In the preceding chapter, we pointed out that the extraordinary rise in female-headed families, particularly among the black poor, is now being viewed in policy circles as a reflection of the failure of federal antipoverty programs. According to this view, liberal welfare policies, especially those associated with the Great Society program (which expanded eligibility for income transfer payments, increased benefit levels, and created or expanded programs such as Medicaid and food stamps) have reduced the incentive to work and to create or maintain stable families. We also attempted to show that much of the empirical research on changing family structure has provided only limited support for this argument. It retains great appeal, nonetheless, because the logic of the association between welfare and family/work disincentives is intuitively compelling and appears largely consistent with aggregate trends in social welfare spending and changes in family structure over time. However, it was not until Charles Murray developed the thesis in his controversial critique of the Great Society, *Losing Ground*, that the welfare thesis was widely discussed in the popular media. [1]

Murray argues that welfare generosity is the fundamental cause of black family disintegration in the inner city and contributes substantially to joblessness among younger black men as well. He contends that in 1970, a poor urban family with one worker literally could improve its financial situation by dissolving its marriage, withdrawing its members from the labor market, and subsisting on welfare. Indeed Murray implies that by 1970 the monetary value of the full welfare benefit package available to unmarried mothers exceeded the minimum-wage earnings from a full forty-hour work week.

Murray illustrates this argument by presenting the case of a fictitious young unmarried couple, Harold and Phyllis, in an "average" city at two points in time—1960 and 1970. Phyllis is pregnant, and the couple must decide between remaining unmarried and thus qualifying for Aid to Families with Dependent Children (AFDC) or marrying and subsisting on Harold's minimum-wage earnings. In 1960, the welfare package would have barely supported Phyllis and her child. Moreover, the law did not permit payment of welfare benefits if the couple were to cohabit, regardless of their marital status. In that situation, Murray argues, Harold and Phyllis would very likely decide to marry and live on his earnings. However, by 1970 the situation had changed—the income from the welfare package would not only exceed Harold's minimum-wage earnings, but it could be collected while the couple cohabited as a family unit provided they were not legally married. Thus, Murray concludes, the couple would tend to eschew marriage and minimum-wage employment in favor of welfare.

There are a number of problems with this presentation. First, Murray's calculations were based on welfare benefits from the state of Pennsylvania, where AFDC payments rose at twice the national average over the 1960s.[2] Hence, the example of "shift in incentives" that Murray presents as "typical" was likely to be far greater than that confronted by most poor families.

Of greater importance is Murray's inadequate attention to trends in the relative advantages of welfare versus work *after 1970*. He states that real AFDC payments, which had risen sharply during the 1960s, continued to grow during the 1970s until about mid-decade, after which average payments "increased little if at all in most states."[3] Real benefit levels, in fact, have fallen dramatically since the early 1970s. Danziger and Gottschalk reveal that by 1980 the real value of AFDC plus food stamps had been reduced by 16 percent from their 1972 levels. By 1984 the combined payments were only 4 percent higher than their 1960 levels and 22 percent less than in 1972.[4] In the words of Greenstein, "no other group in American society experienced such a sharp decline in real income since 1970 as did AFDC mothers and their children."[5]

Finally, the 1975 enactment of the Earned Income Tax Credit further increased the incentives for members of low-income households to work. Thus, Greenstein estimates that Harold's 1980 minimum-wage income plus in-kind transfers would have been one-third higher in Pennsylvania (and higher still in other states) than the family's welfare payments and other benefits. Accordingly, he concludes, "if perverse welfare incentives in the late 1960s actually led to family dissolution and black unemployment, as Murray contends, then these trends should have reversed themselves in the 1970s, when the relative advantage of work over welfare increased sharply. They didn't. The number of female-headed households continued to surge, and black employment declined."[6]

As shown in the previous chapter, much research supports Greenstein's claim that changes in welfare benefit levels alone cannot explain family disintegration. Although Murray does not discuss much of this literature, he does cite the Income Maintenance Experiments as evidence of strong welfare effects on family structure. The Seattle/Denver experiments (which were the most comprehensive and best administered) indicated that guaranteed incomes significantly reduced the stability or frequency of marriage. The effects were not consistent across payment levels, however: at the highest income level, the payments (or guarantees) had no effect on marital stability. In addition, the experimental conditions differed substantially from those under which states actually dispense AFDC payments (the primary source of public assistance to families), thereby jeopardizing generalizations from one to the other. For example, the experiments provided income support to two-parent as well as one-parent families, but, unlike the AFDC program, adjusted payments (or guarantees) were also provided to *both* adults (and the children) in cases of marital splits. Finally, as Cain notes, the effects of the income transfers were confounded with those of the experimental training program, which was shown to have increased marital instability; thus the magnitude and direction of the effects of income transfers alone are unclear.[7]

Thus, neither Murray's comparisons nor the empirical literature establishes the claim that liberal welfare policies are the major cause of changing family structure among blacks. An alternative hypothesis on the role of joblessness was presented in the previous chapter.

The Family, Joblessness, and Changes in Economic Organization: "The Male Marriageable Pool" and Family Structure by Region

In chapter 3 we argued that when jobless figures among black men are combined with the men's relatively high rates of incarceration and premature mortality,[8] it becomes clear that the ability of black men to provide economic support is even lower than official employment statistics convey. The full dimensions of the problem were depicted with an index that showed the ratio of employed men to women of the same age and race. Designated as a "male marriageable pool index" (MMPI), this measure is intended to reveal the marriage market conditions facing women, on the assumption that to be marriageable a man needs to be employed.[9] The men and women are matched by age and race, since most people marry within their own race and near their own age.

If it is correct to assume that most of the black men escaping census coverage are jobless, then their omission from the MMPI exerts little bias on the analyses.

Trends in the MMPI for the nation as a whole showed that unlike white women, black women, particularly younger black women, are confronting a shrinking pool of economically stable, or "marriageable," men. This finding supports the hypothesis that the rise of black female-headed families is directly related to increasing black male joblessness. Data presented below on both MMPI and family status by region over the 1960–80 period afford a more direct test of this hypothesis.

The trends in the MMPI reveal that changes in the ratios of employed men to women among whites have been minimal, with modest declines only among northern whites (see table 4.1). On the other hand, the ratios for blacks have declined substantially in all regions but the West. The northern regions averaged losses of more than 11 employed black men per 100 women among persons aged twenty to forty-four, with even greater losses if the youngest men (ages sixteen to forty-four) are included.[10] The South averaged a loss of more than 6 employed men per 100 women in the twenty to forty-four age category, and almost as many when the youngest men are included. The "marriageable pool" of black men in the West, however, declined only by about the same amount as that of northern whites. On the basis of these trends, we would expect growth in female-headed families to be greatest among blacks in the northern regions, followed by the South, and to be least among whites and western blacks.

Table 4.2 presents figures on female family headship by race and region for women under age forty-five in 1960 and 1980. We focus on female family heads under age forty-five because that group is the fastest growing and it is economically the most disadvantaged of women householders.[11] They are also more likely to have borne their children outside of marriage and therefore have more difficulty obtaining child support.[12] Two measures describe changes in female headship: the proportion of all family heads under age forty-five who are women and the proportion of all women under age forty-five who head families. While the first measure (which describes trends in family type by sex of head) is useful because it is the conventional index of female headship, the second measure (which describes trends in family headship among women) is important as well because it does not vary with changes in the number of male-headed families.

Trends in joblessness and family structure by race and region largely conform to our expectations: as table 4.3 shows, a large drop in the MMPI tends to be associated with a sizable increase in female-headed

TABLE 4.1
Male Marriageable Pool Index (employed men per 100 women) by Race, Age, and Region, 1960 and 1980

	NORTHEAST				NORTH CENTRAL			
	White		Black		White		Black	
	1960	1980	1960	1980	1960	1980	1960	1980
16–19	43.8	45.1	31.2	22.7	50.5	51.4	27.4	25.5
20–24	77.9	74.1	59.1	48.1	81.6	77.4	58.0	49.0
25–34	89.5	87.9	67.7	57.8	93.4	90.3	69.0	57.6
35–44	88.1	88.4	71.4	60.4	92.2	90.4	73.8	61.3
16–44	80.8	78.1	63.0	50.3	84.5	81.0	63.0	50.7
20–44	86.9	84.7	67.5	56.3	90.6	87.0	68.8	56.3

	SOUTH				WEST			
	White		Black		White		Black	
	1960	1980	1960	1980	1960	1980	1960	1980
16–19	44.2	50.7	38.9	29.2	48.1	51.3	NA	29.6
20–24	75.9	78.7	70.5	58.0	77.8	76.6	57.7	57.3
25–29	85.8	89.6	71.1	68.2	90.0	88.9	69.1	69.0
35–44	87.0	89.3	71.6	67.7	90.0	91.8	76.2	73.1
16–44	78.1	81.1	65.2	59.7	82.0	81.4	NA	60.5
20–44	84.4	86.8	71.2	65.1	87.7	86.8	69.7	67.0

Sources: U.S. Bureau of the Census, *U.S. Census of Population, 1960: Characteristics of the Population*, pt. 1, U.S. Summary (Washington, D.C.: Government Printing Office, 1961); and idem, *Census of Population: Detailed Characteristics of the Population*, pt. 1, U.S. Summary (Washington, D.C.: Government Printing Office, 1980).

Note: The 1960 figures for 16- to 19-year-olds refer to nonwhites rather than to blacks. This has a sizable effect only for western blacks. In 1960, blacks made up only 49 percent of all western nonwhites, while in all other regions, blacks comprised over 95 percent of all nonwhites.

families. The proportion of black women under forty-five heading families grew most substantially in the northeastern and north-central regions (+12.0 and +12.1), followed by the South (+9.1), and then the West (+8.7). On the other hand, the smaller proportions of younger white women heading families varied little by region.

Data based on the first measure, the proportion of families headed by women, also largely conformed to our expectations among blacks in the northern regions and the South. We did not expect, however, the

TABLE 4.2
Indicators of Family Status by Race and Region, 1960 and 1980, Family Heads, and
Women Ages Fifteen to Forty-four

	Proportion of Families Headed by Women		Proportion of Women Heading Families	
	Black	White	Black	White
Northeast				
1960	24.2	6.1	13.4	3.5
1980	48.6	12.3	25.4	6.5
Change 1960–80	+24.4	+ 6.2	+12.0	+3.0
North Central				
1960	22.7	4.8	13.4	2.9
1980	49.0	10.6	25.5	6.2
Change 1960–80	+26.3	+ 5.8	+12.1	+3.3
South				
1960	21.6	6.1	10.0	3.7
1980	37.2	10.0	19.1	6.1
Change 1960–80	+15.6	+ 3.9	+ 9.1	+2.4
West				
1960	21.5	7.5	14.1	4.7
1980	39.5	16.9	22.9	7.9
Change 1960–80	+18.0	+ 9.4	+ 8.7	+3.2

Sources: U.S. Bureau of the Census, *U.S. Census of Population, 1960: Characteristics of the Population,* pt. 1, U.S. Summary (Washington, D.C.: Government
Printing Office, 1961); and idem, *Census of Population: Detailed Characteristics of
the Population,* pt. 1, U.S. Summary (Washington, D.C.: Government Printing
Office, 1980).

West to show a faster rate of growth in the proportion of black families
headed by women than did the South (+18 and +15.6, respectively),
nor did we expect so sharp a rise in the proportion of black women
heading families in the West.

A number of characteristics unique to western blacks, four-fifths of
whom live in California, may help to explain these findings. Representing less than 9 percent of the total black population, western blacks are
far more likely to be recent migrants and to have higher levels of income and education than blacks in other regions of the country. Beyond that, the social and economic characteristics of black women who
head families in California are closer to those of white female heads
than to those of other black female heads. For instance they become
family heads more frequently through divorce than through separation
and out-of-wedlock births, and have higher average incomes and lower
rates of poverty. They also receive less welfare than women heading

TABLE 4.3
Change in the Male Marriageable Pool Index and Indicators of Family Status by
Race and Region, 1960–1980

	MMPI	Families Headed by Women	Proportion of Women Heading Families
Northeast			
Black	−11.2	+24.4	+12.0
White	− 2.2	+ 6.2	+ 3.0
North Central			
Black	−12.5	+26.3	+12.1
White	− 3.6	+ 5.8	+ 3.3
South			
Black	− 6.1	+15.6	+ 9.1
White	+ 2.4	+ 3.9	+ 2.4
West			
Black	− 2.7	+18.0	+ 8.7
White	− 0.9	+ 9.4	+ 3.2

Source: See table 4.1.

families in northern regions (in the South, AFDC eligibility levels are low and welfare recipiency is restricted), despite the fact that AFDC payment guarantees in California are the highest in the continental United States.[13]

If the social and economic traits of California's black female family heads are more like those of white female heads, the reasons for their respective high rates of marital dissolution may be similar. In their landmark study of female-headed families, Ross and Sawhill suggested that the relatively high rates of marital dissolution among western whites could be a function of selective migration.[14] Divorce is also significantly higher among blacks in the West than among blacks in other regions; indeed, the differential exceeds that between western and nonwestern white women.[15] Trends in female family headship among whites as well as among blacks in the West, moreover, appear to be unrelated to changes in the MMPI. The proportion of white families headed by women grew significantly higher in the West than in the other three regions, despite the fact that the white MMPI rose in the West and declined in the other three regions (see tables 4.1 and 4.2). It therefore seems quite reasonable to hypothesize that female family headship among western blacks, as among western whites, is significantly bolstered by the influx of relatively well-off migrants among whom marital dissolution is relatively high.

Nonetheless, although the MMPIs for blacks in the West changed only slightly from 1960 to 1980, they are still significantly lower than those of western whites. While deterioration of employment conditions cannot explain the growth of black female-headed families in the West, the substantial black-white difference in male employment is quite plausibly one of the major reasons for the racial gap in female headship in the West. Moreover, in the three regions in which more than 90 percent of the nation's blacks reside, the MMPI remains a powerful predictor of the phenomenal rise of black female-headed families.

Changing Economic Organization and Black Male Joblessness

If we have good reason to believe that black male joblessness is strongly related to changes in black family structure, it is also reasonable to hypothesize that the rapid contraction of the black "male marriageable pool" is related to basic changes in economic organization that have occurred in recent decades. The shift in economic activity from goods production to services has been associated with changes in the location of production: first, an interregional movement of industry from the North to the South and West; and second and more important, a movement of certain industries away from the older central cities where blacks are concentrated.

We have shown that the ratio of employed black men per one hundred black women of the same age decreased most rapidly in the two northern regions. As table 4.4 reveals, these areas have experienced substantially less employment growth than the rest of the country.[16] Moreover, these trends are concentrated in sectors where "employment conditions typically do not require substantial education: manufacturing, retail, and wholesale trade." Between 1970 and 1980, for example, 701,700 manufacturing jobs were lost from the economies of these regions.[17]

Data on the decrease in manufacturing, wholesale, and retail employment by region, however, do not reveal another pattern that appears especially relevant to the drop in the black MMPI ratios across the country: the decline of these jobs in the nation's largest cities, where blacks are heavily concentrated. Between 1947 and 1972, the central cities of the thirty-three most populous metropolitan areas (according to 1970 figures) lost 880,000 manufacturing jobs, while manufacturing employment in their suburbs grew by 2.5 million. The same cities lost 867,000 jobs in retail and wholesale trade at the same time

TABLE 4.4
Employment Growth by Region

	Time Period	
Region	1950–77	1970–77
Northwest		
New England	44.6	6.3
Middle Atlantic	28.4	−1.1
North Central		
East North Central	52.8	8.5
West North Central	71.8	15.6
South		
South Atlantic[a]	128.1	20.1
East South Central	107.5	21.9
West South Central	133.0	29.8
West		
Mountain	185.5	36.8
Pacific	155.0	21.0
U.S. Total	70.3	8.6

Source: Bernard L. Weinstein and Robert E. Firestine, *Region Growth and Decline in the United States* (New York: Praeger, 1978), table 1.5.

[a] Between 1970 and 1977, all southern states experienced job growth of at least 10 percent while the District of Columbia had a loss of 16.1 percent.

that their suburbs gained millions of such positions.[18] While the black populations of these central cities were growing substantially, white and middle-class residents migrated to the suburbs. Between 1950 and 1980, populations in these central cities lost more than 9 million whites and added more than 5 million blacks,[19] many of them from the rural South.[20]

The decline in demand for the designated types of unskilled labor has been most severe in the older central cities of the North. The four largest (New York, Chicago, Philadelphia, and Detroit), which in 1982 accounted for more than one-quarter of the nation's central-city poor, lost more than a million jobs in manufacturing, wholesale, and retail enterprises between 1967 and 1976 alone,[21] at the same time that their populations were rapidly becoming minority dominant. By 1980, blacks and Hispanics accounted for virtually half of New York City's population, 57 percent of Chicago's, 67 percent of Detroit's, and 43 percent of Philadelphia's. The major portion of this minority population, especially in the latter two cities, is black.

The decline in blue-collar employment in the central city has been partly offset by expansion in "knowledge-intensive" fields such as advertising, finance, brokering, consulting, accounting, and law. For example, between 1953 and 1984 New York City lost about 600,000 jobs in manufacturing but gained nearly 700,000 jobs in white-collar service industries; Philadelphia lost 280,000 jobs in manufacturing but added 178,000 jobs in white-collar service industries; Baltimore lost 75,000 jobs in manufacturing but gained 84,000 jobs in white-collar service industries; and St. Louis lost 127,000 jobs in manufacturing but added 51,000 jobs in white-collar service industries.[22]

However, the research on the decline of entry-level jobs in the inner city (reported in chap. 2) provides more direct evidence that these demographic and employment trends have produced a serious mismatch between the skills of inner-city blacks and the opportunities available to them. As pointed out earlier, substantial job losses have occurred in the very industries in which urban minorities have the greatest access, and substantial employment gains have occurred in the higher-education-requisite industries that are beyond the reach of most minority workers. If one examines recent data presented by Kasarda on central-city educational attainment by race, the extent to which inner-city blacks are poorly matched for these employment trends is readily apparent. Trichotomizing attainment into less than high school, high school completion only, and some college, Kasarda finds that whereas a plurality of central-city white men (ages sixteen to sixty-four) have attended at least some college, the modal category among black men is less than high school for all regions of the country except the West.[23] "This mismatch is one major reason why both unemployment rates and labor-force dropout rates among central city blacks are much higher than those of central city white residents," states Kasarda, "and why black unemployment rates have not responded well to economic recovery in many northern cities."[24]

However, Kasarda's measure of "lower education requisite" jobs and "higher education requisite" jobs does not address the question of the actual relevance of levels of education to real job performance. Many jobs identified as "higher education" jobs because of the average level of education of the workforce may not really require "higher educational" training. For example, a number of people have observed that the new high technology is "user friendly" and can be operated in most cases by people who have mastered the "3Rs."[25] Nonetheless, if jobs in the high growth industry depend on a mastery of the 3Rs, and if employers tend to associate such skills with higher levels of formal education, then they will tend to favor those with more, not less, formal education, thereby institutionalizing "job requirements." Moreover, many inner-city minorities face an additional problem when access to jobs is increasingly based on education criteria. Samuel Bowles and Herbert Gintis, in a provocative study of the history of education in the United States, have argued that consignment to inner-city schools helps guarantee the future economic subordinacy of minority students.[26] More specifically, inner-city schools train minority youth so that they feel and appear capable of only performing jobs in the low wage sector. Citing a recent study of disadvantaged workers which indicated that appearance was between two and three times as important to potential employees as previous work experience, high school diplomas or test scores, Bowles and Gintis contend that students in ghetto schools are not encouraged to develop the levels of self-esteem or the styles of presentation which employers perceive as evidence of capacity or ability. Secondly, schools adopt patterns of socialization which reflect the background and/or future social position of their students. Those schools with a high concentration of poor and minorities have radically different internal environments, methods of teaching and attitudes toward students than predominantly white, upper middle class suburban schools. Bowles and Gintis state that:

> Blacks and minorities are concentrated in schools whose repressive, arbitrary, generally chaotic internal order, coercive authority structures and minimal possibilities for advancement mirror the characteristics of inferior job situations. Similarly, predominantly working-class schools tend to emphasize behavioral control and rule following, while schools in well-to-do suburbs employ relatively open systems that favor greater student participation, less direct supervision, more electives and in general a value system stressing internalized standards of control.[27]

If the characteristics of inferior job situations are mirrored in the internal order of ghetto schools, then the transformation of the urban economy from jobs perceived to require lower education to those perceived to require higher education or the mastery of the 3Rs is even more problematic for inner-city residents.

The change in the MMPI of younger black men presents a particular problem of interpretation. Although the overall decline in the proportion of black marriageable men in the South is not nearly so great as that in the northern regions, the shrinkage in the "male marriageable pool" for ages sixteen to twenty-four is actually greater there than in the North. In a recent study of the decline in black teenage em-

ployment from 1950 to 1970, Cogan argues that "the decline in the
demand for low-skilled agricultural labor" was "the driving force behind the sizable reductions in the aggregate black teenage employment
ratio during the period 1950–1970."[28] If the primary source of employment for black teenagers in the South was drastically reduced by
mechanization of agricultural production, it is reasonable to assume
that many southern black men aged twenty to twenty-four suffered the
same fate.

The substantial decline in the MMPI for black youth outside the
South cannot be explained by the mechanization of agriculture, since
the vast majority of nonsouthern blacks are living in metropolitan
areas. However, the changes in economic organization affecting central
cities, where more than three-quarters of all metropolitan blacks reside, are likely to have had a significant impact on the employment of
black youth. Research has shown that youth employment problems are
concentrated among the less educated as well as among blacks.[29] In
turn, central-city and poverty-area or ghetto residence has also been
found to depress youth employment.[30] These findings are consistent
with the implications of Kasarda's research: shifts in employment mix
should have their greatest impact on low-skilled workers in the central
cities. Finally, evidence suggests that these declines in employment of
low-skilled workers accelerated during the 1970s.[31] Decennial employment ratios of black youth show that while joblessness among
southern youth increased more rapidly during the 1960s than the
1970s, among northern youth the increase was more substantial over
the latter decade. The timing of these two trends is consistent with the
interpretation that changes in economic organization have had an impact on the employment of black youth.

Conclusion: Race, Family Structure, and Public Policy

We have attempted in this chapter to show that Murray's thesis in
Losing Ground does not begin to come to grips with the complex problem of the rising number of female-headed families and out-of-wedlock
births because he overemphasizes the role of liberal welfare policies
and plays down what is perhaps the most important factor in the rise of
black female-headed families—the extraordinary rise in black male
joblessness. We have shown here that the decline in the incidence of
intact marriages among blacks is associated with the declining economic
status of black men. In chapter 3 we demonstrated that black women
nationally, especially young black women, are facing a shrinking pool of

"marriageable" (i.e., employed) black men. This finding supports the hypothesis that the sharp rise of black female-headed families is directly related to increasing black male joblessness. Regional longitudinal data on female headship and the "male marriageable pool" were presented in this chapter to provide a further test of this hypothesis.

The trends in the MMPI reveal that whereas changes in the ratios of employed men to women among whites have been minimal for all age categories and in all regions of the country from 1960 to 1980, the ratios for blacks have declined substantially in all regions except the West. On the basis of these trends, we expected the most rapid growth in the number of black female heads to be in the northern regions, followed by the South and the West. The data conformed to our expectations, except for the larger-than-expected increase in black female-headed families in the West. Our explanation of this latter finding focused on the pattern of selective black migration to the West. The smaller proportions of white women heading families varied little by region.

The MMPI can be constructed only on the basis of aggregate racial data, rather than by race and income class as we would prefer. Nevertheless, as we have shown, the rise of the female-headed family has had its major impact on the impoverished. Work cited in chapter 3 indicated that black female-headed families were poorer, more permanent, and more welfare-dependent than families led by white women. In a similar vein, recent work by Bane with the Michigan Panel Study of Income Dynamics showed that unlike whites, the majority of blacks experiencing a transition into a female-headed family were poor afterward.[32] Around two-thirds of those were in poverty, however, even *before* experiencing such a transition. Such findings increase our confidence that the incidence of female-headed families among blacks, more so than among whites, is related to conditions of economic deprivation.

We conclude, therefore, that the problem of joblessness should be a top-priority item in any public policy discussion focusing on enhancing the status of families. Unfortunately, in recent years joblessness has received very little attention among policymakers concerned about the plight of families in the United States. Even the perceptive Daniel Patrick Moynihan, an early advocate of this point of view, failed to emphasize this issue in his Harvard University Godkin lectures on the family and nation.[33] Instead he chose to focus on measures to aid poor families, such as establishing a national benefit standard for child welfare aid, indexing benefits to inflation, and enlarging personal and dependent tax exemptions. These are all constructive suggestions, but they need to be included in a more comprehensive reform program designed to create a tight labor market that enhances the employment opportunities of both poor men and women. Such an undertaking will, we believe, do far more in the long run to enhance the stability and reduce the welfare dependency of low-income black families than will cutting the vital provisions of the welfare state.

We emphasize the need to create employment opportunities for both sexes, even though our focus in this chapter is on the problem of black male joblessness. To identify black male joblessness as a major source of black family disintegration is not to suggest that policymakers should ignore the problems of joblessness and poverty among current female heads of families. Rather we underline the point that the tragic decline of intact black households cannot be divorced from the equally tragic decline in the black male "marriageable pool" in any serious policy deliberations on the plight of poor American families.

2

The Ghetto Underclass
and Public Policy

5   Race-specific Policies and the Truly Disadvantaged

In the period following the thirtieth anniversary of the 1954 Supreme Court decision against racial separation, Brown v. the Board of Education of Topeka, Kansas, and the twentieth anniversary of the 1964 Civil Rights Act, a troubling dilemma confronts proponents of racial equality and social justice. The dilemma is that while the socioeconomic status of the most disadvantaged members of the minority population has deteriorated rapidly since 1970, that of advantaged members has significantly improved. This is perhaps most clearly seen in the changes that have occured within the American black population in recent years.

In several areas, blacks have not only improved their social and economic positions in recent years, but have made those improvements at a relatively faster rate than the reported progress of comparable whites. The most notable gains have occurred in professional employment, income of married-couple families, higher education, and home ownership. The number of blacks in professional, technical, managerial, and administrative positions increased by 57 percent (from 974,000 to 1,533,000) from 1973 to 1982, while the number of whites in such positions increased by only 36 percent.[1] The median annual income for black married-couple families in 1982 was $20,586, compared to $26,443 for white married-couple families. The gap was even narrower in households where both husband and wife were employed; this was especially true for couples between the ages of twenty-four and thirty-five, where the difference in annual income between blacks and whites was less than $3,000. And the fraction of black families earning $25,000 or more (in 1982 dollars) increased from 10.4 percent in 1960 to 24.5 percent in 1982. Meanwhile, the number of blacks enrolled full time at American colleges and universities nearly doubled between 1970 and 1980 (going from 522,000 to over 1 million).[2] Blacks recorded a 47 percent increase in home ownership during the 1970s (from 2.57 million to 3.78 million), compared to a 30 percent increase for whites.[3]

But for millions of other blacks, most of them concentrated in the ghettos of American cities, the past three decades have been a time of regression, not progress. As indicated in chapters 1 and 2, these low-income families and individuals are, in several important respects, more socially and economically isolated than before the great civil rights victories, particularly in terms of high joblessness and the related problems of poverty, family instability, and welfare dependency.

These changes are reflected in a growing economic schism between lower-income and higher-income black families. As shown in table 5.1, the percentage of total black family income attributable to the lowest two-fifths of black families declined from 15.8 percent in 1966 to 13.4 percent by 1981; the upper two-fifths of black families contributed 67.3 percent of the total in 1966, but 70.6 percent in 1981. The lowest two-fifths of white families, on the other hand, contributed 18.2 percent to the total white family income in 1966, and 17.1 percent in 1981; the upper two-fifths of white families contributed 64 percent in 1966, and 65.4 percent in 1981. The index of income concentration (a statistical measure of income inequality ranging from zero, which indicates perfect equality, to one, which reveals perfect inequality) reveals that income inequality is greater and has increased at a faster rate among black families than among white families from 1966 to 1981.

As indicated in the previous chapters, the factors associated with the growing woes of low-income blacks are exceedingly complex and go beyond the narrow issue of contemporary discrimination. Indeed, it would not be unreasonable to contend that the race-specific policies emanating from the civil rights revolution, although beneficial to more advantaged blacks (i.e., those with higher income, greater education and training, and more prestigious occupations), do little for those who are truly disadvantaged. The Harvard black economist Glenn Loury has argued in this connection that

> It is clear from extensive empirical research on the effect of affirmative action standards for federal contractors, that the positive impact on blacks which this program has had accrues mainly to those in the higher occupations. If one examines the figures on relative earnings of young black and white men by educational class, by far the greater progress has been made among those blacks with the most education. If one looks at relative earnings of black and white workers by occupation going back to 1950, one finds that the most dramatic earning gains for blacks have taken place in the professional, technical, and managerial occupations, while the least significant gains have come in the lowest occupations, like laborer and service work-

TABLE 5.1
Share of Aggregate Income by Each Fifth of Families, by Percentage of Distribution
of Aggregate Income by Race

Selected Family Positions	1966	1976	1981
Black and other races			
Lowest fifth	4.9	4.4	4.0
Second fifth	10.9	9.6	9.4
Middle fifth	16.9	15.9	16.0
Fourth fifth	25.0	25.2	25.5
Highest fifth	42.3	44.9	45.1
Top 5%	14.6	16.1	16.0
Index of income concentration	.377	.411	.418
White			
Lowest fifth	5.6	5.8	5.4
Second fifth	12.6	12.1	11.7
Middle fifth	17.8	17.7	19.5
Fourth fifth	23.7	23.9	24.2
Highest fifth	40.3	40.6	41.2
Top 5%	15.4	15.4	15.1
Index of income concentration	.346	.349	.359

Source: U.S. Bureau of the Census, Current Population Reports, series P-60, no.
137, "Money Income of Households, Families and Persons in the United States,
1981" (Washington, D.C.: Government Printing Office, 1983).

er. Thus a broad array of evidence suggests, at least to this observer,
that better placed blacks have simply been able to take more advantage of the opportunities created in the last twenty years than have
those mired in the underclass.[4]

The crucial point is not that the deteriorating plight of the ghetto
underclass is associated with the greater success enjoyed by advantaged blacks as a result of race-specific programs, but rather that these
programs are mistakenly presumed to be the most appropriate solution
to the problems of all blacks regardless of economic class. In the following sections this argument is explored in some detail, beginning with a
critical discussion of the basic assumptions associated with two liberal
principles that underlie recent, but entirely different, policy approaches to problems of race, namely, equality of individual opportunity, which stresses the rights of minority individuals, and equality of
group opportunity, which embodies the idea of preferential treatment
for minority groups.

Egalitarian Principles of Race and Disadvantaged Members of Minorities

The goals of the civil rights movement have changed considerably in the last fifteen to twenty years. This change has been reflected in the shift in emphasis from the rights of minority individuals to the preferential treatment of minority groups. The implementation of the principle of equality of group rights results in the formal recognition of racial and ethnic groups by the state, as well as economic, educational, and political rewards based on formulas of group membership.[5] Although many of the proponents of this principle argue that preferential treatment is only a temporary device to overcoming the effects of previous discrimination, this shift in precepts has long divided the civil rights movement, which, in the early 1960s, was unified behind the principle of equality of individual opportunity.

However, neither programs based on equality of individual opportunity nor those organized in terms of preferential group treatment are sufficient to address the problems of truly disadvantaged minority group members. Let us consider, first of all, the principle of equality of individual rights which dominated the early phases of the civil rights movement.

At mid-twentieth century, liberal black and white leaders of the movement for racial equality agreed that the conditions of racial and ethnic minorities could best be improved by an appeal to the conscience of white Americans to uphold the American creed of egalitarianism and democracy. These leaders directed their efforts to eliminating Jim Crow segregation statutes through Supreme Court litigation, pressing for national legislation to outlaw discrimination in employment and housing, and breaking down the extralegal obstacles to black voting in the South.[6]

It was assumed that the government could best protect the rights of individual members of minority groups not by formally bestowing rewards and punishments based on racial or ethnic categories, but by using antidiscrimination legislation to enhance individual freedom of choice in education, employment, voting, and public accommodations. The individual, therefore, was "the unit of attribution for equity considerations,"[7] and the ultimate goal was to reward each citizen based on his or her merits and accomplishments. In short, equality of opportunity meant equality for citizens.

Thus, from the 1950s to 1970, emphasis was on the equality of individual opportunity, or freedom of choice; the approved role of government was to ensure that people were not formally categorized on the basis of race. Antidiscrimination legislation was designed to eliminate racial bias without considering the actual percentage of minorities in certain positions. These actions upheld the underlying principle of equality of individual rights, namely, that candidates for positions stratified in terms of prestige or other social criteria should be judged solely on individual merit and therefore ought not be discriminated against on the basis of race or ethnic origin.

It would be ideal if programs based on this principle were sufficient to address problems of inequality in our society because they are consistent with the prevailing ideals of democracy and freedom of choice, do not call for major sacrifices on the part of the larger population, and are not perceived as benefiting certain groups at the expense of others. The "old" goals of the civil rights movement, in other words, were more in keeping with "traditional" American values, and thus more politically acceptable than the "new" goals of equal opportunity for groups through a system of collective racial and ethnic entitlements. However, programs based solely on the principle of equality of individual opportunity are inadequate to address the complex problems of group inequality in America.

More specifically, as James Fishkin appropriately points out, this principle does not address the substantive inequality that exists at the time the bias is removed.[8] In other words, centuries or even decades of racial subjugation can result in a system of racial inequality that may linger on for indefinite periods of time after racial barriers are eliminated. This is because the most disadvantaged minority group members, who have been crippled or victimized by the cumulative effects of both race and class subordination (including those effects passed on from generation to generation), are disproportionately represented among that segment of the total population that lacks the resources to compete effectively in a free and open market. The black columnist William Raspberry recognized this problem when he stated: "There are some blacks for whom it is enough to remove the artificial barriers of race. After that, their entry into the American mainstream is virtually automatic. There are others for whom hardly anything would change if, by some magical stroke, racism disappeared from America. Everyone knows this of course. And yet hardly anyone is willing to say it. And because we don't say it, we wind up confused about how to deal with the explosive problems confronting the American society, confused about what the problem really is."[9]

It is important to recognize that in modern industrial society the removal of racial barriers creates the greatest opportunities for the better-trained, talented, and educated segments of the minority population—those who have been crippled the least by the weight of past discrimination. This is because they possess the resources that allow them to compete freely with dominant group members for valued positions. In this connection, as Leroy D. Clark and Judy Trent Ellis have noted,

> there must be a recognition that civil rights legislation can only benefit those in a position to take advantage of it. To the extent that some members of minority groups have been denied education and certain work experience, they will be able to compete for only a limited number of jobs. Certain disabilities traceable in general to racism may deprive some minority members of the qualifications for particular jobs. Title VII, however, protects only against arbitrary use of race or its equivalents as barrier to work; it does not assure one of employment or promotion if legitimate qualifications are lacking.[10]

In short, the competitive resources developed by the advantaged minority members—resources "resulting from the income, family stability, peer groups, and schooling that their parents can make available to them"[11]—result in their benefiting disproportionately from policies that promote the rights of minority *individuals*, policies that remove artificial barriers and thereby enable individuals to compete freely and openly for the more desirable and prestigious positions in American society.

However, since 1970, government policy has tended to focus on the equitable distribution of *group* rights, so that people have been formally categorized or recognized on the basis of race or ethnicity. Formal programs have been designed and created not only to prevent discrimination, but also to ensure that minorities are adequately represented in certain positions. Thus emphasis has shifted from equality of opportunity, stressing individual rights, to equality of condition, emphasizing group rights. Between the mid-1950s and 1970, the elimination of existing discrimination was the sole concern of liberal policymakers; since 1970, however, serious attention has also been given to negating the effects of past discrimination. This has resulted in a move from the simple investigation and adjudication of complaints of racial discrimination by fair employment practices commissions and civil rights commissions to government-mandated affirmative action programs designed to ensure minority representation in employment, in public programs, and in education.[12]

Nonetheless, if the more advantaged minority members profit disproportionately from policies built on the principle of equality of individual opportunity, they also reap disproportionate benefits from policies of preferential treatment based solely on their group membership. I say this because minority individuals from the most advantaged families are likely to be disproportionately represented among the minority members most qualified for preferred positions—such as higher-paying jobs, college admissions, promotions, and so forth. Accordingly, if policies of preferential treatment for such positions are conceived not in terms of the actual disadvantages suffered by individuals but rather in terms of race or ethnic group membership, then these policies will further enhance the opportunities of the more advantaged without addressing the problems of the truly disadvantaged. In other words, programs such as affirmative action "can be very effective in increasing the rate of progress for minorities who are doing reasonably well."[13] Special admission programs that enlarge the number of minorities in law schools and medical schools, and special programs that increase minority representation in high-level government jobs, in the foreign service, and on university faculties not only favor minorities from advantaged backgrounds but require a college education to begin with. To repeat: programs of preferential treatment applied merely according to racial or ethnic group membership tend to benefit the relatively advantaged segments of the designated groups. The truly deprived members may not be helped by such programs.

Nonetheless, as William L. Taylor has argued, "the focus of much of the [affirmative action] effort has been not just on white collar jobs, but also on law enforcement, construction work, and craft and production jobs in large companies—all areas in which the extension of new opportunities has provided upward mobility for less advantaged minority workers." Taylor also notes that "studies show that of the increased enrollment of minority students in medical schools during the 1970s, significant numbers were from families of low income and job status, indicating that the rising enrollments of minorities in professional schools stemming from affirmative action policies reflects increased mobility, not simply changing occupational preferences among middle-class minority families."[14] However, although affirmative action programs do in fact create opportunities for some less advantaged minority individuals, ghetto underclass individuals are severely underrepresented among those who have actually benefited from such programs. In other words, upon close examination what we really see is a "creaming" process in the sense that those with the greatest economic, educational, and social resources among the less advantaged individuals are the ones who are actually tapped for higher paying jobs and higher education through affirmative action.

It has been argued, however, that group preferential treatment based on race, although more directly beneficial to advantaged minority members, will "trickle down" to the minority poor. Thus, a government policy favoring minority business would ultimately lead to greater employment opportunities for the black poor. Affirmative action programs designed to increase the number of blacks in medical schools would thus ultimately result in improved medical care for low-income blacks. Indeed, these programs are often justified on the ground that they would improve the black poor's chances in life. "The question should be raised though as to how the black poor are to be benefited by the policy actions extracted from the system in their name," observes Glenn Loury. "The evidence of which I am aware suggests that, for many of the most hotly contested public policies advocated by black spokesmen, not much of the benefit 'trickles down' to the black poor. There is no study, of which I am aware, supporting the claim that set-asides for minority businesses have led to a significant increase in the level of employment among lower class blacks."[15]

But what about the argument, often heard during the heated debate over the *Bakke* decision, that increasing the percentage of blacks in medical schools will result in improvements in medical care for lower-income blacks? Although there is virtually no definitive research on this question, I believe that we would not improve the health of the ghetto underclass, in either the long or the short run, even if we tripled the number of black physicians in our large central cities.

This is not to say that a sharp increase in the number of black physicians would have no impact in the black community. Blacks who can afford to pay for adequate medical care would certainly have more black physicians to choose from, and poor blacks would undoubtedly witness the opening of more clinics, staffed by black physicians, in their neighborhoods. But the ultimate determinant of black access to medical care is not the supply of black physicians, even if an overwhelming majority choose to practice in the black community,[16] but the availability of programs such as Medicaid, Medicare, National Health Insurance, or other benefits designed, regardless of race, to give people who lack economic resources access to expensive medical care. There are plenty of doctors for those who can afford them.

However, there does exist a third liberal philosophy concerned with equality and social justice, namely, what Fishkin has called the principle of equality of life chances. According to this principle, if we can predict with a high degree of accuracy where individuals will end up in the competition for preferred positions in society "merely by knowing their race, sex, or family background, then the conditions under which

their talents and motivations have developed must be grossly unequal." Supporters of this principle believe that a person "should not
be able to enter a hospital ward of healthy newborn babies and, on the
basis of class, race, sex, or other arbitrary native characteristics, predict the eventual positions in society of those children." In other
words, it is unfair that some individuals "are given every conceivable
advantage while others never really have a chance, in the first place, to
develop their talents."[17]

Proponents of equality of life chances recognize not only that those
from higher social strata have greater life chances or more-than-equal
opportunities, but that "they also have greater than equal influence on
the political process and greater than equal consideration from the
health care and legal systems." The major factor that distinguishes the
principle of equality of life chances from the principles of equality of
individual opportunity and equality of group opportunity is the recognition that the problems of truly disadvantaged individuals—class
background, low income, a broken home, inadequate housing, poor
education, or cultural or linguistic differences—may not be clearly related to the issue of previous discrimination. Nevertheless, "children
growing up in homes affected by these disadvantages may be deprived
of an equal life chance because their environments effectively inhibit
the development of their talents or aspirations."[18]

Accordingly, programs based on this principle would not be re-
strictively applied to members of certain racial or ethnic groups but
would be targeted to truly disadvantaged individuals regardless of their
race or ethnicity. Thus, whereas poor whites are ignored in programs
of reverse discrimination based on the desire to overcome the effects of
past discrimination, they would be targeted along with the truly disadvantaged minorities for preferential treatment under programs to
equalize life chances by overcoming present class disadvantages.

Under the principle of equality of life chances, efforts to correct family background disadvantages through such programs as income redistribution, compensatory job training, compensatory schooling, special
medical services and the like would not "require any reference to past
discrimination as the basis for justification."[19] All that would be required is that the individuals targeted for preferred treatment by ob-
jectively classified as disadvantaged in terms of the competitive
resources associated with their economic-class background.

Ironically, the shift from preferential treatment for those with certain
racial or ethnic characteristics to those who are truly disadvantaged in
terms of their life chances would not only help the white poor, but would
also address more effectively the problems of the minority poor. If the

life chances of the ghetto underclass are largely untouched by programs of preferential treatment based on race, the gap between the haves and have-nots in the black community will widen, and the disproportionate concentration of blacks within the most impoverished segments of our population will remain. As Fishkin appropriately points out, programs based on the principle of equality of life chances would not be mistargeted to those who are already relatively affluent.[20]

Targeted Programs and the Problems of Political Support

Despite the emphasis placed on helping disadvantaged members of minority groups through programs based on the principle of equality of individual opportunity and those based on the principle of equality of group opportunity (as brought out in the previous section), only programs based on the principle of equality of life chances are capable of substantially helping the truly disadvantaged. Nonetheless, even these, however comprehensive and carefully constructed, may not represent the most efficacious or viable way to lift the truly disadvantaged from the depths of poverty today. In the next section of this chapter and in the following chapter, I discuss the effectiveness of targeted programs in a stagnant economy. For now let me focus on the problem of generating and sustaining public support for such programs.

An important consideration in assessing public programs targeted at particular groups (whether these groups are defined in terms of race, ethnicity, or class) is the degree of political support those programs receive, especially when the national economy is in a period of little growth, no growth, or decline. Under such economic conditions, the more the public programs are perceived by members of the wider society as benefiting only certain groups, the less support those programs receive. I should like to deal with the implications of this argument by briefly contrasting the institutionalization of the programs that emanated from the New Deal legislation of the Roosevelt administration with the demise of the Great Society programs of the Johnson administration, bearing in mind that Johnson's Great Society program was the most ambitious effort in our nation's history to implement the principle of equality of life chances. [21]

In 1932 Franklin D. Roosevelt received a popular mandate to attack the catastrophic economic problems created by the Great Depression. He then launched a series of programs—such as Social Security and unemployment compensation—designed to protect all citizens against sudden impoverishment. One of these programs was Aid to Families with Dependent Children (AFDC), the current symbol of income-tested public welfare programs. Aid to Families with Dependent Children, however, was conceived not as a permanent alternative to working but as a temporary means of support for families that were, at the time they applied for aid, clearly unemployable. Indeed, the "safety net" of Roosevelt's New Deal emphatically included the creation of public works projects designed to forestall the formation of a permanent welfare class. It was not necessary to satisfy a means test to work in these projects; the only requirement was that the applicant be unemployed, want a job, and be able to work. Furthermore, no one was denied eligibility for these jobs as a result of being either over-skilled or underskilled; the programs attempted to match jobs with individual abilities. [22]

Thus, jobs for able individuals, Social Security, and unemployment compensation for the unemployed were to provide a modicum of security for all. Economic stability was not tied to the dole. By contrast, nearly all of the Great Society programs *were* tied to the dole. Job training, legal aid, and Medicaid levied income tests. In effect, one had to be on welfare to be eligible. Unlike the New Deal programs, the Great Society programs were modeled on the English poor laws. Although these programs improved the life chances of many of their recipients—because job-training programs enabled many long-term welfare recipients to find their first jobs, Medicaid enabled many to receive decent medical care for the first time, and legal aid gave many access to capable lawyers—the programs were increasingly perceived in narrow terms as intended for poor blacks. In the cities, especially, the Great Society programs established what amounted to separate legal and medical systems—one public and predominantly black, the other private and predominantly white. The real problem, however, was that the taxpayers were required to pay for legal and medical services that were provided to welfare recipients but not to the tax-payers—services many taxpayers could not afford to buy for themselves. In other words, this system amounted to taxation to pay for programs that were perceived to benefit mostly minorities, programs that excluded taxpayers perceived to be mostly white. [23] Thus, these programs were cut back or phased out during the recent periods of recession and economic stagnation because they could not sustain sufficient political support. [24]

From the New Deal to the 1970s, the Democrats were able to combine Keynesian economics and prosperity for the middle class with social welfare programs and pressures for integrating the poor and minorities into the mainstream of American economic life. The MIT economist Lester Thurow reminds us that "in periods of great economic progress when [the incomes of the middle classes] are rising rapidly, they are willing to share some of their income and jobs with those less fortunate than themselves, but they are not willing to reduce their real standard of living to help either minorities or the poor."[25]

In the face of hard economic times, Pres. Ronald Reagan was able to persuade the middle classes that the drop in their living standards was attributable to the poor (and implicitly, minorities), and that he could restore those standards with sweeping tax and budget cuts. In short, the New Deal coalition collapsed when Reagan was elected. In 1980 the only groups that did not leave the Democratic party in significant numbers were blacks, Hispanics, and the poor—groups that constitute only a quarter of the American population, hardly enough to win a national election,[26] and certainly not enough to sustain programs, incorrectly perceived as benefiting only the minority poor, based on the principle of equality of life chances. What is interesting, however, is that the Reagan administration has shown far less willingness to cut significantly the much more expensive universal programs such as Social Security and Medicare, programs that are not income tested and therefore are available to people across class lines. In this connection, one of the reasons why western European social welfare programs enjoy wide political support (especially in countries such as the Federal Republic of Germany, France, Austria, Sweden, the Netherlands, Belgium, and Norway) is that they tend to be universal—applied across class and racial/ethnic lines—and therefore are not seen as being targeted for narrow class or racially identifiable segments of the population.[27]

I am convinced that, in the last few years of the twentieth century, the problems of the truly disadvantaged in the United States will have to be attacked primarily through universal programs that enjoy the support and commitment of a broad constituency. Under this approach, targeted programs (whether based on the principle of equality of group opportunity or that of equality of life chances) would not necessarily be eliminated, but would rather be deemphasized—considered only as offshoots of, and indeed secondary to, the universal programs. *The hidden agenda is to improve the life chances of groups such as the ghetto underclass by emphasizing programs in which the more advantaged groups of all races can positively relate.*

In the final section of this chapter, I should like to amplify and support this position by focusing on what I consider to be one of the most important universal programs of equality—an economic policy to address the problems of American economic organization.

The Case for a Universal Program

I believe that many of the problems plaguing the truly disadvantaged minorities in American society can be alleviated by a program of economic reform characterized by rational government involvement in the economy.[28] I have in mind a general economic policy that would involve long-term planning to promote both economic growth and sustained full employment, not only in higher-income areas but in areas where the poor are concentrated as well. Such a policy would be designated to promote wage and price stability, favorable employment conditions, and the development and integration of manpower training programs with educational programs. As I see it, the questions usually ignored when ad hoc strategies to promote employment are discussed and proposed should be systematically addressed. These questions include the relative impact of proposed strategies on labor markets in different areas of the country; the type, variety, and volume of jobs to be generated; the extent to which residents in low-income neighborhoods will have access to these jobs; the quality of these jobs in terms of stability and pay; the extent to which proposed strategies enhance the employment opportunities of both new entrants into the labor market and the currently unemployed; and whether the benefits from economic development and employment provide reasonable returns on public investment.[29]

Although the basic features of such a program are designed to benefit all segments of society, I believe the groups that have been plagued by severe problems of economic dislocation, such as the ghetto underclass, would be helped the most. I say this because the low-income minority community is disadvantaged not simply by cyclical economic stagnation but by profound structural economic changes. The widely heralded shift from goods-producing to service-producing industries is polarizing the labor market into high-wage and low-wage sectors. Technological innovations in industry are affecting the number and types of jobs available. Manufacturing industries are relocating from the central city to the suburbs, to other parts of the country, and even to foreign countries. As was shown in previous chapters, while these changes adversely affect segments of the poor and working classes in general, they have been especially devastating for low-income blacks and other minorities because these groups are concentrated in the central areas that have been hardest hit by economic dislocation.

Accordingly, those who argue that the deteriorating economic plight of the truly disadvantaged minorities can be satisfactorily addressed simply by confronting the problems of current racial bias fail to recognize how the fate of these minorities is inextricably connected with the structure and function of the modern American economy. The net effect is the recommendation of programs that do not confront the fundamental causes of poverty, underemployment, and unemployment. In other words, policies that do not take into account the changing nature of the national economy—including its rate of growth and the nature of its variable demand for labor; the factors that affect industrial employment, such as profit rates, technology, and unionization; and patterns of institutional and individual migration that result from industrial transformation and shifts—will not effectively handle the economic dislocation of low-income minorities.

But it is not only disadvantaged minorities who would benefit from a program of economic reform designed to promote full employment and balanced economic growth. Even the trained, talented, and educated minorities could not really benefit from the removal of racial barriers if the economy lacked sufficient positions to absorb either them or any new entrants into higher-paying or valued positions. In other words, deracialization, or the removal of racial barriers, has far greater meaning when positions are available or become available to enhance social mobility. Indeed, the significant movement of blacks into higher-paying manufacturing positions from 1940 to the 1960s had much more to do with fairly even and steady economic growth in the manufacturing sector than with equal employment legislation. It is noteworthy, however, that the uneven economic growth since the latter half of the 1960s resulted in a much more rapid rate of social mobility for trained and educated blacks than for the untrained and uneducated. While deindustrialization was subjecting the latter to the gradual reduction of the more desirable blue-collar positions into which workers can enter without special skills or higher education, the former, that is, trained and educated blacks, were experiencing increasing job opportunities in the expanding corporate and government sectors.[30]

Thus, the necessary factor for minority mobility is the availability of positions. For example, affirmative action programs have had little impact in a slack labor market where the labor supply is greater than the labor demand. This has been the case with higher-paying blue-collar positions in which employment opportunities for the lesser-trained and less-experienced blacks remain restricted due to increases in plant closings, labor-saving technology, and the efforts of unions to protect remaining jobs. On the other hand, the impact of antibias programs to enhance minority jobs tends to be greater in a tight labor market. This argument should come as no surprise.[31]

In a tight labor market, job vacancies are numerous, unemployment is of short duration, and wages are higher. Moreover, the labor force becomes larger because increased job opportunities not only reduce unemployment but also draw into the labor force those workers who, in periods when the labor market is slack, respond to fading job prospects by dropping out of the labor force altogether. Thus, the status of minority workers improves in a tight labor market because unemployment is reduced and better jobs are available.

Affirmative action and other antibias programs are accordingly more successful in tight labor markets than in slack ones. Not only are there sufficient positions for many qualified workers, but also employers faced with a labor shortage are not as resistant to affirmative action. Furthermore, in a favorable economic climate, those who support affirmative action are encouraged to push such programs because they perceive greater chances for success. Finally, nonminority employees are less likely to oppose affirmative action when there are sufficient jobs available because they are less likely to see minorities as a threat to their own employment.

In a slack labor market, on the other hand, employers tend to be more selective in recruiting and in promoting; they can afford to demand greater experience, skills, and education than a job actually requires. They are thus more resistant to affirmative action pressures. And the longer the labor market is slack, the less pressure they receive from supporters of affirmative action, who become increasingly discouraged in the face of shrinking resources. The situation is exacerbated by increased hostility to affirmative action by dominant-group workers who fear the loss of their own jobs to minority competition. In short, the success of affirmative action and other antidiscrimination programs is in no small measure related to the state of the economy.

Thus, unlike programs based on equality of individual opportunity and equality of group opportunity, a universal program of economic reform would benefit both advantaged and disadvantaged minority members as well as nonminority groups, including women.

However, to embrace the idea of a universal program of reform does not mean a shift in focus away from the current suffering of racial minorities. Many of their problems, especially those of the truly disadvantaged among them, call for immediate attention and therefore cannot wait for the launching of long-term programs. Short-term programs consistent with the principle of equality of life chances (such as manpower job training and education for the disadvantaged, and public assistance) are needed now. But such programs are hardly a solution to the current woes of groups such as the ghetto underclass. Although they provide some short-term relief, these programs do not address problems of economic organization (e.g., plant closings and layoffs due to deindustrialization), that impact heavily on disadvantaged groups in society. Moreover, as I have tried to show in the previous section, without a tight labor market or a full-employment situation the very survival of targeted programs for low-income groups is threatened. To repeat: income-tested programs are much less likely to be introduced or to receive continuing support in a stagnant economy. Although sustained full employment and balanced economic growth would ultimately render targeted programs for the able-bodied superfluous, they would create the economic climate to help preserve such programs when they are needed in the short run.

Moreover, without full employment it is much more difficult to shift from income-tested and stigmatized public assistance programs to the kinds of universal programs of social welfare (e.g., family allowances) found in Western European democracies. Universal welfare programs, usually tied to employment and labor market policies, depend on conditions approximating full employment so that workers can combine their income from transfers with income from employment, maximize tax revenues, and thereby reduce the strain on the welfare budget inflated by the broad coverage of transfer payments.

In short, to speak of the need for long-term economic reform in the United States is not to disregard the need for short-term targeted programs for the disadvantaged. Rather, it is to recognize that the more effective the universal program of reform, the less targeted programs are required.

In the final analysis, the question of reform is a political one. Accordingly, if the issues are couched in terms of promoting economic security for all Americans, if the essential political message underscores the need for economic and social reform that benefits all groups in society, not just poor minorities, a basis for generating a broad-based political coalition to achieve such reform would be created. Minority leaders could play an important role in this coalition once they fully recognize the need to shift or expand their definition of racial problems in America and to broaden the scope of suggested policy programs to address them. This would certainly not mean the abandonment of race-specific policies the embody either the principle of equality of individual rights or that of group rights. It would simply mean that such programs are no longer central to advancing the cause of minorities, especially the cause of the truly disadvantaged such as the ghetto underclass.

6   The Limited Visions of Race
       Relations and the War on Poverty

In the mid-1960s a series of insightful articles were written by black and white intellectuals that raised questions about the direction and goals of the black protest movement.[1] Basically, the authors of these articles made it clear that from 1955 to 1965 the chief objectives of the civil rights movement were to integrate public accommodations and to eliminate black disfranchisement. These were matters of constitutional rights and basic human dignity, matters that affected blacks and other minorities exclusively and therefore could be defined and addressed simply as problems of civil rights. However, these authors noted that despite the spectacular victories in the area of civil rights, by the latter half of the 1960s a more complex and fundamental set of problems had yet to be attacked—problems of jobs, education, and housing that affected not only blacks but other minorities and whites as well.

A consistent theme running throughout these articles is that in the period from 1955 to 1963, all blacks, regardless of their station in life, were concerned about the banning of discrimination in public accommodations and in voting. As Bayard Rustin observed, "Ralph Bunch was as likely to be refused service in a restaurant or a hotel as any illiterate sharecropper. This common bond prevented the latent class differences and resentments from being openly expressed."[2] However, it did not take long to realize that the group that had profited the most from the civil rights legislation up to 1965 was middle-class blacks—blacks who had competitive resources such as steady incomes, education, and special talents. As Kenneth Clark argued in 1967, "The masses of Negroes are now starkly aware of the fact that recent civil rights victories benefited a very small percentage of middle-class Negroes while their predicament remained the same or worsened."[3]

What these observers were telling us in the mid-1960s is that a close examination of ghetto black discontent, most dramatically seen in the riots of that period, reveals issues that transcend the creation and implementation of civil rights laws. "To the segregation by race," Bayard

Rustin observed, "was now added segregation by class, and all the problems created by segregation and poverty—inadequate schooling, substandard and overcrowded housing, lack of access to jobs and job training, narcotics and crime—were greatly aggravated."[4] In short, for ghetto blacks the problems move beyond the issue of civil rights. The late Martin Luther King, Jr., recognized this point in 1968 when shortly before his death he asked, "What good is it to be allowed to eat in a restaurant if you can't afford a hamburger?"[5] It would not be unfair to suggest that he was probably influenced by the thoughts of Bayard Rustin, who, four years earlier in his now-classic article "From Protest to Politics," phrased the matter in much the same way: "What is the value of winning access to public accommodations for those who lack money to use them?"[6]

Thus, these perceptive civil rights advocates recognized in the 1960s that removing artificial racial barriers would not enable poor blacks to compete equally with other groups in society for valued resources because of an accumulation of disadvantages flowing from previous periods of prejudice and discrimination, disadvantages that have been passed on from generation to generation. Basic structural changes in our modern industrial economy have compounded the problems of poor blacks because education and training have become more important for entry into the more desirable and higher-paying jobs and because increased reliance on labor-saving devices has contributed to a surplus of untrained black workers. In short, once the movement faced these more fundamental issues, argued Rustin in 1965, "it was compelled to expand its vision beyond race relations to economic relations, including the role of education in society."[7]

The Problem of the Race Relations Vision

During the same period in which problems of structural inequality were being raised, scholars such as Kenneth Clark, Lee Rainwater, and Elliot Liebow were also raising important issues about the experiences of inequality.[8] As I pointed out in chapter 1, what was both unique and important about these studies in the 1960s was that discussions of the experiences of inequality were inextricably tied to discussions of the structure of inequality. Thus, in reading these works one received a clear understanding of how the economic and social situations into which so many poor blacks are born produce modes of adaptation and create subcultural patterns that take the form of a "self-perpetuating pathology."[9] In other words, and in sharp contrast to approaches that simply "blame the victim" or that use a "culture-of-poverty" thesis to explain group disadvantages, the works of scholars such as Clark, Rainwater, and Liebow not only presented a sensitive portrayal of the destructive features of ghetto life, they also provided a comprehensive analysis of the deleterious structural conditions that produce these features.

However, arguments stressing economic relations in determining the structure of inequality and in significantly influencing the experiences of inequality began to compete with a new definition, description, and explanation of the black condition. This new approach, proclaimed as the "black perspective," revealed an ideological shift from interracialism to racial solidarity. It first gained currency among militant black spokespersons in the late 1960s and became a theme in the writings of young black academics and intellectuals by the early 1970s (see chap. 1). Although the "black perspective" represented a variety of views and arguments on issues of race, the trumpeting of racial pride and self-affirmation was common to all the writings and speeches on the subject. Thus interracial cooperation and integration were being challenged by the ideology of racial solidarity, and the rhetoric of black militancy, symbolized by the cry of Black Power, gradually moved from expressions of selective to generalized hostility toward whites.

The complex factors associated with this shift in emphasis cannot be reviewed in full detail here, but I should like to point out that the declining support for interracialism and the rising emphasis on black solidarity in the late 1960s was typical of a pattern that has been repeated throughout the history of dominant-subordinate group relations in multiethnic societies.

More specifically, in a multiracial society such as the United States where racial groups share the same social order (i.e., where an interdependent relationship exists between the racial groups), sentiments for integration and interracialism tend to emerge when the struggle against racial inequality appears hopeful. Such periods have included the three decades following the emancipation of slaves in the North in the early nineteenth century, the Reconstruction era, the New Deal era, and the era of successful nonviolent resistance movements during the late 1950s and early 1960s. On the other hand, sentiments for racial separation and racial solidarity tend to emerge when minority race members perceive the struggle against racial inequality as hopeless or when they experience intense disillusionment and frustration immediately following a period of optimism or heightened expectations.[10] Such periods have included the disheartening decades of the 1850s in the United States when nationalistic sentiment among free blacks in the North reached its peak before the Civil War; the violent period of Jim Crow segregation and biological racism in the late nineteenth and early twentieth centuries when the movements of Booker T. Washington, Bishop Turner, Marcus Garvey, and the Harlem Renaissance emerged; and the "law and order" period of the late 1960s and early 1970s, when the Black Power movement crystallized and black cultural nationalism flourished.

Consistent with the dominant focus on racial solidarity in the late sixties was an emphasis on we versus they and black versus white. Since the accent was on race, little attention was paid to the social-economic differences within the black community and the implications they had for different public policy options, and little discussion was devoted to problems with the economy and the need for economic reform. Thus, the promising move in the early and mid-1960s to pursue programs of economic reform by defining the problems of American economic organization and outlining their effect on the minority community was offset by slogans calling for "reparations," or "black control of institutions serving the black community." This is why Orlando Patterson was led to proclaim in a later analysis that black ethnicity had become "a form of mystification, diverting attention from the correct kinds of solutions to the terrible economic conditions of the group," thereby making it difficult for blacks to see the inextricable connection between their own fate and the structure of the modern American economy.[11]

Meanwhile, during this period of racial solidarity, significant events, such as those detailed in chapter 2, were unfolding in inner-city communities across the nation that profoundly affected the lives of millions of blacks and dramatically revealed that the problems earlier described by observers such as Clark and Rustin had reached catastrophic proportions.

However, because the government not only adopted and resolutely implemented antidiscrimination legislation to enhance minority individual rights but also mandated and purposefully enforced affirmation and related programs to promote minority group rights, it was clear that by 1980 many thoughtful American citizens, including civil rights supporters, were puzzled by recent developments in the black community. Despite the passage of antidiscrimination legislation and the creation of affirmative action programs, they sensed that conditions were getting worse, not better, for a significant segment of black Americans. This perception had emerged because of the constant flow of pessimistic reports concerning the sharp rise in black unemployment, the substantial decline of blacks in the labor force, the steady drop in the black-white family income ratio, the consistent increase in the percentage of blacks on the welfare rolls, the remarkable growth of single-parent households, and the persistent problems of black crime and black victims of crime. The perception was reinforced by the almost uniform cry among black leaders that conditions were deteriorating and white Americans had abandoned the cause of blacks as well. In the face of these developments, there were noticeable signs (even before Ronald Reagan was elected president and well before his administration adopted a conspicuously laissez-faire attitude toward civil rights) that demoralization had set in among many blacks who had come to believe that "nothing really works" and among many whites who were otherwise committed to social reform.

These recent developments in the black community will remain puzzling, and the feeling that "nothing really works" will likely become more widespread if advocates of minority rights fail in significant numbers to understand that many contemporary problems of race cannot be satisfactorily addressed, as I tried to show in the previous chapter, solely by race-specific programs to eliminate racial discrimination and eradicate racial prejudices.

A Parallel Development: The Problem of the War on Poverty Vision

The War on Poverty emerged paradoxically during an era of general economic prosperity and economic growth. In the early 1960s a budget surplus existed, and economists, optimistic about continued economic growth, predicted that this surplus would continue to rise throughout the latter half of the decade. As Daniel Patrick Moynihan argued, federal revenues were growing so rapidly that may economists (not foreseeing the Vietnam War buildup) were concerned that if new expenditures could not be generated to reduce the growing tax surplus, it would ultimately slow economic growth.[12] Accordingly, despite high levels of unemployment in the inner city and in other low-income areas, it was not difficult for the key advisers in the Kennedy and Johnson administrations to see minority poverty as a problem unrelated to the national economy. As Weir, Orloff, and Skocpol have argued, when the United States started to face the problems associated with the concentration of minorities in large urban ghettos, members of the Council of Economic Advisers discussed these problems not within the realm of central economic concerns but as "marginal issues of 'poverty' to be addressed by much less academically prestigious groups of labor economists and sociologists." [13]

Accordingly, increasing black joblessness was viewed as a problem of poverty and discrimination, not of American economic organization, and therefore could be addressed by antipoverty measures (such as compensatory job training, compensatory schooling, income redistribution) and antidiscrimination legislation. In the succinct words of Lawrence Mead, "the main impetus of Great Society policy, therefore, was to give the disadvantaged the income and skills they needed to function in the free market, not change the economic rules in their favor."[14]

The separation of antipoverty measures from national economic policy was respected by the newly created and expanding network of "poverty researchers" who, throughout the 1960s and 1970s, tended to ignore the effects of fundamental economic processes on the work histories of the poor while paying considerable attention to the question of individual work incentives and the association between the work efforts of the poor and income maintenance programs.[15] As Walter Korpi has pointed out, in his perceptive critique of approaches to the study of poverty in this country from a European perspective, "efforts to explain poverty and inequality in the United States . . . appear primarily to have been sought in terms of the characteristics of the poor." Whereas American poverty analysts have produced volumes of research on the work motivation of the poor, problems of human capital (whereby poverty is seen as a reflection of insufficient education and occupational skills), and the effects of income maintenance programs on the labor supply, they have largely neglected the impact of the extremely high levels of postwar unemployment on the poor. "In Europe, where unemployment has been considerably lower," states Korpi, "the concerns of politicians as well as researchers have been keyed much more strongly to the question of unemployment. It is an intellectual paradox that living in a society that has been a sea of unemployment, American poverty researchers have concentrated their research interests on the work motivation of the poor."[16]

Since changes in the rate of poverty in the United States are very closely related to changes in overall economic performance, this research orientation presents a problem for those seeking a comprehensive explanation of minority poverty. Recent research by the economists Rebecca Blank and Alan Blinder of Princeton reveals that a downturn in the economy, measured in this case by a 1 percent increase in the baselevel unemployment (unemployment rate for white males), results in an additional increase in unemployment among black males that is 2 percent to 2.5 percent greater than an additional increase in unemployment among white males.[17] Low-income groups, particularly black males, are especially hard hit when unemployment rises and real wages decline.[18]

It was only a short step to move from an analysis that segregates the economic woes of underemployed or unemployed minorities in the category of poverty-related programs to one that associates the crystal-lization of a ghetto underclass or the explosion of minority female-headed households not with the "more inclusive economic or institu-tional insufficiencies in American life"[19] but with ghetto-specific values or family background. Thus, as shown in chapter 3, research on the relationship between the growth of income transfers and in-kind bene-fits and the increase of black female-headed families has dwarfed research on the relationship between joblessness and black female-headed families in recent years.

In the final analysis, the policy agenda set by the architects of the Great Society, that is, the labor economists and sociologists who fash-ioned the War on Poverty in the 1960s, established the vision for the subsequent research and analysis of minority poverty. Although this vision attributed the behavioral problems of the poor to adverse social conditions, the emphasis was mainly on the environments of the poor, "the disarray at the bottom of society" where ignorance is widespread, crime is rampant, positive role models are lacking, and apathy is en-demic.[20] Since this vision did not consider poverty as a problem of American economic organization, efforts to alter the characteristics of individuals through employment and training programs were seen as the most efficacious way to fight poverty. "After 1960," states Law-rence Mead,

poverty and disadvantaged seemed rooted mostly in the limited skills of the poor themselves, yet government could do little to raise skills simply with benefits. Politically, that left unpalatable alter-natives. Either equality must be achieved by a leveling of income or status without regard to the capacities of the poor, the prescription of the far left, or the poor themselves must be seen as malingerers or congenitally incompetent. Sociological analysis offered a way out. It defined a set of less obvious social barriers permitting further re-formism. By providing further benefits and services, it was argued government could push back the barriers of "disadvantage" without either embracing revolutionary change or blaming the poor for their condition.[21]

However, just as the rate of poverty is in large measure determined by the state of the economy, particularly the levels of wages and unemployment, so too does the effectiveness of training, education, and employment programs depend on a favorable economic climate. If gainful employment is problematic because of a stagnant economy, as was frequently the case throughout the 1970s, participants in these programs understandably lose interest. Indeed, it would be surprising if program participants took training seriously when there is little or no chance for placement.

Given the most comprehensive civil rights legislation and the most comprehensive antipoverty program in the nation's history, it becomes difficult for liberals (who have adopted either the race relations vision in addressing the problems of the minority poor or the vision of the War on Poverty) to explain the sharp increase in inner-city poverty, joblessness, female-headed families, and welfare dependency since 1970 without reference to individual or group deficiencies. By the end of the 1970s these liberals were on the defensive, and their position made it easy for the more conservative policy analysts, such as Charles Murray, to argue that liberal programs have been ineffective and misdirected and that emphasis should now be placed on forcing value and behavior changes, particularly among ghetto residents.

Just as the architects of the War on Poverty failed to relate the problems of the poor to the broader processes of American economic organization, so too have the advocates for minority rights failed in significant numbers to understand that many contemporary problems of race, especially those that engulfed the minority poor, emanate from the broader problems of societal organization and therefore cannot be satisfactorily addressed by race-specific programs to eliminate racial discrimination and eradicate racial prejudices. What is presently lacking is a comprehensive and integrated framework—in other words, a holistic approach—that shows how contemporary racial problems in America, or issues perceived to be racial problems, are often part of a more general or complex set of problems whose origin and/or development may have little or no direct or indirect connection with race.

A Holistic Approach: Racial Problems
and Societal Organization

The development of a holistic approach involves an attempt to relate problems associated with race to the broader issues of societal organization. By the term *societal organization* I refer to the working arrangements of society, including those that have emanated from previous arrangements, that specifically involve processes of ordering relations and actions with respect to given social ends, and that represent the material outcomes of those processes. These working arrangements can be best described in terms of their institutional and technological dimensions. The institutional dimensions of societal organization (such as the economic, political, and educational) embody modes of social interaction that are structured by a constellation of statuses and roles and guided by norms and values. They therefore represent the social, normative, and cultural orders of society. The technological dimensions of societal organization (e.g., stages of industrialization and the degree of urbanization) represent the material outcomes of systematic and goal-directed social relations and action.

At any given time, groups can be stratified in terms of the benefits and privileges they receive from existing working arrangements and in terms of the influence they yield because of these arrangements. And group variation in behavior, norms, and values will reflect variation in access to organizational channels of privilege and influence. Support of existing societal working arrangements will therefore vary depending upon the degree to which groups are stratified in relation to them. And these arrangements may be quite satisfactory for one group and exceedingly problematic for another. Accordingly, to speak of problems of societal organization is to speak of the way that existing working arrangements (ranging from the way relations and actions are ordered to levels of technology, rates of economic growth, and rates of unemployment) adversely affect certain groups in society, even though other groups may be unaffected or may even benefit from these arrangements. And the number and size of groups adversely affected are indications of the problems of societal organization.

To study problems of race in terms of societal organization, therefore, entails a detailed investigation of not only the political, economic, and other institutional dimensions of societal organization that affect intra- and intergroup experiences, but also the technological dimensions. The basic theoretical argument I am proposing is that the dimensions of societal organization impose constraints on intergroup interaction whereby intergroup relations are structured, racial antagonisms are channeled, and racial group access to rewards and privileges is differentiated. And the changes in the institutional dimensions of societal organization or in the technological dimensions often bring about changes in the patterns of intergroup interaction. Moreover, significant changes in *intragroup* experiences accompany changes in societal organization. Let me demonstrate how the principal ideas in this brief theoretical discussion can illuminate recent problems associated with race in America and suggest new approaches to public policy.

Problems of Race, Societal Organization, and Public Policy

Since World War II, both political changes of the state and structural changes in the economy have contributed to a gradual and continuous process of deracialization in the economic sector; in other words, a process in which racial distinctions gradually lose their importance in determining individual mobility in the United States. The expansion of the economy, on the one hand, facilitated the movement of blacks from southern rural areas to the industrial centers of the nation and created job opportunities leading to greater occupational differentiation within the black community. On the other hand, the state, instead of reinforcing the racial barriers that were created during the previous periods, has, in recent years, promoted racial equality. Partly in response to the pressure of increased black political resources (resulting from the growing concentration of blacks in large industrial cities) and partly in response to the pressures of black protest movements (in many ways, a manifestation of greater black political strength), the government has consistently intervened on behalf of blacks with the enactment and enforcement of antidiscrimination legislation. In short, a combination of changes in political and economic dimensions of societal organization created greater economic mobility opportunities for a substantial segment of the black population.[22]

The curious paradox, however, is that whereas economic growth since World War II enabled many blacks to experience occupational mobility, recent structural shifts in the economy have diminished mobility opportunities for others. And whereas antidiscrimination legislation has removed many racial barriers, not all blacks are in a position to benefit from it. Indeed, as I have attempted to show in previous chapters, the position of the black underclass has actually deteriorated during the very period in which the most sweeping antidiscrimination legislation and programs have been enacted and implemented. The net effect is a growing economic schism between poor and higher-income blacks.

Accordingly, people who argue that *current* racial bias is the major cause of the deteriorating economic plight of the black poor fail to recognize how the fate of poor blacks is inextricably connected with the structure and functioning of the modern American economy. The net effect is that policy programs are recommended that do not confront the fundamental cause of poverty—underemployment and unemployment. In other words, policies that do not take into account the changing nature of the national economy will not effectively handle the economic dislocation of low-income blacks. Factors that must be considered are the economy's rate of growth and the nature of its variable demand for labor; matters that affect industrial employment, such as profit rates, technology, and unionization; and patterns of institutional and individual migration that are a result of industrial transformation and shifts.

For example, a recent study by the Illinois Advisory Committee to the United States Commission on Civil Rights reported that among the 2,380 firms in their statewide sample that had left the central cities and relocated in the suburbs between 1975 and 1978, black employment decreased by 24.3 percent compared to a white employment drop of only 9.8 percent. This study also found that although minorities were 14.1 percent of the statewide work force between 1975 and 1978, they were 20 percent of the formerly employed workers in the firms that shut down.[23] Furthermore, a recent study on the effects of deindustrialization on the national labor force found that blacks are disproportionately concentrated in industries that have "borne the brunt of recent" plant closings, such as the automobile, rubber, and steel industries.[24] Moreover, industries that were most adversely affected (lowered job opportunities) by the impact of foreign trade from 1964 to 1975 had an average minority work force of 11.5 percent compared to one of 7.4 percent in industries that were favorably affected. And, finally, the detrimental effects of the decline in central-city industries that employ a substantial number of young workers were concentrated among the black males.[25]

Thus minorities, particularly poor and working-class minorities, are not only adversly affected by periodic recessions, they are also vulnerable to the structural economic changes of the past two decades because of their disproportionate concentration in industries with the largest number of layoffs due to economic cutbacks, plant closings, and the relocation of firms to cheaper labor sites and to the suburbs.

Other problems that have been defined in race-specific terms (such as the quality of inner-city schools, school desegregation, and residential segregation) have also been partly created and exacerbated by nonracial factors such as demographic changes responding to industrial shifts or tranformations. Just as the changes in the economy have fundamentally altered the job market situation for inner-city blacks, so too has the class and racial composition of urban public schools and residential neighborhoods been affected by population movements responding to economic changes. The technological and economic shifts of the post–World War II period precipitated the movement toward decentralization and residential development in the suburbs. Once these processes were under way, they became part of a vicious cycle of metropolitan change and relocation. The flight of the more affluent families to the suburbs has meant that the central cities are becoming increasingly the domain of the poor and the stable working class. Thus, in major cities, such as New York, Chicago, Atlanta, Washington, D.C., Philadelphia, St. Louis, and Detroit, not only have public schools become overwhelmingly populated with minority students, but the background of both minority and white students is primarily working or lower class. And in certain underclass neighborhoods in the inner city, neither children from middle-class families nor those from working-class families are represented in the public schools. The more affluent white and minority families are increasingly opting to send their children to parochial or private schools if they remain in the central city or to suburban schools if they move to the metropolitan fringe.

Moreover, changes in societal organization have created situations that enhance racial antagonisms between those groups that are trapped in central cities and are victimized by deteriorating services and institutions that serve the city. In addition to problems experienced by poor minorities, inner-city white ethnics have encountered mounting difficulties in maintaining their quality of life. Many of these people originally bought relatively inexpensive homes near their industrial jobs. Because of the deconcentration of industry, the racially changing neighborhood bordering their communities, the problems of neighborhood crime, and the surplus of inner-city housing created by the population shift to the suburbs, housing values in their neighborhoods have failed to keep pace with those in the suburbs. As the industries in which they are employed become suburbanized, a growing number of inner-city white ethnics find that not only are they trapped in the inner city because of the high costs of suburban housing, but they are physically removed from job opportunities.[26] This situation increases the potential for racial tensions as white European ethnics compete with blacks and the rapidly growing Hispanic population for access to and control of the remaining decent schools, housing, and neighborhoods. And explanations that their negative response to minority encroachment is due to racial prejudice hardly capture the dynamic factors of societal organization that channel racial antagonisms.

Finally, policymakers must understand how some aspects of American societal organization have direct consequences for group cultural behavior. The more unequal the distribution of scarce resources among groups in a society, the more differentiation there is in group social participation in the institutions of society and in group culture. Group variation in behavior, norms, and values reflects variation in group access to organizational channels of privilege and influence.

Since class background and race are two major factors in determining group access to such channels, the opportunities available to the ghetto underclass, a group that represents the combination of both race and class subordination, are therefore more limited and the structural constraints are greater. Ghetto-specific culture is a response to these structural constraints and limited opportunities.

However, the notion of a ghetto subculture is not to be equated with the popular conception of *culture of poverty*. In chapter 2, I distinguished the concept *culture of poverty* from the concept *social isolation* to highlight the association between the ghetto subculture and structural constraints and opportunities. Nonetheless, some readers may still have difficulty distinguishing the two concepts because the very meaning of *social isolation* implies that ghetto-specific cultural traits are not irrelevant in understanding the behavior of inner-city residents. But, what distinguishes the two concepts is that although they both emphasize the association between the emergence of certain cultural traits and the structure of social constraints and opportunities, *culture of poverty*, unlike *social isolation*, places strong emphasis on the autonomous character of the cultural traits once they come into existence. In other words, these traits assume a "life of their own" and continue to influence behavior even if opportunities for social mobility improve. As Oscar Lewis puts it, "By the time slum children are age six or seven, they have usually absorbed the basic values and attitudes of their subculture and are not psychologically geared to take full advantage of changing conditions or increased opportunities which may occur in their lifetime."[27] Although Lewis later modified his position by placing more weight on external societal forces than on self-perpetuating cultural traits to explain the behavior of the poor, conservative social scientists have embellished the idea that poverty is a product of "deeply ingrained habits" that are unlikely to change following improvements in external conditions.[28] On the other hand, *social isolation* is one of several concepts included in my discussion of the social transformation of the inner city (see chapter 2) that link ghetto-specific behavior with the problems of societal organization. More specifically, concepts such as *social buffer, concentration effects,* and *social isolation* are used to describe the social and institutional mechanisms that enhance patterns of social dislocations originally caused by racial subjugation but that have been strengthened in more recent years by such developments as the class transformation of the inner city and changes in the urban economy. As I have tried to emphasize, the significance of increasing social isolation is not that ghetto culture went unchecked following the removal of higher income fami-

lies from many inner-city neighborhoods, but that the increasing exodus of these families made it more difficult to sustain the basic
institutions in these neighborhoods (including churches, stores,
schools, recreational facilities, etc.) in the face of increased joblessness
caused by the frequent recessions during the 1970s and early 1980s and
changes in the urban job structure. As the basic institutions declined,
the social organization of inner-city neighborhoods (sense of community, positive neighborhood identification, and explicit norms and sanctions against aberrant behavior) likewise declined. This process
magnified the effects of living in highly concentrated urban poverty
areas—effects that are manifested in ghetto-specific culture and
behavior.

If my concept of *social isolation* does not imply self-perpetuating
cultural traits, am I completely ruling out the possibility that some
cultural traits may in fact take on a life of their own for a period of time
and thereby become a constraining or liberating factor in the life of
certain individuals and groups in the inner city? It would be dogmatic
to rule out this possibility, however, as pointed out in chapter 1, as
economic and social situations change, cultural traits, created by previous situations, likewise *eventually* change even though it is possible
that some will linger on and influence behavior for a period of time.[29]
Accordingly, the key conclusion from a public policy perspective is that
programs created to alleviate poverty, joblessness, and related forms of
social dislocation should place primary focus on changing the social and
economic situations, not the cultural traits, of the ghetto underclass.

Conclusion

To hold, as I do, that changes in social and economic situations will
bring about changes in behavior and norms raises the issue of what
public policy can deal effectively with the social dislocations that have
recently plagued the ghetto underclass. In this chapter I have outlined
a holistic approach emphasizing the problems of societal organization.
My purpose is to show not only the complexities of the issue currently
associated with race and to explain why they cannot be firmly grasped
by focusing solely or even mainly on racial discrimination but also to
reinforce the argument underlined in the previous chapter, namely,
that it is necessary to move beyond race-specific public policy to address the problems of the truly disadvantaged. For example, I argued
in this chapter that (1) the vulnerability of poor urban minorities to
changes in the economy since 1970 has resulted in sharp increases in

joblessness, poverty, female-headed families, and welfare dependency despite the creation of Great Society programs, and despite anti-discrimination and affirmative action programs; (2) the War on Poverty and race relations visions failed to relate the fate of poor minorities to the functionings of the modern American economy and therefore could not explain the worsening conditions of inner-city minorities in the post–Great Society and post–civil rights periods; (3) liberals whose views embody these visions have not only been puzzled by the recent increase of inner-city social dislocations, they have also lacked a convincing rebuttal to the forceful arguments by conservative scholars that erroneously attribute these problems to the social values of the ghetto underclass; and (4) the growing emphasis on social values deflects attention from the major source of the rise of inner-city social dislocations since 1970—changes in the nation's economy.

Any significant reduction of the problems of black joblessness and the related problems of crime, out-of-wedlock births, single-parent homes, and welfare dependency will call for a far more comprehensive program of economic and social reform than what Americans have usually regarded as appropriate or desirable. In short, it will require a radicalism that neither Democratic nor Republican parties have as yet been realistic enough to propose. This program is discussed in some detail in the next chapter.

7   The Hidden Agenda

The inner city is less pleasant and more dangerous than it was prior to 1960. As pointed out in chapter 1, despite a high rate of poverty in inner-city areas during the first half of this century, rates of joblessness, out-of-wedlock births, single families, welfare dependency, and serious crime were significantly lower than they are today and did not begin to rise rapidly until after the mid-1960s, with extraordinary increases during the 1970s. The questions of why social problems in the inner city sharply increased when they did and in the way they did, and why existing policy programs assumed to be relevant to such problems are either inappropriate or insufficient, were addressed in the preceding chapters. In this chapter I should like, by way of summary and conclusion, to outline some of the central substantive and theoretical arguments presented in this study on the ghetto underclass and social change in the inner city and to draw out in sharper relief the basic policy implications of my analysis.

The Ghetto Underclass and Social Dislocations

Why have the social conditions of the ghetto underclass deteriorated so rapidly in recent years? Racial discrimination is the most frequently invoked explanation, and it is undeniable that discrimination continues to aggravate the social and economic problems of poor blacks. But is discrimination really greater today than it was in 1948, when black unemployment was less than half of what it is now, and when the gap between black and white jobless rates was narrower?

As for the poor black family, it apparently began to fall apart not before but after the mid-twentieth century. Until publication in 1976 of Herbert Gutman's *The Black Family in Slavery and Freedom*, most scholars had believed otherwise. Stimulated by the acrimonious debate over the Moynihan report, Gutman produced data demonstrating that the black family was not significantly disrupted during slavery or even during the early years of the first migration to the urban North, beginning after the turn of the century. The problems of the modern black family, he implied, were associated with modern forces.

Those who cite discrimination as the root cause of poverty often fail to make a distinction between the effects of *historic* discrimination (i.e., discrimination prior to the mid-twentieth century) and the effects of *contemporary* discrimination. Thus they find it hard to explain why the economic position of the black underclass started to worsen soon after Congress enacted, and the White House began to enforce, the most sweeping civil rights legislation since Reconstruction.

The point to be emphasized is that historic discrimination is more important than contemporary discrimination in understanding the plight of the ghetto underclass—that in any event there is more to the story than discrimination (of whichever kind). Historic discrimination certainly helped create an impoverished urban black community in the first place. In his recent *A Piece of the Pie: Black and White Immigrants since 1880* (1980), Stanley Lieberson shows how, in many areas of life, including the labor market, black newcomers from the rural South were far more severely discriminated against in northern cities than were the new white immigrants from southern, central, and eastern Europe. Skin color was part of the problem but it was not all of it.

The disadvantage of skin color—the fact that the dominant whites preferred whites over nonwhites—is one that blacks shared with the Japanese, Chinese, and others. Yet the experience of the Asians, who also experienced harsh discriminatory treatment in the communities where they were concentrated, but who went on to prosper in their adopted land, suggests that skin color per se was not an insuperable obstacle. Indeed Lieberson argues that the greater success enjoyed by Asians may well be explained largely by the different context of their contact with whites. Because changes in immigration policy cut off Asian migration to America in the late nineteenth century, the Japanese and Chinese population did not reach large numbers and therefore did not pose as great a threat as did blacks.

Furthermore, the discontinuation of large-scale immigration from Japan and China enabled those Chinese and Japanese already in the United States to solidify networks of ethnic contacts and to occupy particular occupational niches in small, relatively stable communities. For blacks, the situation was different. The 1970 census recorded 22,580,000 blacks in the United States but only 435,000 Chinese and 591,000 Japanese.

If different population sizes accounted for a good deal of the difference in the economic success of blacks and Asians, they also helped determine the dissimilar rates of progress of urban blacks and the new European arrivals. European immigration was curtailed during the 1920s, but black migration to the urban North continued through the 1960s. With each passing decade there were many more blacks who were recent migrants to the North, whereas the immigrant component of the new Europeans dropped off over time. Eventually, other whites muffled their dislike of the Poles and Italians and Jews and directed their antagonism against blacks.

In addition to the problem of historic discrimination, the black migration to New York, Philadelphia, Chicago, and other northern cities—the continued replenishment of black populations there by poor newcomers—predictably skewed the age profile of the urban black community and kept it relatively young. The number of central-city black youths aged sixteen to nineteen increased by almost 75 percent from 1960 to 1969. Young black adults (aged twenty to twenty-four) increased in number by two-thirds during the same period, three times the increase for young white adults. In the nation's inner cities in 1977, the median age for whites was 30.3, for blacks 23.9. The importance of this jump in the number of young minorities in the ghetto, many of them lacking one or more parents, cannot be overemphasized.

Age correlates with many things. For example, the higher the median age of a group, the higher its income; the lower the median age, the higher the unemployment rate and the higher the crime rate (more than half of those arrested in 1980 for violent and property crimes in American cities were under twenty-one). The younger a woman is, the more likely she is to bear a child out of wedlock, head up a new household, and depend on welfare. In short, part of what had gone awry in the ghetto was due to the sheer increase in the number of black youth.

The population explosion among minority youth occurred at a time when changes in the economy were beginning to pose serious problems for unskilled workers. Urban minorities have been particularly vulnerable to the structural economic changes of the past two decades: the shift from goods-producing to service-producing industries, the increasing polarization of the labor market into low-wage and high-wage sectors, innovations in technology, and the relocation of manufacturing industries out of the central cities.

Most unemployed blacks in the United States reside within the central cities. Their situation, already more difficult than that of any other major ethnic group in the country, continues to worsen. Not only are there more blacks without jobs every year; men, especially young males, are dropping out of the labor force in record proportions. Also, more and more black youth, including many who are no longer in school, are obtaining no job experience at all.

However, the growing problem of joblessness in the inner city exacerbates and is in turn partly created by the changing social composition of inner-city neighborhoods. These areas have undergone a profound social transformation in the last several years, as reflected not only in their increasing rates of social dislocation but also in the changing class structure of ghetto neighborhoods. In the 1940s, 1950s, and even the 1960s, lower-class, working-class, and middle-class black urban families all resided more or less in the same ghetto areas, albeit on different streets. Although black middle-class professionals today tend to be employed in mainstream occupations outside the black community and neither live nor frequently interact with ghetto residents, the black middle-class professionals of the 1940s and 1950s (doctors, lawyers, teachers, social workers, etc.) resided in the higher-income areas of the inner city and serviced the ghetto community. The exodus of black middle-class professionals from the inner city has been increasingly accompanied by a movement of stable working-class blacks to higher-income neighborhoods in other parts of the city and to the suburbs. Confined by restrictive covenants to communities also inhabited by the urban black lower classes, the black working and middle classes in earlier years provided stability to inner-city neighborhoods and perpetuated and reinforced societal norms and values. In short, their very presence enhanced the social organization of ghetto communities. If strong norms and sanctions against aberrant behavior, a sense of community, and positive neighborhood identification are the essential features of social organization in urban areas, inner-city neighborhoods today suffer from a severe lack of social organization.

Unlike in previous years, today's ghetto residents represent almost exclusively the most disadvantaged segments of the urban black comunity—including those families that have experienced long-term spells of poverty and/or welfare dependency, individuals who lack training and skills and have either experienced periods of persistent unemployment or have dropped out of the labor force altogether, and individuals who are frequently involved in street criminal activity. The term *ghetto underclass* refers to this heterogeneous group of families and individuals who inhabit the cores of the nation's central cities. The term suggests that a fundamental social transformation has taken place in ghetto neighborhoods, and the groups represented by this term are collectively different from and much more socially isolated than those that lived in these communities in earlier years.

The significance of changes embodied in the social transformation of the inner city is perhaps best captured by the concepts *concentration effects* and *social buffer*. The former refers to the constraints and opportunities associated with living in a neighborhood in which the population is overwhelmingly socially disadvantaged—constraints and opportunities that include the kinds of ecological niches that the residents of these communities occupy in terms of access to jobs, availability of marriageable partners, and exposure to conventional role models. The latter refers to the presence of a sufficient number of working- and middle-class professional families to absorb the shock or cushion the effect of uneven economic growth and periodic recessions on inner-city neighborhoods. The basic thesis is not that ghetto culture went unchecked following the removal of higher-income families in the inner city, but that the removal of these families made it more difficult to sustain the basic institutions in the inner city (including churches, stores, schools, recreational facilities, etc.) in the face of prolonged joblessness. And as the basic institutions declined, the social organization of inner-city neighborhoods (defined here to include a sense of community, positive neighborhood identification, and explicit norms and sanctions against aberrant behavior) likewise declined. Indeed, the social organization of any neighborhood depends in large measure on the viability of social institutions in that neighborhood. It is true that the presence of stable working- and middle-class families in the ghetto provides mainstream role models that reinforce mainstream values pertaining to employment, education, and family structure. But, in the final analysis, a far more important effect is the institutional stability that these families are able to provide in their neighborhoods because of their greater economic and educational resources, especially during periods of an economic downturn—periods in which joblessness in poor urban areas tends to substantially increase.

In underlining joblessness as an important aspect of inner-city social transformations, we are reminded that in the 1960s scholars readily attributed poor black family deterioration to problems of employment. Nonetheless, in the last several years, in the face of the overwhelming attention given to welfare as the major source of black family breakup, concerns about the importance of joblessness have diminished, despite the existence of evidence strongly suggesting the need for renewed scholarly and public policy attention to the relationship between the disintegration of poor black families and black male labor-market experiences.

Although changing social and cultural trends have often been said to explain some of the dynamic shifts in the structure of the family, they appear to have more relevance for changes in family structure among whites. And contrary to popular opinion, there is little evidence to support the argument that welfare is the primary cause of family out-of-wedlock births, breakups, and female-headed households. Welfare does seem to have a modest effect on separation and divorce, particularly for white women, but recent evidence indicates that its total effect on the proportion of all female householders is small.

By contrast, the evidence for the influence of joblessness on family structure is much more conclusive. Research has demonstrated, for example, a connection between an encouraging economic situation and the early marriage of young people. In this connection, black women are more likely to delay marriage and less likely to remarry. Although black and white teenagers expect to become parents at about the same ages, black teenagers expect to marry at later ages. The black delay in marriage and the lower rate of remarriage, each associated with high percentages of out-of-wedlock births and female-headed households, can be directly tied to the employment status of black males. Indeed, black women, especially young black women, are confronting a shrinking pool of "marriageable" (that is economically stable) men.

White women are not experiencing this problem. Our "male marriageable pool index" shows that the number of employed white men per one hundred white women in different age categories has either remained roughly the same or has only slightly increased in the last two decades. There is little reason, therefore, to assume a connection between the recent growth of female-headed white families and patterns of white male employment. That the pool of "marriageable" white men has not decreased over the years is perhaps reflected in the earlier age of first marriage and the higher rate of remarriage among white women. It is therefore reasonable to hypothesize that the rise in rates of separation and divorce among whites is due mainly to the increased economic independence of white women and related social and cultural factors embodied in the feminist movement.

The argument that the decline in the incidence of intact marriages among blacks is associated with the declining economic status of black men is further supported by an analysis of regional data on female headship and the "male marriageable pool." Whereas changes in the ratios of employed men to women among whites have been minimal for all regions of the country regardless of age from 1960 to 1980, the ratios among blacks have declined significantly in all regions except the West, with the greatest declines in the northeastern and north-central regions of the country. On the basis of these trends, it would be expected that the growth in numbers of black female-headed households would occur most rapidly in the northern regions, followed by the South and the West. Regional data on the "male marriageable pool index" support this conclusion, except for the larger-than-expected increase in black female-headed families in the West—a function of patterns of selective black migration to the West.

The sharp decline in the black "male marriageable pool" in the northeastern and north-central regions is related to recent changes in the basic economic organization in American society. In the two northern regions, the shift in economic activity from goods production to services has been associated with changes in the location of production, including an interregional movement of industry from the North to the South and West and, more important, a movement of certain industries out of the older central cities where blacks are concentrated. Moreover, the shrinkage of the male marriageable pool for ages sixteen to twenty-four in the South from 1960 to 1980 is related to the mechanization of agriculture, which lowered substantially the demand for low-skilled agricultural labor, especially during the 1960s. For all these reasons, it is often necessary to go beyond the specific issue of current racial discrimination to understand factors that contribute directly to poor black joblessness and indirectly to related social problems such as family instability in the inner city. But this point has not been readily grasped by policymakers and civil rights leaders.

The Limits of Race-specific Public Policy

In the early 1960s there was no comprehensive civil rights bill and Jim Crow segregation was still widespread in parts of the nation, particularly in the Deep South. With the passage of the 1964 Civil Rights Bill there was considerable optimism that racial progress would ensue and that the principle of equality of individual rights (namely, that candidates for positions stratified in terms of prestige, power, or other social criteria ought to be judged solely on individual merit and therefore should not be discriminated against on the basis of racial orgin) would be upheld.

Programs based solely on this principle are inadequate, however, to deal with the complex problems of race in America because they are not designed to address the substantive inequality that exists at the time discrimination is eliminated. In other words, long periods of racial oppression can result in a system of inequality that may persist for indefinite periods of time even after racial barriers are removed. This is because the most disadvantaged members of racial minority groups, who suffer the cumulative effects of both race and class subjugation (including those effects passed on from generation to generation), are disproportionately represented among the segment of the general population that has been denied the resources to compete effectively in a free and open market.

On the other hand, the competitive resources developed by the *advantaged minority members*—resources that flow directly from the family stability, schooling, income, and peer groups that their parents have been able to provide—result in their benefiting disproportionately from policies that promote the rights of minority individuals by removing artificial barriers to valued positions.

Nevertheless, since 1970, government policy has tended to focus on formal programs designed and created both to prevent discrimination and to ensure that minorities are sufficiently represented in certain positions. This has resulted in a shift from the simple formal investigation and adjudication of complaints of racial discrimination to government-mandated affirmative action programs to increase minority representation in public programs, employment, and education.

However, if minority members from the most advantaged families profit disproportionately from policies based on the principle of equality of individual opportunity, they also reap disproportionate benefits from policies of affirmative action based solely on their group membership. This is because advantaged minority members are likely to be disproportionately represented among those of their racial group most qualified for valued positions, such as college admissions, higher paying jobs, and promotions. Thus, if policies of preferential treatment for such positions are developed in terms of racial group membership rather than the real disadvantages suffered by individuals, then these policies will further improve the opportunities of the advantaged without necessarily addressing the problems of the truly disadvantaged such as the ghetto underclass.[1] The problems of the truly disadvantaged may require *nonracial* solutions such as full employment, balanced economic growth, and manpower training and education (tied to—not isolated from—these two economic conditions).

By 1980 this argument was not widely recognized or truly appreciated. Therefore, because the government not only adopted and implemented antibias legislation to promote minority individual rights, but also mandated and enforced affirmative action and related programs to enhance minority group rights, many thoughtful American citizens, including supporters of civil rights, were puzzled by recent social developments in black communities. Despite the passage of civil rights legislation and the creation of affirmative action programs, they sensed that

conditions were deteriorating instead of improving for a significant segment of the black American population. This perception had emerged
because of the continuous flow of pessimistic reports concerning the
sharp rise in black joblessness, the precipitous drop in the black-white
family income ratio, the steady increase in the percentage of blacks on
the welfare rolls, and the extraordinary growth in the number of female-
headed families. This perception was strengthened by the almost uniform cry among black leaders that not only had conditions worsened,
but that white Americans had forsaken the cause of blacks as well.

Meanwhile, the liberal architects of the War on Poverty became
puzzled when Great Society programs failed to reduce poverty in
America and when they could find few satisfactory explanations for the
sharp rise in inner-city social dislocations during the 1970s. However,
just as advocates for minority rights have been slow to comprehend
that many of the current problems of race, particularly those that
plague the minority poor, derived from the broader processes of societal organization and therefore may have no direct or indirect connection with race, so too have the architects of the War on Poverty failed
to emphasize the relationship between poverty and the broader processes of American economic organization. Accordingly, given the
most comprehensive civil rights and antipoverty programs in America's
history, the liberals of the civil rights movement and the Great Society
became demoralized when inner-city poverty proved to be more
intractable than they realized and when they could not satisfactorily
explain such events as the unprecedented rise in inner-city joblessness
and the remarkable growth in the number of female-headed households. This demoralization cleared the path for conservative analysts to
fundamentally shift the focus away from changing the environments of
the minority poor to changing their values and behavior.

However, and to repeat, many of the problems of the ghetto underclass are related to the broader problems of societal organization, including economic organization. For example, as pointed out earlier,
regional differences in changes in the "male marriageable pool index"
signify the importance of industrial shifts in the Northeast and Midwest. Related research clearly demonstrated the declining labor-market opportunities in the older central cities. Indeed, blacks tend to be
concentrated in areas where the number and characteristics of jobs
have been most significantly altered by shifts in the location of production activity and from manufacturing to services. Since an overwhelming majority of inner-city blacks lacks the qualifications for the high-
skilled segment of the service sector such as information processing,
finance, and real estate, they tend to be concentrated in the low-skilled

segment, which features unstable employment, restricted opportunities, and low wages.

The Hidden Agenda: From Group-specific to Universal Programs of Reform

It is not enough simply to recognize the need to relate many of the woes of truly disadvantaged blacks to the problems of societal organization; it is also important to describe the problems of the ghetto underclass candidly and openly so that they can be fully explained and appropriate policy programs can be devised. It has been problematic, therefore, that liberal journalists, social scientists, policymakers, and civil rights leaders were reluctant throughout the decade of the 1970s to discuss inner-city social pathologies. Often, analysts of such issues as violent crime or teenage pregnancy deliberately make no references to race at all, unless perhaps to emphasize the deleterious consequences of racial discrimination or the institutionalized inequality of American society. Some scholars, in an effort to avoid the appearance of "blaming the victim" or to protect their work from charges of racism, simply ignore patterns of behavior that might be construed as stigmatizing to particular racial minorities.

Such neglect is relatively recent. During the mid-1960s, social scientists such as Kenneth B. Clark, Daniel Partick Moynihan, and Lee Rainwater forthrightly examined the cumulative effects of racial isolation and class subordination on inner-city blacks. They vividly described aspects of ghetto life that, as Rainwater observed, are usually not discussed in polite conversations. All of these studies attempted to show the connection between the economic and social environment into which many blacks are born and the creation of patterns of behavior that, in Clark's words, frequently amounted to "self-perpetuating pathology."

Why have scholars tended to shy away from this line of research? One reason has to do with the vitriolic attack by many blacks and liberals against Moynihan upon publication of his report in 1965—denunciations that generally focused on the author's unflattering depiction of the black family in the urban ghetto rather than on the proposed remedies or his historical analysis of the black family's social plight. The harsh reception accorded *The Negro Family* undoubtedly dissuaded many social scientists from following in Moynihan's footsteps.

The "black solidarity" movement was also emerging during the latter half of the 1960s. A new emphasis by young black scholars and intellectuals on the positive aspects of the black experience tended to crowd out older concerns. Indeed, certain forms of ghetto behavior labeled pathological in the studies of Clark and colleagues were redefined by some during the early 1970s as "functional" because, it was argued, blacks were displaying the ability to survive and in some cases flourish in an economically depressed environment. The ghetto family was described as resilient and capable of adapting creatively to an oppressive, racist society. And the candid, but liberal writings on the inner city in the 1960s were generally denounced. In the end, the promising efforts of the early 1960s—to distinguish the socioeconomic characteristics of different groups within the black community, and to identify the structural problems of the United States economy that affected minorities—were cut short by calls for "reparations" or for "black control of institutions serving the black community."

If this ideologically tinged criticism discouraged research by liberal scholars on the poor black family and the ghetto community, conservative thinkers were not so inhibited. From the early 1970s through the first half of the 1980s, their writings on the culture of poverty and the deleterious effects of Great Society liberal welfare policies on ghetto underclass behavior dominated the public policy debate on alleviating inner-city social dislocations.

The Great Society programs represented the country's most ambitious attempt to implement the principle of equality of life chances. However, the extent to which these programs helped the truly disadvantaged is difficult to assess when one considers the simultaneous impact of the economic downturn from 1968 to the early 1980s. Indeed, it has been argued that many people slipped into poverty because of the economic downturn and were lifted out by the broadening of welfare benefits. Moreover, the increase in unemployment that accompanied the economic downturn and the lack of growth of real wages in the 1970s, although they had risen steadily from 1950 to about 1970, have had a pronounced effect on low-income groups (especially black males).

The above analysis has certain distinct public policy implications for attacking the problems of inner-city joblessness and the related problems of poor female-headed families, welfare dependency, crime, and so forth. Comprehensive economic policies aimed at the general population but that would also enhance employment opportunities among the truly disadvantaged—both men and women—are needed. The research presented in this study suggests that improving the job prospects of men will strengthen low-income black families. Moreover, underclass absent fathers with more stable employment are in a better position to contribute financial support for their families. Further-more, since the majority of female householders are in the labor force, improved job prospects would very likely draw in others.[2]

I have in mind the creation of a macroeconomic policy designed to promote both economic growth and a tight labor market.[3] The latter affects the supply-and-demand ratio and wages tend to rise. It would be necessary, however, to combine this policy with fiscal and monetary policies to stimulate noninflationary growth and thereby move away from the policy of controlling inflation by allowing unemployment to rise. Furthermore, it would be important to develop policy to increase the competitiveness of American goods on the international market by, among other things, reducing the budget deficit to adjust the value of the American dollar.

In addition, measures such as on-the-job training and apprenticeships to elevate the skill levels of the truly disadvantaged are needed. I will soon discuss in another context why such problems have to be part of a more universal package of reform. For now, let me simply say that improved manpower policies are needed in the short run to help lift the truly disadvantaged from the lowest rungs of the job market. In other words, it would be necessary to devise a national labor-market strategy to increase "the adaptability of the labor force to changing employment opportunities." In this connection, instead of focusing on remedial pro-grams in the public sector for the poor and the unemployed, emphasis would be placed on relating these programs more closely to oppor-tunities in the private sector to facilitate the movement of recipients (including relocation assistance) into more secure jobs. Of course there would be a need to create public transitional programs for those who have difficulty finding immediate employment in the private sector, but such programs would aim toward eventually getting individuals into the private sector economy. Although public employment programs continue to draw popular support, as Weir, Orloff, and Skocpol point out, "they must be designed and administered in close conjunction with a nationally oriented labor market strategy" to avoid both becoming "enmeshed in congressionally reinforced local political patronage" and being attacked as costly, inefficient, or "corrupt."[4]

Since national opinion polls consistently reveal strong public support for efforts to enhance work in America, political support for a program of economic reform (macroeconomic employment policies and labor-market strategies including training efforts) could be considerably stronger than many people presently assume.[5] However, in order to draw sustained public support for such a program, it is necessary that training or retraining, transitional employment benefits, and relocation assistance be available to all members of society who choose to use them, not just to poor minorities.

It would be ideal if problems of the ghetto underclass could be adequately addressed by the combination of macroeconomic policy, labor-market strategies, and manpower training programs. However, in the foreseeable future employment alone will not necessarily lift a family out of poverty.[6] Many families would still require income support and/or social services such as child care. A program of welfare reform is needed, therefore, to address the current problems of public assistance, including lack of provisions for poor two-parent families, inadequate levels of support, inequities between different states, and work disincentives. A national AFDC benefit standard adjusted yearly for inflation is the most minimal required change. We might also give serious consideration to programs such as the Child Support Assurance Program developed by Irwin Garfinkel and colleagues at the Institute for Research on Poverty at the University of Wisconsin, Madison.[7] This program, currently in operation as a demonstration project in the state of Wisconsin, provides a guaranteed minimum benefit per child to single-parent families regardless of the income of the custodial parent. The state collects from the absent parent through wage withholding a sum of money at a fixed rate and then makes regular payments to the custodial parent. If the absent parent is jobless or if his or her payment from withholdings is less than the minimum, the state makes up the difference. Since all absent parents regardless of income are required to participate in this program, it is far less stigmatizing than, say, public assistance. Moreover, preliminary evidence from Wisconsin suggests that this program carries little or no additional cost to the state.

Many western European countries have programs of family or child allowances to support families. These programs provide families with an annual benefit per child regardless of the family's income, and regardless of whether the parents are living together or whether either or both are employed. Unlike public assistance, therefore, a family allowance program carries no social stigma and has no built-in work disincentives. In this connection, Daniel Patrick Moynihan has recently observed that a form of family allowance is already available to American families with the standard deduction and the Earned Income Tax Credit, although the latter can only be obtained by low-income families. Even though both have been significantly eroded by inflation, they could represent the basis for a more comprehensive family allowance program that approximates the European model.

Neither the Child Support Assurance Program under demonstration in Wisconsin nor the European family allowances program is means tested; that is, they are not targeted at a particular income group and therefore do not suffer the degree of stigmatization that plagues public assistance programs such as AFDC. More important, such universal programs would tend to draw more political support from the general public because the programs would be available not only to the poor but to the working-and middle-class segments as well. And such programs would not be readily associated with specific minority groups. Nonetheless, truly disadvantaged groups would reap disproportionate benefits from such programs because of the groups' limited alternative economic resources. For example, low-income single mothers could combine work with adequate guaranteed child support and/or child allowance benefits and therefore escape poverty and avoid public assistance.

Finally, the question of child care has to be addressed in any program designed to improve the employment prospects of women and men. Because of the growing participation of women in the labor market, adequate child care has been a topic receiving increasing attention in public policy discussions. For the overwhelmingly female-headed ghetto underclass families, access to quality child care becomes a critical issue if steps are taken to move single mothers into education and training programs and/or full- or part-time employment. However, I am not recommending government-operated child care centers. Rather it would be better to avoid additional federal bureaucracy by seeking alternative and decentralized forms of child care such as expanding the child care tax credit, including three- and four-year-olds in preschool enrollment, and providing child care subsidies to the working-poor parents.

If the truly disadvantaged reaped disproportionate benefits from a child support enforcement program, child allowance program, and child care strategy, they would also benefit disproportionately from a program of balanced economic growth and tight-labor-market policies because of their greater vulnerability to swings in the business cycle and changes in economic organization, including the relocation of plants and the use of labor-saving technology. It would be shortsighted to conclude, therefore, that universal programs (i.e., programs not targeted at any particular group) are not designed to help address in a fundamental way some of the problems of the truly disadvantaged, such as the ghetto underclass.

By emphasizing universal programs as an effective way to address problems in the inner city created by historic racial subjugation, I am recommending a fundamental shift from the traditional race-specific approach of addressing such problems. It is true that problems of joblessness and related woes such as poverty, teenage pregnancies, out-of-wedlock births, female-headed families, and welfare dependency are, for reasons of historic racial oppression, disproportionately concentrated in the black community. And it is important to recognize the racial differences in rates of social dislocation so as not to obscure problems currently gripping the ghetto underclass. However, as discussed above, race-specific policies are often not designed to address fundamental problems of the truly disadvantaged. Moreover, as also discussed above, both race-specific and targeted programs based on the principle of equality of life chances (often identified with a minority constituency) have difficulty sustaining widespread public support.

Does this mean that targeted programs of any kind would necessarily be excluded from a package highlighting universal programs of reform? On the contrary, as long as a racial division of labor exists and racial minorities are disproportionately concentrated in low-paying positions, antidiscrimination and affirmative action programs will be needed even though they tend to benefit the more advantaged minority members. Moreover, as long as certain groups lack the training, skills, and education to compete effectively on the job market or move into newly created jobs, manpower training and education programs targeted at these groups will also be needed, even under a tight-labor-market situation. For example, a program of adult education and training may be necessary for some ghetto underclass males before they can either become oriented to or move into an expanded labor market. Finally, as long as some poor families are unable to work because of physical or other disabilities, public assistance would be needed even if the government adopted a program of welfare reform that included child support enforcement and family allowance provisions.

For all these reasons, a comprehensive program of economic and social reform (highlighting macroeconomic policies to promote balanced economic growth and create a tight-labor-market situation, a nationally oriented labor-market strategy, a child support assurance program, a child care strategy, and a family allowances program) would have to include targeted programs, both means tested and race-specific. However, the latter would be considered an offshoot of and indeed secondary to the universal programs. The important goal is to construct an economic-social reform program in such a way that the universal programs are seen as the dominant and most visible aspects by the general public. As the universal programs draw support from a wider population, the targeted programs included in the comprehensive reform package would be indirectly supported and protected. According-

ly, the hidden agenda for liberal policymakers is to improve the life chances of truly disadvantaged groups such as the ghetto underclass by emphasizing programs to which the more advantaged groups of all races and class backgrounds can positively relate.

I am reminded of Bayard Rustin's plea during the early 1960s that blacks ought to recognize the importance of fundamental economic reform (including a system of national economic planning along with new education, manpower, and public works programs to help reach full employment) and the need for a broad-based political coalition to achieve it. And since an effective coalition will in part depend upon how the issues are defined, it is imperative that the political message underline the need for economic and social reforms that benefit all groups in the United States, not just poor minorities. Politicians and civil rights organizations, as two important examples, ought to shift or expand their definition of America's racial problems and broaden the scope of suggested policy programs to address them. They should, of course, continue to fight for an end to racial discrimination. But they must also recognize that poor minorities are profoundly affected by problems in America that go beyond racial considerations. Furthermore, civil rights groups should also recognize that the problems of societal organization in America often create situations that enhance racial antagonisms between the different racial groups in central cities that are struggling to maintain their quality of life, and that these groups, although they appear to be fundamental adversaries, are potential allies in a reform coalition because of their problematic economic situations.

The difficulties that a progressive reform coalition would confront should not be underestimated. It is much easier to produce major economic and social reform in countries such as Sweden, Norway, Austria, the Netherlands, and West Germany than in the United States. What characterizes this group of countries, as demonstrated in the important research of Harold Wilensky,[8] is the interaction of solidly organized, generally centralized, interest groups—particularly professional, labor, and employer associations with a centralized or quasi-centralized government either compelled by law or obliged by informal agreement to take the recommendations of the interest groups into account or to rely on their counsel. This arrangement produces a consensus-making organization working generally within a public framework to bargain and produce policies on present-day political economy issues such as full employment, economic growth, unemployment, wages, prices, taxes, balance of payments, and social policy (including various forms of welfare, education, health, and housing policies).

In all of these countries, called "corporatist democracies" by Wilensky, social policy is integrated with economic policy. This produces a situation whereby, in periods of rising aspirations and slow economic growth, labor—concerned with wages, working conditions, and social security—is compelled to be attentive to the rate of productivity, the level of inflation, and the requirements of investments, and employers—concerned with profits, productivity, and investments— are compelled to be attentive to issues of social policy.[9]

The corporatist democracies, which are in a position to develop new consensus on social and economic policies in the face of declining economies because channels for bargaining and influence are firmly in place, stand in sharp contrast to the decentralized and fragmented political economies of the United States, Canada, and the United Kingdom. In these latter countries—none of which is a highly progressive welfare state—the proliferation of interest groups is not restrained by the requisites of national trade-offs and bargaining, which therefore allows parochial single issues to move to the forefront and thereby exacerbates the advanced condition of political immobilism. Reflecting the rise of single-issue groups has been the steady deterioration of political organizations and the decline of traditional allegiance to parties among voters. Moreover, there has been a sharp increase in the influence of the mass media, particularly the electronic media, in politics and culture. These trends, typical of all Western democracies, are much more salient in countries such as the United States, Canada, and the United Kingdom because their decentralized and fragmented political economies magnify the void created by the decline of political parties—a void that media and strident, single-issue groups rush headlong to fill.[10]

I raise these issues to underline some of the problems that a political coalition dedicated to developing and implementing a progressive policy agenda will have to confront. It seems imperative that, in addition to outlining a universal program of reform including policies that could effectively address inner-city social dislocations, attention be given to the matter of erecting a national bargaining structure to achieve sufficient consensus on the program of reform.

It is also important to recognize that just as we can learn from knowledge about the efficacy of alternative bargaining structures, we can also benefit from knowledge of alternative approaches to welfare and employment policies. Here we fortunately have the research of Alfred J. Kahn and Sheila Kamerman, which has convincingly demonstrated that countries that rely the least on public assistance, such as Sweden, West Germany, and France, provide alternative income transfers (family allowances, housing allowances, child support, unemployment assistance), stress the use of transfers to augment both earnings and transfer income, provide both child care services and day-care programs, and emphasize labor-market policies to enhance high employment. These countries, therefore, "provide incentives to work, supplement the use of social assistance generally because, even when used, it is increasingly only one component, at most, of a more elaborate benefit package." By contrast, the United States relies more heavily than all the other countries (Sweden, West Germany, France, Canada, Austria, the United Kingdom, and Israel) on public assistance to aid poorer families. "The result is that these families are much worse off than they are in any of the countries."[11]

In other words, problems such as poverty, joblessness, and long-term welfare dependency in the United States have not been addressed with the kinds of innovative approaches found in many western European democracies. "The European experience," argue Kamerman and Kahn, "suggests the need for a strategy that includes income transfers, child care services, and employment policies as central elements." The cornerstone of social policy in these countries is employment and labor-market policies. "Unless it is possible for adults to manage their work and family lives without undue strain on themselves and their children," argue Kamerman and Kahn, "society will suffer a significant loss in productivity, and an even more significant loss in the quantity and quality of future generations."[12]

The social policy that I have recommended above also would have employment and labor-market policies as its fundamental foundation. For in the final analysis neither family allowance and child support assurance programs, nor means-tested public assistance and manpower training and education programs can be sustained at adequate levels if the country is plagued with prolonged periods of economic stagnation and joblessness.

A Universal Reform Package and the Social Isolation of the Inner City

The program of economic and social reform outlined above will help address the problems of social dislocation plaguing the ghetto underclass. I make no claims that such programs will lead to a revitalization of neighborhoods in the inner city, reduce the social isolation, and thereby recapture the degree of social organization that characterized these neighborhoods in earlier years. However, in the long run these programs will lift the ghetto underclass from the throes of long-term poverty and welfare dependency and provide them with the economic and educational resources that would expand the limited choices they now have with respect to living arrangements. At the present time many residents of isolated inner-city neighborhoods have no other option but to remain in those neighborhoods. As their economic and educational resources improve they will very likely follow the path worn by many other former ghetto residents and move to safer or more desirable neighborhoods.

It seems to me that the most realistic approach to the problems of concentrated inner-city poverty is to provide ghetto underclass families and individuals with the resources that promote social mobility. Social mobility leads to geographic mobility. Geographic mobility would of course be enhanced if efforts to improve the economic and educational resources of inner-city residents were accompanied by legal steps to eliminate (1) the "practice at all levels of government" to "routinely locate housing for low-income people in the poorest neighborhoods of a community where their neighbors will be other low-income people usually of the same race"; and (2) the manipulation of zoning laws and discriminatory land use controls or site selection practices that either prevent the "construction of housing affordable to low-income families" or prevent low-income families "from securing residence in communities that provide the services they desire."[13]

This discussion raises a question about the ultimate effectiveness of the so-called self-help programs to revitalize the inner city, programs pushed by conservative and even some liberal black spokespersons. In many inner-city neighborhoods, problems such as joblessness are so overwhelming and require such a massive effort to restablize institutions and create a social and economic milieu necessary to sustain such institutions (e.g., the reintegration of the neighborhood with working- and middle-class blacks and black professionals) that it is surprising that advocates of black self-help have received so much serious attention from the media and policymakers.[14]

Of course some advocates of self-help subscribe to the thesis that problems in the inner city are ultimately the product of ghetto-specific culture and that it is the cultural values and norms in the inner city that must be addressed as part of a comprehensive self-help program.[15] However, cultural values emerge from specific circumstances and life chances and reflect an individual's position in the class structure. They therefore do not ultimately determine behavior. If ghetto underclass minorities have limited aspirations, a hedonistic orientation toward life, or lack of plans for the future, such outlooks ultimately are the result of restricted opportunities and feelings of resignation originating from bitter personal experiences and a bleak future. Thus the inner-city social dislocations emphasized in this study (joblessness, crime, teenage pregnancies, out-of-wedlock births, female-headed families, and welfare dependency) should be analyzed not as cultural aberrations but as symptoms of racial-class inequality.[16] It follows, therefore, that changes in the economic and social situations of the ghetto under-class will lead to changes in cultural norms and behavior patterns. The social policy program outlined above is based on this idea.

Before I take a final look, by way of summary and conclusion, at the important features of this program, I ought briefly to discuss an alternative public agenda that could, if not challenged, dominate the public policy discussion of underclass poverty in the next several years.

A Critical Look at an Alternative Agenda: New-Style Workfare

In a recent book on the social obligations of citizenship, Lawrence Mead contends that "the challenge to welfare statesmanship is not so much to change the extent of benefits as to couple them with serious work and other obligations that would encourage functioning and thus promote the integration of recipients." He argues that the programs of the Great Society failed to overcome poverty and, in effect, increased dependency because the "behavioral problems of the poor" were ig-nored. Welfare clients received new services and benefits but were not told "with any authority that they ought to behave differently." Mead attributes a good deal of the welfare dependency to a sociological logic ascribing the responsibilities for the difficulties experienced by the dis-advantaged entirely to the social environment, a logic that still "blocks government from expecting or obligating the poor to behave differ-ently than they do."[17]

Mead believes that there is a disinclination among the underclass to either accept or retain many available low-wage jobs. The problem of nonwhite unemployment, he contends, is not a lack of jobs, but a high turnover rate. Mead contends that because this kind of joblessness is not affected by changes in the overall economy, it would be difficult to blame the environment. While not dismissing the role discrimination may play in the low-wage sector, Mead argues that it is more likely that the poor are impatient with the working conditions and pay of menial jobs and repeatedly quit in hopes of finding better employment. At the present time, "for most jobseekers in most areas, jobs of at least a rudimentary kind are generally available." For Mead it is not that the poor do not want to work, but rather that they will work only under the condition that others remove the barriers that make the world of work difficult. "Since much of the burden consists precisely in acquiring skills, finding jobs, arranging child care, and so forth," states Mead, "the effect is to drain work obligation of much of its meaning."[18]

In sum, Mead believes that the programs of the Great Society have exacerbated the situation of the underclass by not obligating the recipients of social welfare programs to behave according to mainstream norms—completing school, working, obeying the law, and so forth. Since virtually nothing was demanded in return for benefits, the underclass remained socially isolated and could not be accepted as equals.

If any of the social policies recommended by conservative analysts are to become serious candidates for adoption as national public policy, they will more likely be based on the kind of argument advanced by Mead in favor of mandatory workfare. The laissez-faire social philosophy represented by Charles Murray is not only too extreme to be seriously considered by most policymakers, but the premise upon which it is based is vulnerable to the kind of criticism raised in chapters 1 and 4, namely, that the greatest rise in black joblessness and female-headed families occurred during the very period (1972–80) when the real value of AFDC plus food stamps plummeted because states did not peg benefit levels to inflation.

Mead's arguments, on the other hand, are much more subtle. If his and similar arguments in support of mandatory workfare are not adopted wholesale as national policy, aspects of his theoretical rationale on the social obligations of citizenship could, as we shall see, help shape a policy agenda involving obligational state programs.

Nonetheless, whereas Mead speculates that jobs are generally available in most areas and therefore one must turn to behavioral explanations for the high jobless rate among the underclass, data presented in chapters 2 and 4 reveal (1) that substantial job losses have occurred in the very industries in which urban minorities are heavily concentrated and substantial employment gains have occurred in the higher-education-requisite industries that have relatively few minority workers; (2) that this mismatch is most severe in the Northeast and Midwest (regions that also have had the sharpest increases in black joblessness and female-headed families); and (3) that the current growth in entry-level jobs, particularly in the service establishments, is occurring almost exclusively outside the central cities where poor minorities are concentrated. It is obvious that these findings and the general observations about the adverse effects of the recent recessions on poor urban minorities (see chap. 2) raise serious questions not only about Mead's assumptions regarding poor minorities, work experience, and jobs, but also about the appropriateness of his policy recommendations.

In raising questions about Mead's emphasis on social values as an explanation of poor minority joblessness, I am not suggesting that negative attitudes toward menial work should be totally dismissed as a contributing factor. The growing social isolation, and the concentration of poverty in the inner city, that have made ghetto communities increasingly vulnerable to fluctuations in the economy, undoubtedly influence attitudes, values, and aspirations. The issue is whether attitudes toward menial employment account in large measure for the sharp rise in inner-city joblessness and related forms of social dislocation since the formation of the Great Society programs. Despite Mead's eloquent arguments the empirical support for his thesis is incredibly weak.[19] It is therefore difficult for me to embrace a theory that sidesteps the complex issues and consequences of changes in American economic organization with the argument that one can address the problems of the ghetto underclass by simply emphasizing the social obligation of citizenship. Nonetheless, there are clear signs that a number of policymakers are now moving in this direction, even liberal policymakers who, while considering the problems of poor minorities from the narrow visions of race relations and the War on Poverty (see chap. 6), have become disillusioned with Great Society–type programs. The emphasis is not necessarily on mandatory workfare, however. Rather the emphasis is on what Richard Nathan has called "new-style workfare," which represents a synthesis of liberal and conservative approaches to obligational state programs.[20] Let me briefly elaborate.

In the 1970s the term *workfare* was narrowly used to capture the idea that welfare recipients should be required to work, even to do make-work if necessary, in exchange for receiving benefits. This idea was generally rejected by liberals and those in the welfare establishment. And no workfare program, even Gov. Ronald Reagan's 1971 program, really got off the ground. However, by 1981 Pres. Ronald Reagan was able to get congressional approval to include a provision in the 1981 budget allowing states to experiment with new employment approaches to welfare reform. These approaches represent the "new-style workfare." More specifically, whereas workfare in the 1970s was narrowly construed as "working off" one's welfare grant, the new-style workfare "takes the form of obligational state programs that involve an array of employment and training services and activities—job search, job training, education programs, and also community work experience."[21]

According to Nathan, "we make our greatest progress on social reform in the United States when liberals and conservatives find common ground. New-style workfare embodies both the caring
commitment of liberals and the themes identified with conservative
writers like Charles Murray, George Gilder, and Lawrence Mead." On
the one hand, liberals can relate to new-style workfare because it creates short-term entry-level positions very similar to the "CETA public
service jobs we thought we had abolished in 1981"; it provides a convenient "political rationale and support for increased funding for education and training programs"; and it targets these programs at the most
disadvantaged, thereby correcting the problem of "creaming" that is
associated with other employment and training programs. On the
other hand, conservatives can relate to new-style workfare because "it
involves a strong commitment to reducing welfare dependency on the
premise that dependency is bad for people, that it undermines their
motivation to self-support and isolates and stigmatizes welfare recipients in a way that over a long period feeds into and accentuates the
underclass mind set and condition."[22]

The combining of liberal and conservative approaches does not, of
course, change the fact that the new-style workfare programs hardly
represent a fundamental shift from the traditional approaches to poverty in America. Once again the focus is exclusively on individual characteristics—whether they are construed in terms of lack of training,
skills, or education, or whether they are seen in terms of lack of motivation or other subjective traits. And once again the consequences of
certain economic arrangements on disadvantaged populations in the
United States are not considered in the formulation and implementation of social policy. Although new-style workfare is better than having
no strategy at all to enhance employment experiences, it should
be emphasized that the effectiveness of such programs ultimately depends upon the availability of jobs in a given area. Perhaps Robert D.
Reischauer put it best when he stated that: "As long as the unemployment rate remains high in many regions of the country, members of
the underclass are going to have a very difficult time competing successfully for the jobs that are available. No amount of remedial education, training, wage subsidy, or other embellishment will make them
more attractive to prospective employers than experienced unemployed workers."[23] As Reischauer also appropriately emphasizes, with
a weak economy "even if the workfare program seems to be placing its
clients successfully, these participants may simply be taking jobs away
from others who are nearly as disadvantaged. A game of musical under-

class will ensue as one group is temporarily helped, while another is pushed down into the underclass."[24]

If new-style workfare will indeed represent a major policy thrust in the immediate future, I see little prospect for substantially alleviating inequality among poor minorities if such a workfare program is not part of a more comprehensive program of economic and social reform that recognizes the dynamic interplay between societal organization and the behavior and life chances of individuals and groups—a program, in other words, that is designed to both enhance human capital traits of poor minorities and open up the opportunity structure in the broader society and economy to facilitate social mobility. The combination of economic and social welfare policies discussed in the previous section represents, from my point of view, such a program.

Conclusion

In this chapter I have argued that the problems of the ghetto underclass can be most meaningfully addressed by a comprehensive program that combines employment policies with social welfare policies and that features universal as opposed to race- or group-specific strategies. On the one hand, this program highlights macroeconomic policy to generate a tight labor market and economic growth; fiscal and monetary policy not only to stimulate noninflationary growth, but also to increase the competitiveness of American goods on both the domestic and international markets; and a national labor-market strategy to make the labor force more adaptable to changing economic opportunities. On the other hand, this program highlights a child support assurance program, a family allowance program, and a child care strategy.

I emphasized that although this program also would include targeted strategies—both means tested and race-specific—they would be considered secondary to the universal program so that the latter are seen as the most visible and dominant aspects in the eyes of the general public. To the extent that the universal programs draw support from a wider population, the less visible targeted programs would be indirectly supported and protected. To repeat, the hidden agenda for liberal policymakers is to enhance the chances in life for the ghetto underclass by emphasizing programs to which the more advantaged groups of all class and racial backgrounds can positively relate.

Before such programs can be seriously considered, however, cost has to be addressed. The cost of programs to expand social and economic opportunity will be great, but it must be weighed against the economic and social costs of a do-nothing policy. As Levitan and Johnson have pointed out, "the most recent recession cost the nation an estimated $300 billion in lost income and production, and direct outlays for unemployment compensation totaled $30 billion in a single year. A policy that ignores the losses associated with slack labor markets and forced idleness inevitably will underinvest in the nation's labor force and future economic growth." Furthermore, the problem of annual budget deficits of around $200 billion dollars (driven mainly by the peacetime military buildup and the Reagan administration's tax cuts), and the need for restoring the federal tax base and adopting a more balanced set of budget priorities have to be tackled if we are to achieve significant progress on expanding opportunities.[25]

In the final analysis, the pursuit of economic and social reform ultimately involves the question of political strategy. As the history of social provision so clearly demonstrates, universalistic political alliances, cemented by policies that provide benefits directly to wide segments of the population, are needed to work successfully for major reform.[26] The recognition among minority leaders and liberal policymakers of the need to expand the War on Poverty and race relations visions to confront the growing problems of inner-city social dislocations will provide, I believe, an important first step toward creating such an alliance.

Appendix

Urban Poverty: A State-of-the-Art Review of the Literature

with Robert Aponte

Before the Civil War, poverty was not widely recognized as a social problem in the United States. The prevalent attitude was that personal misfortunes were personal affairs, that poverty was an individual problem that neither could nor should be alleviated by society. Thus, people unable to make it in the East were advised to go West; the general feeling was that individuals had only themselves to blame if they were mired in poverty. In a largely rural society provided with an abundance of vacant fertile land, this view could be developed and sustained. However, the dislocations that accompanied industrialization in the post–Civil War period prompted changes in this attitude. In the face of massive unemployment, poor working conditions, inadequate wages, and inferior housing, preindustrial conceptions of poverty eroded and efforts to combat these problems evolved into major social reforms. They included the regulation of working hours, working conditions, and child employment. Laws concerned with public health and housing were passed. By the turn of the century, social reform was a dominant theme in the fight against poverty.[1]

A number of early descriptive studies of urban poverty emanated from this social reform movement. Most notable were Jacob Riis's vivid description of life in the tenements of New York, and Jane Addams's and Sophonisba Breckinridge's works on poverty and housing in Chicago.[2] Although these studies detailed the deleterious conditions of urban poverty, they provided little in the way of analytical insights on the relationship between poverty and the social organization of an industrializing society. However, appearing at roughly the same time as these fact-finding social reform inquiries were a series of ethnographic studies on urban life conducted by sociologists at the University of Chicago. In 1918, W. I. Thomas collaborated with Florian Znaniecki in writing the first volume of a classic five-volume work, *The Polish Peasant*.[3] This work, plus the research of Robert E. Park on human behavior in an urban environment, helped establish Chicago as the main center of urban sociological research in the earlier twentieth century.[4]

Much of this research focused on urban poverty and related problems.[5] Although many of the Chicago studies incorporated data collected by the social reformers, their discussions of urban poverty were informed by sociological insights into the nature and processes of urban life in a changing industrial society.[6]

However, the early interest in urban poverty research was not sustained, despite the heightened public awareness of poverty generated by the depression of the 1930s and the nationwide discussion and debate concerning the New Deal antipoverty programs (e.g., Aid to Dependent Children, unemployment compensation, Social Security, and old-age assistance). By the late 1930s, scholarly research on urban poverty and social dislocation was on the wane. Ironically, "the Depression had the effect of arresting some of the questions that had given urban ethnography its impetus," argued Gerald Suttles. "Contemporary poverty and social disorder, and the reason for them, were so obviously social in origin that there was little mystery that would incline ethnographers to go into our cities as if they were almost foreign lands. Ethnography became mostly something done by anthropologists, and that mostly in genuinely foreign and obscure places."[7] Furthermore, in the 1930s urban ethnographic studies began to compete with, and in the 1940s eventually gave way to, studies that employed more sophisticated techniques of data gathering and analysis. In short, the decline of urban ethnography amounted to a decline in the study of urban poverty. But there were other factors involved in the shift away from poverty studies. The onset of World War II created interest in issues other than poverty, and the generally prosperous decade of the 1950s was hardly a stimulus to social scientists and policymakers to recognize and address the problems of a growing concentration of citizens in our nation's central-city slums and ghettos.

Rediscovery of Poverty

If interest in the fate of the poor declined following World War II, in the late 1950s and early 1960s there was notable political activity on behalf of disadvantaged groups, even though the issue of poverty was not explicitly raised. Following the 1954 Supreme Court decision on school segregation, Pres. Dwight D. Eisenhower sent national guardsmen into Little Rock, Arkansas, in 1957 to force compliance with that decision, and the United States Congress passed the first civil rights law in eighty years. In 1959 the Kerrs-Mills Act increased funds for health care for the aged; in 1961 Pres. John F. Kennedy approved a pilot food stamp program and expanded and liberalized the surplus commodity program; and in 1962 Congress passed the Manpower Development and Training Act and soon broadened its coverage to include the disadvantaged.[8]

By 1963 poverty began to receive explicit attention in the New Frontier administration of John F. Kennedy with the recognition that "public receptiveness to the issues of poverty amid plenty could provide a rallying point for the coming election of 1964." In May 1963, Walter Heller, chairman of President Kennedy's Council of Economic Advisors, wrote a memorandum to the president concluding that certain large segments of the poor (families headed by women, the aged, and the disabled) would remain poor even if full employment in the economy were reached. In response to this memorandum President Kennedy instructed his executive agency heads to develop a case for a major policy effort to confront poverty. That fall he requested that antipoverty proposals be included in the legislative program of 1964.[9]

After the assassination of President Kennedy in late 1963, the interest in poverty at the federal level was sustained by Lyndon Baines Johnson. His 1964 economic report included a detailed statement on poverty in the United States and a number of proposals for attacking poverty. The report was followed by the creation of an independent agency within the House of Representatives to draft a bill consistent with the ideas expressed in the economic report. In 1964 the War on Poverty was officially approved by Congress, with emphasis on job-training programs, and community participation and development.[10]

This rediscovery of poverty by officials at the federal level and the emergence of the Great Society programs occurred, paradoxically, during an era of general prosperity and economic growth. Following the publication of John Kenneth Galbraith's classic study, *The Affluent Society,* generally acknowledged as providing the initial impetus to the revival of interest in poverty, came Michael Harrington's celebrated work, *The Other America.*[11] It was Harrington's passionate portrayal of poverty in America that actually launched the poverty program prominently into the public consciousness. Stimulated by Galbraith's study, Harrington argued that at least 40 million, or a fifth of the population, were poor; that much of this population was invisible partly because it included large numbers of children and the elderly (groups unlikely to stray far from home) as well as nonwhites (who were becoming increasingly isolated in urban ghettos); that motivational deficiencies (e.g., fatalistic attitudes) resulting from prolonged poverty were impeding the economic advancement of the poor; and, therefore, that poverty had become a vicious cycle for millions of Americans.

According to Dorothy Buchton James, the studies by Galbraith and Harrington spurred Kennedy's administration to formulate proposals to combat the problems of poverty in America.[12] J. L. Sundquist, an administration insider, suggests that these works helped the Kennedy team to see poverty as underlying a number of other social ills (e.g., juvenile delinquency, illiteracy, urban blight) that were being unsuccessfully addressed by government programs at that time. However, it would be a mistake to assume that the emergence of the Great Society was due solely to thoughtful studies of the American poor. Sundquist is careful to note that during the early 1960s the timing and intellectual climate were right for new ideas and new approaches to the study of poverty and related social problems.[13] In the 1960s the high level of confidence in social science theorizing and empirical research resulted in an unprecedented incorporation of the ideas of social scientists in the federal antipoverty thrust.[14]

Even more significantly, as pointed out in chapter 6, a budget surplus existed in the early 1960s and economists then predicted, in the face of widespread optimism about economic growth, that it would rise steadily throughout the latter part of the decade. Indeed, federal revenues were increasing so rapidly that many economists (not anticipating the Vietnam War buildup) were fearful that the growing tax surplus would ultimately slow economic growth if new expenditures could not be generated to reduce the surplus.[15] Finally, as Friedman and Aaron have argued, the great power of the presidency, at a peak under the early Johnson administration, was also an important element in the federal antipoverty initiatives.[16] According to Aaron, the combination of the death of Johnson's predecessor and the weakness of his opponent "led to the electoral landslide of 1964. The nature and quantity of legislation dealing with poverty . . . that followed were determined in no small measure by the political adroitness of the new president."[17]

The foregoing arguments collectively represent the "conventional view" on the rediscovery of poverty and the emergence of the Great Society programs. Little attention was given to the importance of the civil rights movement and the heightened public awareness of poverty and related problems in the inner city. Moynihan, Sundquist, Yarmolinsky, and Levine argue that although there was some discussion of the problems of black poverty, the focus of attention shortly before and immediately after the assassination of Pres. John F. Kennedy was disproportionately on white Appalachian poverty.[18]

However, several other writers, representing divergent views and philosophies, attribute greater significance to issues of race in the development of the War on Poverty.[19] Nathan Glazer, for example, ar-

gues forcefully that "the race problem" was "the chief reason why poverty has become a major issue in this country. . . . It is true that the
statistics show that only one-quarter of the poor . . . are Negroes. But
this . . . is in part a statistical artifact. The poorest, as defined by the
public assistance rolls, are in much larger proportion Negro, Mexican
American, and Puerto Rican. It is the civil rights revolution that makes
poverty a great issue in America, not merely poverty."[20] Furthermore,
Levitan suggests that "the civil rights movement, which had become a
potent power by 1963, could have supplied the political pressure for a
program in aid of the poor."[21] Moreover, Raab notes that even before
the antipoverty legislation was passed in 1964 there were discussions
with city representatives on the central involvement of racial and ethnic communities.[22] Finally, Piven and Cloward, in their elaborate and
controversial thesis, argue that the federal antipoverty program was an
attempt to foster the political allegiance of ghetto residents.[23]

The preceding arguments reveal the complexity of the events leading to the rediscovery of poverty and the emergence of the Great Society programs. Until a definitive social history of these developments is
established, perhaps the most judicious approach is to consider the
merits of all of these arguments as background information for understanding the nature and direction of the proliferation of urban poverty
research since the mid-1960s.

The Resurgence of Poverty Research

As we indicated in a previous section, virtually no poverty research was
undertaken in the scholarly community during the post–Warld War II
period. Indeed, the dearth of research was so pronounced that in the
early months of the Johnson administration a task force assembled to
study the problem of poverty in America began "almost from scratch"
and had to rely upon a bibliography running "less than two pages."[24]
So little research had been conducted that "when the poverty issue
arose," states Bell, "nobody was really prepared, nobody had any data,
nobody knew what to do."[25]

Yet after the issue of poverty reached the public consciousness and
especially after the campaign against poverty was launched by the
federal government, research mushroomed dramatically. A turning
point seems to be 1965. Prior to that year, only a handful of publications on poverty were available, many were government documents,[26]
and most were post-1960 products. But after 1965, an explosion of research occurred. For example, a study by Kerbo revealed that the

number of articles on poverty published annually in five prestigious sociology journals increased from three in 1965 to an average of ten a year in the early 1970s.[27] In 1966 *Poverty and Human Resources Abstract,* a journal devoted to studies of poverty, was created (the word *poverty* was dropped from the title in 1975 at a time of declining interest in poverty). Conferences with a poverty theme proliferated throughout the late 1960s and generated numerous publications.[28] Issues of intense interest and contention at that time include the controversy over the "culture-of-poverty" thesis,[29] and the debate over the disintegration of the black family.[30] Research on how poverty related to education, health, housing, the law, and public welfare was also vigorously pursued. Moreover, a substantial number of studies were published on the research, development, and evaluation of federal antipoverty initiatives.[31] Indeed, a comprehensive bibliography of poverty studies centered on the 1960s filled well over five-hundred printed pages, and most of the entries were published toward the latter years of the decade.[32]

Defining and Measuring Poverty

The resurgence of scholarly interest in poverty in America is also reflected in the increased attention to problems of definition and adequate measurement of the concept *poverty*. The official poverty line, formulated in 1964 by the Social Security Administration, was drawn by combining a set of rock-bottom food allowances (i.e., cheapest cost of feeding a given family yearly) with estimated proportions of yearly family income directed to food purchasing. Except for a few modifications, such as pegging changes in the poverty schedules to general inflation, the official poverty line has remained fundamentally as originally formulated. Despite its widespread use, the official poverty statistic has come under heavy criticism in the literature. The most-often-cited criticism is that in-kind government transfers are not considered income in computing the poverty line. A recent government publication, produced specifically to address this issue, indicates that the inclusion of in-kind income reduces the official 1982 poverty figure, at most, by about one-third (from 34.4 million to 22.9 million persons).[33] Yet even this figure could be substantially reduced if adjusted for underreporting of income.

However, other critics suggest that the official poverty statistic understates the problem. Some writers argue that an "absolute" poverty line (i.e., changing only with inflation) is fundamentally inappropriate because even though the poverty schedules rise with inflation, they remain fixed in constant dollars. In times of economic growth, this neglects the rising real incomes of the nonpoor, thereby allowing for a greater gap between the standard of living of the poor and the nonpoor.[34] Other writers maintain that the poverty schedules are far too stringent to be taken seriously. They remind us that the poverty thresholds were initially based on an "economy" food budget deemed sufficient to maintain individuals only through "temporary" or "emergency" times.[35] Rodgers points out that the 1975 poverty line for a nonfarm family of four was drawn at $5,500. That same year the Bureau of Labor Statistics, which also generates yearly series on the costs of living, found that a "moderate" life-style for a nonfarm family of four would require $15,138, whereas an "austere" standard of living called for as much as $8,588.[36] As Schiller succinctly put it: "The line we have drawn separating the poor from the nonpoor does not indicate what is enough—it only asserts with confidence what is too little."[37]

It could be argued that the two most recognized shortcomings of the poverty figures, the omission of in-kind income and the stringency of the income cutoffs, counteract one another. Few analysts take both problems into account when adjusting the poverty figure. Generally, only the omission of in-kind income is adjusted for. However, a recent government study to assess the impact of in-kind transfers on poverty contains statistics for 1979 to 1983 that allow the consideration of both problems simultaneously. This study demonstrates that raising the income cutoffs by 25 percent and adjusting for the impact of in-kind income by the method of estimation most favorable to poverty reduction—the "market value" approach which assigns the highest values to in-kind transfers—would result in only a slight decrease in the poverty figures for 1979 and 1980, and an actual *increase* of 5 percent and 4.5 percent in 1981 and 1982 respectively.[38] Thus, on balance, it appears that the extent of poverty is not exaggerated by the official poverty formula. Furthermore, in spite of its flaws, the formula yields an accurate account of gross trends over time; retains the strengths of wide recognition, public access, and extensive use; and provides a rich array of detailed series such as poverty trends by race, residence, and family type.

The Urbanization of Poverty

On the basis of the official definition of poverty, the number of poor persons in the United States decreased from 39.5 million in 1959 to 25.4 million in 1968, a reduction of 36 percent. During this same period the proportion of persons living in poverty dropped from 22 percent in 1959 to 12.8 percent in 1968, that is, by nearly half. Because the total population in the United States steadily increased during these nine years, the absolute decrease in the *number* of those in poverty produced an even greater decline in the *proportion* of poor persons.[39]

In metropolitan areas the number of poor persons dropped by 24 percent, from 17 million in 1959 to 12.9 million in 1968. Moreover, the proportion of individuals below the poverty level decreased from 15.3 percent in 1959 to 10 percent in 1968 (or by 35 percent). Record levels of economic prosperity in the 1960s, combined with a number of public policies to combat poverty, effectively reduced the number of poor persons both in and outside of metropolitan areas.

However, the sharp decline in both the absolute number and the relative proportion of the poor did not extend beyond the 1960s. Indeed the number and proportion of poor people actually increased respectively from 24.1 million (12.1 percent) in 1969 to 34.4 million (15 percent) in 1982. Nonetheless, changes in the incidence of poverty have been conspicuously uneven when metropolitan areas are compared with nonmetropolitan areas. The number and proportion of poor people in nonmetropolitan areas continued to decline from 1969 to 1979—from 11 million (17.9 percent) in 1969 to 9.9 million (13.8 percent) in 1979—but increased to 13.2 million (17.8 percent) by 1982. In contrast, the number of poor people in metropolitan areas increased steadily from 13.1 million in 1969 to 21.2 million in 1982 (a 62 percent increase), and the proportion of persons in poverty rose from 9.5 percent to 13.6 percent (a 43 percent gain), with a substantial part of this increase occuring between 1979 and 1982.

The central cities accounted for most of the metropolitan increase in poverty. The number of central-city poor climbed from 8 million in 1969 to 12.7 million in 1982 (or by 59 percent) while the proportion in poverty increased from 12.7 million to 19.9 million (or by 57 percent). Accordingly, to say that poverty has become increasingly urbanized is to note a *remarkable change in the concentration of poor people in the United States in only slightly more than a decade.* During this period poverty rose among both urban blacks and whites. Specifically, while the number of poor central-city blacks increased by 74 percent (from 3.1 million in 1969 to 5.4 million in 1982), the number of poor central-city whites increased by 42 percent (from 4.8 million to 6.8 million). And while the proportion of central-city blacks in poverty increased by 52 percent (from 24.3 million to 36.9 million), the proportion of poor central-city whites increased by 49 percent (from 9.7 million to 14.5 million).[40]

However, these figures do not reveal some fundamental transformations in the makeup and characteristics of the urban poverty population, transformations that have been the subject of a number of research studies, including those that detected the beginnings of a qualitative shift in urban poverty in the mid-1960s.

Urban Poverty and the Structure of the Family

Although the official poverty figures show that whites constitute a majority of the poor population, even in urban areas, as has been shown in previous chapters, many of the social dislocations related to poverty (e.g., crime, out-of-wedlock births, female-headed families, and welfare dependency) reflect a sharply uneven distribution by race. This is most clearly revealed in the studies on the changing relationship between urban poverty and family structure.

The subject of urban poverty and family structure became a topic of widespread discussion and debate following the release of Daniel Patrick Moynihan's report on the Negro family. Moynihan argued that "the Negro community is dividing between a stable middle-class group that is steadily growing stronger and more successful and an increasingly disorganized and disadvantaged lower-class group." He stressed that the disintegration of the black family—as seen in the increasing rates of marital dissolution, female-headed homes, out-of-wedlock births, and welfare dependency among urban blacks—was one of the central problems plaguing the black lower class. And he argued that the problems of the lower-class black family, which seriously impeded the black movement toward equality, stemmed from previous patterns of racial oppression that began with slavery and were sustained by years of discrimination. Moynihan concluded his report by recommending a shift in the focus of civil rights activities to "bring the Negro American to full and equal sharing in the responsibilities and rewards of citizenship" and thereby to increase the "stability and resources of the Negro American family."[41] Although the report integrated familiar themes,[42] it nonetheless drew fire from many outraged parties.[43] However, aside from some problems in historical accounting,[44] Moynihan's analysis, as clearly shown in previous chapters, proved to be prophetic.

Although serious scholarship on these sensitive issues was temporarily curtailed during the aftermath of the controversy over the Moynihan report, a number of studies have addressed issues that relate either directly or indirectly to the report. In the late 1960s and early 1970s the focus of attention was on family life-style,[45] the question of a matriarchal subculture among blacks,[46] and the effects of absent fathers on the well-being of offspring.[47] A recurrent theme in this literature is that the disorganization of urban black families in poverty is not a function of any inherent matriarchal tendency, but a rational, adaptational response to conditions of deprivation.[48]

The most recent studies on black female-headed families are largely unconcerned with questions about black matriarchy or adaptation. Rather, they give more attention to the strong association between female-headed families and poverty;[49] to the effects of family disorganization on children;[50] to demographic and socioeconomic factors that are correlated with different single-parent statuses—separated, divorced, and never married;[51] to empirical variables (rates of contraception, frequency of premarital sex, indexes of deprivation, etc.) that predict different rates of illegitimacy among different groups;[52] and to the connection between the economic status of black men and the rise in the number of black female-headed families.[53]

In short, this collection of studies has shown that female-headed families are heavily represented in the poverty population, are highly urbanized, and are disproportionately black; that black female heads are much less likely to marry if single, or to remarry if divorced or widowed, and therefore that female-headed families among whites tend to be of relatively short duration, whereas among blacks they tend to be prolonged; that teenage pregnancies are strongly associated with being reared in female-headed families, poverty, and ghetto residence; that black children are increasingly growing up in families without fathers not only because more black women are getting divorced, separated, or are becoming widows, but also because more black women are not marrying; and that the increasing joblessness of black men is one of the major reasons black women tend not to be married. This research strongly suggests that the urban core has spawned a sizable and growing black underclass of marginally productive and unattached men, and of women and children in female-headed homes. How well this view is upheld by the recent longitudinal survey research is a subject to which we now turn.

The Underclass, Intergenerational Transmission of Poverty, and Persistent Poverty

Although poverty and socioeconomic mobility had been discussed in a number of earlier studies,[54] the problems of intergenerational and persistent poverty did not receive detailed empirical and systematic attention until it became possible to track the actual experiences of poor individuals over time with adequate longitudinal data such as that provided by the Michigan Panel Study of Income Dynamics (PSID). Using data from the PSID for the years 1968 to 1976, Levy examined the poverty status, receipt of welfare, and labor-market characteristics of young adults who had been teenagers living at home at the outset of the survey, but who had formed independent households by the last year of the survey. Levy found only weak support for the arguments that poverty and welfare dependency were transmitted across generations. Only three of every ten young adults reared in poverty homes, compared to one of ten reared in nonpoverty homes, set up poverty households on their own; even using the "worst-case" background situation (being black and reared in a low-income, welfare-supported, female-headed household), the probability of a young woman forming her own welfare-dependent household was only about one in three.[55]

The issues of intergenerational transmission of poverty and welfare were also explored, using a fourteen-year segment of the Michigan PSID, by Hill and Ponza. Drawing from a sample of offspring who were living with panel families in 1968 but who had formed their own households by 1981, these authors found "a great deal of income mobility from one generation to the next, even among the poorest households." Although there is an association between the economic circumstances of the parents and those of the children, Hill and Ponza report that there is only a very limited form of intergenerational transmission of long-term welfare dependency among whites and none among blacks, and that "parental attitudes and values had little effect on children's later economic outcomes and welfare dependence."[56]

However, McLanahan, who used ten years of data from the PSID to examine the relationship between family structure and the reproduction of persistent poverty, reinforced the intergenerational-transmission-of-poverty thesis by finding that regardless of parents' race, education, or place of residence, children who lived in female-headed households were significantly more likely to have dropped out of high school than those who lived in husband-wife households. The major reason for this relationship was not the long-term absence of a male role model, but the income differences that exist between female-headed and married-couple families.[57]

Perhaps the most surprising findings from the research based on the PSID data are those involving the issue of persistent poverty. One essential conclusion of this work is that a considerably smaller proportion of Americans in poverty are persistently poor, year in and year out, than the poverty statistics imply. For example, using the official definition of poverty, Coe found only 1 percent and Hill only 3 percent of the population to be poor throughout the time span (nine and ten years, respectively) of their studies;[58] Corcoran, Duncan, and Gurin found only 2.2 percent of the population to be poor eight of the ten years (1968–78) that covered their PSID time span. Moreover, their findings indicate that although 62 percent of the persistently poor are black and 61 percent are members of female-headed households, the proportion of the persistently poor residing in large cities is substantially smaller than the proportion of those living in rural areas or small towns.[59]

If students of poverty question whether or not these findings really reflect the depths of the problems of persistent poverty in urban America, they are provided with powerful ammunition from two PSID studies by Bane and Ellwood. These authors point out that other studies using PSID data to determine the length of time that people are in poverty or on welfare normally observe the poor or welfare recipients over a fixed time frame—say, eight or ten years—and then ascertain what proportion was poor or on welfare for a specific period (one, two, five, or ten years) during this time frame. However, they emphasize that this approach fails to take account of the fact that some individuals who appear to have short spells of poverty or welfare dependency are actually *beginning or ending long spells.* Thus, describing them as having short spells of poverty or welfare dependency can lead both to underestimations of the average length of their spells and to inaccurate descriptions of the characteristics of those who are experiencing either short-term or long-term spells.[60]

By estimating the duration of spells from ten years of PSID data with a special methodology (that identifies spells of poverty or welfare, calculates exit probabilities by year, and uses these probabilities "to generate distributions of spell length for new spells, and for completed and uncompleted spells observed at a point in time"), Bane and Ellwood found that although most people who become poor at some point in their lives endure poverty for only one or two years, *a substantial subpopulation remains poor for a very long time.* Indeed, their findings indicate that at any given point in time, these long-term poor represent about 60 percent of the poverty population and are in the midst of a poverty spell that will last at least eight years. These conclusions are similar to those reported in their study of "welfare spells." This latter study reveals that even though most AFDC mothers experience brief spells of welfare dependency, "the bulk of person-years of AFDC receipt and the bulk of the AFDC expenditures are accounted for by women who have spells of eight years or more."[61] These long-term welfare mothers tend to be nonwhites, unwed, and high school dropouts.

Thus, despite the optimistic findings that characterize some of the reports based on the PSID data,[62] there is still a firm basis for accepting the notion that a ghetto underclass has emerged and embodies the problems of long-term poverty and welfare dependency.[63]

Urban Poverty and Migration

The relationship between migration and the emergence of an urban underclass has received a good deal of attention in the sociological literature. One of the major questions discussed is the extent to which joblessness and related problems, such as rising welfare expenditures, are associated with in-migration of the poor.[64] Using 1970 census data to test for migration status, receipt of welfare, and official poverty status by family head in six large cities (Chicago, New York, Philadelphia, Washington, D.C., Los Angeles, and Detroit), all with at least a half million blacks, Long provided the first rigorous test of this question. Contrary to conventional wisdom, black families with *nonmigrant* heads had higher welfare participation rates and higher poverty rates than did families with heads originating in the South. On the other hand, the opposite, and expected, relationship was found for white families (i.e., families with heads originating in the South fared less well economically than families with nonmigrant heads).[65]

In a second and more elaborate study on this subject, Long and Heltman utilized measures of income, rather than receipt of welfare and poverty status, as the main dependent variable, and considered the effects of education, labor-force participation, occupation, and extent of unemployment. They found that southern blacks earned more than northern blacks even after controlling for education. Black southern migrants not only had higher labor-force participation rates, but, except for the most recent migrants, had lower unemployment rates as well. The gap between the black migrants and nonmigrants was especially noticeable among the least educated. Long and Heltman suggested that since the "cost" of dropping out of the labor force is minimal at the lowest levels of education, northern-born, uneducated blacks may be more easily induced to pursue other alternatives (e.g., welfare) than to work for minimal pay. On the other hand, the southern black may have a different point of reference—southern wages—and thus may be more willing to take the dead-end jobs usually available to the uneducated. White southern migrants at the lowest educational levels also had higher incomes than comparable northerners. However, overall, white migrants earned slightly less than the nonmigrants.[66]

Although these two studies have not escaped criticism, the criticisms have been mainly technical and methodological in nature and the main finding—blacks migrating north experience greater economic success in terms of employment rates, earnings, and welfare dependency than northern-born blacks—has withstood the scrutiny of critical reviews.[67] Moreover, a study by Ritchey, that analyzes rural-to-urban migration and poverty, reached compatible conclusions, namely, that "urban poverty and the plight of the cities are the consequences of broader structural features of our society—the handicap of age, being a female head of household, or . . . the status ascribed to blacks—and not the product of rural to urban migration."[68]

These studies refer to the relationship between poverty and relatively recent migration. Many present-day problems in the ghetto are partly the result of the heavy black urban migration that occurred throughout most of the first half of this century. As Lieberson has appropriately pointed out, because substantial black migration to the metropolises continued several decades after the early Asian and new European migration ceased, urban blacks, their ranks continually replenished with poor migrants, found it much more difficult to follow the path of both the Asian immigrants and the new Europeans in overcoming the effects of discrimination.[69] Thus, the issue is not whether the migrants have contributed to the growth of the urban ghetto, but whether recent sharp increases in poverty and welfare dependency, associated with the crystallization of a ghetto underclass, can be tied to urban migration. The evidence suggests otherwise. Indeed, recent data amassed by Farley and Allen suggest that black migration to the largest metropolitan areas has substantially declined. Of the fourteen metropolitan areas that have been among the top ten in black population at one time or another in recent census years (1960, 1970, 1980), only two of those in the North (Newark, New Jersey, and Detroit, Michigan) gained blacks through migration between 1970 and 1980, and the gains were proportionately small. The largest gains were experienced by such "boomtown" metro areas as Houston, Atlanta, Los Angeles, and Dallas–Fort Worth. Indeed, their tally of the welfare status of black in-migrants to the North and West reveals that only 8 percent of the pre-1975 black male migrants aged twenty-five to sixty-four reported any public assistance income for 1979. And as little as 3 percent of the post-1975 migrants (compared with 7 percent among nonmigrant males) listed public assistance income.[70]

On the whole then, this research suggests that the big "urban crisis" cities such as Chicago, New York, Philadelphia, Cleveland, and Detroit are now gaining little or no black population via migration. They appear to be losing more poor through out-migration than they are receiving through in-migration, and this may be true for blacks as well as for whites. Moreover, the arriving blacks appear increasingly less likely to be on public assistance.

If black migration to urban areas is generally on the wane, the "new immigrant" migration is on the upswing. As Massey has shown, the new immigrants tend to come from Asia and Latin America, with virtually all the illegal immigration from the latter region. The incidence of poverty is well known to be highest among the Mexican "illegals." Whereas the size and distribution of the illegal immigrant population is not known exactly, it is believed to number between 3 million to 6 million and to follow a pattern of settlement similar to the legal Mexican immigrants. Mostly working-age males, they are generally employed in agricultural production or, when urbanized, in the "secondary labor market" (small-scale enterprises with low wages, irregular employment, and little chance for advancement).[71] However, recent research has shown that despite their image as an overly exploited underclass, "illegals" are increasingly gravitating to urban areas and, in the process, escaping the employer-exploitation burdens more prevalent in agricultural production.[72] The migration process "does not uproot random individuals into totally unfamiliar contexts," states Waldinger, "rather migration is a social process that is mediated by long-standing family, friendship and community ties that facilitate moving and ease the migrants integration into the new environment." In short, legal and illegal immigration from Mexico tends to occur by way of a "chain" migration largely insuring a process that "operates swiftly and effectively, often netting the migrants a job shortly after arrival."[73] Nonetheless, exploitation and poverty can accompany migrants even into urban areas. One report, cited by Waldinger, showed that around one-third of the 826 employed illegals surveyed in Los Angeles were underpaid. Moreover, illegals tend to find employment in the secondary labor market where their prospects for advancement are slim.[74]

The question of urban poverty and the new immigration is also relevant to recent changes in the Asian population. As revealed in data released by the United States Census Bureau, Asians, who constitute less than 2 percent of the nation's population were the fastest-growing American ethnic group in the 1970s. Following the liberalization of the United States immigration policies, immigrants from Taiwan, China, and, especially, Hong Kong have poured into urban areas and upset the social organization of "Chinatowns." Most of these newcomers speak little English and are at a competitive disadvantage in their quest for jobs, housing, and other resources in the broader society. As a result, poverty and overcrowding, problems even before the new immigration, have substantially increased.[75]

That poverty is a severe problem in "Chinatowns" is seen in figures revealing, for example, that recently in San Francisco 27 percent of Chinatown housing was cited as substandard, compared to 10 percent in the city at large; in Boston the infant mortality rate in Chinatown is two-and-one-half times higher than the rate for the city as whole; in New York 43 percent of Chinatown families reported incomes of under $4,000 annually in 1969, compared with only 21 percent reported for the city as a whole.[76] Gang activity has also sharply increased in the Chinatowns of the large metropolises.[77] Indeed, once homogeneous and stable, Chinatowns are now suffering from problems that have plagued inner-city black neighborhoods, such as joblessness, violent street crimes, gang warfare, school dropouts, and overcrowding. Although there is no systematic research to show the extent to which the new immigrant contributes to these problems, it would appear to be a substantial factor.[78] The core area of San Francisco's Chinatown, for example, by the late 1970s consisted mainly of immigrants and was the most densely populated area in Chinatown.[79]

Urban Poverty and Structural Changes in the Economy

The relationship between migration and urban poverty is ultimately shaped by the state of the economy. The United States has entered a postindustrial revolution characterized by a capital-intensive restructuring of the industrial and manufacturing sector and a phenomenal growth of the service sector. Neither the emerging technical fields nor the traditional heavy industries are likely to be a major source for new jobs. Instead, the expansion of the labor market will take place mainly in the service sector—government, food services, sales, and maintenance.[80] The implications of these changes for urban poverty have not been the subject of a heavy research agenda. However, there are a few important studies that relate these changes to the life chances of economically disadvantaged groups in urban areas.

John Kasarda, in particular, has shown that poor inner-city minorities have been especially vulnerable to the structural transformation occurring in urban metropolises—from centers of production and distribution of physical goods to centers of administration, information exchange, trade, finance, and government services. This process has wiped out millions of wholesale, retail, and manufacturing jobs in the nation's central cities since 1948, a process that has accelerated since 1967. Simultaneously, in urban areas, "postindustrial-society" occupational positions that usually require levels of education and training beyond the reach of poor inner-city residents have significantly increased. Shifts in the urban job structure have accompanied changes in the demographic composition of large central cities from predominantly European white to predominantly black and Hispanic, resulting in a decrease in both the total population of central cities and aggregate person-income levels.[81]

The cumulative effect of these economic and population changes, as Kasarda carefully outlines, has been deeper "ghettoization," solidification of high levels of poverty, mounting institutional problems in the inner city (e.g., poorer municipal services and declining quality of public schools), and an increase in social dislocations (joblessness, crime, female-headed families, teenage pregnancies, and welfare dependency).[82]

The ascendancy of service occupations apparently presents only limited opportunities for the inner-city poor. A recent study by Stanback and Noyelle, identifying "some of the critical dimensions of the change undergone by metropolitan labor markets during the 1970s," reveals that despite the growth of jobs in the service sector, the urban labor market has actually become more polarized—with the poorly paid service workers, laborers, and clericals facing increasingly restricted opportunities for advancement in the face of "the relative dearth of 'middle-layer'" service jobs and the training and education required for well-paying professional, managerial, and technical positions.[83]

Relating the problems of poverty in the inner city to the broader issues of American economic organization, a recent government publication complements several of the points raised by Kasarda. More specifically, this study indicates that many of the newly "dislocated workers" (victims of plant shutdowns, technological displacements, etc.), especially those in the northeastern and north-central industrial regions, will not be reabsorbed in the industrial sector because of the modernization of production, import competition, and changes in consumer demand.[84] For example, it is estimated that the spread of microtechnology alone will result in the loss of 3 million manufacturing jobs by 1990, and increased automation and import competition are expected to decrease automobile manufacturing by 200,000 jobs between 1982 and 1985.[85] It takes little imagination to recognize the relevance of these projections for current and future problems of urban joblessness and poverty.

Theoretical Issues in Studies of Urban Poverty

During the past two decades social scientists have debated the relative importance of culture versus environment (or social situation) in accounting for the experiences and behavior of impoverished urban Americans. The debate was generated in large measure by the work of the anthropologist Oscar Lewis, who coined the concept *culture of poverty*. Relying on participant observation and life-history collections, Lewis described the culture of poverty as "both an adaptation and a reaction of the poor to their marginal position in a class-stratified, highly individuated, capitalistic society."[86] It represents, in other words, efforts to cope with feelings of despair and hopelessness that invariably accompany poor people's realization of the overwhelming odds against their achieving success in terms of the values and goals of mainstream society. The net result is a series of special adaptations to existential circumstances, including a sense of resignation and passivity because of enduring poverty; a present-time orientation because of the pressures of day-to-day survival; feelings of fatalism and powerlessness because of separation from the political process; low aspirations because of lack of opportunity; feelings of inferiority because of the larger society's contempt and aversion for the poor; and creation of female-headed families because of the inability of poor men to be adequate breadwinners.[87] Lewis maintained that basic structural changes in society may alter some of the cultural characteristics of the poor and that, if the poor become involved in an active trade-union movement or become class conscious, "they are no longer part of the culture of poverty although they still may be desperately poor."[88] Lewis's conceptions were expanded by a number of social scientists,[89] and some have used them to suggest that the poor have to be rehabilitated culturally before they can advance in society.[90]

Critics of the culture-of-poverty thesis, especially the later versions proffered by conservative theorists, argued that it places blame on the victim and therefore conceals the social causes of poverty and leads to social policies that focus on changing the attitudes and behavior of the poor rather than on reforming the society. These critics tend to believe that the poor share the aspirations and values of the larger society and that the so-called pathological consequences of poverty will disappear when the poor are provided with decent jobs and other resources that facilitate social mobility.[91] As Herbert Gans has observed, "the arguments between those who think that poverty can best be eliminated by providing jobs and other resources and those who feel that cultural obstacles and psychological deficiencies must be overcome as well is ultimately an argument about social change, about the psychological readiness of people to respond to change, and about the role of culture in change."[92] In other words, the advocates of resources, those who advance a situational view of social change (and of personality), feel that people's behavior and attitudes change when opportunities and situations available to them change.[93] The proponents of the centrality of culture, those who advance a cultural view of social change, maintain that prior values and patterns of behavior determine how people will react to change, and therefore only changes that are congruent with one's culture will be adopted.[94] The acrimonious debate over these issues during the past several years has often resulted in rigid either/or positions;[95] but the truth, as Herbert Gans suggests, probably "lies somewhere in between."[96]

Clearly, the poor are not monolithic. Considerable variations among them suggest that responses to situational changes will vary. The poor range from those who have only periodic experiences with poverty to those who have been poor for several generations; from those who are upwardly mobile to those who are downwardly mobile; from those who embrace middle-class values to those who share working-class values.[97] We are beginning to gather data on these variations (see the discussion of the Michigan PSID research above), and sufficient data exist to demonstrate divergence between behavioral norms and aspirations among the poor.[98] More research is needed on both micro- and macroprocesses to help explain variations and similarities in responses to changing situations not only among the poor, but also between segments of the poor and others in the larger society.

A reasonable hypothesis developed by Gans is that the gap between behavior norms and aspirations among affluent people is narrower than that among poor people. Even if the affluent fail to fulfill occupational aspirations, he argues, they are often able to satisfy other aspirations, such as those for their families. Because the poor have fewer options, and because they lack the economic resources to fulfill their aspirations, they are forced to develop behavioral norms that diverge from mainstream areas of life, even though they still retain many of the aspirations and values of the affluent society. For all these reasons, research on the cultural patterns of the poor should focus on behavioral norms, aspirations, and other values. "The norms must be studied because they indicate how people react to their present existence," states Gans, "but limiting the analysis to them can lead to the assumption that behavior would remain the same under different conditions when there is no reliable evidence, pro or con, to justify such an assumption."[99]

Urban Poverty, Dependency, and Public Policy Research

There is a growing suspicion in many quarters that liberal welfare policies—especially those associated with the Great Society program
(which extended eligibility for income transfer programs, increased
benefit levels, and created new programs such as food stamps and
Medicaid)—have had adverse effects on the norms and aspirations of
large segments of the urban poor in the sense that they now have little
incentive either to work or to create and maintain stable families and
are therefore increasingly dependent on welfare.[100]
    These concerns have helped provide the impetus and direction for a
good deal of public policy research on the extent to which public assistance creates work and family disincentives. A number of studies
have attempted to measure the effects of Aid to Families with Dependent Children (AFDC) on the supply of labor;[101] with the exception of
the study by Masters and Garfinkel,[102] all found that AFDC payments
had small but significant negative effects on labor-force participation.
However, Danziger, Haveman, and Plotnick uncovered a variety of
methodological problems that plague this body of research. These included "reliance on statutory instead of effective tax rates (Garfinkel
and Orr, Levy), poor or missing measures of unearned non-AFDC income (Garfinkel and Orr, Saks, Williams, Masters and Garfinkel), neglect of administrative and/or local labor market variables (all but
Garfinkel and Orr), and poor measures of the dependent variables
(Barr and Hall)."[103]
    There are also difficulties with the research on welfare and family
disincentives. Before the Seattle-Denver Income Maintenance Experiments (SIME-DIME), most researchers and policymakers believed
that a program of welfare that would support both intact and split families would result in fewer marital dissolutions than a program that only
supported split families.[104] However, when early reports on the
SIME-DIME revealed that marital splits were greater in the experimental group (i.e., the group receiving negative income tax payments)
than in the control group,[105] support for extending welfare to intact
families decreased among policymakers.[106] As revealed in the final report of the SIME-DIME, "the NIT increased the proportion of families headed by single females. For blacks and whites, the increase was
due to the increase in dissolution; for Chicanos, the increase was due to
the decrease in the marital formation rate. For all three-ethnic groups,
the net effect is increased welfare costs because the proportion of the
population most likely to depend upon welfare rises."[107] Nonetheless,
a careful review of the original SIME-DIME analysis by Cain ques-

tions the validity of the findings because the effects of experimental training programs were confounded with those of the experimental Negative Income Tax program; the effects on childless couples (who are ineligible for AFDC) were not distinguished from those of couples with children; the possibility that the results were biased by the different attrition between experimentals and controls was incorrectly ruled out; and the experiment focused arbitrarily on couples enrolled for five years and thereby excluded two-thirds of the sample, which were enrolled for only three years.[108]

Additional research examining the effect of income transfers on intact families in natural urban settings or combined urban/rural settings offers mixed results. Honig found a significant positive association between the level of AFDC payments and rates of female family headship for both blacks and whites in forty-four metropolitan areas in 1960, but by 1970 the relationship had diminished and was significant only for blacks.[109] Ross and Sawhill, using cross-sectional 1970 census data for forty-one cities, found small but significant effects of AFDC payment levels (including average food stamp benefits) on the rate of female family headship for nonwhites, but not for whites.[110] In research based on both urban and rural samples, Minarik and Goldfarb found nonsignificant effects of AFDC payment levels on marital instability.[111] However, Hoffman and Holmes found a significant positive effect of AFDC-level payments on marital instability.[112]

Thus, despite popular opinion and theoretical assumptions on the negative impact of public assistance, the studies described above not only fail to provide definitive conclusions on the general association between the level of AFDC payments and the rate of female-headed households, they also yield virtually no information on the extent to which levels of benefits stimulate marital dissolution, discourage remarriage, or deter marriage.

These problems were addressed, however, in a recently completed landmark study on the effects of AFDC on family structure and living arrangements. The authors of this study correctly pointed out that previous nonexperimental studies "included a variety of measured variables to control for state differences. But generally they did little to erase any problems caused by unmeasured differences across states that might be correlated with benefit levels." Using three different methods based on different data sets (Survey of Income and Education, aggregate national data from the census and *Vital Statistics Reports,* aggregate census data by state) to control these unmeasured differences and to provide a "check for consistency across method," Elwood and Bane found that AFDC has virtually no effect on the fertility of unmarried black and white women, only a modest effect on separation and divorce among young married mothers, and a substantial impact on the living arrangements in the sense that it increases the movement of single mothers from subfamilies to their own independent households. In short, "welfare simply does not appear to be the underlying cause in the dramatic changes in family structure of the past few decades."[113]

The results of Ellwood and Bane's research and the inconsistent findings of other studies on the relationship between welfare and family structure and on welfare and illegitimate births seriously undermine claims that changes in welfare policies are at the root of the decreased proportion of intact families and increased proportion of out-of-wedlock births.

Finally, the effects of the Reagan budget cuts (the Omnibus Budget Reconciliation Act of 1981 [OBRA]) on the poor, particularly the working poor, have been the subject of recent research by Joe, Joe et al., and Moscovice and Craig.[114] These studies placed special emphasis on the effects of the AFDC regulatory changes on working women and their children. These changes affected the "tax" on earned income and imposed lower ceilings on the income criteria for AFDC eligibility. One immediate consequence was a punitive effect for working. But the more important consequences were the millions of partially dependent families either completely removed from the welfare rolls or made to sustain severe declines in living standards. For example, Joe estimated that under the OBRA, average disposable income of working AFDC families (including net earnings, benefits, and food stamps) for the nation declined from 101 percent of the poverty line to 81 percent. And average AFDC benefits were reduced from $186 to only $20 monthly.[115] Thus, as Bawden and Palmer appropriately argue, the rise in official poverty between 1979 and 1982 is not simply due to macroeconomic conditions (mild recession of 1980, high inflation, then deep recession), but is also a function of fundamental changes in the federal government's response to conditions of poverty.[116]

Conclusion

There has been an ebb and flow in the study of urban poverty in America. The social reform movement of the early twentieth century, responding to the dislocations that accompanied rapid industrialization, prompted a number of descriptive and muckraking studies on poverty in urban areas. At roughly the same time, sociologists at the

University of Chicago conducted a prodigious volume of research on urban life, including a number of ethnographic studies on poverty that were far more analytical and systematic than those of the social reformers. By the late 1930s, scholarly research on urban poverty was on the wane, only to be revived again in the 1960s following the rediscovery of poverty and the emergence of the Great Society programs.

The subject of urban poverty and the structure of the family has drawn considerable attention from researchers since the mid-1960s and has helped raise the level of national interest in the problems of the inner city and the crystallization of a sizable ghetto underclass. However, with the emergence of longitudinal data sets, many assumptions about the intergenerational transmission of poverty and persistent poverty in the inner city have been challenged. Likewise, research on urban poverty and migration has raised questions and generated new insights on the contribution of the urban migrant to the current problems of inner-city poverty and social dislocations. And several recent studies, possibly representing a trend in urban poverty research, have provided significant insights on the relationship between poverty in the inner city and the broader problems of American economic organization.

The study of urban poverty is not blessed with elaborate and definitive theoretical schemes. Nonetheless, a synthesis of the cultural and situational perspectives reveals a coherent theoretical framework that relates to a good deal of the substantive research, including recent public policy research, on the relationship between poverty and welfare dependency. The results of the public policy research are so mixed, however, that it would be risky to draw policy recommendations from them. On the other hand, the most recent studies on the effects of the OBRA on the working poor are clear and consistent: they reveal the nature of the federal government's dramatic retreat from the Great Society programs of the 1960s.

Notes

Preface

1. Herbert J. Gans, "The Negro Family: Reflections on the Moynihan Report," in *The Moynihan Report and the Politics of Controversy*, ed. Lee Rainwater and William L. Yancey (Cambridge, Mass: MIT Press, 1967), p. 449.

Chapter 1

1. Kenneth B. Clark, *Dark Ghetto: Dilemmas of Social Power* (New York: Harper and Row, 1965); Lee Rainwater, "Crucible of Identity: The Negro Lower-Class Family," *Daedalus* 95 (Winter 1966): 176–216; Daniel P. Moynihan, *The Negro Family: The Case for National Action* (Washington, D.C.: Office of Policy Planning and Research, U.S. Department of Labor, 1965); and idem, "Employment, Income and the Ordeal of the Negro Family," in *The Negro American*, ed. Talcott Parsons and Kenneth B. Clark (Boston: Beacon Press, 1965), pp. 134–59.

2. David L. Lewis, *When Harlem Was in Vogue* (New York: Alfred A. Knopf, 1981); Clark, *Dark Ghetto*; and Thomas Sowell, *Civil Rights: Rhetoric or Reality?* (New York: William Morrow, 1984).

3. See St. Clair Drake and Horace R. Cayton, *Black Metropolis: A Study of Negro Life in a Northern City*, vol. 2 (New York: Harper and Row, 1945).

4. Clark, *Dark Ghetto*, p. 27.

5. Rainwater, "Crucible of Identity," p. 173.

6. Clark, *Dark Ghetto*, p. 81.

7. See, e.g., Roger D. Abrahams, *Deep Down in the Jungle* (Hatboro, Pa.: Folklore Associates, 1964); Clark, *Dark Ghetto*; Rainwater, "Crucible of Identity"; and Elliot Liebow, *Tally's Corner: A Study of Negro Streetcorner Men* (Boston: Little, Brown, 1967).

8. Moynihan, *Negro Family*.

9. Richard McGahey, "Poverty's Voguish Stigma," *New York Times*, March 12, 1982, p. 29. Also see, Michael B. Katz, *In the Shadow of the Poorhouse: A Social History of Welfare in America* (New York: Basic Books, 1986), esp. pp. 274–75.

10. For a discussion of recent conservative analyses of the underclass, see Ken Auletta, *The Underclass* (New York: Random House, 1982).

11. Drake and Cayton, *Black Metropolis*.

12. Moynihan, *Negro Family*. See, e.g., Joyce Ladner, ed., *The Death of White Sociology* (New York: Random House, 1973); Robert B. Hill, *The Strength of Black Families* (New York: Emerson Hall, 1972); Nathan Hare, "The Challenge of a Black Scholar," *Black Scholar* 1 (1969): 58–63; Abdul Hakim Ibn Alkalimat [Gerald McWorter], "The Ideology of Black Social Science," *Black Scholar* 1 (1969): 28–35; and Robert Staples, "The Myth of the Black Matriarchy," *Black Scholar* 2 (1970): 9–16.

13. Clark, *Dark Ghetto*; E. Franklin Frazier, *The Negro Family in the United States* (Chicago: University of Chicago Press, 1939); Moynihan, *Negro Family*; Rainwater, "Crucible of Identity."

14. Orlando Patterson, *Ethnic Chauvinism: The Reactionary Impulse* (New York: Stein and Day, 1977), p. 155. Also see Martin Kilson, "Black Social Classes and Intergenerational Poverty," *Public Interest* 64 (Summer 1981): 58–78.

15. Martha S. Hill, "Some Dynamic Aspects of Poverty," in *Five Thousand American Families: Patterns of Economic Progress*, ed. M. S. Hill, D. H. Hill, and J. N. Morgan, vol. 19 (Ann Arbor: Institute for Social Research, University of Michigan Press, 1981).

16. Mary Corcoran and Greg J. Duncan, "Demographic Aspects of the Underclass," paper presented at the Annual Meeting of the Population Association of American, Pittsburgh, Pa., 1983.

17. See, e.g., Katz, *Shadow of the Poorhouse*.

18. Mary Jo Bane and David T. Ellwood, "Slipping into and out of Poverty: The Dynamics of Spells," working paper no. 1199, National Bureau of Economic Research, Cambridge, Mass., 1983; idem, *The Dynamics of Dependence: The Routes to Self-Sufficiency* (Washington, D.C.: U.S. Department of Health and Human Services, 1983).

19. Bane and Ellwood, *Slipping into and out of Poverty,* p. 36.

20. Kenneth B. Clark, "The Role of Race," *New York Times Magazine*, October 5, 1980, p. 109.

21. Carl Gershman, "Carl Gershman Responds," *New York Times Magazine*, October 5, 1980, p. 33.

22. See William Julius Wilson, *The Declining Significance of Race: Blacks and Changing American Institutions*, 2d ed. (Chicago: University of Chicago Press, 1980).

23. See, e.g., Clark, "Role of Race"; Alphonoso Pinkney, *The Myth of Black Progress* (Boston: Cambridge University Press, 1984); and Charles V. Willie, "The Inclining Significance of Race," *Society* 15 (July/August 1978): 10, 12–15.

24. Michael Harrington, *The New American Poverty* (New York: Holt, Rinehart and Winston, 1984), p. 140.

25. Barry Bluestone and Bennett Harrison, *The Deindustrialization of America: Plant Closings, Community Abandonment, and the Dismantling of Basic Industry* (New York: Basic Books, 1982).

26. Oscar Lewis, "The Culture of Poverty," in *On Understanding Poverty: Perspectives from the Social Sciences*, ed. Daniel Patrick Moynihan (New York: Basic Books, 1968), pp. 187–200. Also see idem, *Five Families: Mexican Case Studies in the Culture of Poverty* (New York: Basic Books, 1959); idem, *The Children of Sanchez* (New York: Random House, 1961); and idem, *La Vida: A Puerto Rican Family in the Culture of Poverty—San Juan and New York* (New York: Random House, 1966).

27. Lewis, "Culture of Poverty," p. 188.

28. Ibid.

29. For a good discussion of these points, see Auletta, *Underclass*, esp. chap. 2.

30. See, e.g., Edward Banfield, *The Unheavenly City*, 2d ed. (Boston: Little, Brown, 1970).

31. For examples of the tone of the more popular and ideological liberal critiques, see Charles A. Valentine, *Culture and Poverty: Critique and Counter Proposals* (Chicago: University of Chicago Press, 1968); and William Ryan, *Blaming the Victim* (New York: Random House, 1971).

32. See Herbert J. Gans, "Culture and Class in the Study of Poverty: An Approach to Anti-Poverty Research," in Moynihan, *On Understanding Poverty*, pp. 201–8; Lee Rainwater, "The Problem of Lower-Class Culture and Poverty-War Strategy," in Moynihan, *Understanding Poverty*, pp. 229–59; Hylan Lewis, "Culture, Class and the Behavior of Low-Income Families," paper prepared for Conference on Views of Lower-Class Culture, New York, N.Y., June 1963; and Stephen Steinberg, *The Ethnic Myth: Race, Ethnicity and Class in America* (New York: Atheneum, 1981). Steinberg's analysis is a succinct restatement of points made by liberal critics in the 1960s.

33. Gans, "Culture and Class"; Rainwater, "Problem of Lower-Class Culture"; Lewis, "Culture, Class and the Behavior of Low-Income Families"; and Steinberg, *Ethnic Myth*.

34. Gans, "Culture and Class," p. 211.

35. See, e.g., Clark, *Dark Ghetto;* Liebow, *Tally's Corner;* Ulf Hannerz, *Soulside: Inquires into Ghetto Culture and Community* (New York: Columbia University Press, 1969); and Lee Rainwater, *Behind Ghetto Walls: Black Families in a Federal Slum* (Chicago: Aldine, 1970).

36. For a discussion of this point, see Stanley Lieberson, *A Piece of the Pie: Black and White Immigrants since 1880* (Berkeley: University of California Press, 1980), chap. 1.

37. For a discussion of this point see William Julius Wilson, "Reflections on the Insiders and Outsiders Controversy," in *Black Sociologists,* ed. James E. Blackwell and Morris Janowitz (Chicago: University of Chicago Press, 1972).

38. James Q. Wilson, *Thinking about Crime* (New York: Basic Books, 1975); George Gilder, *Wealth and Poverty* (New York: Basic Books, 1981); Sowell, *Civil Rights;* Charles Murray, *Losing Ground: American Social Policy, 1950–1980* (New York: Basic Books, 1984).

39. "Losing More Ground," *New York Times,* February 3, 1985, p. 22.

40. See, e.g., Robert Greenstein, "Losing Faith in 'Losing Ground,'" *New*

Republic, March 25, 1985, pp. 12–17; Robert Kuttner, "A Flawed Case for Scrapping What's Left of the Great Society," *Washington Post Book World*, December 17, 1984, pp. 34–35; David Ellwood and Lawrence Summers, "Poverty in America: Is Welfare the Answer or the Problem?" paper presented at a conference on Poverty and Policy: Retrospect and Prospects, Williamsburg, Va., December 6, 1984; Christopher Jencks, "How Poor Are the Poor?" *New York Review of Books*, May 9, 1985, pp. 41–49; and Sheldon Danziger and Peter Gottschalk, "Social Programs—A Partial Solution to, But Not a Cause of Poverty: An Alternative to Charles Murray's View," *Challenge Magazine*, May/June 1985.

41. Danziger and Gottschalk, "Social Programs," p. 36.

42. Greenstein, "Losing Faith," p. 14.

43. Ibid.; Danziger and Gottschalk, "Social Programs"; and Jencks, "How Poor Are the Poor?"

44. Greenstein, "Losing Faith," p. 14.

45. Ibid., p. 15; Danziger and Gottschalk, "Social Programs"; Kuttner, "Flawed Case"; Jencks, "How Poor Are the Poor"; and Ellwood and Summers, "Poverty in America."

Chapter 2

1. For an excellent discussion of the Moynihan report and the controversy surrounding it, see Lee Rainwater and William L. Yancey, eds., *The Moynihan Report and the Politics of Controversy* (Cambridge, Mass.: MIT Press, 1967).

2. E. Franklin Frazier, *The Negro Family in the United States* (Chicago: University of Chicago Press, 1939); Kenneth B. Clark, *Youth in the Ghetto: A Study of the Consequences of Powerlessness and a Blueprint for Change,* Harlem Youth Opportunities (HARYOU) Report, 1964; and Bayard Rustin, "From Protest to Politics: The Future of the Civil Rights Movement," *Commentary* 39 (1965): 25–31.

3. Daniel P. Moynihan, *The Negro Family: The Case for National Action* (Washington, D.C.: Office of Policy Planning and Research, U.S. Department of Labor, 1965), pp. 5–6.

4. Ibid., p. 48.

5. It is interesting to point out that Pres. Lyndon B. Johnson's widely heralded Howard University commencement speech on human rights, which was partly drafted by Moynihan, drew heavily from the Moynihan report when it was still an in-house document. The speech was uniformly praised by black civil rights leaders.

6. U.S. Department of Health and Human Services, National Center for Health Statistics, "Advanced Report of Final Natality Statistics, 1982," *Monthly Vital Statistics Report*, vol. 33, no. 6, suppl. (Washington, D.C.: Government Printing Office, 1984); and U.S. Bureau of the Census, *Current Population Reports*, Series P-20, no. 398, "Household and Family Characteristics, March 1984" (Washington, D.C.: Government Printing Office, 1985).

7. U.S. Department of Justice, *Uniform Crime Reports for the United States, 1984* (Washington, D.C.: Government Printing Office, 1985); and Norval Morris and Michael Tonry, "Blacks, Crime Rates and Prisons—A Profound Challenge," *Chicago Tribune*, August 18, 1980, p. 2.

8. For my discussion of violent crime in Chicago I am indebted to Rick Greenberg, "Murder Victims: Most Blacks, Latinos Now Surpassing Whites," *Chicago Reporter: A Monthly Information Service on Racial Issues in Metropolitan Chicago* 10, no. 1 (January 1981): 1, 4–7.

9. The murder rate represents the number of murders committed per 100,000 population. In 1974 the rate in Chicago was 30.8, in Detroit 51.8, in Cleveland 46.3, in Washington 38.3, and in Baltimore 34.1. See Greenberg, "Murder Victims."

10. Chicago Police Department, *Murder Analysis, 1983* (Chicago: Chicago Police Department, 1984).

11. Chicago Police Department, *Statistical Summary, 1983* (Chicago: Chicago Police Department, 1984).

12. Ibid.

13. Nathaniel Sheppard, Jr., "Chicago Project Dwellers Live under Siege," *New York Times*, August 6, 1980, p. A14.

14. Chicago Housing Authority, *Statistical Report, 1983* (Chicago: Chicago Housing Authority Executive Office, 1984).

15. Sheppard, "Chicago Project Dwellers," p. A14.

16. Chicago Housing Authority, *Statistical Report, 1983*.

17. Paul Galloway, "Nine Weeks, Ten Murders," *Chicago Sun-Times*, March 22, 1981, pp. 66–67.

18. Chicago Housing Authority, *Statistical Report, 1983*.

19. U.S. Bureau of the Census, *Current Population Reports*, Series P-23, no. 107, "Families Maintained by Female Householders, 1970–79" (Washington, D.C.: Government Printing Office, 1980); and idem, "Household and Family Characteristics, March 1984."

20. Ibid.

21. Ibid.

22. U.S. Bureau of the Census, *Current Population Reports*, Series P-60, no. 146, "Money Income of Households, Families, and Individuals in the United States, 1983" (Washington, D.C.: Government Printing Office, 1985).

23. Based on calculations from U.S. Bureau of the Census, *Current Population Reports*, Series P-60, no. 147, "Characteristics of the Population below the Poverty Level, 1983" (Washington, D.C.: Government Printing Office, 1985).

24. Based on calculations from U.S. Bureau of the Census, "Characteristics of the Population below the Poverty Level, 1983"; and idem, *Current Population Reports*, Series P-20, nos. 218, 340, 398, "Household and Family Characteristics, March 1970/1978/1984" (Washington, D.C.: Government Printing Office, 1971, 1979, 1985).

25. U.S. Department of Health and Human Services, National Center for Health Statistics, "Final Natality Statistics, 1982," *Monthly Vital Statistics Re-*

port, vol. 33, no. 6, suppl. (Washington, D.C.: Government Printing Office, 1981).

26. However, despite the sharp increase in out-of-wedlock teenage births, the overall rate of teenage childbearing has been declining in recent years. For example, there were almost 100,000 fewer children born to teenagers in 1983 than there were in 1960. And what is significant is that this decline in the absolute number of births to teenage mothers occurred despite a 33 percent increase in the teenage population from 1960 to 1983. The result was a sharp drop in the nation's teenage birth rate (ages 15 to 19) from 89 per 1,000 in 1960 to 52 per 1,000 in 1983.

Although it is true that the absolute number of births to black teenagers increased by 9 percent (from 133,000 to 142,000) from 1960 to 1983, there were actually 37,000 fewer births to black teenagers in 1983 than there were in 1970. Moreover, the actual black teenage birth rate in 1983 (95.5) was 35 percent less than in 1970 (147.7) and 40 percent less than in 1960 (158.2). The real problem, therefore, is not the rate of teenage childbearing, which is steadily declining, but the proportion of teenage births that are out of wedlock, which has substantially increased.

27. U.S. Department of Health and Human Services, Social Security Administration, Office of Policy, "Aid to Families with Dependent Children, 1977," in *Recipient Characteristics Study* (Washington, D.C.: Government Printing Office, 1980); and *Local Community Fact Book: Chicago Metropolitan Area 1970–1980* (Chicago: Chicago Review Press, 1984).

28. U.S. Department of Health and Human Services, "Aid to Families with Dependent Children."

29. Kristin Moore and Steven B. Caldwell, "Out-of-Wedlock Pregnancy and Childbearing," working paper no. 999-02, Urban Institute, Washington, D.C., 1976.

30. William Julius Wilson, *The Declining Significance of Race: Blacks and Changing American Institutions*, 2d ed. (Chicago: University of Chicago Press, 1980); and idem, "The Black Community in the 1980s: Questions of Race, Class, and Public Policy," *Annals of the American Academy of Political and Social Science* 454 (1981): 26–41.

31. Charles C. Killingsworth, Jr., *Jobs and Income for Negroes* (Ann Arbor: University of Michigan Press, 1963).

32. Alfred Blumstein, "On the Racial Disproportionality of United States' Prison Populations," *Journal of Criminal Law and Criminology* 73, no. 3 (1983): 1259–81, quote on p. 1281.

33. Michael J. Hindelang, "Race and Involvement in Common Law Personal Crimes," *American Sociological Review* 43, no. 1 (February 1978): 93–109; and idem, *Criminal Victimization in Eight American Cities: A Descriptive Analysis of Common Theft and Assault* (Cambridge, Mass.: Ballinger, 1976).

34. Blumstein, "Racial Disproportionality," p. 1278.

35. Herbert Gutman, *The Black Family in Slavery and Freedom, 1750–1925* (New York: Pantheon, 1976), quote on p. xvii.

36. U.S. Bureau of the Census, "Characteristics of the Population below the Poverty Level, 1983."

37. Stanley Lieberson, *A Piece of the Pie: Black and White Immigrants since 1880* (Berkeley: University of California Press, 1980), quotes on pp. 368–69.

38. Some social scientists, attempting to explain the deterioration of the position of urban blacks as their numbers increased, have argued that there was a shift in the "quality" of the migrants. But, as Lieberson points out, "there is evidence to indicate that southern black migrants to the North in recent years have done relatively well when compared with northern-born blacks in terms of welfare, employment rates, earnings after background factors are taken into account, and so on." Ibid., p. 374.

39. Ibid., p. 380.

40. As Philip M. Hauser has noted: "Data from the census indicate that blacks who migrate from nonmetropolitan areas are now going to the metropolitan centers of the South and West rather than to those of the urban North as they had in earlier decades." "The Census of 1980," *Scientific American* 245, no. 5 (1981): 61.

41. U.S. Bureau of the Census, "Social and Economic Characteristics, 1977 and 1970."

42. Hauser, "Census of 1980," p. 61.

43. U.S. Bureau of the Census, *Census of the Population, 1980*, PC 80-1-B1, U.S. Summary (Washington, D.C.: Government Printing Office, 1985).

44. For a good discussion of socioeconomic differences among Hispanics, see Joseph P. Fitzpatrick and Lourdes Traviesco Parker, "Hispanic-Americans in the Eastern United States," *Annals of the American Academy of Political and Social Sciences* 454 (1981): 98–124.

45. Ralph Blumenthal, "Gunmen Firing Wildly Kill Three in Chinatown Bar," *New York Times*, December 24, 1982, pp. 1, 13; Richard Bernstein, "Tension and Gangs Mar the Chinatown Image," *New York Times*, December 24, 1982, p. 13; and Robert Lindsey, "Asian Americans See Growing Bias," *New York Times*, September 10, 1983, pp. 1, 9.

46. Thomas Sowell, *Ethnic America: A History* (New York: Basic Books, 1981).

47. U.S. Bureau of the Census, *Current Population Reports*, Series P-23, no. 37, "Social and Economic Characteristics of the Population in Metropolitan and Nonmetropolitan Areas, 1970 and 1960" (Washington, D.C.: Government Printing Office, 1971).

48. U.S. Bureau of the Census, "Social Economic Characteristics, 1977 and 1970."

49. U.S. Department of Justice, *Uniform Crime Reports, 1984*.

50. Social Security Administration, *Social Security Bulletin*, Annual Statistical Supplement, 1983 (Washington, D.C.: Government Printing Office, 1983); U.S. Bureau of the Census, *Current Population Reports*, Series P-25, no. 965, "Estimates of the Population of the United States by Age, Sex, and Race, 1980 to 1984" (Washington, D.C.: Government Printing Office, 1985).

51. James Q. Wilson, *Thinking about Crime* (New York: Basic Books, 1975), pp. 16, 17.

52. Ibid., p. 17. Also see Arnold Barnett, David J. Kleitman, and Richard C. Larson, "On Urban Homicide," working paper WP-04-74, Operations Research Center, MIT, Cambridge, Mass., 1974; and Theodore Ferdinand, "Reported Index Crime Increases between 1950 and 1965 Due to Urbanization and Changes in the Age Structure of the Population Alone," in *Crimes of Violence*, ed. Donald J. Mulvihail and Melvin Tumin, Staff Report to the National Commission on the Causes and Prevention of Violence, vol. 2 (Washington, D.C.: Government Printing Office, 1969).

53. Wilson, *Thinking about Crime*, pp. 17, 18.

54. Dennis Roncek, Ralph Bell, and Jeffrey M. A. Francik, "Housing Projects and Crime: Testing a Proximity Hypothesis," *Social Problems* 29 (1981): 151.

55. Ibid., p. 152. See also Lee Rainwater, *Behind Ghetto Walls: Black Life in a Federal Slum* (Chicago: Aldine, 1970).

56. Roncek, "Dangerous Places"; and Newman, *Defensible Space* and *Community of Interest*.

57. John D. Kasarda, "Urban Change and Minority Opportunities," in *The New Urban Reality*, ed. Paul E. Peterson (Washington, D.C.: The Brookings Institution, 1985), p. 33. See also idem, "Urbanization, Community, and the Metropolitan Problem," in *Handbook of Contemporary Urban Life*, ed. David Street (San Francisco: Jossey-Bass, 1978), pp. 27–57; and idem, "The Implications of Contemporary Redistribution Trends for National Policy," *Social Science Quarterly* 61 (1980): 373–400.

58. John D. Kasarda, "The Regional and Urban Redistribution of People and Jobs in the U.S.," paper prepared for the National Research Council Committee on National Urban Policy, National Academy of Science, 1986.

59. Ibid., p. 24.

60. Ibid., pp. 26–27.

61. Ibid., p. 31.

62. Ibid., p. 37. For a recent discussion of the disproportionate growth in employment at the lower extreme of the wage-scale distribution, see Barry Bluestone and Bennett Harrison, *The Great American Job Machine: The Proliferation of Low Wage Employment in the U.S. Economy*, a study prepared by the Joint Economic Committee of the U.S. Congress (Washington, D.C.: Government Printing Office, 1986).

63. Brian Becker and Stephen Hills, "Today's Teenage Unemployed—Tomorrow's Working Poor?" *Monthly Labor Review* 102 (1979): 67–71.

64. Frank Levy, "Poverty and Economic Growth," unpublished manuscript, School of Public Affairs, University of Maryland, College Park, Maryland, 1986, quotes on pp. 8, 9, 19, and 20.

65. U.S. Bureau of the Census, *1970 Census of the Population: Low Income Areas in Large Cities* PC (2)-9B (Washington, D.C.: Government Printing Office, 1973); and *1980 Census of the Population: Low Income Areas in Large Cities* PC-2-8D (Washington, D.C.: Government Printing Office, 1985).

66. Richard Nathan, of Princeton University, introduced the concept *extreme-poverty areas* in private communication.

67. About one-fifth of the population in each of the cities of New York, Chicago, Philadelphia, and Detroit was poor in 1980. In Los Angeles about one-sixth of the total population was poor. There are some notable differences in the proportion of people living in poverty areas in these five large central cities, ranging from 29 and 33 percent, respectively, in New York and Los Angeles to 39 percent in Chicago and to 43 and 48 percent respectively in Philadelphia and Detroit. However, the really sharp contrast is in the differences in the proportion of the population living in high- and extreme-poverty areas in Los Angeles, on the one hand, and in these large Northeast and Midwest central cities, on the other hand. In the latter metropolises, roughly one-fourth of the population in each city resided in high-to-extreme poverty areas (at least 30 percent poor), and 13 percent in Philadelphia and 9 percent in Detroit lived in extreme-poverty areas (at least 40 percent poor). In Los Angeles, however, only 14 percent of the population resided in high-poverty areas and only 13 percent lived in extreme-poverty areas. Thus, when one speaks of the growing concentration of poverty in large central cities, these figures suggest that the dimensions of the problem are greater in the larger cities of the Midwest and Northeast than in the West.

68. Sheldon Danziger and Peter Gottschalk, "Earnings Inequality, the Spatial Concentration of Poverty, and the Underclass." Paper presented at the Annual Meeting of the American Economic Association, New Orleans, 1986, p. 5.

69. A *community area* includes a number of adjacent census tracts. Accordingly, it should not be confused with the U.S. Census designation of *poverty area* because the latter refers to only one census tract. Because a number of census tracts are included in a given included poverty area, the upper range of the poverty rates in community poverty areas is lower than that of poverty areas. Also, poverty areas are determined on the basis of the percentage of individuals living below the poverty line, whereas community poverty areas are determined on the basis of the percentage of households with incomes below the poverty level. Nonetheless, in the following discussion I shall continue to use the terms "high" and "extreme" to refer to community poverty areas that have, respectively, rates of poverty that are in the 30-percent range and at least in the 40-percent range.

70. *Local Community Fact Book: Chicago Metropolitan Area, 1970 and 1980* (Chicago: Chicago Review Press, 1984), p. 321.

71. William Julius Wilson, "Cycles of Deprivation and the Underclass Debate," annual *Social Service Review* lecture, University of Chicago, May 1985. The revised version of this lecture appears as chap. 1 in this volume.

72. See, for example, Nicholas Lemann, "The Origins of the Underclass," *Atlantic Monthly*, June 1986, pp. 31–61; and Staff of the *Chicago Tribune, The American Millstone: An Examination of the Nation's Permanent Underclass* (Chicago: Contemporary Books, 1986). In this connection, Lemann states (in the September issue of the *Atlantic Monthly* following the publication of his

two articles on the "Origins of the Underclass"): "I should have mentioned in my articles an essay by William Julius Wilson, the chairman of the sociology department at the University of Chicago. . . . Wilson strongly emphasized the negative effects on the ghettos of the exodus of the black working and middle classes, which has left the ghettos 'increasingly isolated socially from mainstream patterns and norms of behavior.' I'm sorry for not having given Wilson the credit he deserves for being the first to publish this theory." *Atlantic Monthly,* September 1986, p. 7.

73. Lemann, "Origins of the Underclass." p. 35.

74. U.S. Department of Labor, "Manpower Report of the President" (1974), p. 95. As I have argued elsewhere, "the hypothesis can be entertained that blacks who leave the South in search of better economic opportunities are more willing both to accept the kind of menial work that northern-born blacks have come to reject and to adapt to an economic arrangement which seems to have created permanent economic proletarians out of a substantial percentage of lower-class residents. If so, this is not unlike the behavior of those migrants from other parts of the world who leave a poorer economy for a more developed economy and who there, in hopes of improving their standard of living, initially tend to accept willingly the kinds of work the indigenous workers have come to reject." Wilson, *Declining Significance of Race,* p. 109.

As pointed out in the appendix, the findings on recent migrants do not contradict Lieberson's thesis (see earlier section, "The Importance of the Flow Migrants") on the effect of the heavy black migration from the South to the central cities in the first half of the century (see "Poverty and Migrants" in the appendix).

75. *The Bottom Line: Chicago's Failing Schools and How to Save Them* (Chicago: Designs for Change, 1985), pp. 2 and 5.

76. Comments from Mark Testa, of the University of Chicago, in private communication.

77. David T. Ellwood, "The Spatial Mismatch Hypothesis: Are There Jobs Missing in the Ghetto?" in *The Black Youth Employment Crisis,* ed. R. B. Freeman and H. J. Holzer (Chicago: University of Chicago Press, 1986).

Chapter 3

1. Kenneth B. Clark, *Dark Ghetto: Dilemmas of Social Power* (New York: Harper and Row, 1965); Lee Rainwater, "Crucible of Identity: The Negro Lower-Class Family," *Daedalus* 95 (Winter 1966): 176–216; and Daniel P. Moynihan, *The Negro Family: The Case for National Action* (Washington, D.C.: Office of Policy Planning and Research, U.S. Department of Labor, 1965).

2. Moynihan, *Negro Family,* p. 48.

3. F. F. Furstenberg, Jr., T. Hershberg, and J. Modell, "The Origins of the Female-Headed Black Family: The Impact of the Urban Experience," *Journal of Interdisciplinary History* 6 (1975): 211–33; E. H. Pleck, "The Two-Parent Household: Black Family Structure in Late Nineteenth-Century Boston," *Journal of Social History* 6 (Fall 1972): 3–31; Reynolds Farley, *The Growth of*

the Black Population (Chicago: Markham, 1970); and R. Farley and A. I. Hermalin, "Family Stability: A Comparison of Trends between Blacks and Whites," *American Sociological Review* 36 (1971): 1–8.

4. E. Franklin Frazier, *The Negro Family in the United States* (Chicago: University of Chicago Press, 1939). Cf. A. H. Walker, "Racial Differences in Patterns of Marriage and Family Maintenance, 1890–1980," in *Feminism, Children, and New Families*, ed. S. M. Dornbush and M. H. Strober (New York: Guilford Press, 1985).

5. Herbert Gutman, *The Black Family in Slavery and Freedom, 1750–1925* (New York: Pantheon Books, 1976).

6. Furstenberg, Hershberg, and Modell, "Origins of Female-Headed Black Family"; C. A. Shifflett, "The Household Composition of Rural Black Families: Louisa County, Virginia, 1880," *Journal of Interdisciplinary History* 6 (1975): 235–60; Pleck, "Two-Parent Household"; P. J. Lammermeier, "The Urban Black Family in the Nineteenth Century: A Study of Black Family Structure in the Ohio Valley, 1850–1880," *Journal of Marriage and the Family* 35 (August 1973): 440–56.

7. Pleck, "Two-Parent Household"; and Furstenberg, Hershberg, and Modell, "Origins of Female-Headed Black Family."

8. Furstenberg, Hershberg, and Modell, "Origins of Female-Headed Black Family."

9. Pleck, "Two-Parent Household."

10. Farley and Hermalin's "Family Stability" age-standardized figures show that between 1940 and 1960 the proportion of widows in the population dropped from 14 percent to 12 percent for white women, and from 24 percent to 17 percent for black women. During these two decades, however, the number of divorced women per 1,000 married women rose from 27.2 to 36.8 for whites, and from 29.1 to 71.3 for blacks. U.S. Bureau of the Census, *Census of the Population* (Washington, D.C.: Government Printing Office, 1943); and idem, *Current Population Reports*, Series P-20, "Marital Status and Family Status, March 1960" (Washington, D.C.: Government Printing Office, 1960).

11. U.S. Bureau of the Census, *Current Population Reports*, Series P-20, no. 388, "Household and Family Characteristics, March 1983" (Washington, D.C.: Government Printing Office, 1984).

12. National Office of Vital Statistics, *Vital Statistics of the United States*, vol. 1 (Washington, D.C.: U.S. Department of Health, Education, and Welfare, 1957); and National Center for Health Statistics, "Advanced Report of Final Natality Statistics, 1980," in *Monthly Vital Statistics Report* (Washington, D.C.: U.S. Department of Health and Human Services, 1982); and U.S. Bureau of the Census, *Current Population Reports*, Series P-20, "Fertility of American Women, June 1981" (Washington, D.C.: Government Printing Office, 1983).

13. U.S. Bureau of the Census, "Marital Status and Family Status, March 1960"; and idem, *Current Population Reports*, Series P-20, "Marital Status and Living Arrangements, March 1980" (Washington, D.C.: Government Printing Office, 1981).

14. M. O'Connell and M. J. Moore, "The Legitimacy Status of First Births to U.S. Women Aged 15–24, 1939–1978," *Family Planning Perspectives* 12 (1980): 16–25; and A. Cherlin, *Marriage, Divorce, Remarriage* (Cambridge, Mass.: Harvard University Press, 1981).

15. U.S. Bureau of the Census, *Current Population Reports*, Series P-20, "Characteristics of Single, Married, Widowed, and Divorced Persons in 1947" (Washington, D.C.: Government Printing Office, 1948); and idem, "Marital Status and Living Arrangements, March 1980."

16. Abundant evidence indicates that whites are more likely to remarry than blacks. For instance, a 1975 Current Population Survey showed that of women ages thirty-five to fifty-four who had been divorced or widowed, 53 percent of whites had remarried and were currently married and living with their husbands, as compared with only 38 percent of blacks (U.S. Bureau of the Census, *Current Population Reports*, Series P-20, "Marriage, Divorce, Widowhood, and Remarriage by Family Characteristics, June 1975" [Washington, D.C.: Government Printing Office, 1977]). In addition, National Center for Health Statistics data show that a higher proportion of white than black marriages are *remarriages*, despite the fact that blacks have higher rates of martial dissolution (National Center for Health Statistics, "Marriage and Divorce," in *Vital Statistics of the United States, 1978*, vol. 3 [Washington, D.C.: U.S. Department of Health and Human Services, 1982]).

17. U.S. Bureau of the Census, "Marital Status and Living Arrangements."

18. U.S. Bureau of the Census, *Current Population Reports*, Series P-25, "Population Estimates" (Washington, D.C.: Government Printing Office, 1965); and idem, *Current Population Reports*, Series P-25, "Population Estimates" (Washington, D.C.: Government Printing Office, 1981).

19. Mary Jo Bane and David T. Ellwood, "The Dynamics of Children's Living Arrangements," working paper, supported by U.S. Department of Health and Human Services grant, contract no. HHS-100-82-0038, 1984.

20. P. Cutright, "Components of Change in the Number of Female Family Heads Aged 15–44: United States, 1940–1970," *Journal of Marriage and the Family* 36 (1974): 714–21.

21. Bane and Ellwood, "Dynamics of Children's Living Arrangements."

22. U.S. Bureau of the Census, *Current Population Reports*, Series P-23, "The Social and Economic Status of the Black Population in the United States: A Historical View, 1790–1978" (Washington, D.C.: Government Printing Office, 1979); and idem, *Current Population Reports*, Series P-20, "Marital Status and Family Status, March 1970" (Washington, D.C.: Government Printing Office, 1971); and idem, "Marital Status and Living Arrangements, March 1980."

23. Bane and Ellwood, "Dynamics of Children's Living Arrangements," p. 3.

24. Ibid., p. 23.

25. Mary Jo Bane and David T. Ellwood, "Single Mothers and Their Living Arrangements," working paper, supported by U.S. Department of Health and Human Services grant, contract no. HHS-100-82-0038, 1984, quote on p. 27.

26. U.S. Bureau of the Census, *Current Population Reports*, Series P-60,

no. 144, "Characteristics of the Population below Poverty Level, 1982" (Washington, D.C.: Government Printing Office, 1983).

27. Ibid.

28. G. J. Duncan, *Years of Poverty, Years of Plenty* (Ann Arbor: Institute for Social Research, University of Michigan, 1984).

29. U.S. Department of Health and Human Services, "Advance Report of Final Natality Statistics, 1980," in *Monthly Vital Statistics Report* (Washington, D.C.: Government Printing Office, 1982).

30. M. Zelnik and J. F. Kantner, "Sexual Activity, Contraceptive Use and Pregnancy among Metropolitan-Area Teenagers, 1971–1979," *Family Planning Perspectives* 12 (1980): 230–37.

31. Dennis P. Hogan, personal communication, 1984.

32. Clark, *Dark Ghetto*, p. 72.

33. Dennis P. Hogan, "Demographic Trends in Human Fertility and Parenting across the Life-Span," paper prepared for the Social Science Research Council Conference on Bio-Social Life-Span Approaches to Parental and Offspring Development, Elkridge, Md., May 1983; and idem, "Structural and Normative Factors in Single Parenthood among Black Adolescents," paper presented at the Annual Meeting of the American Sociological Association, San Antonio, Tx., August 1984.

34. Hogan, personal communication, 1984.

35. Hogan, "Structural and Normative Factors," p. 21.

36. Dennis P. Hogan and Evelyn M. Kitagawa, "The Impact of Social Status, Family Structure, and Neighborhood on the Fertility of Black Adolescents," *American Journal of Sociology* 90 (1985): 825–55.

37. Hogan, "Demographic Trends."

38. R. Easterlin, *Birth and Fortune: The Impact of Numbers on Personal Welfare* (New York: Basic Books, 1980); Dennis P. Hogan, *Transitions and Social Change: The Early Lives of American Men* (New York: Academic Press, 1981); and M. D. Evans, "Modernization, Economic Conditions and Family Formation: Evidence from Recent White and Nonwhite Cohorts," Ph.D. dissertation, University of Chicago, 1983. Cf. Hogan, "Demographic Trends."

39. Zelnik and Kantner, "Sexual Activity."

40. S. Hoffman and J. Holmes, "Husbands, Wives, and Divorce," in *Five Thousand American Families: Patterns of Economic Progress*, ed. J. N. Morgan, vol. 4 (Ann Arbor: Institute for Social Research, University of Michigan Press, 1976); S. Danziger, G. Jakubson, S. Schwartz, and E. Smolensky, "Work and Welfare as Determinants of Female Poverty and Household Headship," *Quarterly Journal of Economics* 97 (August 1982): 519–34; and H. L. Ross and I. Sawhill, *Time of Transition: The Growth of Families Headed by Women* (Washington, D.C.: Urban Institute, 1975).

41. U.S. Bureau of the Census, *Census of the Population, 1980* (Washington, D.C.: Government Printing Office, 1984).

42. Ibid.

43. U.S. Bureau of the Census, "Characteristics of the Population below Poverty Level, 1982."

44. Charles Murray, *Losing Ground: American Social Policy, 1950–1980* (New York: Basic Books, 1984).

45. Cited in M. Feldstein, ed., *The American Economy in Transition* (Chicago: University of Chicago Press, 1980), p. 341.

46. P. Cutright, "Illegitimacy and Income Supplements," *Studies in Public Welfare*, paper no. 12 prepared for the use of the Subcommittee on Fiscal Policy of the Joint Economic Committee, Congress of the United States (Washington, D.C.: Government Printing Office, 1973); C. R. Winegarden, "The Fertility of AFDC Women: An Economic Analysis," *Journal of Economics and Business* 26 (1974): 159–66; A. Fechter and S. Greenfield, "Welfare and Illegitimacy: An Economic Model and Some Preliminary Results," working paper 963-37 (Washington, D.C.: Urban Institute, 1973); Kristin Moore and Steven B. Caldwell, "Out-of-Wedlock Pregnancy and Childbearing," working paper no. 999-02, Urban Institute, Washington, D.C., 1976; and D. R. Vining, Jr., "Illegitimacy and Public Policy," *Population and Development Review* 9 (1983): 105–10.

47. Vining, "Illegitimacy and Public Policy," p. 108.

48. Cutright, "Illegitimacy and Income Supplements"; David T. Ellwood and Mary Jo Bane, "The Impact of AFDC on Family Structure and Living Arrangements," prepared for the U.S. Department of Health and Human Services under grant no. 92A-82, 1984.

49. P. J. Placek and G. E. Hendershot, "Public Welfare and Family Planning: An Empirical Study of the 'Brood Sow' Myth," *Social Problems* 21 (1974): 660–73; H. B. Presser and L. S. Salsberg, "Public Assistance and Early Family Formation: Is There a Pronatalist Effect?" *Social Problems* 23 (1975): 226–41; S. Polgar and V. Hiday, "The Effect of an Additional Birth on Low-Income Urban Families," *Population Studies* 28 (1974): 463–71; and Moore and Caldwell, "Out-of-Wedlock Pregnancy and Childbearing."

50. G. Cain, "The Effect of Income Maintenance Laws on Fertility in Results from the New Jersey–Pennsylvania Experiment," in *Final Report of the Graduated Work Incentive Experiment in New Jersey and Pennsylvania* (Madison, Wis., and Princeton, N.J.: Institute for Research on Poverty, University of Wisconsin, and Mathematica Policy Research, 1974).

51. M. C. Keeley, "The Effects of Negative Income Tax Programs on Fertility," *Journal of Human Resources* 9 (1980): 303–22.

52. Cutright and Madras, "AFDC and the Marital and Family Status of Ever-Married Women"; J. J. Minarik and R. S. Goldfarb, "AFDC Income, Recipient Rates, and Family Dissolution: A Comment," *Journal of Human Resources* 11 (Spring 1976): 243–50; M. Honig, "AFDC Income, Recipient Rates, and Family Dissolution," *Journal of Human Resources* 9 (Summer 1974): 303–22; and Ross and Sawhill, *Time of Transition*.

53. Honig, "AFDC Income, Recipient Rates, and Family Dissolution"; Minarik and Goldfarb, "AFDC Income, Recipient Rates, and Family Dissolution: A Comment"; Ross and Sawhill, *Time of Transition*; and Cutright and Madras, "AFDC and the Marital and Family Status of Ever-Married Women."

54. D. T. Ellwood and M. J. Bane, "Impact of AFDC on Family Structure

and Living Arrangements," report prepared for the U.S. Department of Health and Human Services under grant no. 92A-82 (John F. Kennedy School of Government, Harvard University, 1984), p. 2.

55. In this connection, Ellwood and Bane state that "women in this group will tend to have married and had children at a very young age. Such marriages tend to be unstable, and thus it is plausible that welfare benefits might have an important impact on this group. Welfare may offer an alternative to an unhappy early marriage. . . . One should keep in mind, however, that even a sizable increase such as this one need not imply a very sizable increase in the number of single mothers. Among younger nonwhite women, divorced or separated mothers represent just 20% of all single mothers. A 50% increase in this group translates to only a 10% increase in the number of single mothers under 24. Thus even though welfare might have a significant impact on ever-married mothers, if welfare does not influence births to nonmarried women, its overall impact on the fraction of all women who are single mothers would be small. . . . By contrast nearly 60% of all young white mothers report themselves as divorced or separated. A 50% increase here implies a much larger change in the number of single mothers. A large impact on divorce and separation then implies a much larger change in the number of women who are single mothers for whites than for nonwhites." Ellwood and Bane, "Impact of AFDC on Family Structure," p. 42.

56. Hoffman and Holmes, "Husbands, Wives, and Divorce"; Ross and Sawhill, *Time of Transition;* and Danziger et al., "Work and Welfare."

57. J. H. Bishop, "Jobs, Cash Transfers, and Marital Instability: A Review and Synthesis of the Evidence," *Journal of Human Resources* 15 (Summer 1980): 301–34; L. P. Groeneveld, M. Hannon, and N. Tuma, *Marital Stability: Final Report of the Seattle-Denver Income Maintenance Experiment,* vol. 1, Design and Result, pt. 5 (Menlo Park, Calif.: SRI International), p. 344; and L. P. Groeneveld, N. B. Tuma, and M. T. Hannon, "The Effects of Negative Income Tax Programs on Marital Dissolution," *Journal of Human Resources* 15 (1980): 654–74.

58. Hogan, "Demographic Trends"; and idem, "Structural and Normative Factors."

59. Ellwood and Bane, "Impact of AFDC on Family Structure," p. 8.

60. U.S. Bureau of the Census, *Census of the Population, 1980.*

61. Ibid.

62. Duncan, *Years of Poverty, Years of Plenty;* U.S. Bureau of the Census, "Social and Economic Status of the Black Population"; and U.S. Bureau of Labor Statistics, *Employment and Earnings* (Washington, D.C.: U.S. Department of Labor, January 1984).

63. W. E. Bakke, *Citizens without Work* (New Haven, Conn.: Yale University Press, 1940); M. Komarovsky, *The Unemployed Man and His Family* (New York: Octagon Books, 1940); G. H. Elder, Jr., *Children of the Great Depression* (Chicago: University of Chicago Press, 1974); Honig, "AFDC Income, Recipient Rates, and Family Dissolution"; Ross and Sawhill, *Time of Transition;* I. Sawhill, G. E. Peabody, C. A. Jones, and S. B. Caldwell, *Income*

Transfers and Family Structure (Washington, D.C.: Urban Institute, 1975); and Hoffman and Holmes, "Husbands, Wives, and Divorce"; Bishop, "Jobs, Cash Transfers, and Marital Instability"; P. Cutright, "Income and Family Events: Marital Instability," *Journal of Marriage and the Family* 33 (1971): 291–306; and A. Cohen, "Economic, Marital Instability and Race," Ph.D. dissertation, University of Wisconsin, Madison, 1979.

64. R. Farley, "Homicide Trends in the United States," *Demography* 17 (May 1980): 177–88; A. Blumstein, "On the Racial Disproportionality of United States' Prison Populations," *Journal of Criminal Law and Criminology* 73 (Fall 1982): 1259–81.

65. Several objections might be raised to these figures. First, it might be argued that the ratios are biased downward because of an undercount of young black men. This may be true, but it would seem that unenumerated men are not counted precisely because they do not have a stable attachment to labor force and family, and thus would be unlikely to be included in these figures even if they had been enumerated. Second, the employment figures are for the civilian labor force only and do not include men in the armed forces. Including men who are in the armed forces would smooth out the graph for men twenty to twenty-four years of age during the late 1960s, and would narrow the black-white gap a little because of slightly higher enlistment levels among blacks, but would not change the basic trends. The slight upturn in the index after 1954 for men twenty to twenty-four is likely to represent the return of men in the armed forces to the civilian labor force following the Korean War. Finally, although some women may marry men other than employed men of their own age and race category, the figures are intended to convey the "marriage market" constraints facing most women.

66. While rising average incomes are likely to have enhanced family stability for black men who are employed, the more dramatic trends in unemployment and labor-force participation have outweighed increases in earnings to produce a net decline in family stability among blacks.

67. Ellwood and Bane, "Impact of AFDC on Family Structure."

68. Cutright and Madras, "AFDC and the Marital and Family Status of Ever-Married Women"; cf. G. S. Becker, E. M. Landes, and R. T. Michael, "An Ecomic Analysis of Marital Instability," *Journal of Political Economy* 85 (1977): 1141–87.

69. Center for the Study of Social Policy, "The 'Flip-Side' of Black Families Headed by Women: The Economic Status of Black Men," working paper, 1984; and Walker, "Racial Differences in Patterns of Marriage and Family Maintenance."

Chapter 4

1. Charles Murray, *Losing Ground: American Social Policy, 1950–1980* (New York: Basic Books, 1984).

2. See, e.g., Robert Kuttner, "A Flawed Case for Scrapping What's Left of the Great Society," *Washington Post Book World*, November 25, 1984, p. 4;

and Robert Greenstein, "Losing Faith in 'Losing Ground,'" *New Republic*, March 25, 1985, pp. 12–17.

3. Murray, *Losing Ground*, p. 165.

4. Sheldon Danziger and Peter Gottschalk, "The Poverty of Losing Ground," *Challenge*, May/June 1985, p. 36.

5. Greenstein, "Losing Faith in 'Losing Ground,'" p. 16.

6. Ibid., p. 14.

7. Glen Cain, "Comments on August 18th Version of Marital Stability Findings, Chapter Three," mimeo, 1981.

8. Alfred Blumstein, "On the Racial Disproportionality of United States' Prison Populations," *Journal of Criminal Law and Criminology* 73 (Fall 1982): 1259–81; Reynolds Farley, "Homicide Trends in the United States," *Demography* 17 (May 1980): 177–88.

9. The MMPI figures include estimates of the number of men in the armed forces by region. The census enumerates men in the armed forces as part of the population of the area in which they are stationed: in these figures, however, they are reallocated among the regions according to the proportion of the total population (by race) residing in each region.

Region	Black		White	
	1960	1980	1960	1980
Northeast	16.0	18.3	26.1	22.5
North Central	18.2	20.1	30.2	27.7
South	60.0	53.0	27.4	31.3
West	5.7	8.5	16.3	18.6

If enlistment rates varied systematically by region, this allocation formula would be biased; unfortunately, the *Selected Manpower Statistics*, published by the Department of Defense, provides no information on enlistment rates by state or region.

While there are slight differences by age and sex in the regional distribution of the population, they are not great enough to distort the index. For instance, of the age-groups with a high proportion of servicemen, the civilian black males ages twenty to twenty-four show the greatest deviation from the distribution of the total black population in 1980.

Region	Total Population	20- to 24-Year-Old Civilian Males
Northeast	18.3	16.9
North Central	20.1	20.8

Region	Total Population	20- to 24-Year-Old Civilian Males
South	53.0	53.2
West	8.5	9.1

However, the MMPI values based on allocation of the servicemen according to this alternative distribution show very little difference from those based on the total population: for the Northeast, the region showing the greatest deviation, the MMPI based on this alternative allocation is 47.4, very close to the 48.1 reported in table 4.1. For the sake of simplicity and comparability, then, an allocation based on total population was chosen.

10. We stress the MMPI for men over nineteen years of age for a number of reasons. First, data for 1960 for black men between the ages of sixteen and nineteen are unavailable. Use of 1960 data for unavailable. Use of 1960 data for nonwhite males is acceptable only for the three regions where well over 90 percent of young nonwhite males were black. In the West in 1960 only about half of all nonwhite males were black. Also, the majority of teenagers are in school, and it is more difficult to suggest that they join the labor force full time to support a family than it is to suggest that older men do so.

11. For instance, poverty rates in 1982 for white and black families headed by women under the age of forty-five were 33 percent and 53 percent respectively, compared to 11 percent and 35 percent for white and black families headed by women ages forty-five and over. U.S. Bureau of the Census, *Current Population Reports*, Series P-60, no. 144, "Characteristics of the Population below Poverty Level, 1982" (Washington, D.C.: Government Printing Office, 1983).

12. One-quarter of all women under forty-five heading families were never married, compared to 8 percent of those forty-five and over. Never-married women have more difficulty getting child support than other women; according to Garfinkel and Uhr, only about 10 percent of all single mothers received child support awards in 1978, compared to half of all separated women and four-fifths of all divorced women. Irwin Garfinkel and Elizabeth Uhr, "A New Approach to Child Support," *Public Interest* 75 (Spring 1984): 111–22.

13. Both blacks and whites in the West are significantly more likely to be recent migrants than blacks and whites elsewhere. According to the 1980 census, for women ages twenty-five to thirty-nine, for example, more than 15 percent of western blacks and about 14 percent of western whites were migrants (the California proportion was about 13 percent for both groups), compared to less than 7 percent in other regions.

While educational attainment by white women was not always greater in the West or in California than in other areas, for blacks in the West greater attainment held consistently for women ages twenty-five to thirty-nine. For example, 85 percent of western black women of those ages were high school graduates, and 13 percent were college graduates (the same as California), compared to 75 percent or fewer in other regions. Less than 12 percent of southern black women and less than 11 percent of northern black women of the same age-group were college graduates.

Western black families had higher incomes than families elsewhere, but more important, this was true for the female-headed families. For example, the median family incomes of black families led by women ages twenty-five to thirty-four and thirty-five to forty-four were $7,543 and $10,596 respectively in the West (in California, incomes were slightly higher). In the north-central region, the region with the second highest average income among black female-headed families, the comparable figures were only $6,488 and $9,922.

Poverty rates were unavailable for the age breakdowns most appropriate to our arguments, but the pattern of lower poverty in the West among black families headed by women under the age of sixty-five holds nevertheless. Among such families with heads ages fifteen to twenty-four years, nearly 70 percent of those in the South, more than 70 percent of those in the northern regions, but only 65 percent of those in the West were poor. Among black families headed by women under age sixty-five, westerners' poverty rates were 39 percent (only 36 percent in California), compared to 45 percent in the Northeast, 46 percent in the North Central, and 48 percent in the South.

Black female family heads in California tend to resemble white female heads more than other black women heading families in their levels of income and education, as noted above. But even from a purely demographic perspective, the relative similarity between these groups of women is apparent. Like the well-established pattern of white female heads (Heather L. Ross and Isabelle Sawhill, *Time of Transition: The Growth of Families Headed by Women* [Washington, D.C.: Urban Institute, 1975]; and Mary Jo Bane and David T. Ellwood, "Single Mothers and Their Living Arrangements," working paper supported by U.S. Department of Health and Human Services grant, contract no. HHS-82-0038, 1983), black women heading families in California are more likely to head families because of a divorce than a separation or illegitimate birth. Not only are black women in California far more prone to divorce than elsewhere, but a far smaller proportion of never-married black California women had ever borne children than was the case among never-married women elsewhere. Never-married black women ages fifteen to forty-four in the West had borne some 52 children per 100 women, compared to 64 in the South and Northeast, and 70 in the north-central region.

The California AFDC program has the highest payment guarantee in the continental United States. (Over 84 percent of western black female-headed families live in California.) Despite this, only 53 percent of western black families headed by women under twenty-five (usually the poorest group) reported any public assistance income in 1979, while 60 percent of such families in the northeastern and north-central regions reported welfare income.

14. Ross and Sawhill, *Time of Transition*.

15. For instance, among ever-married women between the ages of twenty-five and thirty-nine, 37 percent of both California and western blacks, but only 28 percent of all such black women nationwide, ever divorced. Among white

women of the same ages, the respective percentages are 33%, 32%, and 26%. U.S. Bureau of the Census, *1980 Census of Population: Detailed Characteristics of the Population*, pt. 1, U.S. Summary (Washington, D.C.: Government Printing Office, 1983).

16. John D. Kasarda, "The Implications of Contemporary Redistribution Trends for National Urban Policy," *Social Science Quarterly* 61 (1980): 303–22; and Bernard L. Weinstein and Robert E. Firestine, *Regional Growth and Decline in the United States* (New York: Praeger, 1978).

17. Kasarda, "Implications of Contemporary Redistribution Trends," p. 384.

18. Ibid.

19. Of the thirty-three largest Standard Metropolitan Statistical Areas in 1970, data on the 1950 population by race were unavailable for three (San Jose; San Bernardino-Riverside-Ontario; and Anaheim, Santa Ana–Garden Grove, in California) and part of one additional SMSA (Everett of Seattle). All of these areas are in the West. We have not argued here that central cities in the West have experienced much loss of low-skilled jobs. Indeed Kasarda ("Urban Change and Minority Opportunities," in *The New Urban Reality*, ed. Paul E. Peterson [Washington, D.C.: Brookings Institution, 1985]) has argued that Sunbelt cities, especially in the West, have tended to experience job growth even in low-skilled jobs. Moreover, as of 1980, these central cities contained only 1.2 million whites and about 74,000 blacks. Finally, the figures we present in the text understate the shifts in population of the other central cities. This is because the 1950 data for blacks are based on counts for nonwhites, thus inflating their 1950 population count, while the data for whites include most Hispanics, another socially disadvantaged group. Hence, the extent of population decline among non-Hispanic whites in the big cities is quite understated. U.S. Bureau of the Census, *U.S. Census Population*, vol. 2: *Characteristics of the Population*, pt. 1, U.S. Summary (Washington, D.C.: Government Printing Office, 1953); idem, *1970 Census of Population: Detailed Characteristics of the Population*, pt. 1, U.S. Summary (Washington, D.C.: Government Printing Office, 1973); and idem, *1980 Census of Population*.

20. C. Horace Hamilton, "The Negro Leaves the South," *Demography* 1 (1964): 273–95; and Neil Fligstein, *Going North: Migration of Blacks and Whites from the South, 1900–1950* (New York: Academic Press, 1981).

21. John D. Kasarda, "Caught in the Web of Change," *Society* 21 (1983): 44.

22. Kasarda, "Regional and Urban Redistribution of People and Jobs in the U.S.," paper prepared for the National Research Council Committee on National Urban Policy, National Academy of Science, 1986. "White-collar service industries" are "defined as those service industries where executives, managers, professionals, and clerical employees exceed more than 50% of the industry workforce." Ibid., pp. 18–19.

23. Ibid.

24. Ibid., p. 27.

25. I would like to thank Sar Levitan for bringing this point to my attention.

26. Samuel Bowles and Herbert Gintis, *Schooling in Capitalist America:*

Education and the Contradictions of Economic Life (New York: Basic Books, 1976).

27. Ibid., p. 132.

28. John Cogan, "The Decline in Black Teenage Employment, 1950–70," *American Economic Review* 72 (September 1982): 621–38, quote on p. 635.

29. Martin Feldstein and David T. Ellwood, "Teenage Employment: What Is the Problem?" in *The Youth Labor Market Problem: Its Nature, Causes, and Consequences,* ed. Richard B. Freeman and David A. Wise (Chicago: University of Chicago Press, 1982); and David T. Ellwood and David A. Wise, "Youth Employment in the Seventies: The Changing Circumstances of Youth Adults," working paper no. 1055, National Bureau of Economic Research, Cambridge, Mass., 1983.

30. D. N. Wescott, "Youth in the Labor Force: An Area Study," *Monthly Labor Review* 99 (1976): 3–9; B. Magnum and R. Seniger, *Coming of Age in the Ghetto* (Baltimore: Johns Hopkins University Press, 1978); S. L. Friedlander, *Unemployment in the Urban Core: An Analysis of Thirty Cities with Policy Recommendations* (New York: Praeger, 1972); Richard B. Freeman, "Economic Determinants of Geographic and Individual Variation in the Labor Market Position of Young Persons," in Freeman and Wise, *Youth Labor Market Problem;* and Albert Rees and Wayne Gray, "Family Effects in Youth Employment," in Freeman and Wise, *Youth Labor Market Problem.*

31. Black male youth employment-to-population ratios by age for the Northeast, North Central, and South for the years 1960–80 are shown here.

	16–19 Years			20–24 Years		
	1960	1970	1980	1960	1970	1980
Northeast	31.4	26.1	19.6	67.3	61.2	48.5
North Central	26.5	27.8	22.3	62.3	62.2	48.0
South	36.0	27.4	25.8	68.3	60.8	55.6

32. Mary Jo Bane, "Household Composition and Poverty: Which Comes First?" revised paper prepared for the conference on Poverty and Policy: Retrospect and Prospects, Williamsburg, Va., December 6–8, 1984.

33. Daniel Patrick Moynihan, *Family and the Nation* (New York: Harcourt Brace Jovanovich, 1986).

Chapter 5

1. U.S. Department of Labor, *Handbook of Labor Statistics* (Washington, D.C.: Government Printing Office, December 1983).

2. Gary Puckrein, "Moving Up," *Wilson Quarterly* 8 (Spring 1984): 74–87.

3. U.S. Bureau of the Census, "Statistical Abstract of the United States, 1982–1983" (Washington, D.C.: Government Printing Office, 1983).

4. Glen C. Loury, "On the Need for Moral Leadership in the Black Community," paper presented at the University of Chicago, sponsored by the Center for the Study of Industrial Societies and the John M. Olin Center, Chicago, Ill., April 18, 1984, pp. 13–14.

5. Milton M. Gordon, "Models of Pluralism: The New American Dilemma," *Annals of the American Academy of Political and Social Sciences* 454 (March 1981): 183.

6. Milton M. Gordon, "Toward a General Theory of Racial and Ethnic Group Relations," in *Ethnicity: Theory and Experience,* ed. Nathan Glazer and Daniel P. Moynihan (Cambridge, Mass.: Harvard University Press. 1975), pp. 84–110.

7. Gordon, "Models of Pluralism."

8. In the following discussion in this section, I am indebted to James S. Fishkin's stimulating book *Justice, Equal Opportunity, and the Family, 1983* (New Haven, Conn.: Yale University Press, 1983).

9. William Raspberry, "Illusion of Black Progress," *Washington Post,* May 28, 1980, p. A19.

10. Leroy D. Clark and Judy Trent Ellis, "Affirmative Action in Recessionary Periods: The Legal Structure," *Adherent: A Journal of Comprehensive Employment Training and Human Resources of Development* 7 (December 1980): 64.

11. Fishkin, *Justice, Equal Opportunity, and the Family, 1983,* p. 92.

12. Raspberry, "Illusion of Black Progress," p. A19.

13. Ibid.

14. William L. Taylor, "*Brown,* Equal Protection, and the Isolation of the Poor," *Yale Law Journal* 95 (July 1986): 1714.

15. Loury, "On the Need for Moral Leadership in the Black Community," p. 14.

16. There is a question as to whether black physicians actually prefer to practice medicine within the black community, especially the poor black community. It is reasonable to assume that the typical black physician, like the typical white physician, would seek out the areas of practice providing the greatest financial and professional rewards. Accordingly, the more opportunities a black physician has to practice in attractive areas, the less likely that he or she will choose to serve poor blacks.

Of course, racial barriers have restricted the movements of many black physicians. It is ironic that the removal of racial barriers would result in a decrease in the percentage of the most qualified black physicians practicing medicine in the black community.

17. Fishkin, *Justice, Equal Opportunity, and the Family, 1973,* p. 4.

18. Ibid., p. 17.

19. Ibid.

20. Ibid.

21. In drawing this comparison I have benefited from Toby Cohen's insightful article, "Reagan's New Deal," *New York Times,* August 19, 1981, p. 23.

22. Ibid.

23. Ibid.

24. A number of political activists have argued against considering seriously potential political resistance on the grounds that it is better to press for the adoption of certain programs, even when it is clear that they are doomed to failure, than to bow to political pressures. But it is one thing to ignore political realities because certain programs are noble; it is quite another thing to channel scarce energy into programs that could have significant long-term payoffs for the truly disadvantaged. The question is not the abandonment of noble programs because of political realities, but the shaping of those programs so that they can achieve noble goals while still receiving vital political support.

25. Lester C. Thurow, "Recession plus Inflation Spells Statis," *Christianity and Crisis,* March 30, 1981, pp. 91–92.

26. Ibid.

27. Sheila Kamerman and Alfred J. Kahn, "Europe's Innovative Family Policies," *Transatlantic Perspectives* 2 (March 1981): 9–12.

28. Many have argued for governmental involvement in economic reform without stipulating the need for "rational" intervention, i.e., systematic long-term planning. Most current planning, whether undertaken by the executive branch, by Congress, or by the Federal Reserve, looks no further than the next election. The results speak for themselves.

29. My recommendation of a general economic policy was originally developed as part of a policy statement on social justice issued by black scholars and leaders (*A Policy Framework for Racial Justice* [Washington, D.C.: Joint Center for Political Studies, June 1983]), and was further elaborated in testimony that I gave on industrial policy and the concern of minorities, before the Subcommittee on Economic Stabilization of the Committee on Banking, Finance, and Urban Affairs, House of Representatives, Washington, D.C., January 25, 1984.

30. William Julius Wilson, *The Declining Significance of Race: Blacks and Changing American Institutions,* 2d ed. (Chicago: University of Chicago Press, 1980).

31. In developing the argument that follows, I have benefited from James Tobin, "On Improving the Economic Status of the Negro," *Daedalus* 94 (Fall 1965): 878–98.

Chapter 6

1. Bayard Rustin, "From Protest to Politics: The Future of the Civil Rights Movement," *Commentary* 39 (February 1964): 25–31; idem, "A Way Out of the Exploding Ghetto," *New York Times Magazine,* August 13, 1967; idem, "The Long Hot Summer," *Commentary* (October 1967): 39–45; Tom Kahn, "Problems of the Negro Movement," *Dissent* 11 (Winter 1964): 108–38; and Kenneth B. Clark, "The Present Dilemma of the Negro," paper presented at the Annual Meeting of the Southern Regional Council, Atlanta, Ga., November 2, 1967.

2. Rustin, "Lessons of the Long Hot Summer," p. 43.

3. Clark, "Present Dilemma of the Negro," p. 8.

4. Bayard Rustin, "The Blacks and the Unions," *Harper Magazine*, May 1971, p. 74.

5. Martin Luther King, Jr., "Showdown for Non-Violence," *Look*, April 16, 1968, p. 24.

6. Rustin, "From Protest to Politics," p. 25.

7. Ibid., p. 25.

8. Kenneth B. Clark, *Dark Ghetto: Dilemmas of Social Power* (New York: Harper and Row, 1965); Lee Rainwater, "Crucible of Identity: The Negro Lower-Class Family," *Daedelus* 95 (Winter 1966): 172–216; and Elliot Liebow, *Tally's Corner: A Study of Negro Streetcorner Men* (Boston: Little, Brown, 1967).

9. Clark, *Dark Ghetto*, p. 27.

10. See William Julius Wilson, *Power, Racism, and Privilege: Race Relations in Theoretical and Sociohistorical Perspectives* (New York: Free Press, 1976).

11. Orlando Patterson, *Ethnic Chauvinism: The Reactionary Impulse* (New York: Stein and Day, 1977), p. 155.

12. Daniel Patrick Moynihan, *Maximum Feasible Misunderstanding* (New York: Free Press, 1970).

13. Margaret Weir, Ann S. Orloff, and Theda Skocpol, "The Future of Social Policy in the United States," in *The Politics of Social Policy in the United States*, ed. Margaret Weir, Ann S. Orloff, and Theda Skocpol (Princeton, N.J.: Princeton University Press, forthcoming). For a good discussion of the Council of Economic Advisers approach to the problem of poverty, see Lawrence M. Mead, *Beyond Entitlement: The Social Obligations of Citizenship* (New York: Free Press, 1986), chap. 3.

14. Mead, *Beyond Entitlement*, p. 35.

15. Weir, Orloff, and Skocpol, "Future of Social Policy in the United States.

16. W. Korpi, "Approaches to the Study of Poverty in the United States: Critical Notes from a European Perspective," in *Poverty and Public Policy: An Evaluation of Social Research*, ed. V. T. Covello (Boston: G. K. Hall, 1980), pp. 305, 306.

17. Rebecca M. Blank and Alan A. Blinder, "Macroeconomics, Income Distribution, and Poverty," in *Fighting Poverty: What Works and What Doesn't*, ed. Sheldon Danziger and Daniel H. Weinberg (Cambridge, Mass.: Harvard University Press, 1986).

18. Robert Greenstein, "Losing Faith in 'Losing Ground,'" *New Republic*, March 25, 1985, pp. 12–17.

19. Weir, Orloff, and Skocpol, "Future of Social Policy in the United States."

20. Mead, *Beyond Entitlement*.

21. Ibid., pp. 55–56.

22. See William Julius Wilson, *The Declining Significance of Race: Blacks*

and Changing American Institutions, 2d ed. (Chicago: University of Chicago Press, 1980).

23. Illinois Advisory Committee, *Shutdown: Economic Dislocation and Equal Opportunity,* report to the United States Commission on Civil Rights, June 1981.

24. Barry Bluestone and Bennett Harrison, *The Deindustrialization of America* (New York: Basic Books, 1982).

25. Richard McGahey and John Jeffries, "Employment, Training, and Industrial Policy: Implications for Minorities," paper prepared for a conference on Industrial Policy and Minority Economic Opportunity, sponsored by the Joint Center for Political Studies and the A. Philip Randolph Educational Fund, New York, N.Y., October 14, 1983.

26. John D. Kasarda, "Urbanization, Community, and the Metropolitan Problem," in *Handbook of Contemporary Urban Life,* ed. David Street et al. (San Francisco: Jossey-Bass, 1978).

27. Oscar Lewis, "Culture of Poverty," in *On Understanding Poverty: Perspectives from the Social Sciences,* Daniel Patrick Moynihan, ed. (New York: Basic Books, 1968), p. 188.

28. For a good discussion of this point see, Stephen Steinberg, *The Ethnic Myth: Race, Ethnicity, and Class in America* (New York: Atheneum, 1981).

29. Herbert Gans, "Culture and Class in the Study of Poverty: An Approach to Anti-Poverty Research," in *On Understanding Poverty: Perspectives from the Social Sciences,* ed. Daniel Patrick Moynihan (New York: Basic Books, 1968), pp. 201–8.

Chapter 7

1. James Fishkin covers much of this ground very convincingly. See his *Justice, Equal Opportunity and the Family* (New Haven, Conn.: Yale University Press, 1983).

2. Kathryn M. Neckerman, Robert Aponte, and William Julius Wilson, "Family Structure, Black Unemployment, and American Social Policy," in *The Politics of Social Policy in the United States,* ed. Margaret Weir, Ann Shola Orloff, and Theda Skocpol (Princeton, N.J.: Princeton University Press, forthcoming).

3. The essential features of such a policy are discussed in chap. 5, "The Case for a Universal Program."

4. Margaret Weir, Ann Shola Orloff, and Theda Skocpol, "The Future of Social Policy in the United States: Political Constraints and Possibilities," in Weir, Orloff, and Skocpol, *Politics of Social Policy in the United States.*

5. Theda Skocpol, "Brother Can You Spare a Job?: Work and Welfare in the United States," paper presented at the Annual Meeting of the American Sociological Association, Washington, D.C., August 27, 1985.

6. Part of the discussion on welfare reform in the next several pages is based on Neckerman, Aponte, and Wilson, "Family Structure, Black Unemployment, and American Social Policy."

7. Irwin Garfinkel and Sara S. McLanahan, *Single Mothers and Their Children: A New American Dilemma* (Washington, D.C.: Urban Institute Press, 1986).

8. Harold L. Wilensky, "Evaluating Research and Politics: Political Legitimacy and Consensus as Missing Variables in the Assessment of Social Policy," in *Evaluating the Welfare State: Social and Political Perspectives*, ed. E. Spiro and E. Yuchtman-Yarr (New York: Academic Press, 1983). I am indebted to Wilensky for the following discussion on corporatist democracies.

9. Ibid.

10. Ibid.

11. Sheila S. Kamerman and Alfred J. Kahn, "Income Transfers, Work and the Economic Well-being of Families with Children," *International Social Security Review* 3 (1982): 376.

12. Sheila S. Kamerman and Alfred Kahn, "Europe's Innovative Family Policies," *Transatlantic Perspectives*, March 1980, p. 12.

13. William L. Taylor, "*Brown*, Equal Protection, and the Isolation of the Poor," *Yale Law Journal* 95 (July 1986): 1729–30.

14. I have in mind the numerous editorials and op-ed columns on self-help in widely read newspapers such as the *Washington Post, New York Times, Wall Street Journal*, and *Chicago Tribune*; articles in national magazines such as *The New Republic* and *Atlantic Monthly*; and the testimony that self-help advocates, particularly black conservative supporters of self-help, have given before the U.S. Congress.

15. The most sophisticated and articulate black spokesperson of this thesis is Harvard University professor Glenn Loury. See, e.g., Glen Loury, "The Need for Moral Leadership in the Black Community," *New Perspectives* 16 (Summer 1984): 14–19.

16. Stephen Steinberg makes a compelling case for this argument in his stimulating book *The Ethnic Myth: Race, Ethnicity and Class in America* (New York: Atheneum, 1981).

17. Lawrence M. Mead, *Beyond Entitlement: The Social Obligations of Citizenship* (New York: Free Press, 1986), pp. 4, 61.

18. Ibid., pp. 73, 80.

19. See, for example, Michael Sosin's excellent review of *Beyond Entitlement* in *Social Service Review* 61 (March 1987): 156–59.

20. R. Nathan, "The Underclass—Will It Always Be with Us?" Paper presented at a symposium on the Underclass, New School for Social Research, New York, N.Y., November 14, 1986.

21. Ibid., p. 18.

22. Ibid., pp. 19–21. Although Lawrence Mead is highly critical of new-style workfare (because it reinforces the sociological view of the disadvantaged by assuming that before the recipients can work, the program has to find the client a job, arrange for child care, solve the client's help problems, and so on), his elaborate theory of the social obligation of citizenship is being adopted by policymakers to buttress the more conservative side of the new workfare programs.

23. Robert D. Reischauer, "America's Underclass: Four Unanswered Ques-

tions," paper presented at The City Club, Portland, Oreg., January 30, 1986.

24. Robert D. Reischauer, "Policy Responses to the Underclass Problem," paper presented at a symposium at the New School for Social Research, November 14, 1986.

25. S. A. Levitan and C. M. Johnson, *Beyond the Safety Net: Reviving the Promising of Opportunity in America* (Cambridge, Mass.: Ballinger Publishing Co., 1984), pp. 169–70.

26. Skocpol, "Brother Can You Spare a Job?"

Appendix

1. R. H. Bremner, *From the Depths: The Discovery of Poverty in the United States* (New York: University Press, 1956); and H. P. Miller, *Poverty American Style* (Belmont, Calif.: Wadsworth Press, 1966).

2. J. Riss, *How the Other Half Lives: Studies among the Tenements of New York* (New York: Scribner, 1890); J. Addams, "The Housing Problem in Chicago," *Annuals of the American Academy of Politics and Social Science* 20 (1902): 97–107; and S. Breckinridge, *The Tenements of Chicago, 1908–35* (Chicago: University of Chicago Press, 1936).

3. W. I. Thomas and F. Znaniecki, *The Polish Peasant in Europe and America*, 5 vols. (Boston: Brager, 1918–20).

4. Robert E. Park, *The City* (Chicago: University of Chicago Press, 1925).

5. N. Anderson, *The Hobo* (Chicago: University of Chicago Press, 1923); idem, *Men on the Move* (Chicago: University of Chicago Press, 1940); F. M. Thrasher, *The Gang* (Chicago: University of Chicago Press, 1927); L. Wirth, *The Ghetto* (Chicago: University of Chicago Press, 1928); H. W. Zorbaugh, *The Gold Coast and the Slum* (Chicago: University of Chicago Press, 1929); R. E. L. Faris and W. Dunham, *Mental Disorder in Urban America* (Chicago: University of Chicago Press, 1931); E. Franklin Frazier, *The Negro Family in Chicago* (Chicago: University of Chicago Press, 1932); and E. H. Sutherland and H. Locke, *20,000 Homeless Men* (Philadelphia: Lippincott, 1936).

6. Gerald D. Suttles, "Urban Ethnography: Situational and Normative Accounts," *Annual Review of Sociology* 2 (1976): 1–8.

7. Ibid., p. 7.

8. R. D. Plotnick and F. Skidmore, *Progress against Poverty: A Review of the 1964–1974 Decade* (New York: Academic Press, 1975).

9. Ibid., p. 2.

10. Ibid.

11. John Kenneth Galbraith, *The Affluent Society* (Boston: Houghton-Mifflin, 1958); and Michael Harrington, *The Other America: Poverty in the United States* (New York: Macmillan, 1962).

12. Dorothy B. James, *Poverty, Politics, and Change* (New York: Prentice-Hall, 1972).

13. J. L. Sundquist, "The Origins of the War on Poverty," in *On Fighting Poverty: Perspectives from Experience*, ed. J. L. Sundquist (New York: Basic Books, 1969).

14. Daniel Patrick Moynihan, *Maximum Feasible Misunderstanding* (New York: Free Press, 1970); L. M. Friedman, "The Social and Political Context of the War on Poverty," in *A Decade of Federal Antipoverty Programs: Achievements, Failures, and Lessons*, ed. R. H. Haveman (New York: Academic Press, 1977), pp. 20–40; and H. J. Aaron, *Politics and Professors: The Great Society in Perspective* (Washington, D.C.: Brookings Institution, 1978).

15. Moynihan, *Maximum Feasible Misunderstanding*.

16. Friedman, "Social and Political Context of War on Poverty"; and Aaron, *Politics and Professors*.

17. Aaron, *Politics and Professors*, pp. 150–51.

18. Daniel Patrick Moynihan, "The Professors and the Poor," in *On Understanding Poverty: Perspectives from the Social Sciences*, ed. D. P. Moynihan (New York: Basic Books, 1968), pp. 3–35; Sundquist, "Origins of War on Poverty"; A. Yarmolinsky, "The Beginning of OEO," in Sundquist, *On Fighting Poverty*, pp. 34–51; and R. A. Levine, *The Poor Ye Need Not Have with You: Lessons from the War on Poverty* (Cambridge, Mass.: MIT Press, 1970).

19. Nathan Glazer, "A Sociologist's View of Poverty," in *Poverty in America*, ed. M. S. Gordon (San Francisco: Chandler Press, 1965), pp. 12–26; E. Raab, "A Tale of Three Wars: What War and Which Poverty," *Public Interest* 3 (1966): 45–56; S. A. Levitan, *The Great Society's Poor Law: A New Approach to Poverty* (Baltimore: Johns Hopkins University Press, 1969); Levine, *Poor Ye Need Not Have with You*; and Frances Fox Piven and R. A. Cloward, *Regulating the Poor: The Functions of Public Welfare* (New York: Academic Press, 1971).

20. Glazer, "Sociologist's View," p. 20.

21. Levitan, *Great Society's Poor Law*, p. 15.

22. Raab, "Tale of Three Wars."

23. Piven and Cloward, *Regulating the Poor*.

24. Yarmolinsky, "Beginnings of OEO," p. 37.

25. D. Bell, "Relevant Aspects of the Social Scene and Social Policy," in *Childrens' Allowances and the Economic Welfare of Children*, ed. E. M. Burns (New York: Committee for the Children of New York, 1968), pp. 163–71, cited in J. T. Patterson, *America's Struggle against Poverty, 1900–1980* (Cambridge, Mass.: Harvard University Press, 1981), p. 78.

26. R. J. Lampman, *The Low Income Population and Economic Growth*, study paper no. 12, Joint Economic Committee, 86th Cong., 1st sess., 1959; M. Orshansky, "Children of the Poor," *Social Security Bulletin* 26 (July 1963): 3–13; and idem, "Counting the Poor: Another Look at the Poverty Profile," *Social Security Bulletin* 28 (1965): 3–29.

27. H. R. Kerbo, "Characteristics of the Poor: A Continuing Focus in Social Research," *Sociology and Social Research* 65 (1981): 323–31.

28. Gordon, *Poverty in America*; L. Fishman, ed., *Poverty amid Affluence* (New Haven, Conn.: Yale University Press, 1966); and Burns, *Childrens' Allowances*.

29. Oscar Lewis, "The Culture of Poverty," *Scientific American* 215 (1966): 19–25; and C. A. Valentine, *Culture and Poverty: Critique and Counter Proposals* (Chicago: University of Chicago Press, 1968).

30. Daniel Patrick Moynihan, *The Negro Family: The Case for National Action* (Washington, D.C.: Office of Policy Planning and Research, U.S. Department of Labor, 1965); and Lee Rainwater and W. L. Yancy, eds., *The Moynihan Report and the Politics of Controversy* (Cambridge, Mass.: MIT Press, 1967).

31. Aaron, *Politics and Professors.*

32. D. C. Tompkins, *Poverty in the United States during the Sixties: A Bibliography* (Berkeley: Institute of Government Studies, University of California Press, 1970).

33. U.S. Bureau of the Census, *Estimates of Poverty including the Value of Non-Cash Benefits,* technical paper no. 51 (Washington, D.C.: Government Printing Office, 1984).

34. J. Huber, "Political Implications of Poverty Definitions," in *The Sociology of American Poverty,* ed. J. Huber and P. Chalfant (Cambridge, Mass.: Schenkman, 1974), pp. 300–323; and W. Korpi, "Approaches to the Study of Poverty in the United States: Critical Notes from a European Perspective," in *Poverty and Public Policy: An Evaluation of Social Science Research,* ed. V. T. Covello (Cambridge, Mass.: Schenkman, 1980), pp. 287–314.

35. H. R. Rodgers, *Poverty amid Plenty* (Reading, Mass.: Addison-Wesley, 1979); and R. Perlman, *The Economics of Poverty* (New York: McGraw-Hill, 1976).

36. H. R. Rodgers, "Hiding versus Ending Poverty," *Politics and Society* 8 (1978): 253–66.

37. B. R. Schiller, *The Economics of Poverty and Discrimination* (Englewood Cliffs, N.J.: Prentice-Hall, 1976), p. 21.

38. U.S. Bureau of the Census, *Estimates of Poverty.*

39. A. Downs, *Who Are the Urban Poor* (New York: Committee on Economic Development, 1970).

40. U.S. Bureau of the Census, *Current Population Reports,* Series P-60, "Characteristics of the Population below the Poverty Level, 1982" (Washington, D.C.: Government Printing Office, 1984).

41. Moynihan, *Negro Family,* pp. 5–6, 48.

42. E. Franklin Frazier, *The Negro Family in the United States* (Chicago: University of Chicago Press, 1939); Kenneth Clark, *Dark Ghetto* (New York: Harper and Row, 1965); Lee Rainwater, "Crucible of Identity: The Negro Lower-Class Family," *Daedalus* 95 (1966): 172–216; and Bayard Rustin, "From Protest to Politics: The Future of the Civil Rights Movement," *Commentary* 39 (1965): 25–31.

43. See Rainwater and Yancey, *Moynihan Report,* for a chronology of the controversy.

44. Cf. H. G. Gutman, *The Black Family in Slavery and Freedom, 1750–1925* (New York: Pantheon Books, 1976).

45. Elliot Liebow, *Tally's Corner: A Study of Negro Streetcorner Men* (Boston: Little, Brown, 1967); D. A. Schultz, "Variations in the Father Role in Complete Families in the Negro Lower Class," *Social Science Quarterly* 49 (1968): 651–59; idem, *Coming Up Black: Patterns of Ghetto Socialization* (Englewood Cliffs, N.J.: Prentice-Hall, 1969); U. Hannerz, *Soulside: Inquiries*

into Ghetto Culture and Community (New York: Columbia University Press, 1969); Lee Rainwater, *Behind Ghetto Walls: Black Families in a Federal Slum* (Chicago: Aldine Books, 1970); J. Heiss, "On the Transmission of Marital Instability in Black Families," *American Sociological Review* 37 (1972): 82–92; and C. Stack, *All Our Kin: Strategies for Survival in a Black Community* (New York: Harper and Row, 1974).

46. H. H. Hyman and J. S. Reed, "'Black Matriarchy' Reconsidered: Evidence from Secondary Analysis of Sample Surveys," *Public Opinion Quarterly* 33 (1969): 346–54; L. Rosen, "Matriarchy and Lower Class Negro Male Delinquency," *Social Problems* 17 (1969): 175–89; W. L. Yancey, "Going Down Home: Family Structure and the Urban Trap," *Social Science Quarterly* 52 (1972): 893–906; and A. S. Berger and W. Simon, "Black Families and the Moynihan Report: A Research Evaluation," *Social Problems* 22 (1974): 145–61.

47. Rosen, "Matriarchy and Lower-Class Negro Male Delinquency"; T. F. Hartnagel, "Father Absence and Self-Conception among Lower-Class White and Negro Boys," *Social Problems* 18 (1970): 152–63; M. Rosenberg and R. G. Simmons, *Black and White Esteem: The Urban School Child* (Washington, D.C.: American Sociological Association, 1972); Joyce Ladner, *Tomorrow's Tomorrow* (New York: Doubleday, 1973); and L. L. Hunt and J. G. Hunt, "Race and the Father-Son Connections: The Conditional Relevance of Father Absence for the Orientations and Identities of Adolescent Boys," *Social Problems* 23 (1975): 35–52.

48. See especially Liebow, *Tally's Corner,* and Stack, *All Our Kin.*

49. D. M. Pearce, "The Feminization of Poverty: Women, Work, and Welfare," *Urban and Social Change Review* 11 (1978): 28–36; idem, "The Feminization of Ghetto Poverty," *Society* 21 (1983): 70–74; K. Auletta, *The Underclass* (New York: Random House, 1982); R. Farley and S. M. Bianchi, "Social and Economic Polarization: Is It Occurring among Blacks," paper presented at the Annual Meeting of the American Sociological Association, San Francisco, 1982; and S. McLanahan, "Family Structure and the Reproduction of Poverty," discussion paper 720A-83, Institute for Research on Poverty, Madison, Wis., 1983.

50. S. G. Kellam, M. E. Ensminger, and R. J. Turner, "Family Structure and the Mental Health of Children," *Archives of General Psychiatry* 34 (1977): 1012–22; L. Earl and N. Lohmann, "Absent Fathers and Black Male Children," *Social Work* 23 (1978): 413–15; and McLanahan, "Family Structure."

51. H. L. Ross and I. V. Sawhill, *Time of Transition: The Growth of Families Headed by Women* (Washington, D.C.: Urban Institute, 1975); Mary J. Bane and David T. Ellwood, "The Dynamics of Children's Living Arrangements," working paper, supported by U.S. Department of Health and Human Services grant, contract no. HHS-100-82-0038, 1984; and idem, "Single Mothers and Their Living Arrangements," working paper, supported by U.S. Department of Health and Human Services grant, contract no. HHS-100-82-0038, 1984; W. A. Darity, Jr. and Samuel L. Myers Jr., "Does Welfare Dependency Cause Female Headship? The Case of the Black Family," *Journal of Marriage and the Family* 46 (1984): 765–79.

52. D. P. Hogan and E. M. Kitagawa, *The Impact of Social Status, Family Structure, and Neighborhood on the Fertility of Black Adolescents* (Chicago: Population Research Center, University of Chicago, 1983); D. P. Hogan, N. M. Astone, and E. M. Kitagawa, *The Impact of Social Status, Family Structure, and Neighborhood on Contraceptive Use among Black Adolescents* (Chicago: Population Research Center, University of Chicago, 1984).

53. T. Joe, *The "Flip-Side" of Black Families Headed by Women: The Economic Status of Men* (Washington, D.C.: Center for the Study of Social Policy, 1982).

54. J. N. Morgan, M. H. David, W. J. Cohen, and H. E. Brazer, *Income and Welfare in the United States* (New York: McGraw-Hill, 1962); L. E. Galloway, "On the Importance of Picking One's Parents," *Quarterly Review of Economics and Business* 6 (1966): 7–15; P. M. Blau and O. D. Duncan, *The American Occupational Structure* (New York: Wiley, 1967); S. Thernstrom, "Poverty in Historical Perspective," in Moynihan, *On Understanding Poverty*, pp. 160–86; and B. R. Schiller, "Stratified Opportunities: The Essence of the 'Vicious Circle,'" *American Journal of Sociology* 76 (1970): 426–42.

55. F. Levy, "The Intergenerational Transfer of Poverty," working paper 1241-02, Urban Institute, Washington, D.C., 1980.

56. M. S. Hill and M. Ponza, "Poverty and Welfare Dependence across Generations," *Economic Outlook U.S.A.* 10 (1983): 64.

57. McLanahan, "Family Structure."

58. R. Coe, "Dependency and Poverty in the Short and Long Run," in *Five Thousand American Families: Patterns of Economic Progress*, vol. 6, ed. G. J. Duncan and J. N. Morgan (Ann Arbor: Institute of Social Research, University of Michigan, 1978), pp. 273–96; M. S. Hill, "Some Dynamic Aspects of Poverty," in M. S. Hill, D. H. Hill, and J. N. Morgan, *Five Thousand American Families*, 9:93–120.

59. M. Corcoran, G. J. Duncan, and P. Gurin, "Psychological and Demographic Aspects of the Underclass," paper presented at the Annual Meeting of the Population Association, Pittsburgh, Pa., 1983.

60. Mary J. Bane and David T. Ellwood, "Slipping into and out of Poverty: The Dynamics of Spells," working paper no. 1199, National Bureau of Economic Research, Cambridge, Mass., 1983; and idem, "The Dynamics of Dependence: The Routes to Self-Sufficiency," working paper, supported by U.S. Department of Health and Human Services grant, contract no. HHS-100-82-0038, 1983.

61. Bane and Ellwood, "Dynamics of Dependence," p. ii.

62. Hill and Ponza, "Poverty and Welfare Dependence"; idem, "Intergenerational Transmission of Poverty: Does Welfare Dependency Beget Dependency?" paper presented at the Annual Meeting of the South Economic Association, Washington, D.C., 1983; and Corcoran, Duncan, and Gurin, "Psychological and Demographic Aspects of the Underclass."

63. S. J. Ball-Rokeach and J. F. Short, Jr., "Collective Violence: The Redress of Grievance," in *American Violence and Public Policy*, ed. L. A. Curtis (New Haven, Conn.: Yale University Press, 1985).

64. C. L. Beale, "Rural-Urban Migration of Blacks: Past and Future," *American Journal of Agricultural Economics* 53 (1971): 302–7; Piven and Cloward, *Regulating the Poor;* and G. F. De Jong and W. L. Donnelly, "Public Welfare and Migration," *Social Science Quarterly* 54 (1973): 329–44.

65. L. H. Long, "Poverty Status and Receipt of Welfare among Migrants and Nonmigrants in Large Cities," *American Sociological Review* 39 (1974): 48.

66. L. H. Long and L. R. Heltman, "Migration and Income Differences between Black and White Men in the North," *American Journal of Sociology* 80 (1975): 1391–1409.

67. W. W. Philliber and R. Seufert, "An Untested Hypothesis: The Effect of Size of Public Assistance Benefits on Migration," *American Sociological Review* 40 (1975): 845–47; Stanley Lieberson, "A Reconsideration of the Income Differences Found between Migrants and Northern-Born Blacks," *American Journal of Sociology* 83 (1978): 940–66; and C. B. Norton, "Comment on Long," *American Sociological Review* 44 (1979): 177–78.

68. P. N. Ritchey, "Urban Poverty and Rural to Urban Migration," *Rural Sociology* 39 (1974): 26.

69. Stanley Lieberson, *A Piece of the Pie: Black and White Immigrants since 1880* (Berkeley: University of California Press, 1980).

70. R. Farley and W. Allen, "Recent Trends in Black Migration in the United States," paper presented at the Annual Meeting of the Population Association of America, Minneapolis, Minn., 1984.

71. D. S. Massey, "Dimensions of the New Immigration to the United States and the Prospects for Assimilation," *Annual Review of Sociology* 7 (1981): 57–85.

72. W. Cornelius, "Mexican Migration to the United States: Causes, Consequences, and U.S. Responses," in *Migration and Development Monograph*, C/78-9 (Cambridge, Mass.: MIT Center for Industrial Studies, 1978); A. Portes, "Illegal Immigration and the International System: Lessons from Recent Legal Mexican Immigrants to the United States," *Social Problems* 26 (1979): 425–37; and R. Waldinger, "The Occupational and Economic Integration of the New Immigrants," *Law and Contemporary Problems* 45 (1982): 197–222.

73. Waldinger, "Occupational and Economic Integration," pp. 212, 213.

74. Ibid.; and Massey, "Dimension of the New Immigration."

75. I. Light and C. C. Wong, "Protest or Work: Dilemmas of the Tourist Industry in American Chinatowns," *American Journal of Sociology* 80 (1975): 1342–68.

76. Ibid.

77. R. Bernstein, "Tension and Gangs Mar the Chinatown Image," *New York Times*, December 24, 1982, p. 13.

78. Light and Wong, "Protest or Work."

79. C. Loo and D. Mar, "Desired Residential Mobility in a Low Income Ethnic Community: A Case Study of Chinatown," *Journal of Social Issues* 38 (1982): 95–106.

80. T. Joe, *The Social Consequences of Economic Neglect* (Washington, D.C.: Center for the Study of Social Policy, 1984).

221 Notes to Pages 181–84

81. John D. Kasarda, "The Implications of Contemporary Redistribution Trends for National Urban Policy," *Social Science Quarterly* 61 (1980): 373–400; and idem, "Caught in the Web of Change," *Society* 21 (1983): 41–47.

82. Kasarda, "Caught in the Web."

83. T. M. Stanback and T. J. Noyelle, *Cities in Transition* (Totowa, N.J.: Allanheld, Osmun, 1982), pp. 1, 128.

84. S. Sheingold, *Dislocated Workers: Issues and Federal Options* (Washington, D.C.: Budget Office, 1982).

85. M. C. Barth, "Dislocated Workers," *Journal of the Institute of Socioeconomic Studies* 7 (1982): 23–35.

86. Lewis, "Culture of Poverty," p. 188.

87. Ibid.; and S. Steinberg, *The Ethnic Myth: Race, Ethnicity, and Class in America* (New York: Atheneum Press, 1981).

88. Lewis, "Culture of Poverty," p. 193.

89. Harrington, *Other America;* W. B. Miller, "Focal Concerns of Lower-Class Culture," in *Poverty in America*, ed. L. A. Ferman, J. L. Kornblum, and A. Haber (Ann Arbor: University of Michigan Press, 1965), pp. 261–70; D. Matza, "The Disreputable Poor," in *Class, Status, and Power: A Reader in Social Stratification*, ed. R. Bendix and S. M. Lipset (New York: Free Press, 1966); and E. Banfield, *The Unheavenly City*, 2d ed. (Boston: Little, Brown, 1970).

90. Cf. Banfield, *Unheavenly City.*

91. Valentine, *Culture and Poverty;* and Steinberg, *Ethnic Myth.*

92. H. J. Gans, "Culture and Class in the Study of Poverty: An Approach to Antipoverty Research," in Moynihan, *On Understanding Poverty*, p. 205.

93. L. Kriesberg, "The Relationship between Socioeconomic Rank and Behavior," *Social Problems* 10 (1963): 334–53; Rainwater, "Crucible of Identity"; idem, "The Problem of Lower-Class Culture and Poverty-War Strategy," in Moynihan, *On Understanding Poverty*, pp. 229–59; and idem, *Behind Ghetto Walls.*

94. Miller, "Focal Concerns of Lower-Class Culture"; and Lewis, "Culture of Poverty."

95. See C. A. Valentine, C. H. Berndt, E. Boissevain, J. H. Bushnell, P. Carstens et al., "Culture and Poverty: Critique and Counter Proposals" (book review and author's precis/reply), *Current Anthropology* 10 (1969): 181–200.

96. Gans, "Culture and Class in the Study of Poverty," p. 206.

97. Ibid.

98. H. Rodman, "The Lower-Class Value Stretch," *Social Forces* 42 (1963): 206–15; U. Hannerz, *Soulside: Inquiries into Ghetto Culture and Community* (New York: Columbia University Press, 1969); and E. Anderson, *A Place on the Corner* (Chicago: University of Chicago Press, 1978).

99. Gans, "Culture and Class in the Study of Poverty," p. 209.

100. Charles A. Murray, *Losing Ground: American Social Policy, 1950–1980* (New York: Basic Books, 1984).

101. I. Garfinkle and L. L. Orr, "Welfare Policy and Employment Rate of

AFDC Mothers," *National Tax Journal* 27 (1974): 275–84; and F. Levy, "The Labor Supply of Female Household Heads, or AFDC Work Incentives Don't Work Too Well," *Journal of Human Resources* 14 (1979): 76–97.

102. S. Masters and I. Garfinkle, *Estimating the Labor Supply Effects of Income Maintenance Alternatives* (New York: Academic Press, 1977).

103. S. Danziger, R. H. Haveman, and R. Plotnick, "How Income Transfer Programs Affect Work, Savings, and the Income Distribution: A Critical Review," *Journal of Economic Literature* 19 (1981): 975–1028, quote on p. 995.

104. I. Garfinkle and R. H. Haveman, "Income Transfer Policy in the United States: A Review and Assessment," discussion paper 701-82, Institute for Research on Poverty, Madison, Wis., 1982.

105. M. T. Hannan, N. B. Tuma, and L. P. Groeneveld, "Income and Marital Events: Evidence from an Income Maintenance Experiment," *American Journal of Sociology* 82 (1977): 1186–1211; and idem, "Income and Independence Effects on Marital Dissolution: Results from the Seattle and Denver Income Maintenance Experiments," *American Journal of Sociology* 84 (1978): 611–33.

106. L. E. Lynn and D. F. Whitman, *The President as Policymaker: Jimmy Carter and Welfare Reform* (Philadelphia: Temple University Press, 1981).

107. L. P. Groeneveld, M. T. Hannon, and N. B. Tuma, *Marital Stability: Final Report of the Seattle-Denver Income Maintenance Experiment*, vol. 1: *Design and Results*, pt. 5 (Menlo Park, Calif.: SRI International, 1983), p. 344.

108. G. Cain, "Comments of August 18th Version of Marital Stability Findings," *SIME-DIME Final Report* (Washington, D.C.: Department of Health and Human Services, 1981).

109. M. Honig, "AFDC Income, Recipient Rates, and Family Dissolution," *Journal of Human Resources* 9 (1974): 303–22.

110. Ross and Sawhill, *Time of Transition.*

111. J. J. Minarik and R. S. Goldfarb, "AFDC Income, Recipient Rates, and Family Dissolution: A Comment," *Journal of Human Resources* 11 (Spring 1976): 243–50.

112. S. Hoffman and J. Holmes, "Husbands, Wives, and Divorce," in Hoffman; and Holmes, *Five Thousand American Families*, vol. 4.

113. D. T. Ellwood and Mary J. Bane, "The Impact of AFDC on Family Structure and Living Arrangements," working paper supported by U.S. Department of Health and Human Services grant no. 92A-82, 1984, pp. 9, 4.

114. T. Joe, *Profiles of Families in Poverty: Effects of the FY 1983 Budget Proposals on the Poor* (Washington, D.C.: Center for the Study of Social Policy, 1982); T. Joe, R. Sarri, M. Ginsberg, A. Mesnikoff, and S. Kulis, *Working Female-Headed Families in Poverty: Three Studies of Low-Income Families Affected by the AFDC Policy Changes of 1981* (Washington, D.C.: Center for the Study of Social Policy, 1984); and I. Moscovice and W. J. Craig, *The Impact of Federal Cutbacks on Working AFDC Recipients in Minnesota* (Minneapolis: Center for Health Services Research, University of Minnesota, 1983).

115. Joe, *Profiles of Families in Poverty.*

116. D. L. Bawden and J. L. Palmer, "Social Policy: Challenging the Welfare State," in *The Reagan Record: An Assessment of America's Changing Domestic Priorities,* ed. J. L. Palmer and I. V. Sawhill (Cambridge, Mass.: Ballinger, 1984), pp. 177–215.

Bibliography

Aaron, H. J. 1978. *Politics and Professors: The Great Society in Perspective.* Washington, D.C.: Brookings Institution.

Abrahams, R. D. 1964. *Deep Down in the Jungle.* Hatboro, Pa.: Folklore Associates.

Addams, J. 1902. "The Housing Problem in Chicago." *Annual of the American Academy of Political and Social Science* 20:97–107.

Alkalimat, Abdul Hakim Ibn [Gerald McWorter]. 1969. "The Ideology of Black Social Science." *Black Scholar* 1:28–35.

Anderson, E. 1978. *A Place on the Corner.* Chicago: University of Chicago Press.

Anderson, N. 1923. *The Hobo.* Chicago: University of Chicago Press.

———. 1940. *Men on the Move.* Chicago: University of Chicago Press.

Auletta, K. 1982. *The Underclass.* New York: Random House.

Bakke, W. E. 1940. *Citizens without Work.* New Haven, Conn.: Yale University Press.

Ball-Rokeach, S. J., and J. F. Short, Jr. 1985. "Collective Violence: The Redress of Grievance." In *American Violence and Public Policy,* ed. L. A. Curtis. New Haven, Conn.: Yale University Press.

Bane, M. J. 1985. "Household Composition and Poverty: Which Comes First?" Revised version of paper prepared for the conference on Poverty and Policy: Retrospect and Prospect, December 6–8, 1984, Williamsburg, Va.

Bane, M. J., and D. T. Ellwood. 1983. "The Dynamics of Dependence: The Routes to Self-Sufficiency." Supported by a U.S. Department of Health and Human Services grant, contract no. HHS-100-82-0038.

———. 1983. "Slipping into and out of Poverty: The Dynamics of Spells." Working paper no. 1199, National Bureau of Economic Research, Cambridge, Mass.

———. 1984. "The Dynamics of Children's Living Arrangements." Working paper, supported by a U.S. Department of Health and Human Services grant, contract no. HHS-100-82-0038.

———. 1984. "Single Mothers and Their Living Arrangements." Working paper, supported by a U.S. Department of Health and Human Services grant, contract no. HHS-100-82-0038.

Banfield, E. 1970. *The Unheavenly City.* 2d ed. Boston: Little, Brown.

Barnett, A., D. J. Kleitman, and R. C. Larson. 1974. "On Urban Homicide."

Working paper WP-04-74, Massachusetts Institute of Technology, Operations Research Center, Cambridge, Mass.

Barr, N., and R. Hall. 1981. "The Probability of Dependence on Public Assistance." *Economica* 48:109–23.

Barth, M. C. 1982. "Dislocated Workers." *Journal of the Institute of Socioeconomic Study* 7:23–35.

Bawden, D. L., and J. L. Palmer. 1984. "Social Policy: Challenging the Welfare State." In *The Reagan Record: An Assessment of America's Changing Domestic Priorities,* ed. J. L. Palmer and I. V. Sawhill. Cambridge, Mass.: Ballinger.

Beale, C. L. 1971. "Rural-Urban Migration of Blacks: Past and Future." *American Journal of Agricultural Economics* 53:302–7.

Becker, B., and S. Hills. 1979. "Today's Teenage Unemployed—Tomorrow's Working Poor?" *Monthly Labor Review* 102:67–71.

Becker, G. S., E. M. Landes, and R. T. Michael. 1977. "An Economic Analysis of Marital Instability." *Journal of Political Economy* 85:1141–87.

Bell, D. 1968. "Relevant Aspects of the Social Scene and Social Policy." In *Children's Allowances and the Economic Welfare of Children,* ed. E. M. Burns. New York: Committee for the Children of New York.

Berger, A. S., and W. Simon. 1974. "Black Families and the Moynihan Report: A Research Evaluation." *Social Problems* 22:145–61.

Bernstein, R. 1982. "Tension and Gangs Mar the Chinatown Image." *New York Times* (December 24):13.

Billingsly, A. 1968. *Black Families in White America.* Englewood Cliffs, N.J.: Prentice-Hall.

Bishop, J. H. 1980. "Jobs, Cash Transfers, and Marital Instability: A Review and Synthesis of the Evidence." *Journal of Human Resources* 15 (Summer):301–34.

Blank, R., and A. A. Blinder. 1986. "Macroeconomics, Income Distribution, and Poverty." In *Fighting Poverty: What Works and What Doesn't,* ed. S. Danziger and D. H. Weinberg. Cambridge, Mass.: Harvard University Press.

Blau, P. M., and O. D. Duncan. 1967. *The American Occupational Structure.* New York: Wiley.

Bluestone, B., and B. Harrison. 1982. *The Deindustrialization of America: Plant Closings, Community Abandonment, and the Dismantling of Basic Industry.* New York: Basic Books.

———. 1986. *The Great American Job Machine: The Proliferation of Low Wage Employment in the U.S. Economy.* A study prepared by the Joint Economic Committee of the U.S. Congress. Washington, D.C.

Blumenthal, R. 1982. "Gunmen Firing Wildly Kill Three in Chinatown Bar." *New York Times* (December 24):1, 13.

Blumstein, A. 1983. "On the Racial Disproportionality of United States' Prison Populations." *Journal of Criminal Law and Criminology* 73 (Fall):1259–81.

Bowles, S., and S. Gintis. 1976. *Schooling in Capitalist America: Education and the Contradictions of Economic Life.* New York: Basic Books.

Breckinridge, S. 1936. *The Tenements of Chicago, 1908–35.* Chicago: University of Chicago Press.

Bremner, R. H. 1956. *From the Depths: The Discovery of Poverty in the United States.* New York: University Press.

Burns, E. M., ed. 1968. *Children's Allowances and the Economic Welfare of Children.* New York: Committee for the Children of New York.

Cain, G. 1974. "The Effect of Income Maintenance Laws on Fertility in Results from the New Jersey–Pennsylvania Experiment." In *Final Report of the Graduated Work Incentive Experiment in New Jersey and Pennsylvania.* Madison, Wis., and Princeton, N.J.: Institute for Research on Poverty, University of Wisconsin, and Mathematica Policy Research.

———. 1981. "Comments on August 18th Version of Marital Stability Findings." In *SIME-DIME Final Report.* Washington, D.C.: Department of Health and Human Services.

Center for the Study of Social Policy. 1984. "The 'Flip Side' of Black Families Headed by Women: The Economic Status of Black Men." Working paper.

Cherlin, A. 1981. *Marriage, Divorce, Remarriage.* Cambridge, Mass.: Harvard University Press.

Chicago Housing Authority. 1981. *Statistical Report, 1980.* Chicago: Chicago Housing Authority Executive Office.

———. 1984. *Statistical Report, 1983.* Chicago: Chicago Housing Authority Executive Office.

Chicago Police Department. 1984. *Murder Analysis, 1983.* Chicago: Chicago Police Department.

———. 1984. *Statistical Summary, 1983.* Chicago: Chicago Police Department.

Clark, K. B. 1964. *Youth in the Ghetto: A Study of the Consequences of Powerlessness and a Blueprint for Change.* Harlem Youth Opportunity [HARYOU] Report.

———. 1965. *Dark Ghetto: Dilemmas of Social Power.* New York: Harper and Row.

———. 1967. "The Present Dilemma of the Negro." Paper presented at the Annual Meeting of the Southern Regional Council, November 2, Atlanta, Ga.

———. 1980. "The Role of Race." *New York Times Magazine* (October 5): 25–33.

Clark, L. D., and J. T. Ellis. 1980. "Affirmative Action in Recessionary Periods: The Legal Structure." *Adherent: A Journal of Comprehensive Employment Training and Human Resources of Development* 7 (64): 54–67.

Coe, R. D. 1978. "Dependency and Poverty in the Short and Long Run." In *Five Thousand American Families: Patterns of Economic Progress,* ed. G. J. Duncan, and J. N. Morgan, vol. 6. Ann Arbor: Institute for Social Research, University of Michigan Press.

Cogan, J. 1982. "The Decline in Black Teenage Employment, 1950–70." *American Economic Review* 72 (September): 621–38.

Cohen, A. 1979. "Economic, Marital Stability and Race." Ph.D. dissertation, University of Wisconsin, Madison.

Cohen, T. 1981. "Reagan's New Deal." *New York Times* (August 19):23.

Corcoran, M., and G. J. Duncan. 1983. "Demographic Aspects of the Underclass." Paper presented at the Annual Meeting of the Population Association of America, Pittsburgh, Pa.

Corcoran, M., G. J. Duncan, and P. Gurin. 1983. "Psychological and Demographic Aspects of the Underclass." Paper presented at the Annual Meeting of the Population Association of America, Pittsburgh, Pa.

Cornelius, W. 1978. "Mexican Migration to the United States: Causes, Consequences, and U.S. Responses." In *Migration and Development Monograph*. C/78-9. Cambridge, Mass.: MIT Center for Industrial Studies.

Covello, V. T., ed. 1980. *Poverty and Public Policy: An Evaluation of Social Research*. Boston: G. K. Hall.

Cutright, P. 1971. "Income and Family Events: Marital Instability." *Journal of Marriage and the Family* 33:291–306.

———. 1973. "Illegitimacy and Income Supplements." In *Studies in Public Welfare*, paper no. 12, pt. 1. Washington, D.C.: Government Printing Office.

———. 1974. "Components of Change in the Number of Female Family Heads Aged 15–44: United States, 1940–1970." *Journal of Marriage and the Family* 36:714–21.

Cutright, P., and P. Madras. 1974. "AFDC and the Marital and Family Status of Ever-Married Women Aged 15–44: United States, 1950–1970." *Sociology and Social Research* 60 (April):314–27.

Danziger, S., and P. Gottschalk. 1985. "The Poverty of Losing Ground." *Challenge*, May/June.

———. 1985. "Social Programs—A Partial Solution to, But Not a Cause of Poverty: An Alternative to Charles Murray's View." *Challenge*, May/June.

———. 1986. "Earnings Inequality, the Spatial Concentration of Poverty, and the Underclass." Paper presented at the Annual Meeting of the American Economic Association, New Orleans, 1986.

Danziger, S., R. H. Haveman, and R. Plotnick. 1981. "How Income Transfer Programs Affect Work, Savings, and the Income Distribution: A Critical Review." *Journal of Economic Literature* 19:975–1028.

Danziger, S., G. Jakubson, S. Schwartz, and E. Smolensky. 1982. "Work and Welfare as Determinants of Female Poverty and Household Headship." *Quarterly Journal of Economics* 97 (August):519–34.

Danziger, S., and D. E. Weinberg, eds. *Fighting Poverty: What Works and What Doesn't*. Cambridge, Mass.: Harvard University Press.

Darity, W. A., and Samuel L. Myers. 1984. "Does Welfare Dependency Cause Female Headship? The Case of the Black Family." *Journal of Marriage and the Family* 46: 765–79.

Davis, A. 1971. "The Motivations of the Underprivileged Worker." In *Industry and Society*, ed. William F. Whyte. Westview, Conn.: Greenwood Press.

De Jong, G. F., and W. L. Donnelly. 1973. "Public Welfare and Migration." *Social Science Quarterly* 54:329–44.

Downs, A. 1970. *Who Are the Urban Poor.* New York: Committee on Economic Development.

Drake, St. C., and H. R. Cayton. 1945. *Black Metropolis: A Study of Negro Life in a Northern City.* New York: Harper and Row.

Duncan, G. J. 1984. *Years of Poverty, Years of Plenty.* Ann Arbor: Institute for Social Research, University of Michigan.

Earl, L., and N. Lohmann. 1978. "Absent Fathers and Black Male Children." *Social Work* 23:413–15.

Easterlin, R. 1980. *Birth and Fortune: The Impact of Numbers on Personal Welfare.* New York: Basic Books.

Elder, G. H., Jr. 1974. *Children of the Great Depression.* Chicago: University of Chicago Press.

Ellwood, D. T. 1986. "The Spatial Mismatch Hypothesis: Are There Teenage Jobs Missing in the Ghetto?" In *The Black Youth Employment Crisis,* ed. R. B. Freeman and H. J. Holzer. Chicago: University of Chicago Press.

Ellwood, D. T., and M. J. Bane. 1984. "The Impact of AFDC on Family Structure and Living Arrangements." Working paper prepared for the U.S. Department of Health and Human Services under grant no. 92A-82.

Ellwood, D. T., and L. Summers. 1984. "Poverty in America: Is Welfare the Answer or the Problem?" Paper presented at conference on Poverty and Policy: Retrospect and Prospects, Williamsburg, Va.

Ellwood, D. T., and D. A. Wise. 1983. "Youth Employment in the Seventies: The Changing Circumstances of Young Adults." Working paper no. 1055, National Bureau of Economic Research, Cambridge, Mass.

Evans, M. D. 1983. "Modernization, Economic Conditions, and Family Formation: Evidence from Recent White and Nonwhite Cohorts." Ph.D. dissertation, University of Chicago.

Faris, R. E. L., and W. Dunham. 1931. *Mental Disorder in Urban America.* Chicago: University of Chicago Press.

Farley, R. 1970. *The Growth of the Black Population.* Chicago: Markham.

———. 1980. "Homicide Trends in the United States." *Demography* 17 (May):177–88.

Farley, R., and W. Allen. 1984. "Recent Trends in Black Migration in the United States." Paper presented at the Annual Meeting of the Population Association of America, Minneapolis, Minn.

Farley, R., and S. M. Bianchi. 1982. "Social and Economic Polarization: Is It Occurring among Blacks." Paper presented at the Annual Meeting of American Sociological Association, San Francisco.

Farley, R., and A. I. Hermalin. 1971. "Family Stability: A Comparison of Trends between Blacks and Whites." *American Sociological Review* 36:1–18.

Fechter, A., and S. Greenfield. 1973. "Welfare and Illegitimacy: An Economic Model and Some Preliminary Results." Working paper no. 963-37, Urban Institute, Washington, D.C.

Feldstein, M., ed. 1980. *The American Economy in Transition.* Chicago: University of Chicago Press.

Feldstein, M., and D. T. Ellwood. 1982. "Teenage Employment: What Is the Problem?" In *The Youth Labor Market Problem: Its Nature, Causes and Consequences,* ed. R. B. Freeman and D. A. Wise. Chicago: University of Chicago Press.

Ferdinand, T. 1969. "Report Index Crime Increases between 1950 and 1965 Due to Urbanization and Changes in the Age Structure of the Population Alone." In *Crimes of Violence,* ed. D. J. Mulvihaill and M. Tumin, vol. 2. Staff Report to the National Commission on the Causes and Prevention of Violence. Washington, D.C.: Government Printing Office.

Fishkin, J. 1983. *Justice, Equal Opportunity and the Family.* New Haven, Conn.: Yale University Press.

Fishman, L., ed. 1966. *Poverty amid Affluence.* New Haven, Conn.: Yale University Press.

Fitzpatrick, J. P., and L. T. Parker. 1981. "Hispanic-Americans in the Eastern United States." *Annals of the American Academy of Political and Social Sciences* 454:98–124.

Fligstein, N. 1981. *Going North: Migration of Blacks and Whites from the South, 1900–1950.* New York: Academic Press.

Frazer, F. 1932. *The Negro Family in Chicago.* Chicago: University of Chicago Press.

Frazier, E. F. 1939. *The Negro Family in the United States.* Chicago: University of Chicago Press.

Freeman, R. B. 1981. "Economic Determinants of Geographic and Individual Variation in the Labor Market Position of Young Persons." In *The Youth Labor Market Problem: Its Nature, Causes and Consequences,* ed. R. B. Freeman and D. A. Wise. Chicago: University of Chicago Press.

Freeman, R. B., and H. T. Holzer. 1986. *The Black Youth Employment Crisis.* Chicago: University of Chicago Press.

Friedlander, S. L. 1972. *Unemployment in the Urban Core: An Analysis of Thirty Cities with Policy Recommendations.* New York: Praeger.

Friedman, L. M. 1977. "The Social and Political Context of the War on Poverty." In *A Decade of Federal Antipoverty Programs: Achievements, Failures, and Lessons,* ed. R. H. Haveman. New York: Academic Press.

Furstenberg, F. F., Jr., T. Hershberg, and J. Modell. 1975. "The Origins of the Female-Headed Black Family: The Impact of the Urban Experience." *Journal of Interdisciplinary History* 6 (2):211–33.

Furstenberg, F. F., Jr., C. W. Nord, J. L. Peterson, and N. Zill. 1983. "The Life Course of Children of Divorce: Marital Disruption and Parental Contact." *American Sociological Review* (October):656–68.

Galbraith, J. K. 1958. *The Affluent Society.* Boston: Houghton-Mifflin.

Galenson, W. 1980. "Does the United States Need an Industrial Policy?" Paper presented at the Annual Meeting of the Social Democrats, New York, N.Y.

Galloway, L. E. 1966. "On the Importance of Picking One's Parents." *Quarterly Review of Economics and Business* 6:7–15.

Galloway, P. 1981. "Nine Weeks, Ten Murders." *Chicago Sun-Times* (March 22):66–67.

Gans, H. J. 1968. "Culture and Class in the Study of Poverty: An Approach to Antipoverty Research." In *On Understanding Poverty: Perspectives from the Social Sciences,* ed. D. P. Moynihan. New York: Basic Books.

Garfinkle, I., and R. H. Haveman. 1982. "Income Transfer Policy in the United States: A Review and Assessment." Discussion paper no. 701-82, Institute for Research on Poverty, Madison, Wis.

Garfinkle, I., and S. S. McLanahan. 1986. *Single Mothers and Their Children: A New American Dilemma.* Washington, D.C.: Urban Institute Press.

Garfinkle, I., and L. L. Orr. 1974. "Welfare Policy and Employment Rate of AFDC Mothers." *National Tax Journal* 27:275–84.

Garfinkle, I., and E. Uhr. 1984. "A New Approach to Child Support." *Public Interest* 75 (Spring):111–22.

Gershman, C. 1980. "Carl Gershman Responds." *New York Times Magazine* (October 5):24, 33, 90–91.

———. 1980. "A Matter of Class." *New York Times Magazine* (October 5):24, 92–105.

Gilder, G. 1981. *Wealth and Poverty.* New York: Basic Books.

Glazer, N. 1965. "A Sociologist's View of Poverty." In *Poverty in America*, ed. M. S. Gordon. San Francisco: Chandler.

Gordon, M. M. 1975. "Toward a General Theory of Racial and Ethnic Group Relations." In *Ethnicity: Theory and Experience*, ed. N. Glazer and D. P. Moynihan. Cambridge, Mass.: Harvard University Press.

———. 1981. "Models of Pluralism: The New American Dilemma." *Annals of the American Academy of Political and Social Sciences* 454:183.

Gordon, M. S., ed. 1965. *Poverty in America.* San Francisco: Chandler.

Greenberg, R. 1981. "Murder Victims: Most Blacks, Latinos Now Surpassing Whites." *Chicago Reporter: A Monthly Information Service on Racial Issues in Metropolitan Chicago* 1 (January):1, 4–7.

Greenstein, R. 1985. "Losing Faith in 'Losing Ground.'" *New Republic* (March 25):12–17.

Groeneveld, L. P., M. T. Hannon, and N. B. Tuma. 1983. *Marital Stability: Final Report of the Seattle-Denver Income Maintenance Experiment.* Vol. 1, *Design and Results*, pt. 5. Menlo Park, Calif.: SRI International.

Groeneveld, L. P., N. B. Tuma, and M. T. Hannon. 1980. "The Effects of Negative Income Tax Programs on Marital Dissolution." *Journal of Human Resources* 15: 654–74.

Gutman, H. G. 1976. *The Black Family in Slavery and Freedom, 1750–1925.* New York: Pantheon.

Hamilton, C. H. 1964. "The Negro Leaves the South." *Demography* 1:273–95.

Hannan, M. T., N. B. Tuma, and L. P. Groeneveld. 1977. "Income and Marital Events: Evidence from an Income Maintenance Experiment." *American Journal of Sociology* 82:1186–1221.

————. 1978. "Income and Independence Effects on Marital Dissolution: Results from the Seattle and Denver Income Maintenance Experiments." *American Journal of Sociology* 84:611–33.

Hannerz, U. 1969. *Soulside: Inquiries into Ghetto Culture and Community.* New York: Columbia University Press.

Hare, N. 1969. "The Challenge of a Black Scholar." *Black Scholar* 1:58–63.

Harrington, M. 1962. *The Other America: Poverty in the United States.* New York: Macmillan.

————. 1984. *The New American Poverty.* New York: Holt, Rinehart and Winston.

Harrison, Bennett. 1986. *The Great American Job Machine: The Proliferation of Low Wage Employment in the U.S. Economy.* Study prepared by the Joint Economic Committee of the U.S. Congress, Washington, D.C.

Hartnagel, T. F. 1970. "Father Absence and Self-Conception among Lower-Class White and Negro Boys." *Social Problem* 18:152–63.

Hauser, P. M. 1981. "The Census of 1980." *Scientific American* 245:61.

Heiss, J. 1972. "On the Transmission of Marital Instability in Black Families." *American Sociological Review* 37:82–92.

Herbers, J. 1981. "Census Finds Blacks Gaining Majorities in Big Cities." *New York Times* (April 16).

Hill, M. S. 1981. "Some Dynamic Aspects of Poverty." In *Five Thousand American Families: Patterns of Economic Progress,* vol. 9, ed. M. S. Hill, D. H. Hill, and J. N. Morgan. Ann Arbor: Institute for Social Research, University of Michigan Press.

Hill, M. S., and M. Ponza. 1983. "Intergenerational Transmission of Poverty: Does Welfare Dependency Beget Dependency?" Revised version of paper presented at Annual Meeting of the Southern Economic Association, Washington, D.C.

————. 1983. "Poverty and Welfare Dependence across Generations." *Economic Outlook U.S.A.* 10:61–4.

Hill, R. B. 1972. *The Strength of Black Families.* New York: Emerson Hall.

Hindelang, M. 1976. *Criminal Victimization in Eight American Cities: A Descriptive Analysis of Common Theft and Assault.* Cambridge, Mass.: Ballinger.

————. 1978. "Race and Involvement in Common Law Personal Crimes." *American Sociological Review* 43 (February):93–109.

Hoffman, S., and J. Holmes. 1976. "Husbands, Wives, and Divorce." In *Five Thousand American Families: Patterns of Economic Progress,* ed. J. N. Morgan, vol. 4. Ann Arbor: Institute for Social Research, University of Michigan Press.

Hogan, D. P. 1981. *Transitions and Social Change: The Early Lives of American Men.* New York: Academic Press.

————. 1983. "Demographic Trends in Human Fertility and Parenting across the Life-Span." Paper prepared for the Social Science Research Council

Conference on Bio-Social Life-Span Approaches to Parental and Offspring Development, Elkridge, Md.

———. 1984. "Structural and Normative Factors in Single Parenthood among Black Adolescents." Paper presented at the Annual Meeting of the American Sociological Association, San Antonio, Tx.

Hogan, D. P., N. M. Astone, and E. M. Kitagawa. 1984. *The Impact of Social Status, Family Structure, and Neighborhood on Contraceptive Use among Black Adolescents.* Chicago: Population Research Center, University of Chicago.

Hogan, D. P., and E. M. Kitagawa. 1983. *The Impact of Social Status, Family Structure, and Neighborhood on the Fertility of Black Adolescents.* Chicago: Population Research Center, University of Chicago.

———. 1985. "The Impact of Social Status, Family Structure, and Neighborhood on the Fertility of Black Adolescents." *American Journal of Sociology* 90:825–55.

Honig, M. 1974. "AFDC Income, Recipient Rates, and Family Dissolution." *Journal of Human Resources* 9 (Summer):303–22.

Huber, J. 1974. "Political Implications of Poverty Definitions." In *The Sociology of American Poverty*, ed. J. Huber and P. Chalfant. Cambridge, Mass.: Schenkman.

Hunt, L. L., and J. G. Hunt. 1975. "Race and the Father-Son Connections: The Conditional Relevance of Father Absence for the Orientations and Identities of Adolescent Boys." *Social Problems* 23:35–52.

Hyman, H. H., and J. S. Reed. 1969. "'Black Matriarchy' Reconsidered: Evidence from Secondary Analysis of Sample Surveys." *Public Opinion Quarterly* 33:346–54.

Illinois Advisory Committee. 1981. *Shutdown: Economic Dislocation and Equal Opportunity.* Report to the United States Commission on Civil Rights.

James, D. B. 1972. *Poverty, Politics, and Change.* New York: Prentice-Hall.

Jencks, C. 1985. "How Poor Are the Poor?" *New York Review of Books* 32 (8):41–49.

Joe, T. 1982. *Profile of Families in Poverty: Effects of the FY 1983 Budget Proposals on the Poor.* Washington, D.C.: Center for the Study of Social Policy.

———. 1984. *The "Flip-Side" of Black Families Headed by Women: The Economic Status of Men.* Washington, D.C.: Center for the Study of Social Policy.

———. 1984. *The Social Consequences of Economic Neglect.* Washington, D.C.: Center for the Study of Social Policy.

Joe, T., R. Sarri, M. Ginsberg, A. Mesnikoff, and S. Kulis. 1984. *Working Female-Headed Families in Poverty: Three Studies of Low-Income Families Affected by the AFDC Policy Changes of 1981.* Washington, D.C.: Center for the Study of Social Policy.

Kahn, T. 1964. "Problems of the Negro Movement." *Dissent* 11 (Winter):108–38.

Kamerman, S., and A. J. Kahn. 1981. "Europe's Innovative Family Policies." *Transatlantic Perspectives* 2:9–12.
Kasarda, J. D. 1978. "Urbanization, Community, and the Metropolitan Problems." In *Handbook of Contemporary Urban Life,* ed. D. Street, and associates. San Francisco: Jossey-Bass.
———. 1980. "The Implications of Contemporary Redistribution Trends for National Urban Policy." *Social Science Quarterly* 61:373–400.
———. 1983. "Caught in the Web of Change." *Society* 21:4–7.
———. 1985. "Urban Change and Minority Opportunities." In *The New Urban Reality,* ed. P. E. Peterson. Washington, D.C.: Brookings Institution.
Katz, M. B. 1986. *In the Shadow of the Poorhouse: A Social History of Welfare in America.* New York: Basic Books.
Katznelson, I. 1984. "Social Policy." In *The Hidden Election: Politics and Economics in the 1980 Presidential Campaign,* ed. T. Ferguson and J. Rogers. New York: Pantheon.
Keeley, M. C. 1980. "The Effects of Negative Income Tax Programs on Fertility." *Journal of Human Resources* 9:303–22.
Kellam, S. G., M. E. Ensminger, and R. J. Turner. 1977. "Family Structure and the Mental Health of Children." *Archives of General Psychiatry* 34:1012–22.
Kerbo, H. R. 1981. "Characteristics of the Poor: A Continuing Focus in Social Research. *Sociology and Social Research* 65:323–31.
Killingsworth, C. C., Jr. 1963. *Jobs and Income for Negroes.* Ann Arbor: University of Michigan Press.
Kilson, M. 1981. "Black Social Classes and Intergenerational Poverty." *Public Interest* 64 (Summer):58–78.
King, M. L., Jr. 1968. "Showdown for Non-Violence." *Look* (April 16):23–25.
Komarovsky, M. 1940. *The Unemployed Man and His Family.* New York: Octagon.
Korpi, W. 1980. "Approaches to the Study of Poverty in the United States: Critical Notes from a European Perspective." In *Poverty and Public Policy: An Evaluation of Social Science Research,* ed. V. T. Covello. Boston: G. K. Hall.
Kriesberg, L. 1963. "The Relationship between Socioeconomic Rank and Behavior." *Social Problems* 10:334–53.
Kuttner, R. 1984. "A Flawed Case for Scrapping What's Left of the Great Society." *Washington Post Book World* (November 25):34–35.
Ladner, J. 1973. *Tomorrow's Tomorrow.* New York: Doubleday.
———, ed. 1973. *The Death of White Sociology.* New York: Random House.
Lammermeier, P. J. 1973. "The Urban Black Family of the Nineteenth Century: A Study of Black Family Structure in the Ohio Valley, 1850–1880." *Journal of Marriage and the Family* 35 (August):440–56.
Lampman, R. J. 1959. *The Low Income Population and Economic Growth.* Study paper no. 12. Joint Economic Committee, 86th Cong., 1st sess.
Lemann, N. 1986. "The Origins of the Underclass." *Atlantic* 257 (June):31–61.
Leonard, J. S. 1983. "The Interaction of Residential Segregation and Employment Discrimination." University of California, Berkeley. Typescript.

Leroy, D. C., and J. T. Ellis. 1980. "Affirmative Action in Recessionary Periods: The Legal Structure." *Adherent: A Journal of Comprehensive Employment Training and Human Resources of Development* 7 (December):64.

Levine, R. A. 1970. *The Poor Ye Need Not Have with You: Lessons from the
War on Poverty*. Cambridge, Mass.: MIT Press.

Levitan, S. A. 1969. *The Great Society's Poor Law: A New Approach to Poverty*. Baltimore: Johns Hopkins University Press.

Levitan, S. A., and C. M. Johnson. 1984. *Beyond the Safety Net: Reviving the
Promising of Opportunity in America*. Cambridge, Mass.: Ballinger.

Levy, F. 1979. "The Labor Supply of Female Household Heads, or AFDC
Work Incentives Don't Work Too Well." *Journal of Human Resources*
14:76–97.

———. 1980. "The Intergenerational Transfer of Poverty." Working paper no.
1241-02, Urban Institute, Washington, D.C.

———. 1986. "Poverty and Economic Growth." College Park, University of
Maryland. Typescript.

Lewis, D. L. 1981. *When Harlem Was in Vogue*. New York: Knopf.

Lewis, H. 1963. "Culture, Class and the Behavior of Low-Income Families."
Paper presented at Conference on Views of Lower-Class Culture, New
York, N.Y.

Lewis, O. 1959. *Five Families: Mexican Case Studies in the Culture of Poverty*.
New York: Basic Books.

———. 1961. *The Children of Sanchez*. New York: Random House.

———. 1966. *La Vida: A Puerto Rican Family in the Culture of Poverty—San
Juan and New York*. New York: Random House.

———. 1968. "The Culture of Poverty." In *On Understanding Poverty: Perspectives from the Social Sciences*, ed. D. P. Moynihan. New York: Basic
Books.

Lieberson, S. 1978. "A Reconsideration of the Income Differences Found between Migrants and Northern-Born Blacks." *American Journal of Sociology*
83:940–66.

———. 1980. *A Piece of the Pie: Black and White Immigrants since 1880*.
Berkeley: University of California Press.

Liebow, E. 1967. *Tally's Corner: A Study of Negro Streetcorner Men*. Boston:
Little, Brown.

Light, I., and C. C. Wong. 1975. "Protest or Work: Dilemmas of the Tourist
Industry in American Chinatowns." *American Journal of Sociology* 80:1342–
68.

Lindsey, R. 1983. "Asian Americans See Growing Bias." *New York Times*
(September 10):1, 9.

Local Community Fact Book: Chicago Metropolitan Area 1970–1980. 1980.
Chicago: Chicago Review Press.

Long, L. H. 1974. "Poverty Status and Receipt of Welfare among Migrants
and Nonmigrants in Large Cities." *American Sociological Review* 39:46–56.

Long, L. H., and L. R. Heltman. 1975. "Migration and Income Differences
between Black and White Men in the North." *American Journal of Sociology* 80:1391–1409.

236   Bibliography

Loo, C., and D. Mar. 1982. "Desired Residential Mobility in a Low Income Ethnic Community: A Case Study of Chinatown." *Journal of Social Issues* 38:95–106.

"Losing More Ground." 1985. *New York Times* (February 3).

Loury, G. C. 1984. "On the Need for Moral Leadership in the Black Community." Paper presented at the University of Chicago, sponsored by the Center for the Study of Industrial Societies and the John M. Olin Center, Chicago, Ill.

Lynn, L. E., and D. F. Whitman. 1981. *The President as Policymaker: Jimmy Carter and Welfare Reform.* Philadelphia: Temple University Press.

McGahey, R. 1982. "Poverty's Voguish Stigma." *New York Times* (March 12): 29.

McGahey, R., and J. Jeffries. 1983. "Employment, Training and Industrial Policy: Implications for Minorities." Paper prepared for a conference on Industrial Policy and Minority Economic Opportunity, sponsored by the Joint Center for Political Studies and the A. Philip Randolph Educational Fund, New York, N.Y. October 14,

McLanahan, S. 1983. "Family Structure and the Reproduction of Poverty." Discussion paper 720A-83, Institute for Research on Poverty, University of Wisconsin, Madison.

Mangum, B., and R. Seninger. 1978. *Coming of Age in the Ghetto.* Baltimore: Johns Hopkins University Press.

Mare, R. D., and C. Winship. 1980. "Changes in the Relative Labor Force Status of Black and White Youths: A Review of the Literature." Special report prepared for the National Commission for Employment Policy. Institute for Research on Poverty, University of Wisconsin, Madison.

Massey, D. S. 1981. "Dimensions of the New Immigration to the United States and the Prospects for Assimilation." *Annual Review of Sociology* 7:57–85.

Masters, S., and I. Garfinkle. 1977. *Estimating the Labor Supply Effects of Income Maintenance Alternatives.* New York: Academic Press.

Matza, D. 1966. "The Disreputable Poor." In *Class, Status, and Power: A Reader in Social Stratification,* ed. R. Bendix and S. M. Lipset. New York: Free Press.

Mead, L. 1986. *Beyond Entitlement: The Social Obligations of Citizenship.* New York: Free Press.

Miller, H. P. 1966. *Poverty American Style.* Belmont, Calif.: Wadsworth.

Miller, W. B. 1965. "Focal Concerns of Lower-Class Culture." In *Poverty in America,* ed. L. A. Ferman, J. L. Kornblum, and A. Haber. Ann Arbor: University of Michigan Press.

Minarika, J. J., and R. S. Goldfarb. 1976. "AFDC Income Recipient Rates, and Family Dissolution: A Comment." *Journal of Human Resources* 11 (Spring): 243–50.

Moore, K. A., and M. R. Burt. 1982. *Private Crisis, Public Cost.* Washington, D.C.: Urban Institute.

Moore, K. A., and S. B. Caldwell. 1976. "Out-of-Wedlock Pregnancy and

Childbearing." Working paper no. 999-02, Urban Institute, Washington, D.C.

Morgan, J. N., M. H. David, W. J. Cohen, and H. E. Brazer. 1962. *Income and Welfare in the United States*. New York: McGraw-Hill.

Morris, N., and M. Tonry. "Blacks, Crime Rates and Prisons—A Profound Challenge." *Chicago Tribune* (August 18):2.

Moscovice, I., and W. J. Crag. 1983. *The Impact of Federal Cutbacks on Working AFDC Recipients in Minnesota*. Minneapolis: Center for Health Services Research, University of Minnesota.

Moynihan, D. P. 1965. "Employment, Income and the Ordeal of the Negro Family." In *The Negro American*, ed. T. Parsons and K. B. Clark. Boston: Beacon Press.

———. 1965. *The Negro Family: The Case for National Action*. Washington, D.C.: Office of Policy Planning and Research, U.S. Department of Labor.

———. 1968. "The Professors and the Poor." In *On Understanding Poverty: Perspectives from the Social Sciences*, ed. D. P. Moynihan. New York: Basic Books.

———. 1970. *Maximum Feasible Misunderstanding*. New York: Free Press.

———. 1973. *The Politics of a Guaranteed Income*. New York: Random House.

———. 1986. *Family and the Nation*. New York: Harcourt Brace Jovanovich.

Murray, C. 1984. *Losing Ground: American Social Policy, 1950–1980*. New York: Basic Books.

Nathan. R. 1986. "The Underclass—Will It Always Be with Us?" Paper presented at a symposium on the underclass, New School for Social Research, New York, N.Y. November.

National Center for Health Statistics. 1968. "Trends in Illegitimacy: United States, 1940–1965." In *Vital and Health Statistics* 21, no. 15. Washington, D.C.: Department of Health and Human Services.

———. 1982. "Advance Report of Final Natality Statistics, 1980." In *Monthly Vital Statistics Report*. Washington, D.C.: Department of Health and Human Services.

———. 1982. "Marriage and Divorce." In *Vital Statistics of the United States, 1978*, vol. 3. Washington, D.C.: Department of Health and Human Services.

———. 1983. "Advanced Report of Final Natality Statistics, 1981." In *Monthly Vital Statistics Report* 32, no. 9. Washington, D.C.: Department of Health and Human Services.

———. 1984. *Vital Statistics of the United States*. Vol. 1: *Natality*. Washington, D.C.: Department of Health and Human Services.

National Office of Vital Statistics. 1957. *Vital Statistics of the United States*. Vol. 1. Washington, D.C.: Department of Health, Education, and Welfare.

Neckerman, K. M., R. Aponte, and W. J. Wilson. 1988. "Family Structure, Black Unemployment, and American Social Policy." In *The Politics of Social*

Policy, ed. M. Weir, A. S. Orloff, and T. Skocpol. Princeton, N.J.: Princeton University Press. Forthcoming.

Newman, O. 1973. *Defensible Space: Crime Prevention through Urban Design.* New York: Collier.

———. 1980. *Community of Interest.* New York: Anchor Books.

Nordhaus, W. 1981. "The New Brand of Economics." *New York Times* (February 22): 2F.

Norton, C. B. 1979. "Comment on Long." *American Sociological Review* 4: 177–78.

O'Connell, M., and M. J. Moore. 1980. "The Legitimacy Status of First Births to U.S. Women Aged 15–24, 1939–1978." *Family Planning Perspectives* 12: 16–25.

Orshansky, M. 1963. "Children of the Poor." *Social Security Bulletin* 26 (July): 3–13.

———. 1965. "Counting the Poor: Another Look at the Poverty Profile." *Social Security Bulletin* 28: 3–29.

Park, R. E. 1925. *The City.* Chicago: University of Chicago Press.

Patterson, J. T. 1981. *America's Struggle against Poverty, 1900–1980.* Cambridge, Mass.: Harvard University Press.

Patterson, O. 1977. *Ethnic Chauvinism: The Reactionary Impulse.* New York: Stein and Day.

Pearce, D. M. 1978. "The Feminization of Poverty: Women, Work, and Welfare." *Urban and Social Change Review* 11: 28–36.

———. 1983. "The Feminization of Ghetto Poverty." *Society* 21:70–74.

Perlman, R. 1976. *The Economics of Poverty.* New York: McGraw-Hill.

Philliber, W. W., and R. Seufert. 1975. "An Untested Hypothesis: The Effect of Size of Public Assistance Benefits on Migration." *American Sociological Review* 40: 845–47.

Phillips, L., H. L. Vatey, Jr., and D. Maxwell. 1972. "Crime, Youth, and the Labor Market." *Journal of Political Economy* 80: 491–504.

Pinkney, A. 1984. *The Myth of Black Progress.* New York: Cambridge University Press.

Piven, F. F., and R. A. Cloward. 1971. *Regulating the Poor: The Functions of Public Welfare.* New York: Academic Press.

Placek, P. J., and G. E. Hendershot. 1974. "Public Welfare and Family Planning: An Empirical Study of the 'Brood Sow' Myth." *Social Problems* 21: 660–73.

Pleck, E. H. 1972. "The Two-Parent Household: Black Family Structure in Late Nineteenth-Century Boston." *Journal of Social History* 6 (Fall): 3–31.

Plotnick, R. D., and F. Skidmore. 1975. *Progress against Poverty: A Review of the 1964–1975 Decade.* New York: Academic Press.

Polgar, S., and B. Hiday. 1974. "The Effect of an Additional Birth on Low-Income Urban Families." *Population Studies* 28: 463–71.

Portes, A. 1979. "Illegal Immigration and the International System: Lessons from Recent Legal Mexican Immigrants to the United States." *Social Problems* 26: 425–37.

Posner, R. A. 1975. "The *DeFunis* Case and the Constitutionality of Preferential Treatment of Racial Minorities." In *The Supreme Court Review, 1974*, ed. P. B. Kurland. Chicago: University of Chicago Press.

Presser, H. B., and L. S. Salsberg. 1975. "Public Assistance and Early Family Formation: Is There a Pronatalist Effect?" *Social Problems* 23: 226–41.

Puckrein, G. 1984. "Moving Up." *Wilson Quarterly* 8: 74–87.

Rabb, E. 1966. "A Tale of Three Wars: What War and Which Poverty." *Public Interest* 3: 45–56.

Rainwater, L. 1966. "Crucible of Identity: The Negro Lower-Class Family." *Daedalus* 95 (Winter): 176–216.

————. 1968. "The Problem of Lower-Class Culture and Poverty-War Strategy." In *On Understanding Poverty: Perspectives from the Social Sciences*, ed. D. P. Moynihan. New York: Basic Books.

————. 1970. *Behind Ghetto Walls: Black Families in a Federal Slum.* Chicago: Aldine.

Rainwater, L., and W. L. Yancey, eds. 1967. *The Moynihan Report and the Politics of Controversy.* Cambridge, Mass.: MIT Press.

Raspberry, W. 1980. "Illusion of Black Progress." *Washington Post* (May 28): A19.

Rees, A., and W. Gray. 1982. "Family Effects in Youth Employment." In *The Youth Labor Market Problem: Its Nature, Causes and Consequences*, ed. R. B. Freeman and D. A. Wise. Chicago: University of Chicago Press.

Reischauer, R. D. 1986. "America's Underclass: Four Unanswered Questions." Paper presented at The City Club, Portland, Oreg., January 30.

————. 1986. "Policy Responses to the Underclass Problem." Paper presented at a symposium at the New School for Social Research, New York, N.Y., November 14.

Riss, J. 1890. *How the Other Half Lives: Studies among the Tenements of New York.* New York: Scribners.

Ritchey, P. N. 1974. "Urban Poverty and Rural to Urban Migration." *Rural Sociology* 39: 12–27.

Rodgers, H. R. 1978. "Hiding versus Ending Poverty." *Political Sociology* 8: 253–66.

————. 1979. *Poverty amid Plenty.* Reading, Mass.: Addison-Wesley.

Rodman, H. 1963. "The Lower-Class Value Stretch." *Social Forces* 42: 206–15.

Roncek, D. 1981. "Dangerous Places: Crime and Residential Environment." *Social Forces* 60: 74–96.

Roncek, D., R. Bell, and J. M. A. Francik. 1981. "Housing Projects and Crime: Testing a Proximity Hypothesis." *Social Problems* 29: 151.

Rosen, L. 1969. "Matriarchy and Lower-Class Negro Male Delinquency." *Social Problems* 17: 175–89.

Rosenberg, M., and R. G. Simmons. 1972. *Black and White Esteem: The Urban School Child.* Washington, D.C.: American Sociological Association.

Ross, H. L., and I. Sawhill. 1975. *Time of Transition: The Growth of Families Headed by Women.* Washington, D.C.: Urban Institute.

Rustin, B. 1965. "From Protest to Politics: The Future of the Civil Rights Movement." *Commentary* (February): 39:25–31.

————. 1967. "The Long Hot Summer." *Commentary* (October): 39–45.

————. 1967. "A Way Out of the Exploding Ghetto." *New York Times Magazine* (August 13).

————. 1971. "The Blacks and the Unions." *Harper Magazine* (May): 73–81.

Ryan, W. 1971. *Blaming the Victim*. New York: Random House.

Saks, D. H. 1975. *Public Assistance for Mothers in an Urban Labor Market*. Princeton, N.J.: Industrial Relations Section, Princeton University.

Sawhill, I., G. E. Peabody, C. A. Jones, and S. B. Caldwell. 1975. *Income Transfers and Family Structure*. Washington, D.C.: Urban Institute.

Schiller, B. R. 1970. "Stratified Opportunities: The Essence of the 'Vicious Circle.'" *American Journal of Sociology* 76:426–42.

————. 1976. *The Economics of Poverty and Discrimination*. Englewood Cliffs, N.J.: Prentice-Hall.

Schulz, D. A. 1968. "Variations in the Father Role in Complete Families of the Negro Lower Class." *Social Science Quarterly* 49: 651–59.

————. 1969. *Coming Up Black: Patterns of Ghetto Socialization*. Englewood Cliffs, N.J.: Prentice-Hall.

Shariff, Z. 1981. "An Oversized Nonissue." *New York Times* (February 24): 23.

Sheingold, S. 1982. *Dislocated Workers: Issues and Federal Options*. Washington, D.C.: Congressional Budget Office.

Sheppard, N., Jr. 1980. "Chicago Project Dwellers Live under Siege." *New York Times* (August 6): A14.

Shifflett, C. A. 1975. "The Household Composition of Rural Black Families: Louisa County, Virginia, 1880." *Journal of Interdisciplinary History* 6 (Autumn): 235–60.

Skocpol, T. 1985. "Brother Can You Spare a Job? Work and Welfare in the United States." Paper presented at the Annual Meeting of the American Sociological Association, Washington, D.C., August 27.

Social Security Administration. 1983. *Social Security Bulletin*. Annual Statistical Supplement. Washington, D.C.: Government Printing Office.

Sowell, T. 1981. *Ethnic America: A History*. New York: Basic Books.

————. 1984. *Civil Rights: Rhetoric or Reality?* New York: William Morrow.

Stack, C. 1974. *All Our Kin: Strategies for Survival in a Black Community*. New York: Harper and Row.

Staff of the Chicago Tribune. 1986. *The American Millstone: An Examination of the Nation's Permanent Underclass*. Chicago: Contemporary Books.

Stanback, T. M., Jr., and T. J. Noyelle. 1982. *Cities in Transition*. Totowa, N.J.: Allanheld, Osman.

Staples, R. 1970. "The Myth of the Black Matriarchy." *Black Scholar* 2: 9–16.

Steinberg, S. 1981. *The Ethnic Myth: Race, Ethnicity, and Class in America*. New York: Atheneum.

Sundquist, J. L. 1969. "The Origins of the War on Poverty." In *On Fighting Poverty: Perspective from Experience*, ed. J. L. Sundquist. New York: Basic Books.

Sutherland, E. H., and H. Locke. 1936. *20,000 Homeless Men*. Philadelphia: Lippincott.

Suttles, G. R. 1976. "Urban Ethnography: Situational and Normative Accounts." *Annual Review of Sociology* 2: 1–8.

Taylor, William L. 1986. "*Brown*, Equal Protection, and the Isolation of the Poor." *Yale Law Journal* 95:1700–35.

Thernstrom, S. 1968. "Poverty in Historical Perspective." In *On Understanding Poverty: Perspectives from the Social Sciences*, ed. D. P. Moynihan. New York: Basic Books.

Thomas, W. I., and F. Znaniecki. 1918–20. *The Polish Peasant in Europe and America*. 5 vols. Boston: Brager.

Thrasher, F. M. 1927. *The Gang*. Chicago: University of Chicago Press.

Thurow, L. C. 1981. "Recession plus Inflation Spells Statis." *Christianity and Crisis* 41: 91–92.

Tobin, J. 1965. "On Improving the Economic Status of the Negro." *Daedalus* 94 (Fall): 878–98.

Tompkins, D. C. 1970. *Poverty in the United States during the Sixties: A Bibliography*. Berkeley: Institute of Government Studies, University of California Press.

U.S. Bureau of the Census. 1902. *Population of the United States*. Pt. 2. Washington, D.C.: Government Printing Office.

———. 1912. *Population of the United States*. Vol. 2, *General Report and Analysis Tables*. Washington, D.C.: Government Printing Office.

———. 1912. *Population of the United States*. Vol. 6, Washington, D.C.: Government Printing Office.

———. 1933. *Population of the United States*. Vol. 2, *General Report Statistics by Subject*. Washington, D.C.: Government Printing Office.

———. 1943. *Census of the Population*. Washington, D.C.: Government Printing Office.

———. 1943. *Population of the United States*. Vol. 4, *Characteristics by Age*. Washington, D.C.: Government Printing Office.

———. 1948. "Characteristics of Single, Married, Widowed, and Divorced Persons in 1947." In *Current Population Reports*. Series P-20, no. 10. Washington, D.C.: Government Printing Office.

———. 1950. *Census of the Population*. Washington, D.C.: Government Printing Office.

———. 1953. *U.S. Census of Population*. Vol. 2, *Characteristics of the Population*, pt. 1. U.S. Summary. Washington, D.C.: Government Printing Office.

———. 1960. "Marital Status and Family Status, March 1960." In *Current Population Reports*. Series P-20. Washington, D.C.: Government Printing Office.

———. 1961. *U.S. Census of Population, 1960: Characteristics of the Population*, pt. 1. U.S. Summary. Washington, D.C.: Government Printing Office.

———. 1965. "Household and Family Characteristics, March 1965." In *Cur-*

rent Population Reports. Series P-20. Washington, D.C.: Government Printing Office.

―――. 1965. "Marital Status and Family Status, March 1965." In *Current Population Reports*. Series P-20. Washington, D.C.: Government Printing Office.

―――. 1965. "Population Estimates." In *Current Population Reports*. Series P-25, no. 310. Washington, D.C.: Government Printing Office.

―――. 1966. "Negro Population, March 1965." In *Current Population Reports*. Series P-20. Washington, D.C.: Government Printing Office.

―――. 1971. "Household and Family Characteristics, March 1970." In *Current Population Reports*. Series P-20. Washington, D.C.: Government Printing Office.

―――. 1971. "Marital Status and Family Status, March 1970." In *Current Population Reports*. Series P-20. Washington, D.C.: Government Printing Office.

―――. 1971. "Social and Economic Characteristics of the Population in Metropolitan and Nonmetropolitan Areas, 1970 and 1960." In *Current Population Reports*. Series P-23, no. 37. Washington, D.C.: Government Printing Office.

―――. 1971. "The Social and Economic Status of the Black Population in the United States." In *Current Population Reports*. Series P-23, no. 38. Washington, D.C.: Government Printing Office.

―――. 1972. "Household and Family Characteristics, March 1971." In *Current Population Reports*. Series P-20. Washington, D.C.: Government Printing Office.

―――. 1973. "Household and Family Characteristics, March 1972." In *Current Population Reports*. Series P-20. Washington, D.C.: Government Printing Office.

―――. 1973. "Household and Family Characteristics, March 1973." In *Current Population Reports*. Series P-20. Washington, D.C.: Government Printing Office.

―――. 1973. *1970 Census of Population: Detailed Characteristics of the Population*, pt. 1. U.S. Summary. Washington, D.C.: Government Printing Office.

―――. 1973. *1970 Census of Population: Low Income Areas in Large Cities*. PC(2)-9B. Washington, D.C.: Government Printing Office.

―――. 1974. "Persons of Spanish Origin in the United States, March 1973." In *Current Population Reports*. Series P-20. Washington, D.C.: Government Printing Office.

―――. 1975. *Historical Statistics of the United States*. Vol. 1. Washington, D.C.: Government Printing Office.

―――. 1975. "Household and Family Characteristics, March 1974." In *Current Population Reports*. Series P-20. Washington, D.C.: Government Printing Office.

―――. 1975. "Marital Status and Living Arrangements, March 1975." In

Current Population Reports. Series P-20. Washington, D.C.: Government Printing Office.

———. 1975. "Persons of Spanish Origin in the United States, March 1974." In *Current Population Reports*. Series P-20. Washington, D.C.: Government Printing Office.

———. 1976. "Household and Family Characteristics, March 1975." In *Current Population Reports*. Series P-20. Washington, D.C.: Government Printing Office.

———. 1976. "Persons of Spanish Origin in the United States, March 1975." In *Current Population Reports*. Series P-20. Washington, D.C.: Government Printing Office.

———. 1977. "Household and Family Characteristics, March 1976." In *Current Population Reports*. Series P-20. Washington, D.C.: Government Printing Office.

———. 1977. "Marriage, Divorce, Widowhood, and Remarriage by Family Characteristics, June 1975." In *Current Population Reports*. Series P-20. Washington, D.C.: Government Printing Office.

———. 1978. "Estimates of the Population of the United States by Age, Sex, and Race, 1970 to 1977." In *Current Population Reports*. Series P-25, no. 721. Washington, D.C.: Government Printing Office.

———. 1978. "Household and Family Characteristics, March 1976." In *Current Population Reports*. Series P-20. Washington, D.C.: Government Printing Office.

———. 1978. "Money Income and Poverty Status of Families and Persons in the United States, 1977." In *Current Population Reports*. Series P-60, no. 116. Washington, D.C.: Government Printing Office.

———. 1978. "Social and Economic Characteristics of the Metropolitan and Nonmetropolitan Population, 1977 and 1970." In *Current Population Reports*. Series P-23, no. 75. Washington, D.C.: Government Printing Office.

———. 1979. "Household and Family Characteristics, March 1978." In *Current Population Reports*. Series P-20. Washington, D.C.: Government Printing Office.

———. 1979. "Money Income and Poverty Status of Families and Persons in the United States, 1978." In *Current Population Reports*. Series P-60, no. 120. Washington, D.C.: Government Printing Office.

———. 1979. "The Social and Economic Status of the Black Population in the United States: A Historical View, 1970–1978." In *Current Population Reports*. Series P-23. Washington, D.C.: Government Printing Office.

———. 1980. "Characteristics of the Population below the Poverty Level, 1978." In *Current Population Reports*. Series P-60, no. 124. Washington, D.C.: Government Printing Office.

———. 1980. "Families Maintained by Female Householders, 1970–1979." In *Current Population Reports*. Series P-23, no. 107. Washington, D.C.: Government Printing Office.

———. 1980. "Household and Family Characteristics, March 1979." In *Cur-

rent Population Reports. Series P-20. Washington, D.C.: Government Printing Office.

———. 1981. "Household and Family Characteristics, March 1980." In *Current Population Reports.* Series P-20. Washington, D.C.: Government Printing Office.

———. 1981. "Marital Status and Living Arrangements, March 1980." In *Current Population Reports.* Series P-20. Washington, D.C.: Government Printing Office.

———. 1981. "Money Income and Poverty Status of Families and Persons in the United States, 1980." In *Current Population Reports.* Series P-60, no. 127. Washington, D.C.: Government Printing Office.

———. 1981. "Population Estimates." *Current Population Reports.* Series P-25. Washington, D.C.: Government Printing Office.

———. 1982. "Household and Family Characteristics, March 1981." In *Current Population Reports.* Series P-20. Washington, D.C.: Government Printing Office.

———. 1982. "Trends in the Child Care Arrangements of Working Mothers." *Current Population Reports.* Series P-23. Washington, D.C.: Government Printing Office.

———. 1983. "Characteristics of the Population below the Poverty Level, 1981." In *Current Population Reports.* Series P-60, no. 138. Washington, D.C.: Government Printing Office.

———. 1983. "Characteristics of the Population below Poverty Level, 1982." In *Current Population Reports.* Series P-60, no. 144. Washington, D.C.: Government Printing Office.

———. 1983. "Estimates of the Population of the United States by Age, Sex, and Race, 1980 to 1982." In *Current Population Reports.* Series P-25. Washington, D.C.: Government Printing Office.

———. 1983. "Fertility of American Women, June 1981." In *Current Population Reports.* Series P-20, no. 378. Washington, D.C.: Government Printing Office.

———. 1983. "Marital Status and Living Arrangements, March 1982." In *Current Population Reports.* Series P-20, no. 380. Washington, D.C.: Government Printing Office.

———. 1983. *1980 Census of Population: Detailed Characteristics of the Population,* pt. 1. U.S. Summary. Washington, D.C.: Government Printing Office.

———. 1983. "Statistical Abstract of the United States, 1982–1983." Washington, D.C.: Government Printing Office.

———. 1984. *Census of the Population, 1980.* Washington, D.C.: Government Printing Office.

———. 1984. "Characteristics of the Population below the Poverty Level, 1982." In *Current Population Reports.* Series P-60, no. 144. Washington, D.C.: Government Printing Office.

———. 1984. *Estimates of Poverty including the Value of Non-Cash Benefits.* Technical paper no. 51. Washington, D.C.: Government Printing Office.

245   Bibliography

———. 1984. "Household and Family Characteristics, March 1983." In *Current Population Reports*. Series P-20, no. 388. Washington, D.C.: Government Printing Office.

———. 1984. "Household and Family Characteristics, March 1984." In *Current Population Reports*. Washington, D.C.: Government Printing Office.

———. 1985. *Census of the Population, 1980*. PC 80-12-B1. U.S. Summary. Washington, D.C.: Government Printing Office.

———. 1985. "Characteristics of the Population below the Poverty Level, 1983." In *Current Population Reports*. Series P-60, no. 147. Washington, D.C.: Government Printing Office.

———. 1985. "Estimates of the Population of the United States by Age, Sex, and Race, 1980 to 1984." In *Current Population Reports*. Series P-25, no. 965. Washington, D.C.: Government Printing Office.

———. 1985. "Household and Family Characteristics, March 1970/1978/1984." In *Current Population Reports*. Series P-20, nos. 218, 340, 398. Washington, D.C.: Government Printing Office.

———. 1985. "Money Income of Households, Families, and Individuals in the United States, 1983." In *Current Population Reports*. Series P-60, no. 146. Washington, D.C.: Government Printing Office.

———. 1985. *1980 Census of the Population: Low Income Areas in Large Cities*. PC-2-8D. Washington, D.C.: Government Printing Office.

U.S. Bureau of Labor Statistics. 1980. *Handbook of Labor Statistics*. Bulletin 2070. Washington, D.C.: Government Printing Office.

———. 1983. *Handbook of Labor Statistics*. Bulletin 2175. Washington, D.C.: Government Printing Office.

———. 1984. *Employment and Earnings*. Washington, D.C.: Department of Labor.

U.S. Department of Health and Human Services. National Center for Health Statistics. 1981. "Final Natality Statistics, 1979." In *Monthly Vital Statistics Report*. Washington, D.C.: Government Printing Office.

———. 1982. "Advance Report of Final Natality Statistics, 1980." In *Monthly Vital Statistics Report*. Washington, D.C.: Government Printing Office.

———. 1984. "Advanced Report of Final Natality Statistics, 1982." In *Monthly Vital Statistics Report*, vol. 33, no. 6, suppl. Washington, D.C.: Government Printing Office.

———. Social Security Administration, Office of Policy. 1980. "Aid to Families with Dependent Children, 1977." In *Recipient Characteristics Study*. Washington, D.C.: Government Printing Office.

U.S. Department of Justice. 1981. *Uniform Crime Reports for the United States, 1980*. Washington, D.C.: Government Printing Office.

———. 1985. *Uniform Crime Reports for the United States, 1984*. Washington, D.C.: Government Printing Office.

U.S. Department of Labor. 1982. *Employment and Training Report of the President*. Washington, D.C.: Government Printing Office.

———. 1983. *Handbook of Labor Statistics*. Washington, D.C.: Government Printing Office.

Valentine, C. A. 1968. *Culture and Poverty: Critique and Counter Proposals.* Chicago: University of Chicago Press.

Valentine, C. A., C. H. Berndt, E. Boissevain, J. H. Bushnell, P. Carstens et al. 1969. "Culture and Poverty: Critique and Counter Proposals." Book review and author's precis/reply. *Current Anthropology* 10:181–200.

Vining, D. R., Jr. 1983. "Illegitimacy and Public Policy." *Population and Development Review* 9:105–10.

Waldinger, R. 1982. "The Occupational and Economic Integration of the New Immigrants." *Law and Contemporary Problems* 45:197–222.

Walker, A. H. 1985. "Racial Differences in Patterns of Marriage and Family Maintenance, 1890–1980." In *Feminism, Children, and the New Families,* ed. S. M. Dornbusch and M. H. Strober. New York: Guilford Press.

Weinstein, B. L., and R. E. Firestine. 1978. *Regional Growth and Decline in the United States.* New York: Praeger.

Weir, M., A. S. Orloff, and T. Skocpol. 1988. "The Future of Social Policy in the United States: Political Constraints and Possibilities." In *The Politics of Social Policy in the United States.* Princeton, N.J.: Princeton University Press. Forthcoming.

Wescott, D. N. 1976. "Youth in the Labor Force: An Area Study." *Monthly Labor Review* 99:3–9.

Wilensky, Harold L. 1983. "Evaluating Research and Politics: Political Legitimacy and Consensus as Missing Variables in the Assessment of Social Policy." In *Evaluating the Welfare State: Social and Political Perspectives,* ed. E. Spiro and E. Yuchtman-Yaar. New York: Academic Press.

Williams, R. 1975. *Public Assistance and Work Effort.* Princeton, N.J.: Industrial Relations Section, Princeton University.

Willie, C. V. 1978. "The Inclining Significance of Race." *Society* 15 (July/August): 10, 12–15.

Wilson, J. Q. 1975. *Thinking about Crime.* New York: Basic Books.

Wilson, W. J. 1972. "Reflections on the Insiders and Outsiders Controversy." In *Black Sociologists,* ed. J. E. Blackwell and M. Janowitz. Chicago: University of Chicago Press.

———. 1976. *Power, Racism, and Privilege: Race Relations in Theoretical and Sociohistorical Perspectives.* New York: Free Press.

———. 1980. *The Declining Significance of Race: Blacks and Changing American Institutions.* 2d ed. Chicago: University of Chicago Press.

———. 1981. "The Black Community in the 1980s: Questions of Race, Class and Public Policy." *Annals of the American Academy of Political and Social Science* 454:26–41.

———. 1984. "The Black Underclass." *Wilson Quarterly* 8:88–99.

Winegarden, C. R. 1974. "The Fertility of AFDC Women: An Economic Analysis." *Journal of Economics and Business* 26:159–66.

Wirth, L. 1928. *The Ghetto.* Chicago: University of Chicago Press.

Yancey, W. L. 1972. "Going Down Home: Family Structure and the Urban Trap." *Social Science Quarterly* 52:893–906.

Yarmolinsky, A. 1969. "The Beginnings of OEO." In *On Fighting Poverty: Perspectives from Experience,* ed. J. L. Sundquist. New York: Basic Books.

Zelnik, M., and J. F. Kantner. 1980. "Sexual Activity, Contraceptive Use and Pregnancy among Metropolitan-Area Teenagers, 1971–1979." *Family Planning Perspectives* 12: 230–37.

Zorbaugh, H. W. 1929. *The Gold Coast and the Slum.* Chicago: University of Chicago Press.

3

Afterword

Reflections on Responses to
The Truly Disadvantaged

William Julius Wilson

T he first edition of *The Truly Disadvantaged* was published twenty-five years ago. However, the economic processes emphasized in the book have continued—the loss of manufacturing jobs, the
movement of jobs from cities to the suburbs and overseas, and even
greater internationalization of the economy, especially through trade liberalization facilitated by free trade agreements in the 1990s. Moreover,
given the expansion of low-wage jobs lacking fringe benefits, and the polarization between high-wage and low-wage occupations, higher education is even more critical for social advancement in the labor market
today. Furthermore, the adverse effects of deindustrialization on inner-
city black employment continue to be severe.

By and large, the conditions described in *The Truly Disadvantaged*
are not qualitatively different twenty-five years later, even though when I
wrote the book urban conditions had been in decline for roughly fifteen
years (i.e. since the early 1970s). There are still major racial differences
in concentrated poverty. Although the country experienced dramatic declines in concentrated poverty in the 1990s, including declines in urban
black neighborhoods, the substantial decreases may simply have been
blips of economic boom in the 1990s rather than permanent trends.[1]
Unemployment and individual poverty rates have increased since 2000,
and there is every reason to assume that concentrated poverty rates are
on the increase again, although complete data on concentrated poverty

I am enormously indebted to Jackelyn Hwang and Jeremy Levine for their excellent review of the roughly 3,500 articles, as well as a number of books, that cited or responded to
The Truly Disadvantaged. Their systematic research on these articles provided the basis for
my discussion and arguments in this afterword. I would also like to thank Anmol Chaddha,
Jackelyn Hwang, Jeremy Levine, James Quane, Loïc Wacquant, and Edward Walker for
their very helpful comments on a previous draft of this afterword. This afterword is original,
although I have included a few partially rewritten paragraphs from my books *More than Just
Race* (copyright © 2009 by William Julius Wilson and used by permission of W. W. Norton
& Co.) and *When Work Disappears* (copyright © 1996 by William Julius Wilson and used by
permission of Alfred A. Knopf, a division of Random House).

will become available only after a more thorough analysis of the 2010 census.

The problems of joblessness have continued and have even gotten worse for low-skilled blacks. The racial employment disparities have persisted. The black/white unemployment ratio seems essentially fixed at 2.0 or greater, which means that even through economic upturns and downturns the black unemployment rate has been at least twice that of the white unemployment rate—although for the first time in five decades, except for the year 1975, the ratio dipped below 2.0 from December 2009 to March 2010 during the current economic crisis. However, at the time of this writing the ratio has once again returned to 2.0.

There have also been some important changes that should be noted. There is greater class polarization among African Americans.[2] The out-migration of middle-class blacks from the inner city continues, but more have moved to the suburbs, including suburban black neighborhoods. And a growing number of poor blacks now live in the suburbs rather than the cities, many in older inner-ring suburbs that feature poverty rates approximating those in the inner cities. Immigration has been very consequential in reshaping cities and urban labor markets, especially low-wage labor markets. Incarceration has sharply increased in the twenty-five years since *The Truly Disadvantaged* was published and has had profound consequences for the urban black poor.[3] There is of course the Great Recession and its aftermath—the current period of very high unemployment, long-term joblessness, and foreclosures. And the surprising election of a black president should certainly be noted. These changes notwithstanding, the basic arguments in *The Truly Disadvantaged* are as relevant and important today as they were when the book was published. I hope this will be clearly demonstrated in the following pages.

The Truly Disadvantaged is one of the most widely cited books in the last half century. Indeed, it created a paradigm that has stimulated hundreds of studies across disciplines. Some of the studies reflect the controversy *The Truly Disadvantaged* has generated; others are more concerned with the empirical and theoretical issues raised in the book. The purpose of this afterword is to reflect on studies that have corroborated, extended, or challenged arguments in the book in insightful ways. In the process I will discuss and reflect on *The Truly Disadvantaged*'s influence in shaping the fields of urban poverty, urban inequality, and race relations, as well as its influence on social policy. I welcome this opportunity to engage the large array of studies that have responded to the book. And I begin by first discussing scholarly reactions to a controversial concept that was featured in *The Truly Disadvantaged*—the concept *underclass*.

The Concept *Underclass*

The use of the concept *underclass* has been the subject of considerable debate among scholars of urban poverty. Many have questioned the meaning of the term and its value as a social category and have reacted critically to the way the term has been appropriated by those intellectuals and journalists whose ideological views and orientations strongly influence their perceptions of the urban poor.[4] However, in their critical commentary many of these scholars have not addressed, in theoretical terms, the scientific import of the concept *underclass*; that is, its role in the description and explanation of social behavior. Rather they have objected to the way the term is used to label a subgroup of the urban poor whose cultural traits are thought to be different from those of the larger society. I discuss the controversy surrounding the concept *underclass* in this section. However, to help readers more clearly distinguish between my use of the concept and how others have used it, in the following section I discuss my theoretical definition of the *underclass*, emphasizing that it denotes a disadvantaged position in the labor market and a social environment of concentrated poverty and social isolation.

In *The Truly Disadvantaged* the relationship between economic restructuring, long-term joblessness, and cultural behavior previously highlighted in the writings of the liberal scholars in the 1960s was once again strongly emphasized.[5] However, in spelling out this relationship, I also explicitly used the concept *underclass*, described as a grouping of individuals and families who are (1) outside the mainstream of the American occupational system—including those "who lack training and skills and either experience long-term unemployment or are not members of the labor force, individuals who are engaged in street crime and other forms of aberrant behavior, and families that experience long-term spells of poverty and/or welfare dependency"—and (2) share the same social milieu.[6]

Regarding the sharing of the same social environment, I stated: "It is true that long-term welfare families and street criminals are distinct groups, but they live and interact in the same depressed community and they are part of the population that has, with the exodus of the more stable working- and middle-class segments, become increasingly isolated from mainstream patterns and norms of behavior."[7] I argued that the behavioral and cultural adaptations of the underclass were often a response to social structural constraints, including constraints imposed by the decreased relative demand for low-skilled labor.

I specifically addressed the controversy surrounding the use of the concept *underclass* in my presidential speech—"Studying Inner-City Social

Dislocations: The Challenge of Public Agenda Research"—at the Annual Meeting of the American Sociological Association in 1990.[8] I chose the theme for the 1990 annual meeting, "Sociology and the Public Agenda," to reflect my interest in the relationship between research and public policy. I had hoped to stimulate and encourage sociological research to focus on issues that are of concern to the general public, research that would more likely attract the attention of the media and policymakers. The theme was particularly appropriate for the site of the annual meeting—Washington, DC. And there was extensive media coverage of my presidential speech, including articles in *Time* and in the *Weekend Review* section of the Sunday *New York Times*, which announced that I had abandoned the use of the term *underclass*. In the early part of my speech, I focused on the controversy that was raging over the use of the concept whereby those on the right claimed that "the underclass is a product of the unwillingness of the black poor to adhere to the American work ethic, among other cultural deficiencies, while those on the left contended that the underclass is a consequence of the developments in post-industrial society, which no longer needs the unskilled poor."[9]

This debate swirled around my book *The Truly Disadvantaged*, where I asserted, as Herbert Gans correctly observed, "this underclass exists mainly because of the large scale and harmful changes in the labor market, and its resulting spatial concentration as well as the isolation of such areas from the more affluent parts of the black community."[10] Gans argued that efforts by scholars to resolve this debate were largely unsuccessful. Meanwhile, the behavioral definition of the underclass had increased in the public discourse, especially among journalists.[11] Reflecting on this situation in my speech, I attempted to move the debate away from the controversy over the underclass, including the simplistic either/or distinction between social structure and culture that had characterized so much of the debate, by substituting the term *ghetto poor* for the word *underclass* in the hope that I would not lose any of the subtle theoretical meaning that the latter term had in my writings.

The crucial question is whether a theoretically defined concept of underclass—as opposed to the nonsystematic and atheoretical usages—can be helpful in social scientific discourse. In the next section of this afterword I present a more refined concept of the *underclass*, which derives its meaning from this theory. In the process I show how a theoretically defined concept of *underclass* can be helpful in social scientific discourse, despite the ongoing controversy and debate concerning its meaning and value as a social category.

A Theory of the Social Transformation of the Inner City

In *The Truly Disadvantaged* I advanced the argument that historical discrimination combined with migration from the rural South to large metropolises kept the urban black population relatively young and created
a problem of weak labor-force attachment that has made this population
particularly vulnerable to the industrial and geographic changes in the
economy since the early 1970s. Innovations in technology, the shift from
goods-producing to service-producing industries, the relocation of manufacturing industries out of central cities, the increasing polarization of
the labor market into low-wage and high-wage sectors, and periodic recessions have elevated the rate of black joblessness (unemployment and
nonparticipation in the labor market), despite the passage of legislation
against discrimination and the creation of affirmative action programs.

The growth in joblessness has in turn helped generate a rise in the concentration of poor blacks, with accompanying increases in single-parent
families and the receipt of welfare. These problems have been particularly noticeable in the inner-city ghetto neighborhoods of large cities, not
only because of the vast concentrations of impoverished minority families
and individuals there, but also because these neighborhoods have become
less diversified and more isolated in ways that make them more vulnerable to the impact of the continuing economic changes.

Since the early 1970s, a significant out-migration of working- and
middle-class families from inner-city neighborhoods combined with rising numbers of poor residents due to escalating rates of joblessness have
resulted in heavy concentrations of ghetto poverty. The number of inner-
city census tracts with high poverty rates has risen precipitously.[12] The diminishing presence of middle- and working-class families has also weakened an important social buffer that served to deflect the full impact of
the prolonged high levels of neighborhood joblessness stemming from
uneven economic growth and periodic recessions.

In earlier decades, most of the adults in ghetto neighborhoods were
employed. And black working and middle classes provided stability in
these neighborhoods. They invested their economic and social resources
by patronizing neighborhood stores, banks, churches, and community organizations and by sending their children to the local public schools. In
the process they reinforced societal values and norms and made it meaningful for the more disadvantaged in these segregated enclaves to envision
the possibility of some upward mobility. However, the inner-city ghetto
today includes a high proportion of residents whose major predicament is
rising joblessness, a trend that is strengthened by growing social isolation.
The contact between groups of different class and racial backgrounds has

decreased because of the out-migration of higher income families, resulting in greater adverse effects from living in impoverished neighborhoods.
These concentration effects, reflected, for example, in the self-limiting
social dispositions of inner-city residents, are created by inadequate access to job networks and employment, lack of access to quality schools,
decreasing availability of suitable marriage partners, and lack of exposure
to conventional role models and informal mainstream social networks.

Accordingly, the arguments presented in *The Truly Disadvantaged* to
account for the recent increases in social dislocations in the inner-city
ghetto are complex. They cannot be reduced to the easy explanations
of racism advanced by those on the left or of "culture of poverty" pos-
ited by those on the right. Although historic racism created the ghetto
and although contemporary discrimination has undoubtedly aggravated
the economic and social woes of its residents, an adequate understanding of the sharp increase in these problems requires the specification of
a complex web of additional factors, including the impact of shifts in the
modern American economy.

It is not explicit in this summary of *The Truly Disadvantaged* that
social, structural, cultural, and social-psychological variables are integrated into my theoretical framework.[13] A more formal statement of this
framework is that a structure of inequality has evolved that is linked to
contemporary behavior in the ghetto by a combination of opportunities, constraints, and social psychology. The exogenous factors, representing the sources of the concentration of black ghetto poverty, include
racial discrimination, changes in the economy that have restructured
occupations and relocated industries away from inner-city neighborhoods, and political processes (affirmative action programs and antibias
legislation) that have had the unanticipated consequence of increasing
the class divisions among urban African Americans.[14] The endogenous
factors created by these exogenous determinants include demographic
variables such as urban migration, age structures, and the pool of marriageable men, as well as economic factors such as employment and income distributions.

The endogenous determinants also include social isolation, which is a
characteristic feature of the social environment of the urban underclass.
Social isolation deprives inner-city ghetto residents not only of economic
and social resources, including conventional role models whose presence
buffers the impact of neighborhood joblessness, but also of cultural learning from mainstream social networks that facilitates economic and social
mobility in modern society. The lack of economic and social resources in
the neighborhood, the declining presence of conventional role models,
and circumscribed cultural learning produce outcomes that restrict social

advancement. Some of these outcomes are structural (weak labor-force attachment and lack of access to informal job networks) and some are social-psychological (limited aspirations and problematic social dispositions).

These theoretical issues should be kept in mind as I attempt to more fully establish the role of the concept *underclass* in the description and explanation of social behavior. Basically, I argued in *The Truly Disadvantaged* that the central problem of the underclass is joblessness, a problem that is rendered even more severe by an increasing social isolation in impoverished neighborhoods, as reflected, for example, in the weakening of the informal job information network systems. In Martha Van Haitsma's conceptual explication of my theory, the relationship between the social environment and experiences in the labor market is more sharply delineated.[15] She distinguished those persons with weak attachment to the labor force and whose social environment "tends to maintain or further weaken this attachment."[16] I would like to incorporate this more explicit conception by referring to the neighborhood as the social environment.

The term weak labor-force attachment as used here does not imply a desire or willingness to work. Rather, weak labor-force attachment refers to the marginal position of people in the labor force because of restricted job opportunities—including those that result from changes in the demand for labor and from racial discrimination—and/or limited access to the informal job network systems. To understand the unique position of members of the underclass, it is important to comprehend how their neighborhood context aggravates their weak attachment to the labor force. "Environments with low opportunity for stable and legitimate employment and high opportunity for alternative income-generating activities, particularly those which are incompatible with regular employment perpetuate weak labor force attachment," stated Van Haitsma.[17] Poor people who reside in areas that support or foster strong labor-force attachment are in a better position to avail themselves of employment opportunities than those with similar educational training and occupational skills living in neighborhoods that reinforce or promote weak labor-force attachment.

Neighborhoods that have inadequate job information networks, few legitimate employment opportunities, and inferior schools not only feature weak labor-force attachment, but they also increase the likelihood that people will turn to deviant or illegal activities for income, resulting in further deterioration of their attachment to the legitimate labor market. The problems associated with the absence of work are most severe for a jobless family in a neighborhood with low rates of employment because they are more likely to be shared and reinforced by other families in this neighborhood through the process of nonconscious or accidental cultural transmission.[18]

Thus, in my formulation the meaning of the concept of *underclass* is derived from a theoretical framework of the social transformation of the inner city, a framework that links structural, cultural, and social-psychological propositions. In this theory, what distinguishes members of the underclass from those of other economically disadvantaged groups is that their neighborhood or social milieu uniquely reinforces their marginal economic position or weak attachment to the labor force. The standard designation "lower class," as typically used by social scientists, does not capture this distinction—the dual problems of weak attachment to the labor force or marginal economic position and social isolation in neighborhoods of highly concentrated poverty.

What the terms *lower class* and *underclass* have in common is that they each connote economic marginality. Where they differ is that unlike the term *underclass*, as theoretically defined here and in the first edition of *The Truly Disadvantaged*, the term *lower class* does not signify the added dimension of neighborhood or social milieu. In America the problems this definition of the underclass connotes—economic marginality and neighborhoods of highly concentrated poverty—are more likely to be present in the inner-city ghettos. In the United States the concept will more often apply to people of color because whites seldom live in ghetto or high-poverty areas. For example, Paul Jargowsky found that in 1990 the proportion of the poor who reside in ghetto neighborhoods in metropolitan areas varied noticeably by race—of the 8 million ghetto poor, areas with poverty rates of at least 40 percent, 4.2 million were African American, 2 million were Latino, and roughly 1.8 million were white.[19]

Thus to speak of the underclass in the United States today is to refer primarily to blacks and Latinos.[20] However, there is nothing in my conceptual definition of the underclass that would restrict its application to people of color. In other societies the combination of weak labor-force attachment and social isolation may exist in certain inner-city neighborhoods even though the levels of concentrated poverty do not match those inherent in American ghettos. For example, there is evidence that the long-term jobless in the Dutch inner cities of Rotterdam and Amsterdam—particularly the immigrants with weak labor-force attachment from Surinam and Indonesia—have experienced sharply decreasing contact with conventional groups and institutions in Dutch society despite levels of ethnic and class segregation far below those of large inner cities in the United States. In response to this development, several Dutch social scientists have discussed the formation of an underclass in the Netherlands in precisely the theoretical terms outlined in *The Truly Disadvantaged*.[21]

Consequently, we need a concept that allows us to describe and highlight the important theoretical linkage between a disadvantaged group's position in the labor market and its social environment. I have shown how the term *underclass* can serve this purpose. Social scientists may choose another concept to capture this relationship. Indeed, as pointed out in the previous section, I now use the term *ghetto poor* to designate the dual problem of weak labor-force attachment and a social milieu featuring concentrated poverty and social isolation. I have made this nominal change because of a concern that even a theoretically derived concept of underclass will be overcrowded in the long run by nonsystematic, arbitrary, and atheoretical usages that often end up as ideological slogans or code words, particularly in journalistic descriptions of patterns of behavior in the inner city.[22]

Important Empirical Studies Responding to *The Truly Disadvantaged*

In response to *The Truly Disadvantaged*, hundreds of empirical studies have been published on the effects of concentrated poverty in neighborhood environments since the late 1980s. In the first part of this section I discuss the issues raised by some researchers on whether decisions to live in poor neighborhoods are mainly a function of individual self-selection. I then focus on an important book by Robert J. Sampson, which reflects on arguments involving individual self-selection. This is followed by a discussion of other important issues raised in Sampson's study, which sets the stage, in the remaining parts of this section, for a systematic examination of research that addresses a number of theoretical arguments in *The Truly Disadvantaged*—economic restructuring and spatial mismatch, persistent poverty and depopulation, social isolation and concentration effects, and the male marriageable pool hypothesis. This section concludes with a discussion of major empirical challenges to *The Truly Disadvantaged*.

Research on Neighborhood Effects: From Individual Level Outcomes to Structuralist Issues

A particular topic that was the focus of significant attention from subsequent researchers was the concept of *neighborhood effects*, which refers to the impact of various social, structural, cultural, and demographic conditions of the neighborhood on the residents. *The Truly Disadvantaged* identified the growth of concentrated poverty as an important new phenomenon, explained how it was caused, and argued that there are "concentration effects" that are above and beyond the separate effects of low income, unemployment, and so on. However, it is important to note that, even though *The Truly Disadvantaged* highlighted a number of structural arguments that are discussed in subsequent parts of this section, much of the earlier research focused on individual-level outcomes. As Robert Sampson put it: "Rereading *The Truly Disadvantaged*, one is struck by its structuralist bent, though this was rather quickly translated by policy-oriented researchers into a prediction about individual outcome."[23]

Basically, the research on neighborhood effects suggests that concentrated poverty increases the likelihood of social isolation from mainstream institutions, joblessness, dropping out of school, lower educational achievement, involvement in crime, unsuccessful behavioral development and delinquency among adolescents, nonmarital childbirth, and unsuccessful family management.[24] In general the research reveals that concentrated poverty adversely affects one's chances in life beginning in infancy and lasting well into adulthood.

However, some scholars have been concerned that these studies reached conclusions about neighborhood effects based on data that do not address the problem of self-selection bias, a term used in research to describe the effect of people grouping themselves together based on common characteristics.[25] These scholars argue that the effects we attribute to poor neighborhoods may instead be caused by the characteristics of families and individuals who end up living there. In other words, they feel that disadvantaged neighborhoods might not be the cause of poor outcomes, but rather that families with the weakest job-related skills, with the lowest awareness of and concern for the effects of the local environment on their children's social development, with attitudes that hinder social mobility, and with the most burdensome personal problems are simply more likely to live in these types of neighborhoods.

For example, as John Quigley and Steven Raphael pointed out, "in interpreting cross-sectional data on the isolation of low-income workers from job concentrations it is likely that those with weaker attachments to the labor force will have chosen to locate in places where employment access is low [e.g., inner-city ghetto neighborhoods]. This is simply because monthly rents are lower in these places."[26] Indeed, some scholars have maintained that neighborhood effects disappear when researchers use appropriate statistical techniques to account for self-selection bias.[27] Since the appropriateness of measures capturing neighborhood effects is not typically discussed as a major problem in such studies, a point that I will soon elaborate, many readers will conclude that structural explanations of concentrated poverty and related problems like discrimination, segregation, and joblessness are less persuasive than those that focus on personal attributes.

The issue of individual self-selection into neighborhoods was addressed in the publication of the research on the Moving to Opportunity (MTO) experiment, a housing pilot program, undertaken by the U.S. Department of Housing and Urban Development (HUD) between 1994 and 1998. The MTO experiment was framed as a test of the arguments presented in *The Truly Disadvantaged* about whether neighborhoods matter in the lives of poor individuals. HUD's MTO demonstration program conducted a lottery that awarded housing vouchers to families living in public housing developments in high-poverty neighborhoods in five cities—Boston, Baltimore, Chicago, Los Angeles, and New York. Families who entered the lottery, thus indicating their desire to move, were randomly assigned to one of three groups—one was awarded housing vouchers that could be used to rent in the private market in any area, one was awarded housing vouchers that were restricted to private rentals in low poverty neighborhoods, and one did not receive either voucher in the lottery and was therefore treated as a control group to be compared with the other two groups.

The MTO interim evaluation studies were considered superior to other research on neighborhood effects because they were based on data from a randomized experimental design that eliminated the self-selection bias "that had made it difficult to clearly determine the association between living in poor neighborhoods and individual outcomes."[28] The reports and publications on the interim evaluation, which was finalized in 2003, provided mixed evidence for neighborhood effects when comparing the group whose MTO vouchers were restricted to low-poverty areas with the group that did not receive vouchers. On the one hand, during the five-year period following random assignment the MTO movers who relocated to low-poverty areas were more likely to experience improvements in mental health and less likely to be obese, and girls experienced a significant reduction in "risky behavior" (that is, drinking, taking drugs, engaging in sex, and so on). On the other hand, research investigators found no evidence of an impact on employment rates and earnings, or of any marked improvement on the educational or physical health outcomes of children and young men. These mixed results have led some, including reporters, to question whether there really are enduring negative effects of living in poor segregated neighborhoods. And they seem to reinforce the view among some scholars that when studies effectively control for self-selection bias, neighborhood effects are weak or disappear.

However, while the research on the MTO experiment is rigorous, there are serious issues with the design of the experiment that limit the extent to which one can generalize about neighborhood effects. First of all, the treatment was weak. That is, the use of the housing voucher was only restricted to one year and relocation considerations were predicated on neighborhood poverty, not racial composition. Indeed, many MTO movers relocated to neighborhoods that were not significantly different from the ones they left. For example, three-fifths of MTO families entered highly segregated black neighborhoods. Such neighborhoods tend to be considerably less advantaged than integrated areas. Sociologist Robert J. Sampson analyzed the neighborhood attainment of all Chicago MTO families and found that after approximately seven years, although the voucher winners resided in neighborhoods with poverty rates somewhat lower than the neighborhoods of control families, both groups clustered in segregated black neighborhoods that were still considerably poorer than what an overwhelming majority of Americans will ever experience (neighborhoods with poverty rates of roughly 30 percent).[29]

Also, at the time of the experiment's interim evaluation, as many as 41 percent of the MTO families who entered low-poverty neighborhoods subsequently moved back to more disadvantaged neighborhoods. Because of such extensive out-migration, these MTO families accumulated relatively little time in areas of low poverty and correspondingly did not have an extended opportunity to experience life in low-poverty neighborhoods that were racially integrated.[30]

Moreover, nearly three-quarters of the children in the MTO experiment remained in the same school district, often in the same schools, at the time of the interim evaluation. Stefanie Deluca's comment on these findings, based on her interviews of MTO parents in Baltimore, reveals that school choice was a low priority for some parents. "It is quite striking," she stated, "how little some parents thought that school mattered for learning, relative to what the child contributed though hard work and a 'good attitude.'"[31] Furthermore, as pointed out by Quigley and Raphael, the experiment did not improve accessibility to employment opportunities for MTO movers, because their new neighborhoods were no closer to areas of employment growth.[32] Finally, a number of the projects that housed many participants prior to their MTO relocation were torn down during the time of the experiment, forcing individuals in the control groups to also move and thus making it difficult to determine differences between voucher families and those without vouchers. Thus, rather than concluding that neighborhoods do not matter based on this research, it would be prudent to simply state that although the MTO research raises questions about the extent to which neighborhoods affect the social outcomes of children and adults, it certainly does not resolve these questions.

I think that overall quantitative studies generate mixed or weak findings about the effects of living in poor segregated neighborhoods because of crude or inadequate measures to capture neighborhood effects.[33] If a random experiment or a nonexperimental study could be generated that would allow researchers to capture the impact of a range of factors that distinguish different neighborhoods, including identifying factors that are cumulative over time, there would be significantly different findings on the impact of living in inner-city ghetto neighborhoods.

Nowhere is this more clearly demonstrated than in Robert J. Sampson's landmark book *Great American City: Chicago and the Enduring Neighborhood Effect*. Sampson's findings flow mainly from a comprehensive research endeavor called the Project on Human Development in Chicago Neighborhoods (PHDCN), which collected longitudinal data on children, families, and neighborhoods. I will have more to say about this study shortly. Let me first focus on his powerful critique of studies that place special emphasis on self-selection bias.

Sampson did not dismiss the role of individual selection effects. Rather he pointed out that neither higher-order structures nor neighborhood mechanisms are subservient to individual selection. Indeed, argued Sampson, "individual selection is embedded in social contexts" and is itself a neighborhood effect. Neighborhoods, he contended, affect individual decisions (selection) and perceptions, which in turn influence mobility and ultimately neighborhood composition and social dynamics. Accordingly, "in a fundamental sense," Sampson proclaimed, "individual selection is both a neighborhood effect and a process of 'structural sorting' bringing full circle the findings of the book that integrate individual, neighborhood, and ultimately structure."[34]

I find Sampson's special emphasis on social structure in the study of neighborhood effects particularly appealing, because it resonates with much of the focus of *The Truly Disadvantaged*. In the various chapters of *Great American City*, Sampson demonstrated a flexible conception of causality, which stands in sharp contrast to the "crucial individual experiment." Rather than a single effect, *Great American City* features a holistic "contextual causality" that captures neighborhood social processes. A family of neighborhood effects is theoretically interpreted, described, observed, and analyzed using a variety of methodologies.

Great American City examines two fundamentally different ways of looking at the world—one sees life in terms of independent self-maximizing individuals, the other focuses on the important collective processes in contextual settings rooted in shared understanding. The first image is powerfully reflected in contemporary America, not only in popular belief systems but also in recent developments in social science disciplines (e.g., rational choice models of human behavior). This book's theoretical thrust elevates the second idea by revealing how the mechanisms of social causality are profoundly shaped by the spatial logic of urban life. In the process the book does not inherently begin at the top (social structure) or bottom (individual behavior) but rather creatively in-tegrates individual, neighborhood, and structural dynamics.

Based on his rich and diverse data sources, which provide a basis for a clear specification of the structural and cultural dimensions of neigh-borhood effects, Sampson demonstrated the powerful effects of ecologi-cally concentrated disadvantage on both individual outcomes and rates of behavior across neighborhoods. These effects—including joblessness, poverty, single-parent families with children, verbal ability, violence, in-carceration, and collective efficacy—are magnified by racial segregation. Sampson carefully pointed out that historical, macroeconomic, and global forces have indeed impacted urban neighborhoods; however, they do not negate the potent "lower order" mechanisms of neighborhoods that help to account for variations in concentrated inequality. These include social-psychological mechanisms that interact with broad cultural processes (e.g., stereotypes and shared expectations and perceptions of disorder) and have played a role in shaping the long-term identities and trajectories of neighborhoods.

Sampson's longitudinal study is the most notable of the many recent studies that have provided important empirical findings that relate to or extend the arguments advanced in *The Truly Disadvantaged.* I highlight Sampson's book here, because its comprehensive coverage of a range of empirical and theoretical issues relevant to *The Truly Disadvantaged* sets the stage for a discussion of studies dealing with more specific topics. Many of these studies also systematically incorporate longitudinal data that represent significant advances in our understanding of the factors that have shaped poor urban neighborhoods and the experiences of in-dividuals who reside in these neighborhoods. Like Sampson's *Great American City*, these studies capture the impact of long-term exposure to concentrated disadvantage, studies, in other words, that provide a tem-poral perspective on neighborhood effects. I discuss these studies and others in the following parts of this section.

Economic Restructuring and Spatial Mismatch

One thing that was not made clear in *The Truly Disadvantaged* is that ten cities accounted for three-fourths of the ghetto poverty in the United States during the 1970s, and they all had two things in common—they were all industrial centers and, except for Atlanta, they were all located in the Northeast and Midwest regions of the United States. By contrast cities in the Sun Belt regions of the country tended to experience job growth in all sectors of the economy (manufacturing, retail/wholesale, white-collar and blue-collar services) during the 1970s and 1980s.[35] As

John Kasarda's research revealed, the cities in the Frost Belt experienced massive industrial restructuring and a loss of blue-collar jobs. These cities suffered overall employment declines, because "growth in their predominantly information processing industries could not numerically compensate for substantial losses in their more traditional industrial sectors, especially manufacturing."[36]

The impact of economic structuring on inner-city neighborhoods was the focus of a number of longitudinal studies. George Galster, Ron Mincy, and Mitchell Tobin drew on data from four sources and measured the impact of economic restructuring on poverty rates in census tracts in metropolitan statistical areas (MSA) from 1980 to 1990.[37] They found that predominantly black census tracts experienced, on average, substantially higher growth in poverty rates during the 1980s. And that most of this increase of black neighborhood poverty was due to "the severe restructuring experienced in the MSAs that contained these tracts."[38] Moreover, MSA restructuring had stronger effects in black neighborhoods than in comparable white neighborhoods.[39]

In another important study, John Iceland analyzed data from the Panel Study of Income Dynamics (PSID) and the U.S. census to gauge the impact of economic structuring on changes in poverty rates in MSA census tracts from 1980 to 1990.[40] His data reveal that even though deindustrialization had a "negligible impact on poor whites," it decreased the likelihood that African Americans residing in metropolitan areas would transition out of poverty. And the impact of industrial shifts remained constant even after he controlled for racial residential segregation. Iceland's findings support the deindustrialization hypothesis, which suggests that manufacturing employment enables poor individuals to escape poverty. "That deindustrialization has a negative impact on African Americans, but not on whites supports previous findings," stated Iceland, "as African Americans have long been overrepresented in blue-collar jobs."[41]

However, as James R. Elliott pointed out in a study based on data from the 1990 decennial census and the Multi-City Survey of Urban Inequality in Atlanta, Boston, and Los Angeles, overall declines in traditional manufacturing jobs in major central cities have accompanied increases in "downgraded" production arrangements, which feature smaller firms, lower profit margins, and diminishing wages and benefits for lower-skilled workers. The results from Elliott's study "suggest that this secondary aspect of deindustrialization, while often overlooked, plays a key role in shaping the labor market outcomes of disadvantaged inner-city workers." [42]

Kevin F. Gotham presented another important extension of the deindustrialization thesis, as outlined in *The Truly Disadvantaged*.[43] Focusing on Kansas City as a case study, Gotham provided both quantitative and qualitative documentation of how the Federal Housing Administration and the real estate industry interacted with the decline of blue-collar industries and the rise of a service-oriented economy to reinforce racial residential segregation and aggravate urban poverty in the city in the 1980s and 1990s. Gotham argued that the white residents of Kansas City are less likely to be impacted by the negative effects of large-scale economic change, because they tend to be located in all parts of the metropolitan area and are not restricted to geographically constrained areas by ongoing housing discrimination and segregation. In contrast, inner-city black residents have borne the brunt of the decentralization of employment not simply because they are heavily concentrated in manufacturing jobs, but also because they reside in the inner city and have been excluded from obtaining affordable housing in the suburban neighborhoods of Kansas City.

Gotham's basic contribution is to show that changes in the national economy interact with changes in federal housing policy to shape patterns of uneven development and residential segregation. "The intersection of housing markets with the shift in both the locus of production and the nature of work concentrates the deleterious effects of residential segregation in the inner city while reducing its effects in suburban areas," stated Gotham. "Thus, the principal dynamics shaping urban development and residential segregation are continuing racial discrimination in the housing and lending industries combined with the changes in federal housing policy in the context of large-scale shifts in the national economy."[44]

As argued in *The Truly Disadvantaged*, the decline of manufacturing in a number of cities has resulted in a gradual movement of jobs to the suburbs, creating a spatial mismatch, the geographic separation of residence from the location of employment, for inner-city residents. Although studies using data collected up to 1970 failed to demonstrate convincingly that spatial mismatch affects black employment,[45] more recent research conducted mainly by labor and urban economists supports the following notions: that central-city blacks have less access to employment in terms of the ratio of jobs to people and of average travel time to and from work than do central-city whites; that unlike most other groups of workers, less-educated blacks receive lower wages in the central city than their counterparts in the suburbs; and that the decline in earnings of central-city blacks is positively associated with the extent of job decentralization in metropolitan areas.[46]

Inner-city black males have been especially hard hit by these changes. Data collected from the Urban Poverty and Family Life Study (UPFLS) that I directed in Chicago show that the efforts by out-of-school inner-city black males to obtain blue-collar jobs in the industries that had previously employed their fathers have been impeded by industrial shifts as evident in the occupational changes of successive cohorts of young men. The most common occupations mentioned shifted from manufacturing jobs (assembler and operator) among the oldest cohorts to service jobs (janitor and waiter) among the younger cohort of respondents ages nineteen to twenty-eight.[47]

In a related study, analyzing national data from decennial census tract tabulations from the population censuses of 1950 to 1990, Lincoln Quillian found a "marked decline in the employment of working-age men in low-income black tracts, both in absolute terms and relative to the employment rate of male residents of other types of tracts."[48] Quillian's research reveals that the rates of working-age male labor-force nonparticipation in low-income black census tracts roughly doubled from 15 percent in 1950 to 44 percent in 1990. Part of this increase was due to the out-migration of higher income blacks from low-income census tracts, but, as I argued in my book *When Work Disappears*, a good deal of it was due to the declining rates of black male employment in manufacturing industries.

Another study by Sabino Kornrich suggests that an important factor in the occupational status of urban blacks is the variation in the quality of available jobs across time and across cities.[49] Areas hardest hit by economic transformations "were often cities with large black populations, such as Detroit, St. Louis and other manufacturing centers of the Midwest."[50] Kornrich's study reveals the importance of considering the structure of labor and job queues—in particular, the types of available jobs and the available workers to fill them in determining black-white inequality. He found that "black workers have better outcomes in queues where blacks are more numerous, though the level of wage inequality in the queue affects the strength of this relationship. Black workers experience the greatest disadvantage in highly unequal queues with low black representation."[51] He also found that the proportion of Latinos and female workers in a queue influences the black and white wage gap, which suggests that when both groups are available, employers prefer Latino and female workers over black workers. Studies show that such discriminatory hiring choices are especially harmful to low-educated black males.[52]

Persistent Poverty and Depopulation

In *The Truly Disadvantaged* I failed to emphasize the impact of the Second Great Migration of African Americans from the rural South to the cities of the Northeast and Midwest, which lasted thirty years—from

1940 to 1970. This mass movement of African Americans was even larger and more sustained than the First Great Migration, which began at the turn of the twentieth century and ended during the Great Depression, and had a more profound impact on the transformation of the inner city.

As the black urban population in the North grew and precipitated greater demands for housing, pressure mounted in white communities to keep blacks out. Suburban communities, with their restrictive covenants and special zoning laws, refused to permit the construction of public housing. And the federal government acquiesced to opposition from organized white neighborhood groups to the construction of public housing in their neighborhoods in the city. Thus low-income subsidized housing was overwhelmingly concentrated in the overcrowded and deteriorating inner-city ghettos—the poorest and least powerful sections of the city and the metropolitan area. "This growing population of politically weak urban poor was unable to counteract the desires of vocal middle- and working-class whites for segregated housing," housing that would keep blacks from white neighborhoods.[53] In short, public housing became a federally funded institution that isolated families by race and class, resulting in high concentrations of poor black families in inner-city ghettos.[54]

In the last quarter of the twentieth century, new developments led to further changes in these neighborhoods. And one of the most significant, as emphasized in *The Truly Disadvantaged*, was the out-migration of middle-income blacks. Before the 1970s African American families had faced extremely strong barriers when they considered moving into white neighborhoods. Not only did many experience overt discrimination in the housing market, some were recipients of violent attacks. Although fair housing audits continue to reveal the existence of discrimination in the housing market, the fair housing legislation, including the Fair Housing Amendments Act of 1988, reduced the strength of these barriers. And middle-income African Americans increased their efforts to move from concentrated black poverty areas to more desirable neighborhoods in the metropolitan area, including white neighborhoods.[55]

In *The Truly Disadvantaged*, I argued that many working- and middle-class blacks exited ghetto neighborhoods to higher income neighborhoods. Because I failed to elaborate on this point, some writers assumed that I was referring to a movement from the inner city to white suburbs, when in fact I had in mind a movement not only to white suburbs but to nonpoor black neighborhoods in other parts of the metropolitan area—central city and suburbs—as well.[56] And it should be pointed out, as Mary Pattillo's subsequent research shows, even if the black middle class exited the ghetto and entered nonpoor neighborhoods, these neighborhoods are still more likely to have a higher proportion of poor families than the neighborhoods of comparable whites. In other words, they are still more likely to be exposed to conditions of poverty and the problems associated with it. Indeed, many of these neighborhoods were former white neighborhoods that had quickly become segregated, and both middle- and lower-income blacks filled the housing vacancies created by the significant white out-migration.[57]

The out-migration of nonpoor blacks from inner-city ghetto neighborhoods contributed to the depopulation of these neighborhoods. This pattern represents an important change in the formation of neighborhoods. In the earlier years communities undergoing racial change from white to black tended to experience an increase in population density, as a result of the black migration from the South. Because of the housing demand, particularly in the late stages of the succession from white to black, homes and apartments in these neighborhoods were often subdivided into smaller units.[58]

However, 1970 marked the end of the Second Great Migration, and two developments affected the course of population movement to the inner cities after that time. Improvements in transportation made it easier for workers to live outside the central city, and industries gradually shifted to the suburbs because of the increased residential suburbanization of the labor force and the lower cost of production. Consequently, inner-city manufacturing jobs were no longer a strong factor pulling migrants to central cities.[59] So with the decline of industrial employment in the inner city, the influx of southern black migration to northern cities ceased and many poor black neighborhoods, especially those in the Midwest and Northeast, changed from densely packed areas of recently arrived migrants to communities gradually abandoned by the working and middle classes.[60]

Several important studies have examined life experiences in these inner-city black neighborhoods since the 1970s. Using data from the Panel Study of Income Dynamics (PSID) from 1979 to 1990, Quillian found that many residents of poor black neighborhoods at a given point in time will still be residing in a poor black area ten years later.[61] Quillian's results reveal significant differences between whites and blacks in the duration of exposure to poor neighborhoods. Whereas 70 percent of blacks who reside in a poor or extremely poor census tract will still be living in a poor or extremely poor census tract ten years later, less than 40 percent of whites who live in such tracts will experience such prolonged exposure, and most of the racial difference cannot be accounted for by differences in household structure or poverty status. Quillian's analysis reveals that a high rate of repeat spells in moderately and extremely poor neighborhoods is a significant factor contributing to "entrapment" in such neighborhoods. "The difficulty of 'escaping' poor neighborhoods for African Americans results as much because of high rates of repeat spells among the recently exited as from low rates of exit," stated Quillian.[62]

Once repeat spells are taken into account, the level of immobility for African Americans in extremely poor tracts (poverty rates of more than 40 percent) is startlingly high. Nearly 50 percent of black residents in extreme poverty tracts in 1970 and 1980 still resided in the same or a different extreme poverty tract ten years later. And much of the entrapment in poor neighborhoods "reflects the fact that persons who exit poor neighborhoods often re-enter a poor tract rather quickly after an exit. The temporal pattern that leads to entrapment in extremely poor neighborhoods then, is not the inability to move out that is most often hypothesized, but the inability to stay out."[63]

In another impressive study that analyzes data from the Panel Study of Income Dynamics (PSID) with methods designed to measure intergenerational economic mobility, Patrick Sharkey found that "more than 70% of black children who are raised in the poorest quarter of American neighborhoods will continue to live in the poorest quarter of neighborhoods as adults."[64] He also found that since the 1970s, a majority of black families have resided in the poorest quarter of neighborhoods in *consecutive generations*, compared to only 7 percent of white families. Thus he concluded that the disadvantages of living in poor black neighborhoods, like the advantages of living in affluent white neighborhoods, are in large measure inherited.[65]

Accordingly, this persistence of neighborhood inequality raises serious questions about studies on neighborhood effects. Many of these studies substantially underestimate the racial inequality in neighborhood environments, because they use a single point in time, generation, or measure of neighborhood poverty or income.[66] Whereas living in the most impoverished neighborhoods is a temporary state for white families, most black families who lived in the poorest neighborhoods in the 1970s continue to live in such neighborhoods today. Sharkey suggested therefore that the focus of the research on neighborhood effects might be shifted to an examination of how the effect of living in poor neighborhoods over two or more generations differs from short-term residence in such neighborhoods. This brings us back to another shortcoming of the MTO experiment. Sharkey stated:

> The difficulty with interpreting the results from the MTO as estimates of "neighborhood effects" lies in the conceptualization of a move to a new neighborhood as a point-in-time "treatment." This perspective ignores the

possibility that the social environments surrounding families over generations have any lagged or cumulative influence on family members, and
it ignores the complex pathways by which this influence may occur. For
instance, the neighborhood may have an influence on an individual's educational attainment in one generation, in turn influencing the individual's
occupational status and income as an adult, the quality of the home environment in which that individual raises a child, and the developmental
trajectory of that child. These indirect pathways are obscured in observa-
tional studies that control for a set of covariates such as education or the
quality of the home environment, and they are impossible to assess in experimental approaches such as MTO.[67]

We should also consider another important study that Sharkey coauthored with senior investigator Robert Sampson and another colleague,
Steven Raudenbush, that examined the durable effects of concentrated
poverty on black children's verbal ability.[68] They studied a representative
sample of 750 African American children, ages six to twelve, who were
growing up in the city of Chicago in 1995, and followed them anywhere
they moved in the United States for up to seven years. The children were
given a reading examination and vocabulary test at three different periods. Their study shows "that residing in a severely disadvantaged neighborhood cumulatively impedes the development of academically relevant
verbal ability in children," so much so that the effects linger on even if
they leave these neighborhoods.[69]

Their research raises important questions "about ways in which neighborhoods may alter growth in verbal ability producing effects that linger
on even if a child leaves a severely disadvantaged neighborhood."[70] They
argue that if researchers were trying to determine the extent to which
neighborhoods affect children's verbal ability by randomly providing
housing vouchers to black children who lived and grew up in inner-city
ghetto neighborhoods and who took a test measuring verbal ability before
they moved, and then compared the results of the same test a few years
later after the children had resided in better neighborhoods, the conclusion would very likely be there are no neighborhood effects. Why? There
would be no difference in verbal ability linked to their movement to a
better neighborhood, simply because their verbal abilities had already
been formed.

Children's verbal ability certainly has consequences for school perfor-
mances, including the completion of high school. Geoffrey T. Wodtke,
David J. Harding, and Felix Elwert's important recent study used the
Panel Study of Income Dynamics (PSID) to examine the effects of long-
term exposure to disadvantaged neighborhoods on high school gradua-

tion.[71] They tracked 4,154 children by measuring their neighborhood context once each year from age one to seventeen and found that continuous exposure to disadvantaged neighborhoods—featuring high rates of poverty, unemployment, female-headed households, and welfare receipt, as well as few well-educated adults—throughout "the entire childhood life course has a devastating impact on the chances of graduating from high school."[72] The authors stated that their findings, which reveal the cumulative impact of growing up in this country's most disadvantaged communities, are "consistent with Wilson's foundational arguments regarding the consequences of spatially concentrated poverty, which motivated nearly all recent studies of neighborhood effects."[73]

The findings presented in these studies suggest that neighborhood effects are not solely structural. Among the effects of living in segregated neighborhoods over extended periods is repeated exposure to cultural traits that emanate from or are the products of racial exclusion— traits, such as verbal skills, that may impede successful maneuvering in the larger society. As Sharkey pointed out "when we consider that the vast majority of black families living in America's poorest neighborhoods come from families that have lived in similar environments for generations . . . continuity of the neighborhood environment, in addition to continuity of individual economic status, may be especially relevant to the study of cultural patterns and social norms among disadvantaged populations."[74]

Steven R. Holloway and Stephen Mulherin also captured the importance of cumulative neighborhood effects in another important longitudinal study.[75] Pointing out that *The Truly Disadvantaged* gave inadequate empirical attention to adolescents, Holloway and Muherin analyzed data from the National Longitudinal Survey of Youth (NLSY) and found that living in poor neighborhoods during adolescence had long-term effects on labor market outcomes, partly caused by the limited ability to accumulate early work experience. Thus, "adolescent neighborhood poverty appears to have an independent and lasting effect on adult labor market experience—an effect that is greater for males than females, yet one that appears to be transmitted though accumulation of work experience more for females than for males."[76]

Finally, the effects of residence in the most disadvantaged neighborhoods on psychological well-being was the subject of a study by Catherine E. Ross, John R. Reynolds, and Karlyn J. Geis.[77] Analyzing survey data from a representative sample of Illinois residents that was linked to census-tract information about neighborhood poverty and stability, the authors found a significant difference in the effects of neighborhood stability in affluent neighborhoods as opposed to poor neighborhoods. Whereas stability, defined as neighborhoods that "have a high percentage of persons who have lived in the same residence (house or apartment) for the past five years," is associated with low levels of distress in affluent neighborhoods, the opposite is true in disadvantaged neighborhoods.[78] Noting that arguments in *The Truly Disadvantaged* linked high rates of poverty and neighborhood stability, that is, the relative inability of poor residents to escape to safer and more affluent neighborhoods, Ross and her colleagues pointed out that residents of poor, stable neighborhoods face much higher levels of stress because of high levels of disorder. "The disorder common in poor, stable neighborhoods mediates much of the joint effect of neighborhood stability and poverty on distress because it increases resident's perceptions that they are powerless to leave dangerous places."[79]

Social Isolation and Concentration Effects

As noted above, two of the key concepts of *The Truly Disadvantaged* are *social isolation* and *concentration effects*. A number of studies have tested and provided support for propositions in the book that incorporate these two concepts.[80] This section focuses on research that extends or advances these propositions.

In a quantitative longitudinal study, Roberto G. Quercia and George G. Galster used my concept of *social isolation* to test their theory on *threshold effects*. They defined a threshold effect as "a dynamic process in which the magnitude of the response changes significantly as the triggering stimulus exceeds threshold effects." And they reviewed and assessed the available empirical research in which thresholds are manifested in neighborhood change to address the following question: "Is there sufficient evidence to adopt neighborhood thresholds as a working hypothesis?"[81] They found evidence of threshold effects that lends support to my argument that poverty concentration effects should result "in an exponential increase in . . . forms of social dislocation,"[82] and their review of the disparate empirical and theoretical literature on threshold effects related to neighborhood change "supports the contention that threshold effects should be adopted as a working hypothesis."[83]

In another quantitative longitudinal study, Kenneth C. Land, Patricia L. McCall, and Lawrence E. Cohen incorporated my concepts of *concentration effects* and *social isolation* in an examination of the structural covariates of homicide rates across time and social space.[84] They showed that the existing empirical studies on the structural covariates of homicide rates have yielded mixed results across different time periods and different geographical regions. Land and his colleagues used *The Truly Disadvantaged*'s theoretical arguments on social isolation and concentration effects to help tease out the problems of previous studies. The authors pointed out that concentration effects and social isolation represent new ideas to explain the problems that previous studies have had in identifying causal effects involving the structural determinants of crime. The authors stated that these concepts help explain the relationship between homicide rates and the persistent covariation of the components of their index of resource-deprivation (e.g., median family income, the percentage of families living below the official poverty line, the Gini index of family income inequality, the percentage of black families in an area, and the percentage of children age eighteen or under not living with both parents).[85]

The impact of social isolation and concentration effects in the inner-city ghetto is clearly demonstrated in a number of qualitative studies. In the qualitative research component of our Urban Poverty and Family Life Study in Chicago, we found that, overall, the personal friendship networks of blacks (both male and female) are very limited.[86] For example, the poor blacks we talked to in our fieldwork were less likely to have at least one employed close friend than were Mexican immigrants of similar income and education. Because these people lacked friends with jobs, they tended to not hear about possible job opportunities or even different types of employment. This form of social isolation handicapped the residents of inner-city black neighborhoods; as many stable working neighbors drifted away, the ties that connected the remaining residents to the world of work came undone. Analysis of our ethnographic data for the remaining poor and often unemployed residents revealed that "social contacts were a useful means of gaining informal work to help make ends meet but far less often successful in helping with steady employment in the formal economy; networks existed but largely lacked the capacity to help lift residents into the formal labor market."[87]

Moreover, our data on job-search behavior revealed that black men and women in the inner city were less likely than Mexican immigrants to report that they received help from a friend or relative in obtaining their current job. The job-search strategies that black inner-city residents most frequently reported using were filling out an application at a place of business and seeking assistance at an employment office. Seldom did anyone report that they had heard about a job from an acquaintance or friend.

A study by Sandra Smith provides yet another perspective to help explain why informal job networks among blacks were less useful in helping jobseekers find employment in the formal economy. She found that distrust on the part of black jobholders and the defensive individualism typical of black jobseekers profoundly affected the use of job referrals in the search for employment. She pointed out that the neighborhoods of the black poor are "characterized by chronic poverty and a history of exploitation" and tend to feed the inclination to distrust, "inhibiting the development of mutually beneficial cooperative relationships such as those that facilitate the job-matching process."[88] The cooperation between jobseekers and jobholders is thwarted by a lack of mutual trust. Thus, low-skilled black jobseekers are frequently unable to use their friendships, acquaintances, and family ties—their informal network—to promote employment. Black jobholders were reluctant to refer their relatives and friends for jobs, because they feared that their own reputations with employers could be jeopardized if the work of the people they recommended was substandard.

On the one hand, jobholders justified denying assistance to their relatives and friends by saying that these individuals lacked motivation and individual responsibility. On the other hand, many low-skilled jobseekers, particularly black males, "cognizant of how they are perceived by others in their social milieu" and concerned about being demeaned for their unemployment, hesitated to approach their peers for referrals.[89] This "go it alone" approach proves to be enormously self-defeating because employers in low-skilled labor markets heavily rely on personal referrals. Smith's analysis provides an excellent example of how cultural frames (shared visions of human behavior developed from the microlevel processes of meaning and decision making) orient action—in this case the limited use of job referrals.

Another extension of the concepts of *social isolation* and *concentration effects* was featured in Alford Young's insightful book *The Minds of Marginalized Black Men*.[90] Based on an ethnographic study of low-income urban black men's perceptions of mobility and opportunity, Young suggested that the impact of social isolation and concentration effects goes beyond access and proximity to individual institutions that promote social advancement. He went on to argue that there are differences in how social isolation and the effects of concentrated disadvantages are experienced among these men.

These differences in turn shape men's worldviews on mobility and structural constraints. In other words, social isolation and the concentration of disadvantaged people within bounded geographic regions facilitate serial patterns of social contact and exposure that become significant factors for how people construct interpretations of social reality. These interpretations are crucial factors for initiating (or, in some cases, inhibiting) individual action on the part of the urban poor.

Nowhere is this more clearly demonstrated than in two notable and illuminating ethnographies by Elijah Anderson and Sudhir Venkatesh.[91] Unlike Young in *The Minds of Marginalized Black Men*, Anderson and Venkatesh did not necessarily challenge or extend the social isolation concept, but rather applied it respectively to the inner-city ghettos of Philadelphia and Chicago. Each author revealed the existence of informal rules in the inner-city ghetto that govern interactions and shape how people engage one another and make decisions in situations imposed by poverty and racial segregation—situations that place severe constraints on social mobility. Over time, these processes lead to the development of informal codes that regulate behavior.

Anderson talked about the "code of the street," an informal but explicit set of rules developed to govern interpersonal public behavior and regulate violence in Philadelphia's inner-city ghetto neighborhoods, where crime is high and police protection is low. Anderson argued that the issue of respect is at the root of the code. In a context of limited opportunities for self-actualization and success, some individuals in the community, most notably young black males, devise alternative ways to gain respect that emphasize manly pride, ranging from simply wearing brand-name clothing to have the "right look" and talking the right way to developing a predatory attitude toward neighbors. Anderson pointed out, however, that no one residing in these troubled neighborhoods is unaffected by the code of the street, especially young people, who are drawn into this negative culture both on the streets and in the schools as they must frequently adopt "street" behavior as a form of self defense. As Anderson put it, "the code of the street is actually a cultural adaptation to a profound lack of faith in the police and the judicial system—and in others who would champion one's personal security."[92]

A related informal but regulated pattern of behavior is described by Sudhir Venkatesh in his study of the underground economy in a ghetto neighborhood on the South Side of Chicago. Venkatesh illustrated how social isolation lends itself to a thriving underground economy; lacking mainstream opportunities and connections to mainstream society, men and women in this neighborhood are forced to look inward to make ends meet. Venkatesh pointed out that "the underground arena is not simply a place to buy goods and services. It is also a field of social relationships that enable off-the-books trading to occur in an ordered and predictable manner."[93] This trading often results in disagreements or breaches because there are no laws on the books, "but the main point is that in situations ostensibly criminal and often threatening to personal security, there is still a structure in place that shapes how people make decisions and engage one another."[94] In other words, informal rules actually govern what would appear on the surface to be random underground activity. These rules stipulate what is expected of those involved in these informal exchanges and where they should meet. Just as Anderson described a "code of the street", Venkatesh talked about a "code of shady dealings."

Like Anderson in his effort to explain the emergence of the code of the street, Venkatesh argued that the code of shady dealings is a response to circumstances in inner-city ghetto neighborhoods, where joblessness is high and opportunities for advancement are severely limited. Furthermore, both Anderson and Venkatesh clearly argued that these cultural codes ultimately hinder integration into the broader society and are therefore dysfunctional. In other words, they contribute to the perpetuation of poverty.

Anderson found that for some young men the draw of the street is so powerful that they cannot avail themselves of legitimate employment opportunities even when they become available. Likewise, Venkatesh maintained that adherence to the code of shady dealings impedes social mobility. The "underground economy enables people to survive but can lead to alienation from the wider world" he stated.[95] For example, none of the work experience accrued in the informal economy can be listed on a resume for job searches in the formal labor market, and time invested in underground work reduces time devoted to accumulating skills or contacts for legitimate employment.

Finally, Mario Small creatively engaged *The Truly Disadvantaged*'s concept of *social isolation* by adding organizational texture to the study of urban inequality.[96] Integrating quantitative data with field research in New York City, Small concluded that an organizational perspective enhances our understanding of the different aspects of social isolation. He introduced the concept *organizational isolate* to describe what is perhaps the most disadvantaged individual in a poor neighborhood.

His research reveals that the organizational isolate is one who is disconnected from neighborhood associations, community centers, childcare centers, schools, political clubs, hobby clubs, and gyms. "This person is effectively unplugged not merely from the most reliable way to form and sustain ties in a time-sensitive society," stated Small, "but also from the organizational apparatus through which grants, information, consumer goods, discounts, political access, and many other resources are transferred." The organizational isolate is handicapped not simply by the lack of friends but by the "absence of contexts in which friends continue to be made." Accordingly, this person not only lacks ties to the bureaucracy, but lacks access to the numerous resources embodied in the organizational sphere, mechanisms that friends are unable to provide. "In a society increasingly structured around formal organizations, the organizational isolate is the person increasingly guaranteed to be left out."[97] Small's notion of *organizational isolate* could very well become a key concept in the study of urban inequality and represents an important extension of the concept *social isolation*.

The Male Marriageable Pool Hypothesis

The Truly Disadvantaged argues that the sharp increase in black male joblessness since 1970 accounts in large measure for the rise in the rate of single-parent families, and that since jobless rates are highest in the inner-city ghetto, rates of single parenthood are also highest there. However, research on the relationship between male employment and rates of marriage and single parenthood is mixed. Although there is a strong association between rates of marriage and both employment status and earnings at any given point in time, national longitudinal studies suggest that these factors account for a relatively small proportion of the overall *decline* in marriage among African-Americans. Harvard professor Christopher Jencks pointed out that the decline in the proportion of African-American men who were married and living with their wives was almost as large among those who had worked throughout the previous years as among black men in general.[98] Also, studies have shown only modest support for the hypothesis linking the sharp rise in poor single-parent families to the declining employment status and income of young black men.[99]

However, most of these studies are based on national data and other highly aggregate data, not data specific to inner-city neighborhoods where many experiences relate to race and poverty. As Daniel J. Lichter, Felicia B. LeClere, and Diane K. McLaughlin pointed out, the use of national data is potentially problematic "because spatial variation in marriage and family behavior is substantial."[100] To address this problem, Lichter and his colleagues used local area data from the 1980 Public Use Microdata sample (D file). Developing measures that represent variations of *The Truly Disadvantaged*'s "male marriageable pool index," their data clearly reinforce my argument that a shortage of economically attractive men in local markets depresses female marriage rates. "The apparent retreat from traditional family structures may be located in black men's deteriorating economic circumstances," they concluded, "particularly in metropolitan central cities where over half of these young African American men today are jobless, employed part time, or working at poverty-level wages."[101]

Support for this conclusion is found in our study of family life and poverty in Chicago, which also used local data and addressed the question of how much of the decline in the black marriage rate in the inner city can be accounted for by the increasing joblessness among black males.[102] Our study was not longitudinal, but we did collect retrospective (or life-history) marriage and employment data that helped us estimate trends over time. An analysis of respondents' retrospective data comparing the employment experiences of different age groups (cohorts) revealed that marriage rates dropped much more sharply among jobless black fathers than among employed black fathers. But this drop applies only to the younger cohorts. Analyzing data from our survey, Mark Testa and Marilyn Krogh found that while employment had no significant effect on the likelihood that black single fathers ages thirty-two to forty-four would eventually marry, it increased the likelihood of legitimation by eight times for those single fathers eighteen to thirty-one years old.[103]

Kathryn Edin and Maria Kefalas's impressive book *Promises I Can Keep: Why Poor Women Put Motherhood Before Marriage* also relied on local data to address the relationship between male employment and marriage. More specifically, Edin and Kefalas collected and analyzed data on low-income black, white, and Puerto Rican single mothers in Camden, New Jersey, one of America's poorest cities, and in eight poor neighborhoods in Philadelphia.[104] The authors found that the low-income young mothers to whom they talked valued motherhood highly. Indeed, their identity, emotional fulfillment, personal success, and hope for the future were tied to motherhood. The thought of not being a parent or of postponing parenting until their thirties, a common practice for middle-class women, was anathema to the women in their study. However, their respondents also valued marriage and hoped to be married some day. Edin and Kefalas forcefully argued that poor women postpone marriage not because they value it lightly but because they feel that they cannot commit to marriage until they are confident of success.

Basically the problem they face is that the men to whom they have access tend not to be marriageable because of a range of problems—poor education, chronic joblessness, low earnings, criminal records, spells of incarceration, drug and alcohol abuse, intimate violence, and chronic infidelity—not solely male employment as argued in *The Truly Disadvantaged*. For example, as Bruce Western and Christopher Wilderman have noted, incarceration severely damages a man's marriageability.[105]

Edin and Kefalas pointed out that there is a short supply of good, decent, trustworthy men in the world of the women in their study. The better-off men pair off with the better-off women. It is not surprising that the relationships these women have with the fathers of their children are plagued with physical abuse, mistrust, and infidelity. The women therefore wait until they can find a man they can trust, a man who has, over time, proven himself to be a dependable and responsible partner and father. Their dreams include financial security and having a house before getting married. And because all of these conditions are so difficult to meet, they become mothers long before they become wives, and some never marry.

Major Empirical Challenges to *The Truly Disadvantaged*

The major objective of *The Truly Disadvantaged* was to explain the deterioration of conditions in the inner-city ghetto since 1970. Accordingly, the book was not a discussion and analysis of the factors that gave rise to the formation of the ghetto, which would certainly involve a detailed discussion of the legacy of historic racism, discrimination, and segregation. Nonetheless, a number of writers failed to note this distinction and proceeded to critique the book for paying insufficient attention to the factor of race in the formation of the black ghetto. Race, of course, continues to be a major problem in exacerbating life experiences in the inner-city ghetto, but as I attempted to show in *The Truly Disadvantaged*, the most powerful factors in the increasing concentration of poverty and related social dislocations since 1970 were structural changes in the economy and the out-migration of higher income families from the inner-city ghetto. A history of racial subjection made the black inner-city poor particularly vulnerable to these changes. As the late black economist Vivian Henderson argued three decades ago, racism put African Americans in their economic place and stepped aside to watch changes in the modern economy make the place in which they find themselves even more precarious.[106]

If I were writing *The Truly Disadvantaged* today, I would fully elaborate and make explicit the important distinction between the legacy of racial subjugation and the more contemporary changes that aggravate the conditions created by this legacy, changes that were the focus of *The Truly Disadvantaged*.

I would also provide a more nuanced and dialectical position on the interaction effects between social structure and cultural constraints. As Loïc Wacquant, and Michèle Lamont and Mario Small, have pointed out, these two dimensions were not clearly distinguished in *The Truly Disadvantaged*, where I tended to discuss culture as if it were solely a by-product of social structural forces.[107] Since the publication of *The Truly Disadvantaged* I have worked to move beyond this position with a more sophisticated discussion of culture that gives it greater analytic autonomy.[108] For example in my book *More than Just Race* I discussed how some cultural patterns in the inner-city ghetto reflect informal rules that shape how individuals interact or engage one another and make decisions.

The decision-making often involves perceptions about how the world works—what we call meaning making. The meaning-making and decision-making processes evolve over time in situations imposed by poverty and racial segregation, situations that impede social mobility. To state this in formal sociological terms, culture *mediates* the impact of structural forces such as poverty and racial segregation. In other words, residents of the ghetto develop ways, often quite creative, to respond and adjust to chronic racial and economic subordination, as reflected in meaning-making and decision-making processes, including those resulting in the creation of informal cultural codes that regulate behavior. My discussion of the works of Elijah Anderson and Sudhir Venkatesh in the previous section provides examples of such cultural codes in inner-city ghetto neighborhoods.

Finally, I would also give more attention to the role of political factors in producing and aggravating these conditions. Indeed, a major and justified criticism of *The Truly Disadvantaged* raised by authors such as Loïc Wacquant is the lack of attention given to the impact of state policies on inner-city neighborhoods.[109] As I emphasized in my recent book *More than Just Race*, federal government policies, even those that are not explicitly racial, have had a profound impact on inner-city neighborhoods. Some of these policies are clearly motivated by racial bias, such as those that represent the legacy of racism, including the FHA's redlining of black neighborhoods in the 1940s and 1950s, and the federal government's decision to confine construction of public housing projects mainly to poor, black, inner-city neighborhoods. In other cases, including those that represent the periods covered in *The Truly Disadvantaged*, it seems that racial bias or concerns about race influenced but were not the sole inspiration for political decisions, such as the fiscal policies of the New Federalism, which resulted in drastic cuts in federal aid to cities whose populations had become more brown and black.

The point of conservative fiscal policy—no matter whose administration promulgated it (Ronald Reagan, George H. W. Bush, or George W. Bush)—was ostensibly to subject government to financial discipline. Nevertheless, the enactment of these policies creates financial constraints that make it difficult to generate the political support to effectively combat problems such as joblessness, drug trafficking, AIDS, family stress, and failing schools—problems that disproportionately affect residents of the inner-city ghetto.

And other policies that range from those that clearly lack a racial agenda to those where the line between racial and nonracial is somewhat gray have had a profound impact on inner cities and their poor black residents: federal transportation and highway policy that created an infrastructure for jobs in the suburbs; mortgage-interest tax exemptions and mortgages for veterans that jointly facilitated the exodus of working- and middle-class white families from inner-city neighborhoods; urban renewal and the building of freeway and highway networks through the hearts of many cities, which led to the destruction of many viable low-income

black neighborhoods; and the absence of effective labor-market policies
to safeguard the real value of the minimum wage, thereby making it more
difficult for the inner-city working poor to support their families. These
developments have occurred in many cities across the country, but they
perhaps have been felt more in the older, central cities of the Midwest
and Northeast—the traditional Rust Belt—where depopulated poverty
areas have experienced even greater problems.

But there have been other major criticisms that address issues actually raised in the book. Roger Waldinger's book *Still the Promised City?*
has been described in a number of circles as a major challenge to *The
Truly Disadvantaged*'s argument on the impact of the decline in manufacturing jobs on black employment.[110] Analyzing data collected in the
city of New York, Waldinger contended that it was the ethnic queuing
process—where the more advantaged ethnic groups are pulled up the
job ladder by economic growth, and the niches left vacant are filled by
lower-ranking groups—and African Americans' preferences for employment in the public sector that contributed to black employment woes,
not industrial restructuring/flight out of the city or technological shifts.
Whereas immigrants in New York were willing to take these lower-level
jobs, argued Waldinger, African Americans who arrived in the city a generation ago, and have job aspirations similar to those of whites, tended to
reject such jobs.

Moreover, employers of minimum-wage jobs find immigrants more
satisfactory than unskilled blacks. Waldinger contended that better-
educated African Americans have carved out niches in the public sector,
which requires skills that lower-educated blacks lack, thus creating an
economic schism whereby public sector employees maintain good jobs,
while the less educated fall further down the economic ladder.

With considerable fanfare, Waldinger used this theory to debunk the
restructuring/deindustrialization thesis. However, he never raised the
question of whether his analysis is applicable to cities other than New
York, particularly those on the East Coast or in the Midwest, where data
from studies, as discussed above, lend strong support to the restructur-
ing/deindustrialization thesis. In this connection, Waldinger argued that
blacks were never hurt by the departure of manufacturing jobs from New
York, because they were never concentrated in the manufacturing sector
of that city. But he neglected to mention other studies that show the disproportionate concentration of blacks in manufacturing in cities like Chicago, Pittsburgh, Detroit, and Philadelphia, just to mention a few. In
short, Waldinger's theory of ethnic niches and labor-market queues as applied to New York should be viewed as an important qualification to the
restructuring/deindustrialization thesis, not a refutation. At the same time

his attention to the role of immigrants in the overall job-selection and hiring process is important, a subject that was not really addressed in *The Truly Disadvantaged*.

Perhaps the most widely discussed challenge to *The Truly Disadvantaged* has been the work of Douglas Massey and his colleagues.[111] I maintained that one of the major factors involved in the growth of ghetto poverty is the out-migration of higher-income residents from certain parts of the inner city, resulting in a higher concentration of residents in ghetto neighborhoods. Research by Massey and his colleagues found that although levels of interclass segregation among blacks increased during the period covered by *The Truly Disadvantaged*, it was not sufficient to account for the rising concentration of urban black poverty. They argued that because of persisting segregation higher income blacks "are less able to separate from the poor than the privileged of other groups." Thus an increase in the poverty rate of a highly segregated group will automatically lead to an increase in concentrated poverty.[112]

The conflicting findings and conclusions in *The Truly Disadvantaged* and in the work of Massey and his colleagues are associated with different measures of the growth of concentrated poverty. Massey and his colleagues use a segregation index to calculate the probability of intraclass contact among groups in metropolitan areas. Although this measure allows for the description of the overall level of concentrated poverty in Standard Metropolitan Statistical Areas (SMSA), it does not identify specific ghetto and nonghetto neighborhoods. However, in a study that did indeed identify ghetto and nonghetto neighborhoods—focusing specifically on the cities of Philadelphia, Milwaukee, Cleveland, and Memphis—Paul Jargowsky and Mary Jo Bane found a significant geographical spreading of ghetto neighborhoods between 1970 and 1980. Areas that had become ghettos during that decade were mixed-income tracts in 1970 that were contiguous to areas identified as ghettos.[113] Their findings clearly support the hypothesis that a major factor in the increase of ghetto poverty since 1970 has been the out-migration of nonpoor from mixed-income areas. The poor also departed these neighborhoods, but the nonpoor left at a faster rate leaving behind a population that was poorer in 1980 than in 1970. As the population spread out from mixed-income areas in 1970 to other areas, the next "ring" of areas that were mostly white and nonpoor became the home of a larger proportion of African Americans, including poor blacks, as nonpoor whites departed these areas, which experienced an overall decline in population.[114]

Unfortunately, the important process involving the geographical spread of ghetto poverty is not captured in studies that focus on the concentration of poverty in SMSAs using a segregation index. Although such studies are important for understanding the role of racial segregation in explaining changes in the level of metropolitan poverty concentration, the data they yield do not provide an appropriate test of the hypothesis that associates the increase of ghetto poverty with the higher-income black exodus from certain inner-city neighborhoods. In fact, I view the important research of Massey and his colleagues as complementary to *The Truly Disadvantaged*, not contradictory. Other writers such as Jeffrey Morenoff and Robert J. Sampson, Lincoln Quillian, and Kevin F. Gotham have reached similar conclusions.[115] For example, Morenoff and Sampson, in discussing my depopulation hypothesis and Massey's segregation hypothesis, stated: "These two viewpoints may appear to be mutually exclusive because one emphasizes the out-migration of blacks from poor neighborhoods, while the other highlights the forces that constrain middle- and upper-income blacks from moving very far away from those areas that have been overridden by poverty and crime. We argue, however, that the two perspectives can be reconciled by recognizing that both demographic mechanisms may be operating simultaneously, but in distinct spatial contexts."[116]

Finally, I would like to discuss the important research of David Harding who critiqued my discussion of social isolation in *The Truly Disadvantaged*. Based on his qualitative study of sixty adolescent boys who grew up in two very poor areas and one working-class area in Boston, Harding maintained that the social isolation of the residents from mainstream institutions and culture is overemphasized. Specifically, rather than featuring the dominance of "ghetto-specific" cultures, disadvantaged neighborhoods are instead characterized by cultural heterogeneity, which represents a variety of conflicting and competing cultural models. Accordingly, Harding stated that his research "is not built upon Wilson's social isolation theory, which emphasizes the mainstream isolation and negative normative values of poor neighborhoods. Rather, it proposes an alternative framework for understanding the cultural context of poor neighborhoods: cultural heterogeneity."[117]

In considering Harding's research, the crucial question is whether a scholar can respect a neighborhood's diversity of cultural frames, modes, and narrative while also appreciating the value of my concept of social isolation. In other words, are the two mutually exclusive? The objective of my theory of the social transformation of the inner city, which includes arguments about the increase of social isolation, was to analyze the structural forces that produced conditions of increased concentrated poverty and joblessness and to examine the implications of these factors for inner-city residents. The arguments associated with my theory did not simply assert that people in the inner city lacked mainstream values; rather, the arguments attempted to provide a theoretical explanation for why conditions in inner-city neighborhoods had changed over time and how social processes in those contexts resulted in increasing social isolation, as well as the behavior associated with it.

My theory of social isolation certainly does not argue that *all* residents of the inner-city ghetto lack mainstream values. Simply describing supposedly contrary evidence showing that, indeed, many people subscribe to mainstream values does not challenge this theory. What the theory attempts to explain is increasing social isolation, increasing poverty concentration, increasing joblessness, and the resultant changes in behavior. Does this mean that I fail to recognize that inner-city people also subscribe to mainstream values, as Harding seems to assert? Of course, it does not. Unlike *The Truly Disadvantaged*, Harding's qualitative study, however theoretically interesting, cannot account for *changing* patterns of behavior. Nonetheless, I think that Harding's work is important, and it certainly would have been good if I had complemented my theoretical arguments by emphasizing the heterogeneity of cultural values in the inner city as I subsequently did in publications such as *When Work Disappears*.[118]

Framing and Policies Influenced Directly and Indirectly by *The Truly Disadvantaged*

In *The Truly Disadvantaged* I argued that a combination of universal and targeted initiatives are needed to improve the life chances of the ghetto poor. However, I also argued that "the latter would be considered an offshoot of and indeed secondary to the universal programs." In other words, "the important goal is to construct an economic-social reform program in such a way that the universal programs are seen as the dominant and most visible aspects by the general public. As the universal programs draw support from a wider population, the targeted programs would be indirectly supported and protected."[119] I thought that given American views about poverty and race, a program that appears to have a colorblind agenda would be the most realistic way to generate the broad political support that would be necessary to enact the required legislation. Harvard political scientist Theda Skocpol, who argued that the best way to combat poverty is through targeting within universalism, supported this position.[120]

However, this position drew criticisms from some scholars. For example, Robert Lieberman argued that "targeting within universalism" will not succeed if institutions are not in place to ensure that the right targets, for example poor blacks, receive the benefits.[121] I accept this criticism. Indeed since writing *The Truly Disadvantaged* my position on framing has changed. In addition to making sure that institutional mechanisms are in place to allow for an equitable distribution of resources, I also feel that in framing public policy we should not shy away from an explicit discussion of the specific issues of race and poverty; on the contrary, we should highlight them in our attempt to convince the nation that these problems should be seriously confronted and that there is an urgent need to address them. The issues of race and poverty should be framed in such a way that not only a sense of fairness and justice to combat inequality is generated, but also people are made aware that our country would be better off if these problems were seriously addressed and eradicated.

In other words, I now feel that appeals to America's sense of fairness and justice will be more effective in the long run than attempting to neutralize the effects of racial biases by highlighting initiatives that seem to benefit all groups. This does not mean that I reject universal programs to combat poverty, such as the stimulus package, which includes programs to address the needs of the poor, including poor people of color. While I no longer support a framing that is specifically and expressly designed to appear race neutral or color blind, I fully support *both* race-specific and universal programs to address racial inequality, including problems of concentrated poverty in the inner city.

However, questions about the issue of framing notwithstanding, there are also questions about *The Truly Disadvantaged*'s actual impact on programs to combat concentrated black poverty. In this connection, officials in the federal government, as well as in certain municipal governments, have used arguments in *The Truly Disadvantaged* on social isolation and concentration effects to help provide the rationale for programs to address problems of concentrated poverty.[122] One of the earliest and more notable of these initiatives is HUD's HOPE VI—launched in the early 1990s to help overcome the adverse effects of public housing projects in blighted neighborhoods, including the revitalization of the worst public housing projects into mixed-income developments. The income mixing aspect of HOPE VI was conceived to address the problem of social isolation.

More recently, under the Obama administration, HUD adopted the Choice Neighborhood program, which in effect is designed to replace HOPE VI. The Choice Neighborhood program goes beyond the rehabilitation of physically deteriorated public housing neighborhoods, the focus of HOPE VI, and includes comprehensive neighborhood investments ranging from early childhood education to employment, safety, and transportation components. Also, as noted previously, HUD's Moving to Opportunity experiment was framed as a test of *The Truly Disadvantaged's* hypotheses on neighborhood effects. In short, as stated by Edward G. Goetz, "concentrated poverty is the organizing framework for much housing policy at the federal and local levels."[123] A number of writers have been critical of this framework as applied to public policy. And some even go so far as to deny that research supports the adverse effects of concentrated poverty, despite overwhelming evidence to the contrary—including the research discussed in this afterword on spatial mismatch, persistent poverty, depopulation, social isolation, and concentration effects.[124] Indeed, one only has to read Robert Sampson's landmark book *Great American City: Chicago and the Enduring Neighborhood Effect* to see that this claim lacks substance.

However, many of the criticisms of the actual policies involving efforts to confront concentrated poverty do in fact have some merit. Most notably, the criticisms of projects that are designed to promote deconcentration of public housing, projects that legitimate displacement and gentrification and often result in the displacement of inner-city residents without sufficient attention given to relocating them to more desirable neighborhoods. As Jeff R. Crump has argued, the plans to demolish public housing projects and replace them with mixed-income housing developments are designed, in many cases, to encourage middle- and upper-class people to relocate to the inner city. In the process former residents of public housing are often moved into private housing within urban ghettos. A number of the critics of this process maintain that *The Truly Disadvantaged* explicitly supports the deconcentration of public housing and is the main driver in this process.[125]

A scholar cannot always be held responsible for how his or her work is used or misused. In *The Truly Disadvantaged* I sought to explain what causes the distinct phenomenon of concentrated poverty. My argument about the structural causes of concentrated poverty does not imply that these neighborhoods should be deconcentrated by displacing poor residents. In fact, one need not speculate about the policy implications of the research in *The Truly Disadvantaged*, since I explicitly propose a series of policy responses to the problems of concentrated poverty in *The Truly Disadvantaged*.

Nowhere do I suggest the forced relocation of the urban poor from housing projects or other centers of concentrated poverty as a policy option. On the contrary, my extended discussion of policy options, which flows from my analysis of the social transformation of the inner city, highlights macroeconomic policy to generate economic growth and tight labor markets; fiscal and monetary policies to stimulate noninflationary growth and increase the competitiveness of American goods on both the domestic and international markets; and a national labor market strategy to make the labor force, including the black labor force, more adaptable to changing economic opportunities. I also advocated a family allowance program, a child support assurance program, and a child-care strategy.

These policies, I maintained, would address the problems of concentrated poverty by providing poor inner-city residents with resources that promote social mobility. I pointed out that social mobility often leads to geographic mobility. And geographic mobility would be enhanced if efforts to improve the economic and educational resources of inner-city residents were accompanied by legal action to effectively eliminate (1) the historic discriminatory government policies that routinely locate public housing for disadvantaged people of color in poor segregated neighborhoods and (2) the manipulation of zoning laws and discriminatory land use controls, or site selection policies, that thwarts the construction of affordable housing for low-income families and severely restricts their residence in communities that provide desirable services.

The point to be emphasized is that I proposed the creation of macroeconomic policy, labor market policy, and family policy to enable poor inner-city families to develop the resources they need to make their own mobility decisions and to remove the historic discriminatory obstacles that would curtail their social and geographic mobility. Given this comprehensive policy discussion, arguments that imply that this book *explicitly* supports the deconcentration of public housing as a policy option—despite the obvious benefits that accrue to poor families that participate in the *successful* programs involving housing vouchers and scattered-site public housing—are, to put it mildly, misplaced.

Conclusion

In many respects my review of the hundreds of studies generated by *The Truly Disadvantaged* has been gratifying. As the historian Thomas J. Sugrue pointed out, "*The Truly Disadvantaged*, published in 1987, was sweeping and synthetic, elegantly weaving together problems often considered separately from each other into an overarching theory of urban inequality."[126] The scope of this theory is reflected in the wide array of empirical research across disciplines to test my propositions, propositions that relate to economic restructuring, neighborhood effects, persistent and concentrated poverty, depopulation, social isolation, and family structure. Most of these studies either support or extend the hypotheses advanced in the book.

However, what is not elaborated in this afterword is the attention the book has received outside of academia by the media, politicians, and the general public. For example, _The Truly Disadvantaged_ received front-page reviews in the _New York Times Book Review_, _Washington Post Book World_, and the _New Republic_. The book also received a featured profile in the _New York Times Week in Review_ section, was selected by the editors of the _New York Times Book Review_ as one of the fifteen best books of 1987, and was one of the winners of the _Washington Monthly's_ Annual Book Award.[127] Hopefully, this new edition of _The Truly Disadvantaged_, with this extended afterword, will once again engage academics, policymakers, and the media concerned with how sociological knowledge can shed light on some of the nation's most important social problems.

Afterword Notes

1. Paul Jargowsky, *Stunning Progress, Hidden Problems: The Dramatic Decline of Concentrated Poverty during the 1990s* (Washington, DC: Brookings Institution, 2003).

2. William Julius Wilson, "The Declining Significance of Race: Revisited and Revised," afterword to *The Declining Significance of Race*, 3rd ed. (Chicago, IL: University of Chicago Press, 2012).

3. See Bruce Western, *Punishment and Inequality in America* (New York: Russell Sage Foundation, 2006).

4. Mark A. Hughes, "Concentrated Deviance and the 'Underclass' Hypothesis," *Journal of Policy Analysis and Management* 8 (1989): 274–82; Robert Aponte, "Definitions of the Underclass: A Critical Analysis," in *Sociology in America*, ed. Herbert J. Gans (Newbury Park, CA: Sage, 1990); Michael B. Katz, "Reframing the 'Underclass Debate,'" in *The "Underclass" Debate: Views from History*, ed. M. B. Katz (Princeton, NJ: Princeton University Press, 1993), 440–78; Herbert J. Gans, *The War Against the Poor: The Underclass and Antipoverty Policy* (New York: Basic Books, 1995); and Alice O'Connor, *Poverty Knowledge: Social Science, Social Policy, and the Poor in Twentieth-Century U.S. History* (Princeton, NJ: Princeton University Press, 2001).

Several empirical assessments of the size and growth of the underclass by social scientists appeared in the late 1980s, but rather than helping to draw attention to the underlying causes of chronic poverty, these studies tended to contribute to the perception that as a group the underclass was synonymous with deviant behavior. See Richard Nathan, "The Underclass—Will It Always Be with Us?" (paper presented at the New School for Social Research, New York, NY, 1996); and Earl R. Ricketts and Isabell Sawhill, "Defining and Measuring the Underclass," *Journal of Policy Analysis and Management* 7 (1988): 316–25.

5. Kenneth B. Clark, *Dark Ghetto: Dilemmas of Social Power* (New York: Harper and Row, 1965); Lee Rainwater, "Crucible of Identity: The Negro Lower-Class Family," *Daedalus* 95 (Winter 1966): 176–216; Elliot Liebow, *Tally's Corner: A Study of Streetcorner Men* (Boston, MA: Little, Brown, 1967); Ulf Hannerz, *Soulside: Inquiries into Ghetto Culture and Community* (New York: Columbia University Press, 1969).

6. William Julius Wilson, *The Truly Disadvantaged: The Inner City, the Underclass, and Public Policy* (Chicago, IL, University of Chicago Press, 1987), 8.

7. Ibid.

8. William Julius Wilson, "Studying Inner-City Social Dislocations: The Challenge of Public Agenda Research," *American Sociological Review* 56 (February 1991): 1–14.

9. Herbert J. Gans, "Deconstructing the Underclass: The Term's Danger as a Planning Concept," *Journal of the American Planning Association* 56 (1990): 272.

10. Ibid.

11. See Myron Magnet, "America's Underclass: What to Do?" *Fortune*, May 11, 1987, 130–50; and Pete Hamill, "Breaking the Silence," *Esquire*, March 1988, 91–102.

12. Social scientists tend to use census tracts as proxies for neighborhoods. Since the publication of this book, social scientists have designated high-poverty or ghetto-poverty areas as those with poverty rates of at least 40 percent. For example, in Chicago Loïc Wacquant and I found that 82 percent of the residents who live in high-poverty census tracts inhabit the South and West Sides of the city in areas, most of which have been overwhelmingly black for half a century and more. These tracts make up the historic core of Chicago's black ghetto. An additional 13 percent live in immediately adjacent tracts. Loïc Wacquant and William Julius Wilson, "The Cost of Racial and Class Exclusion in the Inner City," *Annals of the American Academy of Political and Social Science* 501 (1990): 8–25.

Using the same rationale on a national level, Paul Jargowsky and Mary Jo Bane stated: "Based on visits to several cities, we found that the 40 percent criterion came very close to identifying areas that looked like ghettos in terms of their housing conditions. Moreover, the areas selected by the 40 percent criterion corresponded rather closely with the judgments of city officials and local census bureau officials about which neighborhoods were ghettos." "Ghetto Poverty in the United States, 1970–1980," in *The Urban Underclass*, ed. C. Jencks and P. E. Peterson (Washington, DC: Brookings Institution, 1991), 235–73.

13. In the ensuing discussion in this section, I benefited from Morris Zelditch's formal explication of *The Truly Disadvantaged*. Morris Zelditch, Jr., "Levels in the Logic of Macro-Historical Explanation" (paper presented at the Annual Meeting of the American Sociological Association, San Francisco, CA, 1989).

14. The point here is that the elimination of racial barriers creates greater opportunities for the talented, more educated, and better-trained minority group members, because, as James Fishkin has pointed out, they possess the resources to compete most effectively. These resources derive from a variety of advantages made possible or provided by their families, including financial means, schooling, and peer groups. However, if the more advantaged members of minority groups profit disproportionately from policies that enhance individual opportunity, they also benefit disproportionately from policies of affirmative action based solely on their racial group membership. Minority individuals from the most advantaged families tend to be more heavily represented among those of their racial group most qualified for college admissions, higher paying jobs, and promotions. James Fishkin, *Justice, Equal Opportunity and the Family* (New Haven, CT: Yale University Press, 1983).

15. Martha Van Haitsma, "A Contextual Definition of the Underclass." *Focus* (newsletter of the Institute for Research on Poverty) 12 (Spring–Summer 1989): 27–31.

16. Ibid., 28.

17. Ibid., 7.

18. Hannerz. *Soulside*; and William Julius Wilson, *When Work Disappears: The World of the New Urban Poor* (New York: Alfred A. Knopf, 1996).

19. Paul Jargowsky, *Poverty and Place: Ghettos, Barrios, and the American City* (New York: Russell Sage Foundation, 1997). Of the large cities in the United States, Boston is unique in that it includes a significant number of whites who live in high-poverty census tracts. Thus the use of the term *white underclass* would be more applicable to Boston than to other metropolises in this country. The term *white underclass*, based on my definition of *underclass*, could also be applied to segments of the white rural poor in the United States. See Cynthia Duncan, *Worlds Apart: Why Poverty Persists in Rural America* (New Haven, CT: Yale University Press, 2000); and Cynthia Duncan, "Understanding Persistent Poverty: Social Class Context in Rural Communities," *Rural Sociology* 61, no. 1 (1996): 103–24.

20. Alejandro Portes and Ruben G. Rumbaut used the term *underclass* to refer to those second generation Latino immigrants who have experienced the downward assimilation path, including residence in barrios, not the more stable and socially organized immigrant enclaves, and whose experiences are similar to those African Americans who reside in ghettos. See Alejandro Portes and Ruben G. Rumbaut, *Legacies: The Story of the Immigrant Second Generation* (Berkeley: University of California Press, 2001).

21. See Kees Schuyt, "The New Emerging Underclass in Europe: The Experience of Long-Term Unemployment in Dutch Inner Cities" (paper presented at the Workshop on Social Policy and the Underclass, University of Amsterdam, the Netherlands, August 1990); Robert C. Kloosterman, "The Making of the Dutch Underclass? A Labour Market View" (paper presented at the Workshop on Social Policy and the Underclass, University of Amsterdam, the Netherlands, August 1990); Godfried Engbersen, "Modern Poverty in the Netherlands" (paper presented at the Workshop on Social Policy and the Underclass, University of Amsterdam, the Netherlands, August 1990); and Godfried Engbersen, Kees Schuyt, and Jaap Timmer, "Cultures of Unemployment: Long-Term Unemployment in Dutch Inner Cities" (working paper 4, Vakgroep Sociologie Rijksuniversiteit, Leiden, the Netherlands, 1990).

22. Hamill, "Breaking the Silence"; and Magnet, "America's Underclass."

23. Robert J. Sampson, "Moving to Inequality: Neighborhood Effects and Experiments Meet Social Structure," *American Journal of Sociology* 114 (July 2008): 189–231 (quote 192).

24. For a discussion of some of the notable studies on neighborhood effects, see Tama Leventhal and Jeanne Brooks-Gunn, "The Neighborhoods They Live In: The Effects of Neighborhood Residence on Child and Adolescent Outcomes," *Psychological Bulletin* 126 (2000): 309–37; and Mario L. Small and Kathryn K.

Newman, "Urban Poverty after *The Truly Disadvantaged*: The Rediscovery of the Family, the Neighborhood, and Culture," *Annual Review of Sociology* 27, no. 1 (2001): 23–45.

25. Marta Tienda, "Poor People and Poor Places: Deciphering Neighborhood Effects on Poverty Outcomes," in *Macro-Micro Linkages in Sociology*, ed. J. Haber (Newbury Park, CA: Sage, 1991), 244–62; and Christopher Jencks and Susan Meyer, "The Social Consequences of Growing Up in a Poor Neighborhood," in *Inner-City Poverty in the United States*, ed. Lawrence Lynn, Jr., and Michael McGeary (Washington, DC: National Academy of Sciences Press, 1990), 111–86.

26. John Quigley and Steven Raphael, "Neighborhoods, Economic Self-Sufficiency, and the MTO," *The Brookings-Wharton Papers on Urban Economics Affairs* 8 (2007), 3.

27. See William N. Evans, Wallace E. Oates, and Robert M. Schwab, "Measuring Peer Group Effects: A Study of Teenage Behavior," *Journal of Political Economy* 100 (1992): 966–91; and Robert Plotnick and Saul Hoffman, "Using Sister Pairs to Estimate How Neighborhoods Affect Young Adult Outcomes," (Working Papers in Public Policy Analysis and Management, No. 93-8, Graduate School of Public Affairs, University of Washington, 1993).

28. Jeffrey R. Kling, Jeffrey B. Lieberman, Lawrence F. Katz, and Lisa Sanbonmatsu, "Moving to Opportunity and Tranquility: Neighborhood Effects on Adult Economic Self-Sufficiency and Health from a Randomized Housing Voucher Experiment," (Princeton IRS Working Paper 481, April 2004, revised October 2004), 31.

29. Sampson, "Moving to Inequality."

30. Ibid.; and Susan Clampet-Lundquist and Douglas S. Massey, "Neighborhood Effects on Economic Self-Sufficiency: A Reconstruction of the Moving to Opportunity Experiment," *American Journal of Sociology* 114 (July 2008): 107–43.

31. Stefanie Deluca, "All Over the Map: Explaining Educational Outcomes of the Moving to Opportunity Program," *Education Next* (Fall 2007): 25.

32. Quigley and Raphael, "Neighborhoods, Economic Self-Sufficiency, and the MTO."

33. It should be pointed out in this connection that a number of studies failing to support the presence of a neighborhood effect include an *operationalization* of neighborhood variables that are not theoretically driven and are therefore unable to identify causality. Several scholars have discussed the problem of arbitrary empirical measures of variables in some studies on neighborhood effects. See Jencks and Meyer, "The Social Consequences of Growing Up in a Poor Neighborhood"; Robert Sampson, Jeffrey Morenoff, and Thomas Gannon-Rowley, "Assessing Neighborhood Effects: Social Processes and New Directions in Research," *Annual Review of Sociology* 28 (2002): 443–78; and Robert J. Sampson, *Great American City: Chicago and the Enduring Neighborhood Effect* (Chicago, IL: University of Chicago Press, 2012), chap. 2 and 3.

34. Sampson, *Great American City*.

35. Wilson, "Studying Inner-City Social Dislocations."

36. John D. Kasarda, "Structural Factors Affecting the Location and Timing of Urban Underclass Growth," *Urban Geography* 11 (1990): 235–64 (quote 241). Paul Jargowsky's important studies of poverty and place also found support for the deindustrialization thesis in northern metropolitan areas. See Jargowsky, *Poverty and Place*.

37. George Galster, Ron Mincy, and Mitchell Tobin. "The Disparate Racial Neighborhood Impacts of Metropolitan Economic Restructuring," *Urban Affairs Review* 32 (1997): 797–825. The data sources included the 1980 and 1990 U.S. Bureau of the Census's Summary Tape File, U.S. Bureau of the Census's USA County File, and the Department of Commerce, Bureau of Economic Analysis's Employment by Detailed Industry File of the Regional Information System. Economic restructuring was measured by changes "in employment/population ratios, shares of manufacturing employment, and shares of MSA manufacturing in a [census] tract's county" (ibid., 797).

38. Ibid., 817.

39. The authors pointed out: "It is tempting to argue that black residential predominance in these areas is responsible for the greater vulnerability to restructuring, because of problems faced by individual blacks in the labor market. However, the data do not support this argument, because the interaction effect between percentage black and restructuring is not statistically significant" (ibid., 815).

40. John Iceland, "Urban Labor Markets and Individual Transitions Out of Poverty," *Demography* 34, no. 3 (1997): 429–41. Iceland measured economic restructuring "with three variables representing the change in the proportion of metropolitan area employment in manufacturing services, and retail/wholesale trade" (ibid., 431).

41. Ibid., 437. Many other studies have also gauged the adverse effects of the loss of manufacturing jobs on city residents. For example, Charles Jaret and his colleagues presented evidence that shows that the black-white income gap is less severe in metropolitan areas with a larger manufacturing base. They found that decreases in manufacturing jobs and increases in low-wage service jobs enlarge black-white income inequality. See Charles Jaret, Lesley W. Reid, and Robert M. Adelman, "Black-White Income Inequality and Metropolitan Socioeconomic Structure," *Journal of Urban Affairs* 25, no. 3 (2003): 305–34.

42. James R. Elliott, "Social Isolation and Labor Market Insulation: Network and Neighborhood Effects on Less-Educated Urban Workers," *The Sociological Quarterly* 40, no. 2 (1999): 213.

43. Kevin Fox Gotham, *Race, Real Estate, and Uneven Development: The Kansas City Experience, 1900–2000* (Albany, New York: SUNY Press, 2002); and Kevin F. Gotham, "Blind Faith in the Free Market: Urban Poverty, Residential Segregation, and Federal Housing Retrenchment, 1970–1995," *Sociological Inquiry* 68, no. 1 (1998): 1–31.

44. Gotham "Blind Faith in the Free Market," 24.

45. David T. Ellwood, "The Spatial Mismatch Hypothesis: Are There Teenage Jobs Missing in the Ghetto?," in *The Black Youth Employment Crisis*, ed.

R. B. Freeman and H. J. Holzer (Chicago, IL: University of Chicago Press, 1986), 147–48.

46. Harry J. Holzer, John M. Quigley, and Steven Raphael, "Public Transit and the Spatial Distribution of Minority Employment: Evidence from a Natural Experiment," *Journal of Policy Analysis and Management* 22, no. 3 (2003): 415–41; Steven Raphael, M. A. Stoll, and Harry J. Holzer, "Are Suburban Firms More Likely to Discriminate Against African Americans?," *Journal of Urban Economics* 48 (2000): 485–508; K. R. Ihlanfeldt and M. V. Young, "The Spatial Distribution of Black Employment between the Central City and the Suburbs," *Economic Inquiry* 34 (1996): 693–707; and H. J. Holzer and R. Ihlanfeldt, "Spatial Factors in the Employment of Blacks at the Firm Level," *New England Economic Review: Federal Reserve Bank of Boston* (May/June 1996): 65–86.

47. Wilson, *When Work Disappears.*

48. Lincoln Quillian, "The Decline of Male Employment in Low-Income Black Neighborhoods, 1950–1990," *Social Science Research* 32 (2003), 244.

49. Sabino Kornrich, "Combining Preferences and Processes: An Integrated Approach to Black-White Labor Market Inequality," *American Journal of Sociology* 15, no. 1(2009): 1–38.

50. Ibid., 6.

51. Ibid., 32. An interesting argument, although not supported directly by empirical research, was advanced by Christopher Jencks. He maintained that economic and demographic shifts (principally declines in urban manufacturing) cannot *fully* account for increased black joblessness since 1965. Instead, he argued, two neglected forces contributed, in part, to the growth of the ghetto: the white middle class, in control of mass media, became more tolerant of deviant behavior, and blacks in the post–civil rights era became far less tolerant of subservient roles. See Christopher Jencks. *Rethinking Social Policy: Race, Poverty, and the Underclass* (Cambridge, MA: Harvard University Press, 1992).

52. William Julius Wilson, *More than Just Race: Being Black and Poor in the Inner City* (New York: Norton, 2009); and Elijah Anderson, ed., *Against the Wall: Poor, Young, and Black* (Philadelphia: University of Pennsylvania Press, 2008).

53. Mark Condon, "Public Housing, Crime and the Urban Labor Market: A Study of Black Youth in Chicago," (Working Paper Series, no. H-91-3, Cambridge, MA, Malcolm Wiener Center, Kennedy School of Government, Harvard University, 1991), 4.

54. Robert Sampson and William Julius Wilson, "Toward a Theory of Race, Crime, and Urban Inequality," in *Crime and Inequality*, ed. John Hagan and Ruth Peterson (Stanford, CA: Stanford University Press, 1995), 37–54. Also see David W. Bartelt, "Housing the 'Underclass,'" in Katz, *The "Underclass" Debate*, 118–57; Robin D. G. Kelly, "The Black Poor and the Politics of Opposition in a New South City, 1929–1970," in Katz, *The "Underclass" Debate*, 293–333; Thomas J. Sugrue, "The Structures of Urban Poverty: The Reorganization of Space and Work in Three Periods of American History," in Katz, *The "Underclass" Debate*, 85–117; Arnold R. Hirsch, *Making the Second Ghetto: Race and Housing in Chicago, 1940–1960* (Cambridge: Cambridge University Press, 1983); and John F.

Bauman, Norman P. Hummon, and Edward K. Muller, "Public Housing, Isolation, and the Urban Underclass," *Journal of Urban History* 17 (1991): 264–92.

55. Lincoln Quillian, "Migration Patterns and the Growth of High-Poverty Neighborhoods, 1970–1990," *American Journal of Sociology* 105 (July 1999): 1–37.

56. See ibid.; Mary Pattillo, *Black Picket Fences: Privilege and Peril among the Black Middle Class* (Chicago, IL: University of Chicago Press, 1999); and Mary Pattillo, *Black on the Block: The Politics of Race and Class in the City* (Chicago, IL: University of Chicago Press, 2007).

57. Pattillo. *Black Picket Fences.*

58. Quillian, "Migration Patterns."

59. Ibid.

60. Ibid.; Wilson, *The Truly Disadvantaged*; and Wilson, *When Work Disappears.*

61. Lincoln Quillian, "How Long Are Exposures to Poor Neighborhoods? The Long-Term Dynamics of Entry and Exit from Poor Neighborhoods," *Population Research and Policy Review* 22 (2003): 221–49.

62. Ibid., 244.

63. Ibid.

64. Patrick Sharkey, "The Intergenerational Transmission of Context," *American Journal of Sociology* 113, no. 4 (January 2008), 933.

65. Sharkey, "Intergenerational Transmission of Context."

66. Ibid.

67. Ibid., 963.

68. Robert J. Sampson, Patrick Sharkey, and Stephen W. Raudenbush, "Durable Effects of Concentrated Disadvantage on Verbal Ability among African-American Children," *Proceedings of the National Academy of Sciences of the United States of America* 105 (January 22, 2008), 845–52.

69. Ibid., 846. Sampson and his colleagues created a composite measure of verbal ability based on results from two widely used tests given to their subjects—the Wide Range Achievement Test reading examination and the Wechsler Intelligence Scale for Children vocabulary test.

70. Ibid., 846.

71. Geoffrey T. Wodtke, David J. Harding, and Felix Elwert, "Neighborhood Effects in Temporal Perspective: The Impact of Long-Term Exposure to Concentrated Disadvantage on High School Graduation." *American Sociological Review* 76, no. 5 (October 2011): 713–36.

72. Ibid., 731. Wodtke, Harding, and Elwert stated, "By measuring neighborhood context throughout childhood, we are able to isolate the total effect of sustained exposure. Second, this study draws on novel methods that were specifically developed to resolve the difficult statistical problems related to dynamic selection into time-varying treatments" (ibid.).

73. Ibid., 732.

74. Sharkey, "The Intergenerational Transmission of Context," 964.

75. Steven R. Holloway and Stephen Mulherin, "The Effect of Adolescent

Neighborhood Poverty on Adult Employment," *Journal of Urban Affairs* 26, no. 4 (2004): 427–54.

76. Ibid., 448. It should be pointed out that despite the adverse effects of long-term residence in poor neighborhoods on adolescents, as reflected in labor market outcomes, one study concludes that most youths in poor neighborhoods are able to complete the developmental tasks of adolescence successfully. See Delbert Elliott, Scott Menard, Bruce Rankin, Amanda Elliott, David Huizinga, and William Julius Wilson, *Good Kids from Bad Neighborhoods: Successful Development in Social Context* (New York: Cambridge University Press, 2006).

77. Catherine E. Ross, John R. Reynolds, and Karlyn J. Geis, "The Contingent Meaning of Neighborhood Stability for Residents' Psychological Well-Being," *American Sociological Review* 65, no. 4 (2000): 581–97.

78. Ibid., 582.

79. Ibid., 595.

80. See Bruce Rankin and James Quane, "Neighborhood Poverty and the Social Isolation of Inner-City African American Families," *Social Forces* 79, no. 1 (2000): 139–64; and Roberto Fernandez and David Harris, "Social Isolation and the Underclass," in *Drugs, Crime, and Social Isolation*, ed. A. V. Harrell and G. E. Peterson (Washington, DC: Urban Institute Press, 1992), 257–93.

It should be pointed out that the following discussion of social isolation and concentration effects focuses on studies of inner-city black neighborhoods, which were the focus of *The Truly Disadvantaged*. Based on his research in the Villa Victoria, a Puerto Rican housing project in South Boston, Mario Small critiqued the implicit assumption in *The Truly Disadvantaged* that high-poverty areas are resource poor. Small argued instead that, even though Villa Victoria is a high-poverty area, it is also rich in resources; though the presence of these resources within the Villa Victoria contributes to social isolation, because the residents have little incentive to venture outside the area. See Mario Small, *Villa Victoria: The Transformation of Social Capital in a Boston Barrio* (Chicago, IL: University of Chicago Press, 2004).

81. Roberto G. Quercia and George G. Galster, "Threshold Effects and Neighborhood Change," *Journal of Planning and Education Research* 20 (2000): 146. Also see George G. Galster, Roberto G. Quercia, and A. Cortes, "Identifying Neighborhood Thresholds: An Empirical Exploration," *Housing Policy Debate* 11, no. 3 (2000): 701–32; George C. Galster, "An Economic Efficiency Analysis of Deconcentrating Poverty Populations," *Journal of Housing Economics* 11 (2002): 303–29; and Roberto G. Quercia, George C. Galster, Jackie M. Cutsinger, and Ron Malega, "The Cost of Concentrated Poverty: Neighborhood Property Markets and the Dynamics of Decline," in *Revisiting Rental Housing: Policies, Programs, and Priorities*, ed. N. Retsinas and E. Belsky (Washington, DC: Brookings Institution Press, 2008), 93–113.

82. Wilson, *The Truly Disadvantaged*, 57.

83. Quercia and Galster, "Threshold Effects and Neighborhood Change," 160.

84. Kenneth C. Land, Patricia L. McCall, and Lawrence E. Cohen, "Structural Covariates of Homicide Rates: Are There Any Invariances across Time and Social Space?," *American Journal of Sociology* 95, no. 4 (1990): 922–63.

299   Notes to Pages 274–79

85. The authors also provided corroborating evidence for my argument "that concentration effects grew more severe from 1970 to 1980 in large cities" (ibid., 945).

86. Wilson, *When Work Disappears*.

87. Sophie Pedder, "Social Isolation and the Labor Market: Black Americans in Chicago" (paper presented at the Chicago Urban Poverty and Family Life Conference, October 10–12, 1991).

88. Sandra Susan Smith, *Lone Pursuit: Distrust and Defensive Individualism among the Black Poor* (New York: Russell Sage Foundation, 2000), 37.

89. Ibid., 23.

90. Alford Young, *The Minds of Marginalized Black Men: Making Sense of Mobility, Opportunity, and Future Life Chances* (Princeton, NJ: Princeton University Press, 2004). Also see Alford Young, "Social Isolation and Concentration Effects: William Julius Wilson Revisited and Re-Applied," *Ethnic and Racial Studies* 26 (November 2003): 1073–87.

91. Elijah Anderson, *Code of the Street: Decency, Violence, and the Moral Life of the Inner-City* (New York: Norton, 1999); and Sudhir Alladi Venkatesh, *Off the Books: The Underground Economy of the Urban Poor* (Cambridge, MA: Harvard University Press, 2006).

92. Anderson, *Code of the Street*, 34.

93. Venkatesh, *Off the Books*, 381.

94. Ibid., 377.

95. Ibid., 385.

96. Mario Small, *Unanticipated Gains: Origins of Network Inequality in Everyday Life* (New York: Oxford University Press, 2009).

97. Ibid., 196–97.

98. Christopher Jencks, "Is the American Underclass Growing?" in *The Urban Underclass*, ed. C. Jencks and P. Peterson (Washington, DC: The Brookings Institution, 1991), 28–102.

99. For a good review of these studies, see David Ellwood and Christopher Jencks, "The Uneven Spread of Single Parent Families in the United States. What Do We Know? Where Do We Look for Answers?," in *Social Inequality*, ed. K. Neckerman (New York: Russell Sage, 2004), 3–78.

100. Daniel T. Lichter, Felicia B. LeClere, and Diane McLaughlin, "Local Marriage Markets and the Marital Behavior of Black and White Women," *American Journal of Sociology* 96, no. 4 (1991): 843–67.

101. Ibid., 865.

102. Wilson, *When Work Disappears*.

103. Mark Testa and Marilyn Krogh, "The Effects of Employment on Marriage among Black Males in Inner-City Chicago," in *The Decline in Marriage among African Americans: Causes, Consequences and Policy Implications*, ed. M. B. Tucker and C. Mitchell-Kernan (New York: Russell Sage Foundation, 1995), 59–95.

104. Kathryn Edin and Maria Kefalas, *Promises I Can Keep: Why Poor Women Put Motherhood Before Marriage* (Berkeley: University of California Press, 2005).

105. Bruce Western and Christopher Wildeman, "The Black Family and Mass Incarceration," *The Annals of the American Academy of Political and Social*

Science 621 (January 2009): 221–42. Also see Western, *Punishment and Inequality*.

106. Vivian Henderson, "Race, Economics and Public Policy," *Crisis* 83 (Fall 1975): 50–55.

107. Loïc Wacquant, "Scrutinizing the Street: Poverty, Morality, and the Pitfalls of Urban Ethnography," *American Journal of Sociology* 107 (May 2002), 1501; and Michèle Lamont and Mario Luis Small, "How Culture Matters for the Understanding of Poverty: Enriching Our Understanding," in *The Color of Poverty: Why Racial and Ethnic Disparities Exist*, ed. by David Harris and Ann Lin (New York: Russell Sage Foundation, 2008).

108. Wilson, *When Work Disappears*; and Wilson, *More than Just Race*.

109. Loic Wacquant, *Urban Outcasts: A Comparative Study of Advanced Marginality* (Cambridge, UK: Polity Press, 2008).

110. Roger Waldinger, *Still the Promised City? African-Americans and New Immigrants in Postindustrial New York* (Cambridge, MA: Harvard University Press, 1996).

111. Douglas Massey and Nancy Denton, *American Apartheid: Segregation and the Making of the Underclass* (Cambridge, MA: Harvard University Press, 1993); Douglas Massey and Mitchell L. Eggers, "The Ecology of Inequality: Minorities and the Concentration of Poverty, 1970–1980," *American Journal of Sociology* 95, no. 5 (1990): 1153–88; Douglas Massey, Andrew B. Gross, and Mitchell L. Eggers, "Segregation, the Concentration of Poverty, and the Life Chances of Individuals," *Social Science Research* 20, no. 4 (1991): 397–420; and Douglas Massey, Andrew B. Gross, and Kumiko Shibuya, "Migration, Segregation, and the Geographic Concentration of Poverty," *American Sociological Review* 59, no. 3 (1994): 425–45.

112. Massey and Eggers, "The Ecology of Inequality," 1186.

113. Jargowsky and Bane. "Ghetto Poverty in the United States." For a comprehensive study that used neighborhood measures instead of metropolitan averages and presented similar findings, see Claudia J. Coulton, Julian Chow, and Shanta Pandey, *An Analysis of Poverty and Related Conditions in Cleveland Area Neighborhoods* (Cleveland, OH: Center for Urban Poverty and Social Change, Case Western Reserve University, 1990).

Paul Jargowsky presents a methodological critique of the measure of economic segregation used by Massey and his colleagues, arguing that their measure confounds changes in the income distribution with spatial changes. See Jargowsky, *Poverty and Place*; and Jargowsky, "Take the Money and Run: Economic Segregation in US Metropolitan Areas," *American Sociological Review* 61, no. 6 (1996): 984–98.

114. Jargowsky and Bane, "Ghetto Poverty in the United States."

115. Jeffrey Morenoff and Robert J. Sampson, "Violent Crime and the Spatial Dynamics of Neighborhood Transition: Chicago, 1970–1990," *Social Forces* 76, no. 1 (1997): 31–64; Gotham, "Blind Faith in the Free Market"; and Quillian, "Migration Patterns."

116. Morenoff and Sampson, "Violent Crime," 36.

117. David Harding, *Living the Drama: Community, Conflict and Culture among Inner-City Boys* (Chicago, IL: University of Chicago Press, 2010), 18–19.

118. See Wilson, *When Work Disappears*, chap. 3.

119. Wilson, *The Truly Disadvantaged*, 154.

120. Theda Skocpol, "Targeting Within Universalism: Politically Viable Strategies to Combat Poverty in the United States," in *The Urban Underclass*, ed. C. Jencks and P. E. Peterson (Washington, DC: Brookings Institution, 1991), 411–36.

121. Robert C. Lieberman, *Shifting the Color Line: Race and the American Welfare State* (Cambridge, MA: Harvard University Press, 2001).

122. According to George Galster, *The Truly Disadvantaged*'s influence on social policy is also evidenced by the number of citations to the book in European journals testing various propositions in the book in studies of neighborhood policy in the European context. See George Galster, "Should Policy Makers Strive for Neighborhood Social Mix? An Analysis of the Western European Evidence Base," *Housing Studies* 22, no. 4 (2007): 523–45.

123. Edward G. Goetz, "The Politics of Poverty Deconcentration and Housing Demolition," *Journal of Urban Affairs* 22, no. 2 (2000), 157.

124. See Herbert J. Gans, "Concentrated Poverty, A Critical Analysis," *Challenge Magazine*, May/June 2010, 82–96.

125. Jeff R. Crump, "The End of Public Housing as We Know It: Public Housing Policy, Labor Regulation and the US City," *International Journal of Urban and Regional Research* 27, no. 1 (2003): 179–87; Mark L. Joseph, Robert J. Chaskin, and Henry S. Webber, "The Theoretical Basis for Addressing Poverty through Mixed-Income Development," *Urban Affairs Review* 42, no. 3 (2007): 369–409; Pauline Lipman, "The Cultural Politics of Mixed-Income Schools and Housing: A Racialized Discourse of Displacement, Exclusion, and Control," *Anthropology and Education Quarterly* 40, no. 3 (2009): 215–36; and Gans, "Concentrated Poverty."

126. Thomas J. Sugrue, *Not Even Past: Barack Obama and the Burden of Race* (Princeton, NJ: Princeton University Press, 2010).

127. For a discussion of the impact of *The Truly Disadvantaged* outside of academia, see William Julius Wilson, "Reflections on a Sociological Career That Integrates Social Science with Social Policy," *Annual Review of Sociology* 37 (2011): 1–18.

Afterword Bibliography

Anderson, E. *Code of the Street: Decency, Violence, and the Moral Life of the Inner-City*. New York: Norton, 1999.

———, ed. *Against the Wall: Poor, Young, and Black*. Philadelphia: University of Pennsylvania Press, 2008.

Bauman, J. F., N. P. Hummon, and E. K. Muller. "Public Housing, Isolation, and the Urban Underclass." *Journal of Urban History* 17 (1991): 264–92.

Clampet-Lundquist, S., and Douglas S. Massey, "Neighborhood Effects on Economic Self-Sufficiency: A Reconstruction of the Moving to Opportunity Experiment." *American Journal of Sociology* 114 (July 2008): 107–43.

Clark, K. B. *Dark Ghetto: Dilemmas of Social Power*. New York: Harper and Row, 1965.

Condon, M. "Public Housing, Crime and the Urban Labor Market: A Study of Black Youth in Chicago." Working Paper Series, no. H-91-3. Cambridge, MA: Malcolm Wiener Center, Kennedy School of Government, Harvard University, 1991.

Coulton, C. J., J. Chow, and S. Pandey. *An Analysis of Poverty and Related Conditions in Cleveland Area Neighborhoods*. Cleveland, OH: Center for Urban Poverty and Social Change, Case Western Reserve University, 1990.

Crump, J. R. "The End of Public Housing as We Know It: Public Housing Policy, Labor Regulation and the US City." *International Journal of Urban and Regional Research* 27, no. 1 (2003): 179–87.

Deluca, S. "All Over the Map: Explaining Educational Outcomes of the Moving to Opportunity Program." *Education Next* (Fall 2007): 29–36.

Duncan, C. "Understanding Persistent Poverty: Social Class Context in Rural Communities." *Rural Sociology* 61, no. 1 (1996): 103–24.

———. *Worlds Apart: Why Poverty Persists in Rural America*. New Haven, CT: Yale University Press, 2000.

Edin, K., and M. Kefalas. *Promises I Can Keep: Why Poor Women Put Motherhood Before Marriage*. Berkeley, CA: University of California Press, 2005.

Elliott, D., S. Menard, B. Rankin, A. Elliott, D. Huizinga, and W. J. Wilson. *Good Kids from Bad Neighborhoods: Successful Development in Social Context*. New York: Cambridge University Press, 2006.

Elliott, J. R. "Social Isolation and Labor Market Insulation: Network and Neighborhood Effects on Less-Educated Urban Workers." *Sociological Quarterly* 40, no. 2 (1999): 199–216.

Ellwood, D. T. "The Spatial Mismatch Hypothesis: Are There Teenage Jobs Missing in the Ghetto?" In *The Black Youth Employment Crisis*, edited by R. B. Freeman and H. J. Holzer, 147–58. Chicago, IL: University of Chicago Press, 1986.

Ellwood, D. T., and C. Jencks. "The Uneven Spread of Single Parent Families in the United States. What Do We Know? Where Do We Look for Answers?" In *Social Inequality*, edited by K. Neckerman, 3–78. New York: Russell Sage, 2004.

Engbersen, G. "Modern Poverty in the Netherlands." Paper presented at the Workshop on Social Policy and the Underclass, University of Amsterdam, the Netherlands, August 1990.

Engbersen, G., K. Schuyt, and J. Timmer. "Cultures of Unemployment: Long-Term Unemployment in Dutch Inner Cities." Working paper 4, Vakgroep Sociologie Rijksuniversiteit, Leiden, the Netherlands, 1990.

Evans, W. N., W. E. Oates, and R. M. Schwab. "Measuring Peer Group Effects: A Study of Teenage Behavior." *Journal of Political Economy* 100 (1992): 966–91.

Fernandez, R., and D. Harris. "Social Isolation and the Underclass." In *Drugs, Crime, and Social Isolation*, edited b A. V. Harrell and G. E. Peterson, 257–93. Washington, DC: Urban Institute Press, 1992.

Fishkin, J. *Justice, Equal Opportunity and the Family*. New Haven, CT: Yale University Press, 1983.

Galster, G. C. "An Economic Efficiency Analysis of Deconcentrating Poverty Populations." *Journal of Housing Economics* 11 (2002): 303–29.

———. "Should Policy Makers Strive for Neighborhood Social Mix? An Analysis of the Western European Evidence Base." *Housing Studies* 22, no. 4 (2007): 523–45.

Galster, G. C., R. G. Quercia, and A. Cortes. "Identifying Neighborhood Thresholds: An Empirical Exploration." *Housing Policy Debate* 11, no. 3 (2000): 303–29.

Galster. G. C., R. Mincy, and M. Tobin. "The Disparate Racial Neighborhood Impacts of Metropolitan Economic Restructuring." *Urban Affairs Review* 32 (1997): 797–825.

Gans, H. J. "Concentrated Poverty, A Critical Analysis." *Challenge Magazine*, May/June 2010, 82–96.

———. "Deconstructing the Underclass: The Term's Danger as a Planning Concept." *Journal of the American Planning Association* 56 (1990): 271–77.

———. *The War Against the Poor. The Underclass and Antipoverty Policy*. New York: Basic Books, 1995.

Goetz, E. G. "The Politics of Poverty Deconcentration and Housing Demolition." *Journal of Urban Affairs* 22, no. 2 (2000): 157–73.

Gotham, K. F. "Blind faith in the free market: Urban poverty, residential segregation, and federal housing retrenchment, 1970–1995." *Sociological Inquiry* 68, no. 1 (1998): 1–31.

———. *Race, Real Estate, and Uneven Development: The Kansas City Experience, 1900–2000*. Albany, NY: SUNY Press, 2002.

Hamill, P. "Breaking the Silence." *Esquire*, March 1988, 91–102.

Hannerz, U. *Soulside: Inquiries into Ghetto Culture and Community*. New York: Columbia University Press, 1969.

Harding, D. J. *Living the Drama: Community, Conflict and Culture among Inner-city Boys*. Chicago, IL: University of Chicago Press, 2010.

Henderson, V. "Race, Economics and Public Policy." *Crisis* 83 (Fall 1975): 50–55.

Hirsch, A. R. *Making the Second Ghetto: Race and Housing in Chicago, 1940–1960*. Cambridge: Cambridge University Press, 1983.

Holloway, S. R., and S. Mulherin. "The Effect of Adolescent Neighborhood Poverty on Adult Employment." *Journal of Urban Affairs* 26, no. 4 (2004): 427–54.

Holzer, H. J., and R. Ihlanfeldt. "Spatial Factors in the Employment of Blacks at the Firm Level." *New England Economic Review: Federal Reserve Bank of Boston* (May/June 1996): 65–86.

Holzer, H. J., J. M. Quigley, and S. Raphael. "Public Transit and the Spatial Distribution of Minority Employment: Evidence from a Natural Experiment." *Journal of Policy Analysis and Management* 22, no. 3 (2003): 415–41.

Hughes, M. "Concentrated Deviance and the 'Underclass' Hypothesis." *Journal of Policy Analysis and Management* 8 (1989): 274–82.

Iceland, J. "Urban Labor Markets and Individual Transitions Out of Poverty." *Demography* 34, no. 3 (1997): 429–41.

Ihlanfeldt, K. R., and M. V. Young. "The Spatial Distribution of Black Employment between the Central City and the Suburbs." *Economic Inquiry* 34 (1996): 693–707.

Jaret, C., L. W. Reid, and R. M. Adelman. "Black-White Income Inequality and Metropolitan Socioeconomic Structure." *Journal of Urban Affairs* 25, no. 3 (2003): 305–34.

Jargowsky, P. *Poverty and Place: Ghettos, Barrios, and the American City*. New York: Russell Sage Foundation, 1997.

———. *Stunning Progress, Hidden Problems: The Dramatic Decline of Concentrated Poverty during the 1990s*. Washington, DC. Brookings Institution, 2003.

———. "Take the Money and Run: Economic Segregation in US Metropolitan Areas." *American Sociological Review* 61, no. 6 (1996): 984–98.

Jargowsky, P., and M. J. Bane. "Ghetto Poverty in the United States, 1970–1980." In *The Urban Underclass*, edited by C. Jencks and P. E. Peterson, 235–73. Washington, DC: Brookings Institution, 1991.

Jencks, C. "Is the American Underclass Growing?" In *The Urban Underclass*, edited by C. Jencks and P. Peterson, 28–102. Washington, DC: The Brookings Institution, 1991.

———. *Rethinking Social Policy: Race, Poverty, and the Underclass*. Cambridge, MA: Harvard University Press, 1992.

Jencks, C., and P. E. Peterson, eds. *The Urban Underclass*. Washington, DC: Brookings Institution Press, 1991.

Jencks, C., and S. Meyer. "The Social Consequences of Growing Up in a Poor Neighborhood." In *Inner-City Poverty in the United States*, edited by Lawrence Lynn, Jr., and Michael McGeary, 111–86. Washington, DC: National Academy of Sciences Press, 1990.

Joseph, M. L., R. J. Chaskin, and H. S. Webber. "The Theoretical Basis for Addressing Poverty through Mixed-Income Development." *Urban Affairs Review* 42, no. 3 (2007): 369–409.

Kasarda, J. D. "Structural Factors Affecting the Location and Timing of Urban Underclass Growth." *Urban Geography* 11 (1990): 235–64.

Katz, M. B. "Reframing the 'Underclass Debate.'" In *The "Underclass" Debate: Views from History*, edited by M. B. Katz, 440–78. Princeton, NJ: Princeton University Press, 1993.

Kling, J. R., J. B. Lieberman, L. F. Katz, and L. Sanbonmatsu. "Moving to Opportunity and Tranquility: Neighborhood Effects on Adult Economic Self-Sufficiency and Health from a Randomized Housing Voucher Experiment." Princeton IRS Working Paper 481, April 2004, revised October 2004.

Kloosterman, R. "The Making of the Dutch Underclass? A Labour Market View." Paper presented at the Workshop on Social Policy and the Underclass, University of Amsterdam, the Netherlands, August 1990.

Kornrich, S. "Combining Preferences and Processes: An Integrated Approach to Black-White Labor Market Inequality." *American Journal of Sociology* 15, no. 1(2009): 1–38

Lamont, M., and M. L. Small. "How Culture Matters for the Understanding of Poverty: Enriching Our Understanding." In *The Color of Poverty: Why Racial and Ethnic Disparities Exist*, edited by D. Harris and A. Lin, 76–102. New York: Russell Sage Foundation, 2008.

Land, K. C., P. L. McCall, and L. E. Cohen. "Structural Covariates of Homicide Rates: Are There Any Invariances across Time and Social Space?" *American Journal of Sociology* 95, no. 4 (1990): 922–63.

Leventhal, T., and J. Brooks-Gunn. "The Neighborhoods They Live In: The Effects of Neighborhood Residence on Child and Adolescent Outcomes." *Psychological Bulletin* 126 (2000): 309–37.

Lichter, D. T., F. B. LeClere, and D. McLaughlin. "Local Marriage Markets and the Marital Behavior of Black and White Women." *American Journal of Sociology* 96, no. 4 (1991): 843–67.

Lieberman, R. C. *Shifting the Color Line: Race and the American Welfare State*. Cambridge, MA: Harvard University Press, 2001.

Liebow, E. *Tally's Corner: A Study of Streetcorner Men*. Boston, MA: Little, Brown, 1967.

Lipman, P. "The Cultural Politics of Mixed-Income Schools and Housing: A Racialized Discourse of Displacement, Exclusion, and Control." *Anthropology and Education Quarterly* 40, no. 3 (2009): 215–36.

Magnet, M. "America's Underclass: What to Do?" *Fortune*, May 11, 1987, 130–50.

Massey, D., A. B. Gross, and K. Shibuya. "Migration, Segregation, and the Geographic Concentration of Poverty." *American Sociological Review* 59, no. 3 (1994): 425–45.

Massey, D., A. B. Gross, and M. L. Eggers. "Segregation, the Concentration of Poverty, and the Life Chances of Individuals." *Social Science Research* 20, no. 4 (1991): 397–420.

Massey, D., and M. L. Eggers. "The Ecology of Inequality: Minorities and the Concentration of Poverty, 1970–1980." *American Journal of Sociology* 95, no. 5 (1990): 1153–88.

Massey, D., and N. Denton. *American Apartheid: Segregation and the Making of the Underclass.* Cambridge, MA: Harvard University Press, 1993.

Morenoff, J. D., and R. J. Sampson. "Violent Crime and the Spatial Dynamics of Neighborhood Transition: Chicago, 1970–1990." *Social Forces* 76, no. 1 (1997): 31–64.

Nathan, R. "The Underclass—Will It Always Be with Us?" Paper presented at the New School for Social Research, New York, NY, 1996.

O'Connor, A. *Poverty Knowledge: Social Science, Social Policy, and the Poor in Twentieth-Century U.S. History.* Princeton, NJ: Princeton University Press, 2001.

Pattillo, M. *Black on the Block: The Politics of Race and Class in the City.* Chicago, IL: University of Chicago Press, 2007.

———. *Black Picket Fences: Privilege and Peril among the Black Middle Class.* Chicago, IL: University of Chicago Press, 1999.

Pedder, S. "Social Isolation and the Labor Market: Black Americans in Chicago." Paper presented at the Chicago Urban Poverty and Family Life Conference, October 10–12, 1991.

Plotnick, R., and S. Hoffman. "Using Sister Pairs to Estimate How Neighborhoods Affect Young Adult Outcomes." Working Papers in Public Policy Analysis and Management, No. 93-8, Graduate School of Public Affairs, University of Washington, 1993.

Portes, A., and R. G. Rumbaut. *Legacies: The Story of the Immigrant Second Generation.* Berkeley: University of California Press, 2001.

Quercia, R. G., and G. C. Galster. "Threshold Effects and Neighborhood Change." *Journal of Planning and Education and Research* 20 (2000): 146–62.

Quercia, R. G., G. C. Galster, J. M. Cutsinger, and R. Malega. "The Cost of Concentrated Poverty: Neighborhood Property Markets and the Dynamics of Decline." In *Revisiting Rental Housing: Policies, Programs, and Priorities*, edited by N. Retsinas and E. Belsky, 93–113. Washington, DC: Brookings Institution Press, 2008.

Quigley, J., and S. Raphael. "Neighborhoods, Economic Self-Sufficiency, and the MTO." *The Brookings-Wharton Papers on Urban Economics Affairs* 8 (2007): 1–46.

Quillian, L. "The Decline of Male Employment in Low-Income Black Neighborhoods, 1950–1990." *Social Science Research* 32 (2003): 1–46.

———. "How Long Are Exposures to Poor Neighborhoods? The Long-Term Dynamics of Entry and Exit from Poor Neighborhoods." *Population Research and Policy Review* 22 (2003): 221–49.

———. "Migration Patterns and the Growth of High-Poverty Neighborhoods, 1970–1990." *American Journal of Sociology* 105 (July 1999): 1–37.

Rainwater, L. "Crucible of Identity: The Negro Lower-Class Family." *Daedalus* 95 (Winter 1966): 176–216.

Rankin, B., and J. Quane. "Neighborhood Poverty and the Social Isolation of Inner-City African American Families." *Social Forces* 79, no. 1 (2000): 139–64.

Raphael, S., M. A. Stoll, and H. J. Holzer. "Are Suburban Firms More Likely to Discriminate against African Americans?" *Journal of Urban Economics* 48 (2000): 485–508.

Ricketts, E. R., and I. Sawhill. "Defining and Measuring the Underclass." *Journal of Policy Analysis and Management* 7 (1988): 316–25.

Ross, C. E., J. R. Reynolds, and K. J. Geis. "The Contingent Meaning of Neighborhood Stability for Residents' Psychological Well-Being." *American Sociological Review* 65, no. 4 (2000): 581–97.

Sampson, R. J. *Great American City: Chicago and the Enduring Neighborhood Effect*. Chicago, IL: University of Chicago Press, 2012.

———. "Moving to Inequality: Neighborhood Effects and Experiments Meet Social Structure." *American Journal of Sociology* 114 (July 2008): 189–231.

Sampson, R. J., J. Morenoff, and T. Gannon-Rowley. "Assessing Neighborhood Effects: Social Processes and New Directions in Research." *Annual Review of Sociology* 28 (2002): 443–78

Sampson, R. J., P. Sharkey, and S. W. Raudenbush. "Durable Effects of Concentrated Disadvantage on Verbal Ability among African-American Children." *Proceedings of the National Academy of Sciences of the United States of America* 105 (January 22, 2008): 845–52.

Sampson, R., and W. J. Wilson. "Toward a Theory of Race, Crime, and Urban Inequality." In *Crime and Inequality*, edited by John Hagan and Ruth Peterson, 37–54. Stanford, CA: Stanford University Press, 1995.

Schuyt, K. "The New Emerging Underclass in Europe: The Experience of Long-Term Unemployment in Dutch Inner Cities." Paper presented at the Workshop on Social Policy and the Underclass, University of Amsterdam, the Netherlands, August 1990.

Sharkey, P. "The Intergenerational Transmission of Context." *American Journal of Sociology* 113, no. 4 (January 2008): 931–69.

Skocpol, T. "Targeting Within Universalism: Politically Viable Strategies to Combat Poverty in the United States." In *The Urban Underclass*, edited by C. Jencks and P. E. Peterson, 411–36. Washington, DC: Brookings Institution, 1991.

Small, M. *Unanticipated Gains: Origins of Network Inequality in Everyday Life*. New York: Oxford University Press, 2009.

———. *Villa Victoria: The Transformation of Social Capital in a Boston Barrio*. Chicago, IL: University of Chicago Press, 2004.

Small, M. L., and K. K. Newman. "Urban Poverty after *The Truly Disadvantaged*: The Rediscovery of the Family, the Neighborhood, and Culture." *Annual Review of Sociology* 27, no. 1 (2001): 23–45.

Smith, S. *Lone Pursuit: Distrust and Defensive Individualism Among the Black Poor*. New York: Russell Sage Foundation, 2007.

Sugrue, T. J. *Not Even Past: Barack Obama and the Burden of Race*. Princeton, NJ: Princeton University Press, 2010.

Testa, M., and M. Krogh. "The Effects of Employment on Marriage among Black Males in Inner-City Chicago." In *The Decline in Marriage Among African*

Americans: Causes, Consequences and Policy Implications, edited by M. B. Tucker and C. Mitchell-Kernan, 59–95. New York: Russell Sage Foundation, 1995.

Tienda, M. "Poor People and Poor Places: Deciphering Neighborhood Effects on Poverty Outcomes." In *Macro-Micro Linkages in Sociology*, edited by J. Haber, 244–62. Newbury Park, CA: Sage, 1991.

Van Haitsma, M. "A Contextual Definition of the Underclass." *Focus* (newsletter of the Institute for Research on Poverty) 12 (Spring–Summer 1989): 27–31.

Venkatesh, S. A. *Off the Books: The Underground Economy of the Urban Poor.* Cambridge, MA: Harvard University Press, 2006.

Wacquant, L. "Scrutinizing the Street: Poverty, Morality, and the Pitfalls of Urban Ethnography." *American Journal of Sociology* 107 (2002): 1468–1532.

———. *Urban Outcasts: A Comparative Study of Advanced Marginality.* Cambridge, UK: Polity Press, 2008.

Wacquant, L., and W. J. Wilson. "The Cost of Racial and Class Exclusion in the Inner City." *Annals of the American Academy of Political and Social Science* 501 (1990): 8–25.

Waldinger, R. *Still the Promised City? African-Americans and New Immigrants in Postindustrial New York.* Cambridge, MA: Harvard University Press, 1996.

Western, B. *Punishment and Inequality in America.* New York: Russell Sage Foundation, 2006.

Western, B., and C. Wildeman. "The Black Family and Mass Incarceration." *Annals of the American Academy of Political and Social Science* 621 (January 2009): 221–42.

Wilson, W. J. "The Declining Significance of Race: Revisited and Revised." Afterword to *The Declining Significance of Race*, 3rd ed., by W. J. Wilson. Chicago, IL: University of Chicago Press, 2012.

———. *More than Just Race: Being Black and Poor in the Inner City.* New York: Norton, 2009.

———. "Reflections on a Sociological Career that Integrates Social Science with Social Policy." *Annual Review of Sociology* 37 (2011): 1–18.

———. "Studying Inner-City Social Dislocations: The Challenge of Public Agenda Research." *American Sociological Review* 56 (February 1991): 1–14.

———. *The Truly Disadvantaged: The Inner City, the Underclass, and Public Policy.* Chicago, IL: University of Chicago Press, 1987.

———. *When Work Disappears: The World of the New Urban Poor.* New York: Alfred A. Knopf, 1996.

Wodtke, T., D. J. Harding, and F. Elwert. "Neighborhood Effects in Temporal Perspective: The Impact of Long-Term Exposure to Concentrated Disadvantage on High School Graduation." *American Sociological Review* 76, no. 5 (October 2011): 713–36.

Young, A. *The Minds of Marginalized Black Men: Making Sense of Mobility, Opportunity, ad Future Life Chances.* Princeton, NJ: Princeton University Press, 2004.

————. "Social Isolation, and Concentration Effects: William Julius Wilson Revisited and Re-applied." *Ethnic and Racial Studies* 26 (2003): 1073–87.

Zelditch, Jr., M. "Levels in the Logic of Macro-Historical Explanation." Paper presented at the Annual Meeting of the American Sociological Association, San Francisco, CA, 1989.

Index

Joblessness (*continued*)
100–104; inner-city, 3, 41–46, 50–57,
100–104, 143–46; and job networks,
60; and labor-force nonparticipation,
3, 267; and public policy, 105–6, 130,
139; teenage, 42–44, 60, 103–4; and
work histories, 60–61, 159–61. *See also*
Inner city
Job market, 150–52
Job mobility, 122
Job networks. *See under* Joblessness
Job training, 151–52
Joe, T., 186
Johnson, Lyndon Baynes, 118;
administration of, 129, 167–68
Joint Economic Committee, 91

Kahn, Alfred J., 156–57
Kamerman, Shelia, 156–57
Kantner, J. F., 73
Kasarda, John, 39, 41–42, 102, 104, 180–
81, 265
Kefalas, Maria, 279
Kennedy, John F., administration of, 129,
166–68
Kerbo, H. R., 170–71
Kerrs-Mills Act, 166
Keynesian economics, 119
King, Martin Luther, Jr., 126
Kitagawa, Evelyn, 75
Kornrich, Sabino, 267
Korpi, Walter, 130
Krogh, Marilyn, 279

Labor, racial division of, 12
Labor-force nonparticipation. *See*
Joblessness
Labor-force participation: of black men,
81–82, 267; in central cities, 39; of
white men, 41–42, 81–89
Labor market: policies, 157; tight, 122–23,
151–53
Lamont, Michèle, 280
Land, Kenneth C., 273–74
LeClere, Felicia B., 278
Lemann, Nicholas, 55
Levine, R. A., 168
Levitan, Saul, 164, 169
Levy, Frank, 44–45, 175
Lewis, Oscar, 13, 137, 182
Liberals, 14–15, 18–19, 148–50; and

discrimination, 114; policy makers, 155,
161; and poverty, 131–32, 139; and
urban analysts, 3–4, 6–13, 21–22; and
workfare, 161–62
Lichter, Daniel J., 278
Lieberman, Robert, 285–86
Lieberson, Stanley, 33–34, 141, 178
Liebow, Elliot, 126–27
Long, L. H., 177
Los Angeles, Calif., 35, 46–49, 55, 177–79
Losing Ground, 16–18, 93, 104
Loury, Glenn, 110–11, 116
Lower class, 258
Lumpen proletariat, 6–7

Macroeconomic policy, 151–57
Madras, P., 91
Male marriageable pool index, 83–92, 95–
106, 145–46, 148, 205n9, 278–79
Manpower: policies, 151; training, 147
Manpower Development and Training
Act, 167
Marriage, 67–71, 145–46, 184–86,
200n16, 203n55. *See also* Family; Male
marriageable pool index
Marx, Karl, 7
Massey, D. S., 179, 283, 284
Masters, S., 184
Matriarchy. *See* Family: female-headed
McCall, Patricia L., 273–74
McLanahan, S., 175
McLaughlin, Diane K., 278
Mead, Lawrence, 130, 131, 159–62
Medicaid, 77, 93, 116, 119
Medicare, 116, 120
Mexicans, immigration of, 179, 274. *See
also* Hispanics
Miami, Fla., 35
Middle class, 119–20, 147; black, 7–8,
55–57, 109–10, 113–15, 125, 143–44,
255, 268–69, 284; white, 109
Migrants. *See* Migration
Migration, 98–99; of Asians, 33, 36; of
blacks, 141–42; of Europeans, 33–34;
of Hispanics, 35–36; from inner city, 50,
55–56, 101, 135–38, 143, 252, 255–56,
268–69; of rural blacks, 33–36, 55, 101,
134, 141–42, 177–80, 195n38, 197n74;
to the West, 206n13
Minarik, J. J., 79, 185
Mincy, Ron, 265

115, 117–18, 120–24, 131, 140–46; and poverty, 49; and public policy, 153–54, 157–59

Unemployment. *See* Joblessness

Uniform Crime Reports, 32

United Kingdom, economic policies of, 156–57

United States, economic policies of, 156–67

University of Chicago, sociological research of, 165–66, 187

Urban Institute, 29

Urban Poverty and Family Life Study, 266, 274, 278

U.S. Census Bureau, 179

U.S. Commission on Civil Rights, 135

Van Haitsma, Martha, 257

Venkatesh, Sudhir, 275–77, 281

Vietnam War, 129, 168

Vining, D. R., Jr., 78

Vital Statistics Reports, 185

Voting, 125

Wacquant, Loïc, 280, 281, 282–83

Waldinger, R., 179

War on Poverty, 129–32, 139, 148, 167. *See also* Great Society

Washington, Booker, T., 128

Washington, D.C., 22, 136, 177

Weir, Margaret, 129–30, 151

Welfare, 55, 91–92, 98–99, 118–24, 150, 154, 177–78; AFDC, 17–18, 25–26, 29, 37, 77–81, 93–95, 99, 118–19, 152–53, 160, 184–86, 207n13; alternative approaches to, 156–57; conservatives' analysis of, 17, 93–95; culture of, 9;

dependency, 9–10, 13, 26–29, 159–60, 175–77, 184–86; and family, 71–81, 90–91, 145; food stamp program, 17, 77, 93, 94, 160, 167; long-term, 8–10; reform, 152, 160–62. *See also* Family: deterioration of

Western, Bruce, 279

Whites: in inner city, 136; middle-class, 109; and poverty, 58–59

Widows, 64–66

Wilderman, Christopher, 279

Wilensky, Harold, 155–56

Williams, R., 184

Wilson, James Q., 37

Wilson, William Julius, 253–54, 266–67, 274, 281, 285

Winegarden, C. R., 78

Wisconsin, 152

Wodtke, Geoffrey T., 271–72

Women: employment and, 27, 83–84, 186; labor-force participation of, 76–77. *See also* Births; Family: female-headed; Male marriageable pool index; Marriage

Work, attitudes toward, 161

Workfare, mandatory, 160–63. *See also* Welfare: reform

Working class: black, 7–8, 55–57, 143–44, 255, 266; white, 136

World War II, 166

Yarmolinsky, A., 216

Young, Alford, 275

Youths: in central city, 36–39; Hispanics, 36–37, 39. *See also* Teenagers

Zelnik, M., 73

Znaniecki, Florian, 165